DE L'ESPRIT;

OR,

𝕰𝖘𝖘𝖆𝖞𝖘

ON

THE MIND,

AND

ITS SEVERAL FACULTIES.

By *C. A. HELVETIUS.*

TRANSLATED FROM THE FRENCH.

TO WHICH IS NOW PREFIXED,

A LIFE OF THE AUTHOR.

LONDON:

PRINTED FOR J. M. RICHARDSON,
SITE THE ROYAL EXCHANGE; AND
AND JONES, PATERNOSTER-ROW.

J.M Vanloo pinx.t

J. Hopwood sculp.t

LIFE

C. A. HELVETIUS.

BIOGRAPHY may be reckoned among the moſt intereſt-ing of literary productions. Its intrinſic value is ſuch, that, though capable of extraordinary embelliſhment from the hand of genius, yet no inferiority of execution can ſo degrade it, as to deprive it of all utility. Whatever relates even to man in ge-neral, conſidered only as an aggregate of active and intelligent beings, has a ſtrong claim upon our notice; but that which relates to him as diſtinguiſhed from the reſt of his ſpecies, as moving in a more exalted ſphere, and towering above them by the reſplendent excellencies of mind, ſeems to me to be pecu-liarly calculated for our contemplation, and ought to form the higheſt pleaſure of our lives. There is a principle of curioſity implanted in us, which leads us, in an eſpecial manner, to in-veſtigate our fellow-creatures; the eager inquiſitiveneſs with which the mechanic ſeeks to know the hiſtory of his fellow-workmen; and the ardour with which the philoſopher, the poet, or the hiſtorian, hunts for details that may familiarize him with Deſcartes or Newton, with Milton, Hume, or Gibbon; ſpring from the ſame ſource. Their object, however, may perhaps vary; for, in the former, it may be for the ſake of detraction, invidious cavil, or malice; in the latter, it is a ſweet homage paid by the human heart to the memory of departed genius.

It has been repeatedly obſerved, that the life of a ſcholar af-fords few materials for biography. This is only negatively true; could every ſcholar have a Boſwell, the remark would vaniſh; or were every ſcholar a Rouſſeau, a Gibbon, or a Cum-berland, it would be equally nugatory. What can preſent higher objects of contemplation—what can claim more forcibly our attention—where can we ſeek for ſubjects of a more precious

nature than in the elucidation of the operations of mind, the ac-
quifitions of knowledge, the gradual expanfion of genius; its
application, its felicities, its forrows, its wreaths of fame, its
cold undeferved neglect? Such fcenes, painted by the artift
himfelf, are a rich bequeft to mankind; even when traced by
the hand of friendfhip or the pencil of admiration, they poffefs
a permanent intereft in our hearts. I cannot conceive a life
more worthy of public notice—more important, more interefting to human nature, than the life of a literary man, were it
executed according to the ideas I have formed of it; did it exhibit
a faithful delineation of the progrefs of intellect, from the cradle
upwards; did it pourtray, in accurate colours, the production
of what we call genius; by what accident it was firft awakened;
what were its firft tendencies; how directed to a particular object; by what means it was nourifhed and unfolded; the gradual progrefs of its operation in the production of a work; its
hopes and fears; its delights; its miferies; its infpirations, and
all the thoufand fleeting joys that fo often inveft its path but
for a moment, and then fade like the dews of the morning.—
Let it contain too a tranfcript of the many namelefs tranfports
that float round the heart, that dance in gay circle before the
ardent gazing eye, when the firft conception of fome future
effort ftrikes the mind; how it pictures undefined delights of
fame and popular applaufe; how it anticipates the bright moments of invention, and dwells with prophetic extacy on the
felicitous execution of particular parts, that already ftart into
exiftence by the magic touch of a heated imagination:—let it
depict the tender feelings of folitude, the breathings of midnight
filence, the fcenes of mimic life, of imaged trial, that often
occupy the mufing mind; let it be fuch a work, fo drawn, fo
coloured, and who fhall pronounce it inferior? who rather will
not confefs that it prefents a picture of human nature, where
every heart may find fome correfponding harmony? When,
therefore, it is faid, that the life of a fcholar is barreh, it is fo
only becaufe it has never been properly delineated; becaufe
thofe parts only have been felected which are common, and fail
to diftinguifh him from the common man; becaufe we have
never penetrated into his clofet, or into his heart; becaufe we
have drawn him only as an outward figure, and left unnoticed
that internal ftructure that would delight, aftonifh, and improve.
And then, when we compare the life of fuch a man with the
more active one of a foldier, a ftatefman, or a lawyer, we pronounce it infipid, uninterefting: true;—the man of ftudy has
never fought for hire, he has never flaughtered at the command
of a mafter; he has never cringed for court favours, and ruined
his country to preferve the fmiles of his monarch; he has never
been the advocate of injuftice, tyranny, or fraud, for a fee; he
has been none of thefe; he would difdain to be fuch: but be
not therefore deceived; though unaccompanied with the glaring
actions of public men, which confound and dazzle by their pub-

licity, but fhrink from the eftimation of moral truth, it would prefent a far nobler picture; yes, and a more inftructive one: the
calm difciple of reafon, he meditates in filence, and while he
meditates, communes with his God; he walks his road with
innoxious humility; he is poor, but his mind is his treafure:
he cultivates his reafon, and fhe lifts him to the pinnacle of
truth; he learns to tear away the veil of felf-love, folly, pride,
and prejudice, and bares the human heart to his infpection; he
corrects and amends; he repairs the breaches made by paffion; the proud man paffes him by, and looks upon him with
fcorn; but he feels his own worth, that ennobling confcioufnefs
which fwells in every vein, and infpires him with true pride,
with manly independence;—to fuch a man I could fooner bow
in reverence, than to the haughtieft, moft fuccefsful, candidate
for the world's ambition, that ever graced the records of a nation. But of fuch men, for the reafon I have already mentioned, our information is fcanty. While of others, who have
commanded a greater fhare of public notoriety, venal or mif-
taken admiration has given more than we wifhed to know.
Among thefe refpected individuals of human nature, I am
led to place Helvetius. My endeavours, indeed, to acquire
many particulars refpecting him have been difappointed; but
from the few that have rewarded my refearches, I am juftified
in viewing him as an amiable member of fociety; as a man no
lefs diftinguifhed for the virtues of his heart, than for the excellencies and errors of his genius. That we are doomed to
remain ignorant of the life of fuch men, fpeaks loudly our dif-
grace; I lament it. Where, indeed, is the literary character,
with the exception of two or three, of whom we poffefs information in any refpect adequate to them, or equal to our curiofity?
Yet, in this particular, we are, I believe, honourably diftinguifhed;
for it is undoubted, that infinitely more biographical works are
publifhed in this country than in France, or perhaps in any other
country. Had Helvetius been an Englifhman, who doubts that
we fhould have poffeffed at leaft ample details of the ufual fubjects
of biographical notice; while all that I have been able to find
among his own countrymen, is a fcanty memoir in a common
dictionary, with fome fcattered facts felected from the literary
men of his age. There may, perhaps, be more copious particulars, but I have not met with them; and fhould there be fuch,
I fhould efteem it a fingular gratification to have them pointed
out to me.

CLAUD ARIAN HELVETIUS was born at Paris in the year
1715. It may be faid of him, that he defcended from a literary
ftock. His grandfather, Adrian Helvetius, was celebrated as a
phyfician. He was born in Holland, and went to Paris, where
he acquired great reputation in his profeffion, and became eminent
by difcovering a cure for the dyfentery, (which was then pre-
valent) by the exhibition of ipecacuanha. Louis XIV. gave

him a thoufand louis d'ors for publishing his method, and made him infpector general of the hofpitals in Flanders, phyfician to the Duke of Orleans, &c. He died in 1721, and was the author of a treatife on the moft common difeafes and their remedies, and other works. The father of the prefent Helvetius was born in 1685, was alfo a phyfician, and ftill more eminent than the former. He became a member of the academy of Sciences at Paris, of the Royal Society of London, of the academies of Pruffia, Florence, and Bologna. He died in 1755, at the age of 70. He was a man amiable in private life, and refpectable as a phyfician; to the poor he was liberal, both of his advice and alms. He publifhed feveral works, which are much efteemed by profeffional men. Voltaire mentions him in his *Siècle de Louis XIV.* among the learned men who flourifhed in that reign, and takes an opportunity alfo of alluding to his fon in thefe words; " il était père d'un vrai philofophe qui renônça à la place de fermier général, pour cultiver les lettres, et qui a eu le fort de plufieurs philofophes, perfecuté pour un livre et pour fa vertu." It appears, indeed, that he was intimate with Voltaire in the latter part of his life, as there is a letter from that celebrated man in his *Correfpondence Générale,* dated about the year 1738, acknowledging one from him.

The name of Helvetius, however, would have been long fince known only to the indefatigable collectors of old books, or to the patient reader of a biographical dictionary, had it not been raifed to fame by the prefent author; and of whom I fhall now proceed to communicate all that I have been able to collect from different fources.

I have already faid that he was born in 1715. His infantile ftudies were carried on under the eye of his father; but he was foon removed to the college of Louis le Grand, where he had for a tutor the famous Porée, who, difcovering in the exercifes of young Helvetius more ideas and images, more power of language, and greater extent of genius, than in his other pupils, was led to beftow a particular attention upon his education. The world has fince feen what were the fruits of this cultivation.

He became early acquainted and connected with the philofophers of France; with Montefquieu he contracted an intimate friendfhip, and we find him correfponding with Voltaire in the year 1738, when he was only twenty-three years old. Voltaire feems to have directed his ftudies; and to have lavifhed upon him all that adulatory language which a mind, unreftrained by true delicacy of feeling, and unacquainted with felf-eftimation, fo copioufly pours forth. At one time he calls him his *young Apollo*; at another, his *fon of Parnaffus*; then *mon aimable petit fils d'Apollon;* and always his *dear philofopher.* And thefe phrafes of admiration are uttered in confequence of fome manufcript poetry which Helvetius handed about among his friends; which has fince been publifhed, and is now forgotten. In this letter, which feems to acknowledge the receipt of one both from the father and the fon, Voltaire fays, with meannefs and falfhood, "the father wifhes only to cure me, but the fon wifhes to give me pleafure,—I am for him; let me languifh, let me fuffer; I confent, provided that your verfes are beautiful." If there be a truly humiliating and indignant fpectacle, it is to behold a man of genius forgetful of his high endowments, and courting praife by the moft abject means.

Helvetius owed much to nature, as well in mind as body.— His exterior was graceful and interefting; he had a vigorous conftitution; and he fought every means of recommending himfelf to the favour of the fair fex. That he was at one time fuccefsful there can be little doubt, when we confider how eafily they facrifice judgment to fenfe, and often pleafe the eye at the expence of the heart.

Nothing has tranfpired that can deferve to be recorded refpecting the early life of Helvetius. It was doubtlefs paffed like that of every other literary man, in the gradual acquifition of knowledge, and in the intercourfe of fociety. One thing is mentioned as a fingularly magnanimous trait of character: he renounced a fplendid income, to which profeffional duties were annexed, that he might purfue undifturbed his literary avocations; but he ftill poffeffed an ample paternal eftate at Voré, adequate to all the luxuries of life. This action, therefore, I am inclined to eftimate as fomewhat lefs fplendid than Voltaire and others have done. Contempt for wealth in an age of artificial wants is undoubtedly a virtue, but to throw away fuperfluity, and retain abundance, appears to me to demand no great energy of foul, and to be entitled to no extravagant eulogies of praife. Voltaire feems to confider it as an "action unique," and worthy of perpetual commemoration; but Voltaire had a filly habit of admiring every thing done by thofe who admired him.

The firft literary attempts of Helvetius confifted of poetry. He wrote fome Epiftles on Happinefs, which he communicated confidentially to his friends. They were not publifhed till after his death. In allufion to thefe verfes, Voltaire calls him, in one of his letters, his brother Apollo; and in another addreffes to him the following lines:

Ne les verrai-je point ces beaux vers que vous faites,
 Ami charmant, fublime auteur?
Le ciel vous anima de ces flammes fecrettes
 Que ne fentit jamais Boileau l'imitateur,
Dans fes triftes beautés fi froidement parfaites.
Il eft des beaux efprits, il eft plus d'un rimeur;
 Il eft rarement des poëtes.
 Le vrai poëte eft créateur;
Peut-être je le fus, et maintenant vous l'êtes."

The modeſt inſinuation of the laſt line, and the magnanimity of friendſhip with which he relinquiſhes ſuch high pretenſions, the fulſome flattery of placing Helvetius above Boileau, and the affectation of the initial lines, afford a true ſpecimen of the minuteneſs of Voltaire's character, and I am ſorry to add, a ſpecimen but too accurate of the diſguſting egotiſm of literary men in general. Voltaire, however, is not content with this; on another occaſion he writes to him, and exclaims:

Vos vers ſemblent écrits par la main d'Apollon;
Vous n'en aurez pour fruit que ma reconnaiſſance, &c.

And at a later period, when grey hairs ſhould have taught him wiſdom, and the ſenſe of merit inſpired dignity, he accompanied a preſent of Semiramis with the following encomiaſtic ſtanza:

Mortal de l'eſpèce très rare
Des ſolides et beaux eſprits,
Je vous offre un tribut qui n'eſt pas d'un grand prix;
Vous pourriez donner mieux, mais vos charmans écrits
Sont le ſeul de vos biens dont vous ſoyez avare.

But this may claim an indulgence which muſt be denied to the others; the laſt line is ſtrictly true: Helvetius publiſhed but one work during his life; and it is well known that he was liberal in acts of charity. But even this truth is ſullied by its accompanying ſervility.

Theſe Épiſtles on Happineſs, which called forth laviſh commendations from the poet of Ferney, were publiſhed after the death of Helvetius, under the title of *Le Bonheur*, to which were appended ſome poetical fragments. An eulogy on the author is prefixed to it, from which I have been enabled to collect ſome of the particulars of this life. Its object is reprehenſible. He endeavours to ſhew, that happineſs does not flow from virtue; but that it reſults from the cultivation of literature and the arts. The poetry of Helvetius is not diſtinguiſhed for felicity of execution; it has ſome fine verſes, but the ſtyle, though often brilliant, is yet forced and turgid; it is too declamatory.

I have anticipated the chronological order of Helvetius's works; but it is of little importance.

Monteſquieu's "Eſprit des Loix" was a favourite book with Helvetius. He ſtudied it deeply, and diſcovered, or thought he diſcovered, a radical defect in it; that it did not embrace the original ideas of the things it contained. He thought, likewiſe, that, before legiſlation itſelf were conſidered, man ought to be ſtudied, and to be viewed in relation to thoſe laws which he muſt ſubmit to from the neceſſity of his nature. This made him reſolve to ſupply the deficiency he fancied he had found in the Preſident's performance. He became full of the magnitude of his plan; he formed important ideas of its utility; he relinquished the situation of farmer-general, that worldly cares might not obtrude upon the sacred silence of meditation and philosophy; he retired to his estates in the country; and after ten years thought and labour, he gave to the world, in 1758, his work entitled *De l'Esprit, &c.* Of this production I have given my opinion in the subjoined criticism, and I shall here only mention the circumstances attending its publication.

The parliament of Paris condemned it immediately; but it was unfortunate in the object of its censure: Helvetius had declared, that, were man provided with a hoof like a horse, he must for ever remain without habitation, without manufactures, without every thing in fact which depends upon manual exertion. The truth of this can be doubted only by those bigots who suppose that, in stating a philosophical fact, the omnipotence of the deity is impeached. Senseless zealots have done more injury to religion than the most determined atheists; by insulting the reason of man, they have driven him to erect a fabric more consistent in its parts than that which we are now called upon to reverence. Voltaire attacked this superstitious mummery with well-directed and effective ridicule.

"It is a little extraordinary," says he*, "that they should have persecuted, disgraced, and harassed, a much-respected philosopher of our days, the innocent, the good Helvetius, for having said that, if men had been without hands they could not have built houses, or worked in tapistry. Apparently those who

---

* " Dictionnaire Philosophique," article *Homme.* The above is preceded by the following satiric lines : the whole is intended to shew how much man owes to cultivation.

> Mon cher Adam, mon gourmand, mon bon père,
> Que fesais-tu dans les jardins d'Eden ?
> Travaillais-tu pour ce sot genre humain ?
> Caressais-tu Madame Eve ma mere ?
> Avouez moi que vous aviez tous deux
> Les ongles longs, un peu noirs et crasseux,
> La chevelure assez mal ordonnée,
> Le teint bruni, la peau rude et tannée.
> Sans propreté l'amour le plus hereux
> N'est plus amour, c'est un besoin honteux.
> Bientôt lassés de leur belle aventure,
> Dessous un chêne ils soupent galamment,
> Avec de l'eau, du millet, et du gland ;
> Le repas fait, ils dorment sur la dure.
> Voila l'état de la pure nature !

The genius of Voltaire was not masculine enough; it had not sufficient sublimity, to render him an advocate for a state of nature.—He was sensual and luxurious; he could form no idea of the simple delights of an uncultivated life, where enjoyments are commensurate to the capacities for enjoyment. It is the forgetting of this single fact that has misled so many with regard to the real happiness of what is called a savage state.

b

have condemned this propofition, have a fecret for cutting ftones and wood, and for fewing with the feet.

" I love the author of the book *De l'Efprit.* He is worth all his enemies together. But I have never approved neither of the errors of his work, nor the trivial truths which he brings forth with fuch pomp. I have taken his part decidedly, when abfurd men have condemned him, even for thefe very truths."

And in another part he fpeaks thus of this injudicious perfecution.

" Who would believe, that, in the eighteenth century, a philofopher would have been dragged before the fecular tribunals, and treated as impious by others, for having faid that men could not have exercifed the arts if they had not had hands. I have no doubt that they will foon condemn to the galleys the firft who fhall have the infolence to fay, that a man cannot think without his head; for, fome bachelor will tell him, the foul is a pure fpirit, the head is nothing but matter; God can place the foul in the nails, as well as in the fcull, therefore I profcribe you as impious.*"

Had the objects of Voltaire's ridicule and fatire been always as legitimate as this, the world would have had lefs reafon to lament the abufe of genius and the degradation of talent. It moves refentment to fee perfecution lift her hand againft the free operations of the human mind, and endeavour to circumfcribe its limits by legal profecutions. When I read fuch inftances of tyranny and oppreffion, I venerate my country tenfold, and feel a prouder confcioufnefs at my heart as I reflect that I am an Englifhman.

The next ftep was to remove Helvetius from the poft which he held of Maître d'Hôtel to the Queen, and it was even with difficulty that his friends were able to refcue him from the fevere profecutions that hung over him.

In 1760, Paliffot de Montenoi produced the comedy of *Les Philofophes,* the object of which was to ridicule the tenets of Helvetius, D' Alembert, Diderot, Duclos, perpetual fecretary of the French Academy, &c. It had a prodigious run. Voltaire, who was the conftant vindicator of infulted genius, and in an efpecial manner the champion of Helvetius, came forth in battle array againft Montenoi. He publifhed an anonymous poem entitled *Le Ruffe à Paris,* and in the perfon of the fuppofed Mufcovite he attacks the illiberality of Montenoi. This dramatic freedom which permits the fatirift to tranfplant the private individual to the boards of the theatre, brings us back to the firft æra of the Greek drama, when Ariftophanes held up to ridicule before the people of Athens, their gods, their heroes, and their poets. But I think it too perfonal; it can be of no avail now; it might, perhaps, be productive of fome good

---

* Dictionnaire Historique, Art. Lettres.

in a rude age, and in a popular government where the public voice gave the bias to public meafures; the ftage might then become an inftrument of party; but when the object is merely to load with unmerited contempt and derifion a fuffering individual; when we would excite a laugh at the expence of the beft feelings of human nature, I can think but lightly of his heart who holds the pen for fuch a purpofe. Perfonal fatire muft always proceed from illaudable motives.

Voltaire, in a note to the poem already mentioned, fays, fpeaking of the *Philofophes* of Montenoi, " il fe reprochera fans doute cette faute toute fa vie;" and afterwards, enumerating the names of thofe whom he had traduced, he concludes with Helvetius; " admirable," adds he, " for a fingle action; he has quitted two hundred thoufand livres per year, to cultivate the belles lettres in peace, and he does good with what remains. The fimplicity and goodnefs of his character have made him hazard in a book, otherwife full of genius, falfe and very reprehenfible pofitions, of which, like the great Fenelon, he was the firft to repent.*"

But Voltaire did not ftop here. Many letters paffed between him and Paliffot de Montenoi upon the fubject. The refult, however, was as ufual; they ceafed with each their own opinions more ftrongly fixed: yet it fhews Voltaire in an advantageous light, to fee him fo unweariedly occupied in vindicating his friend. He forefaw what would be the refult of fuch a free inquiry; he knew that the government would not permit it to pafs unreproved, and he had experienced in his own perfon the effects of fecular and religious perfecution. Soon after the publication of his work, he wrote to Helvetius a letter, confifting of profe and poetry, in which are thefe lines:

" Votre livre eft dicté par la faine raifon;
Partez vite, et quittez la France."

The event verified his expectations, and Helvetius, to remove from the tempeft he had raifed, took a journey into England in the year 1764, and another into Pruffia in 1765. He was well received in England; and Frederic lodged him in his palace, and had him always at his table. The ferment, however, was not eafily allayed. In July 1769 we find Voltaire writing to Helvetius, and begging him to leave France. " In your place," fays he, " I fhould not hefitate a moment to fell all that I have in France; there are fome excellent eftates in my neighbourhood, and there you might cultivate in peace the arts you love."

Thus conftant, thus unfhaken, was the friendfhip of Voltaire toward Helvetius; and it appears that he did not efcape cenfure for this fteady perfeverance.† His numerous enemies chofe it

---

* Le Ruffe à Paris, note r.
† See "Sur un écrit anonyme à Ferney, 20 Avril, 1772." *Mélanges Littéraires.*

for a subject of accusation, and Voltaire had not dignity of character enough to despise their malice. If there be any occasion
when we are imperiously called upon to preserve a stern silence
towards our antagonists, it is when they attempt to convert
our virtues into vices, for the attempt itself must carry depra-
vity on its face; it stands condemned as soon as known; every
heart spurns at it. Hume should have known this when he suffered D'Alembert to draw up his *Exposé Succinct* against
Rousseau.

The immediate and necessary consequence of this persecution
was, with regard to the work, an uncommon notoriety. It
rose to an almost unprecedented popularity. The world were
anxious to read a book which had called forth the animadver-
sions of public bodies; they read and wondered. They saw,
indeed, many opinions not conformable to reason; they saw a
constant attempt to strip mankind of all nobility of motive; they
saw some principles disseminated which in their consequences
led to fatalism; but in all this they only beheld the reveries of a
philosopher; the fanciful dogmas of a mind fevered with the
thirst of fame. There was nothing that affected the immediate
interests of society either morally, religiously, or politically;
there was no attempt to propagate heresies; no people were
called upon to renounce their present rulers, to discard their present notions; the book was merely a calm and speculative inquiry into some recondite points of metaphysics, mingled indeed
with error, but yet containing many sublime and interesting
truths; containing a singular penetration of judgment and an
acute estimation of the probable incentives to human conduct.
In all this they looked in vain for an adequate object of persecution. What injury had been committed? None! What
injury could be committed by the silent introduction of a metaphysical book? None! Men are drawn into action by more
powerful motives than abstruse reasonings. Public curiosity
was excited; the book continued to sell; its principles continued to be canvassed, and its author gained precisely what he
wished, a noisy and extensive reputation. Opinion, however,
varied as to its merits. Voltaire thought it full of trivial thoughts,
too pompously delivered; others condemned its anecdotic frivolity; it was, they thought, too trifling for a work of that kind;
some too fancied that the language was often forced, that it
abounded with misplaced figures and ornaments, and often be-
trayed a false warmth of colouring. To all these opinions
truth cannot be denied; yet with all its imperfections, it is the
work of a man of genius, and a work that will preserve an un-
diminished interest in perusal, from its copiousness of narrative,
when its principles will no longer be received or contended.

About the period of the publication of this work, Helvetius
corresponded with Hume. He had mentioned the English philosopher frequently in the course of his work, and Hume's vanity was gratified by it. In a letter to Dr. Robertson, dated

London, March 12, 1759, he says, " I believe I mentioned to
you a French gentleman, Monsieur Helvetius, whose book
De l'Esprit was making a great noise in Europe. He is a
very fine genius, and has the character of a very worthy man.
My name is mentioned several times in his work, with marks
of esteem ; and he has made me an offer if I would translate his
work into English, to translate anew all my philosophical writings into French. He says, that none of them are well done,
except that on the Natural History of Religion, by Monsieur
Matigny, a counsellor of state. He added, that the Abbé
Prevost, celebrated for the *Memoires d'un homme d'Honneur*,
and other entertaining books, was just now translating my history. This account of Helvetius engaged me to send him over
the new editions of all my writings : and I have added your history, which I told him was here published with great applause ;
adding, that the subject was interesting, and the execution ma-
terly ; and that it was probable some men of letters at Paris
may think that a translation of it would be agreeable to the
public."

It is pleasing thus to penetrate into the closets of celebrated
men, to see how they are influenced by ordinary motives, and
what striking analogies there are in the human heart With
what eagerness Hume embraced the proposal of a new translation of his works, and how readily he becomes the pander to
his own fame; and probably had these translations been executed, he would have been among the first to propagate the circumstance as a proof of his reputation; as a thing of which he had
not the least presentiment ; as an event which had happened in
the usual course of literary celebrity. There is something mechanical in this bargaining of authors; it is as if a butcher
should say to a baker, recommend my beef, and i'll recommend
your loaves. Men of real merit should be superior to this; the
only assistance which genius ought to lend towards the acquisition of its own fame, should be the excellence of its productions ; beyond that all is servile: to wait with silent pride the
gradually swelling echoes of renown, retired and superior as it
were to the very splendour it adores, is the task of true dignity,
the post of a perfectly elevated character.

This mercantile scheme did not, however, succeed. Hume
at the conclusion of the letter says, " I have got a good reason
or pretence for excusing me to M. Helvetius with regard to
the translation of his work. A translation of it was previously
advertised here."

This additionally justifies the expression that Hume was a
pander to his own fame. Helvetius offers to translate Hume's
works *anew*, considering any antecedent translations as no reason
why he should decline his; but Hume, while he sends off immediately new editions of all his works, to be translated by
Helvetius, thinks himself exonerated from the mutual obligation, because a translation was already advertised. Whether

Helvetius penetrated into this fubterfuge I know not; but from fome motive or other, the intended tranflation never was executed. Hume, in another letter to Adam Smith, a month fubfequent to the former, fays, " I believe I have mentioned to you already Helvetius' book *De l'Efprit*. It is worth your reading, not for its philofophy, which I do not highly value, but for its agreeable compofition." He adds a circumftance which will not be eafily reconciled : " I had a letter from him a few days ago, wherein he tells me, that my name was much oftener in the manufcript, but that the cenfor of books at Paris obliged him to ftrike it out." It is difficult to conceive that the name of an individual fhould be profcribed in a country where his works are publicly fold; and the very perfon offering to give a new tranflation of writings, from which he was not permitted by the public cenfor, to make fuch copious extracts as he wifhed. I muft here fufpect the fincerity of the Frenchman, who probably wifhed to compliment at the expence of truth.

After his return to France from Pruffia, in 1765, Helvetius retired to his eftate at Voré, and lived remote from the noife and buftle of the world. He paffed his time in ftudy, in felect fociety, and in acts of beneficence. " The fight of mifery which he could not relieve," fays the author of his *Eloge*, " rendered Paris difagreeable to him." He was a man of great humanity; he loved to affift indigent merit; he allowed a penfion of two thoufand livres to Marivaux, and one of three thoufand to M. Saurin of the French academy. In the country he practifed extenfive benevolence: but it was performed without oftentation; almoft indeed with an affectation of fecrecy. Every day were introduced to him, with the moft cautious privacy, fome new objects of charity. Often in their prefence he would fay to his valet, " I forbid you to fpeak of what you now fee, even after my death." And when it was fometimes pointed out to him that he beftowed his bounty upon perfons undeferving of it, he replied, " If I were a king I would correct them, but as I am only rich, and they are poor, I do my duty in relieving them."

In his domestic relations he appears to us in a very amiable light. He was married, and proved a good hufband, feeling, affectionate, and liberal. At his table were feen the moft celebrated men of all nations. His economy was regular; his life not luxurious or effeminate. It is faid he maintained his feudal rights with jealoufy towards his tenants and dependents; but if ever they met with misfortune, if poverty approached them, then his heart was prompt to pity, his tongue to confole, his purfe to relieve. How fuperior is fuch a character; and how inadequate the praife we beftow upon him, when we confider him only as an acute, an interefting, and an eloquent, writer !

Of the laft moments of Helvetius, I have not been able to learn any thing. It is only recorded that his death was occa-

fioned by an attack of the gout in his head and ftomach, which
terminated his life in December 1771, in the fifty-fixth year of
his age.   The vigour of his conftitution had led his friends and
the world to hope for a longer duration of exiftence.   Voltaire
lived to fee the man expire whom he had fo warmly and fo uni-
formly vindicated and fupported through life.   Such events may be
reckoned among the miferies of old age; we live to fee our-
felves alone; we feel a cheerlefs defolation take poffeffion of
our hearts, as we reflect that the grave has torn from us the
friends of our youth, the companions of our ftruggles, the folace
of our decrepitude.   It is this that renders death, all unlovely
as he is, an afylum, a refuge, from the melancholy confcioufnefs of folitude, at the moment when moft we need the con-
folations of fociety.

I have already remarked, that Helvetius was largely favoured
by nature in perfonal endowments.   He was well made, had a
prepoffeffing addrefs, and an interefting countenance.   His eyes
expreffed what his prevailing character was; mildnefs and benevolence.   He was particularly ambitious of the notice of the
fair fex, and fought every means likely to attain his end; but,
contrary to the ufual procefs, he transferred his attention, for
this purpofe, from his perfon to his mind.   He fought to cap-
tivate them by intellectual endowments; that he fucceeded I am
doubtful; he was led into the error by miftaking their love of
eccentricity for a genuine admiration of genius.   In the *Eloge*
prefixed to his poem of *Le Bonheur*, the following anecdote is
related:—" He was walking alone in one of our public gardens,
when he perceived, furrounded by a circle of young and interefting females, a fingular figure.   It was M. de Maupertuis,
who, dreffed in a fantaftic and grotefque manner, which added to
his natural originality, feemed to occupy their whole care and
attention."   Helvetius paufed; he interrogated his heart; he
fancied he had difcovered a new avenue to female affection:
whether, like Maupertuis, he adopted a ridiculous drefs I know
not; nor am I prepared to fay whether he was more fuccefsful
as a votary of reafon, than as a difciple of folly and fafhion.

He poffeffed a firm and intrepid character, and one which
might be faid naturally to revolt againft injuftice and oppreffion.   He had a rooted averfion to what are called great men: I
mean perfons poffeffing titles, ribbons, garters, &c. and who
think they conftitute a right to exact homage and refpect from
individuals who can boaft no fuch diftinctions.   In the following work he expreffes his fentiments upon connections of this
kind.   " Whoever is born," fays he, " to do honour to the
age in which he lives, is always on his guard againft the great."
They who know the weaknefs, egotifm, vanity, frivolity, and
bloated pride of thofe ufually termed great; who, without one
individual claim to notice from perfonal merit, exact a fervile
humiliating attention from thofe whom they deem inferior;
who, with minds barren as a defert, with hearts often corrupt as

an ulcerous fore, think they cover the moft difgufting vices of our nature by oftentatious fplendour, and a poor parade of empty titles; they, I fay, who know this, will, though not " born to do honour to their age," preferve a dignified indifference to connections which rarely reflect real honour, but more frequently demand a facrifice of princi le, feeling, and character.

A French writer, fpeaking of Helvetius, fays, that no one ought to have been more convinced than himfelf, that, to fucceed in any thing, it is only neceffary vigoroufly to refolve upon it. " He became a good dancer, an able fencer, an expert markfman, an enlightened fi ancier, a good poet, a great philofopher, the moment he wifhed to be fo." There is no doubt, that, when the power is commenfurate to an undertaking, there is nothing wanting to enfure fuccefs to that undertaking but the fteady refolution of perfeverance; but it does not follow that we can attain whatever we wifh, however ardent the wifh may be. It is obferved by Bolingbroke, that we can conceive what we cannot accomplifh, and this is not only true of human nature in general, but of every man in particular. We are all confcious of cherifhing ideas of excellence, which fometimes means, fometimes ability, fometimes opportunity, forbid us to attain.

The above mentioned writer relates further of Helvetius, " that he loved the fex much, but that it was without fentiment; he was propelied entirely by the fenfes. In friendfhip he had no exclufive preference; the connection in his breaft was devoid of tendernefs*. His friends, when in trouble, found him feeling, becaufe he was good; but in the ordinary courfe of his life they were not neceffary to him. His converfation was often that of a man full of his own ideas; he loved difpute; he advanced paradoxes to fee them combated. He delighted to make thofe think whom he imagined capable of it; he ufed to fay that he was going with them to *a chace of ideas.* He had the greateft refpect for the felf-love of others; and he fhewed his own fuperiority fo little, that many intelligent men, who frequently faw him, have been a long time before they difcovered it. He loved glory with ardour, for it was the only paffion he felt."

After his death were publifhed *Le Bonheur,* a poem already mentioned, and *De l'Homme*—" A Treatife on Man, his intellectual faculties and his education," in two volumes octavo. The reafon he affigned for its being a pofthumous production is, " that had he publifhed this book in his life-time, he fhould, in all probability, have expofed himfelf to perfecution, without the profpect of any perfonal advantage." This work is no lefs bold than that on the Mind; it may indeed be confidered as a farther amplification of the principles of that work. The paradox of

---

* He appears to have felt as he wrote; and if fo, he felt as a cynic; not as a man. I am forry to find this recorded of Helvetius; it interrupts the harmony of his character. Read his definition of friendfhip, and judge if he did not draw from his own bofom.

original genius is here confidered in every poffible point of view. He paints man fuch as nature and fociety have made him in all times an in all places. He fhews his ufual acutenefs in detecting the intricacies of human paffion.

In 1792 the municipality of Paris gave the name of Helvetius to St. Anne's-ftreet; a common revolutionary teftimony of regard to the memory of thofe writers whofe production it was thought had contributed to that aftonifhing event.

I had intended to take fome notice here of the curious plagiarifm from Mafon's Elfrida to be found in Helvetius, and which is mentioned in the Life of Gray.* It is, perhaps, as fingular an inftance as any to be found in modern literature. I am not fatisfied with Mafon's explanation of the affair; and in many inftances, where he endeavours to trace parallel paffages, he has only fhewn fuch accidental coincidences as muft always occur when different minds are employed upon fimilar fubjects. I abftain, however, from extending this memoir by copying the paffages in queftion; becaufe the Life of Gray is in every body's hands, and to many it would therefore be fuperfluous; to thofe who are unacquainted with it, I refer them to that part of Gray's Correfpondence pointed out in the note below.

In clofing this Life of Helvetius, it may finally be obferved, that, for ingenuity, intereft, eloquence, and reafoning, the "Effays on the Mind" ftand confpicuous; it has blemifhes, but imperfection is faftened on our natures; its excellencies greatly preponderate, and no man can rife from the perufal without feeling that he has learnt to eftimate, with greater precifion, the actions of human nature.

---

* See Mason's Life of Gray, Sec. iv. Let. 44.

C

PREFACE.

THE subject I propose to examine in this work is new and interesting. People have hitherto considered the Mind only under some of its views: for great writers have no more than cast a rapid glance over it; and this has emboldened me to treat of the subject.

The knowledge of the Mind, when we consider it in its utmost extent, is so closely connected with the knowledge of the heart, and of the passions of men, that it was impossible to write on this subject, without treating, on that part of morality at least, which is common to men of all nations, and which in all governments can have no other object in view than the public advantage.

The principles I establish on this subject are, I think, conformable to the general interest, and to experience. It is by facts that I have ascended to causes. I imagined that morality ought to be treated like all the other sciences, and founded on experiment, as well as natural philosophy. I have adhered to this idea, from the persuasion that all morality, where its principles are of use to the public, is necessarily conformable to the morals of religion, which are only the perfection of human morals. For the rest, if I am deceived, and if, contrary to my expectation, some of my principles are not conformable to the general interest, this proceeds from an error of my judgment, and not of my heart; and I declare, before hand, that I disown them.

I desire but one favour of my reader, that is, to hear, before he condemns me; to follow the chain that unites all my ideas together; to be my judge, and not of my party. This request is not the effect of a foolish confidence, for I have too often found that to be bad at night, which I have thought to be good in the morning, to have an high opinion of my own abilities.

Perhaps I have treated of a subject above my strength: but what man knows himself so well, as not to presume too much? I cannot, however, reproach myself with not having used my utmost endeavours to merit the approbation of the public; and if I do not obtain it, I shall be more afflicted than surprised. In this case, to desire is not sufficient to obtain.

In every thing I have said, I have sought only for the truth, not merely for the honour of delivering it, but because truth is useful to man. If I have deviated from it, I shall find, even in my errors themselves, motives of consolation. " If men," as M. de Fontenelle observes, " cannot, on any subject whatsoever, arrive at what is rational, till after having, in that very subject, exhausted all imaginable folly," my errors will then be of use to my fellow-citizens : I shall have pointed out the rock by my shipwreck. " How many absurdities," adds M. de Fontenelle, " should we not now utter, if the ancients had not already said them before us, and had in a manner delivered us from them ?"

I repeat then, that I shall warrant in my work nothing but the purity and rectitude of my intentions. In the mean time, however assured we may be of our intentions, the voice of envy is so favourably heard, and its frequent declamations are so adapted to seduce the minds that are equally honest and enlightened, that we cannot write in a manner without trembling. The discouragement given to men of

genius from imputations frequently filled with ca-
lumny, seem already to presage the return of the
age of ignorance. It is in every instance, only in
mediocrity of talents that people find an asylum
against the pursuits of the envious. Mediocrity is
now become a protection, and I have probably obtained that protection in spite of myself.

Besides, I believe that it will be difficult for envy
to impute to me the desire of wounding my fellow-
citizens. This kind of work, in which I consider no
man in particular, but men and nations in general,
ought to shelter me from all suspicion of malignity.
I shall even add, that, in reading these discourses, it
will be perceived that I love men, and desire their
happiness, without hating or despising any of them in
particular.

Some of my ideas will perhaps appear too bold.
If the reader think them false, I desire him to recollect, while he condemns them, that it is only by
the boldest attempts that the greatest truth can sometimes be discovered; and that the fear of advancing
an error, ought not to deter us from proceeding in
the search of truth. In vain would base and cowardly men proscribe it, and sometimes give it the
name of odious and licentious; in vain do they repeat, that truth is often dangerous. Supposing that
this is sometimes the case, to what still greater danger would that nation be exposed, which should consent to continue in ignorance? Every nation without knowledge, when it has ceased to be fierce and
savage, is degraded, and will sooner or later be subdued. It was less the valour, than the military knowledge, of the Romans that triumphed over the Gauls.

If the knowledge of such a truth, might, at such
an instant. be attended with some inconveniences;
that instant being past, that very truth will again
become useful to all ages and nations.

Such is the fate of human things: there is none

that may not at certain moments become dangerous; but it is only on this condition that we enjoy them. Woe to him that would from this motive deprive mankind of them.

At the very moment when they forbid the knowledge of certain truths, it will no longer be permitted to mention any. A thousand men in power, who have often ill intentions, under the pretence that it is sometimes wise to conceal the truth, would banish it entirely from the universe. Thus the enlightened part of the public, who alone know all its value, incessantly desire it: they are not afraid to expose themselves to uncertain evils to enjoy the real advantages it procures. Among the qualities of mankind, that which they esteem the most is, that elevation of soul which refuses to submit to the meanness of a lie. They know how useful it is to think and speak every thing; and that errors cease to be dangerous, when permitted to contradict them.— They are soon known to be errors; they sink of themselves into the abyss of forgetfulness, and truth alone swims over the vast extent of ages.

CONTENTS.

———

ESSAY I.

OF THE MIND CONSIDERED IN ITSELF.

THIS discourse is to prove, that natural sensibility and memory are the productive causes of all our ideas; and that all our false judgments are the effect of our passions, or our ignorance.

CHAP. I.

CHAP. II.

CHAP. III.

In this chapter, it is proved, that the second source of our errors consists in the ignorance of the facts of comparison on which, in every instance depends the justness of our decisions.

CHAP. IV.

Some examples of the errors occasioned by the ignorance of the signification of words.

It follows from this discourse, that our passions and our ignorance are the sources of our errors; that all our false judgments are the effects of accidental causes, that do not suppose in the mind a faculty of judging distinct from that of sensation.

ESSAY II.

OF THE MIND RELATIVELY TO SOCIETY.

IT is proposed to prove, in this discourse, that the same interest which influences the judgment we form of actions, and makes us consider them as virtuous, vicious, or allowable according as they are useful, prejudicial, or indifferent, with respect to the public, equally influences the judgment we form of ideas; and that, as well in subjects of morality, as in those of genius, it is interest alone that dictates all our judgments; a truth that cannot be perceived in its full extent, without considering probity and genius, relatively, 1. to an individual; 2. to a small society; 3. to a nation; 4. to different ages and countries, and 5. to the whole world.

CHAP. I.

CHAP. II.

CHAP. III.

It is proved by facts, that we esteem in others, only the ideas that we have an interest in esteeming.

CHAP. IV.

It is also proved in this chapter, that we are always, through indolence and vanity, forced to proportion our esteem for the ideas of others, to the analogy and conformity of those ideas with our own.

CHAP. V.

The design of this chapter is to shew that particular societies give the name of worthy only to such actions as are useful: now the interest of these societies being often found to be opposite to the public interest, they must frequently apply the term worthy to actions really prejudicial to the public; they must then, by the praise of these actions, frequently seduce the probity of the most worthy men, and, unknown to themselves, lead them astray from the path of virtue.

CHAP. VI.

In this chapter is pointed out how a person may repel the insinuations of a particular society, resist their seductions, and preserve a virtue not to be shaken by the shock of a thousand private interests.

CHAP. VII.

It is here shewn, that society weighs in the same balance the merit of the ideas and actions of men. Now the interest of those societies not being always conformable to the general interest, they must, in consequence of this, form very different judgments of the same subjects from those of the public.

CHAP. VIII.

In consequence of the difference observable between the interest of the public and that of particular societies, it is proved, in this chapter, that these societies must affix a great esteem to what is called good breeding and polite conversation.

CHAP. IX.

The public cannot have the same esteem for polite conversation and genteel address as particular societies.

CHAP. X.

It is proved, that in this respect the difference between the judgment of the public and particular societies depend on their different interests.

CHAP. XI.

In consequence of the principles above established, it is shewn that the general interest regulates the judgment formed by the public of the actions of men.

CHAP. XII.

In this chapter it is proved that the esteem of the public for the ideas of men is always proportioned to the interest people have in esteeming them.

CHAP. XIII.

It is proposed to shew, in this chapter, that people have, in all ages and all countries, agreed to give the name of virtuous only to such actions as were, or at least they believed to be, of use to the public. To throw the greater light upon this subject, virtue is distinguished in this chapter into two different kinds.

CHAP. XIV.

We understand by prejudicial virtues, or those that arise from prejudice, such where the exact observance of them does not in the least contribute to the public happiness; and by true virtues, those the practice of which secures the felicity of the people. In consequence of these two different kinds of virtue, a distinction is made in this chapter between two different kinds of the corruption of manners; the one religious, the other political: a knowledge proper to diffuse new light over the science of morality.

CHAP. XV.

The design of this chapter is to prove, that the virtues or vices of the people depend on the goodness or badness of the legislation; and that most moralists, in the paintings they make of the vices, seem less inspired by the love of the public welfare than by personal interest or private hatred.

CHAP. XVI.

The unfolding of the preceding principles.

CHAP. XVII.

These principles give individuals, nations, and even legislators, more clear ideas of virtue; facilitate the reformation of the laws: inform us that the science of morality is the science even of the legislation; and, in short, furnish us with the means of rendering people more happy, and empires more durable.

CHAP. XVIII.

The exposition of the subject of inquiry in the following chapters.

CHAP. XIX.

CHAP. XX.

In conformity to the plan of this discourse, it is here shewn that interest among all nations, is the dispenser of the esteem granted to the ideas of men; and that nations, always faithful to the interest of their vanity, esteem in other nations only such ideas as are analogous to their own.

CHAP. XXI.

After having proved that nations despise manners, customs, and practices, different from their own, it is added, that their vanity makes them consider, as a gift of nature, the superiority some of them have over others; a superiority that is solely owing to the political constitution of the state.

CHAP. XXII.

In this chapter it is shewn that vanity rules nations as well as individuals; that every one obeys the law of interest; and that if consequently each nation has not such an esteem for morality as it ought to have for that science, it is because morality is still in its cradle, and seems to be hitherto of no use to the world.

CHAP. XXIII.

CHAP. XXIV.

CHAP. XXV.

CHAP. XXVI.

This chapter is to shew that there are ideas which are of use to Mankind, and that the ideas of this species are the only ones that can make us obtain the esteem of nations.

The general conclusion of this discourse is, that interest, as we propose to prove, is the only dispenser of the esteem and contempt affixed to the actions and ideas of men.

ESSAY III.

WHETHER GENIUS OUGHT TO BE CONSIDERED AS A NATURAL GIFT, OR AS AN EFFECT OF EDUCATION.

In order to solve this problem, inquiry is made in this discourse, whether nature has endued men with an equal ability of mind, or whether she has favoured some more than others; and it is examined whether all the men who are well organized have not in themselves the natural powers of acquiring the most lofty ideas, when they have motives sufficient to surmount the pain of application.

CHAP. I.

CHAP. II.

CHAP. III.

CHAP. IV.

It is proved in this chapter that nature has endued all men commonly well organized with a capacity of attention necessary for the acquisition of the most lofty ideas: it is at length observed, that attention is a fatigue and pain, from which people would always free themselves, were they not animated by a passion proper to change this pain into pleasure; hence the question is reduced to the inquiry whether all men are by nature susceptible of passions so strong as to endue them with that degree of attention to which superiority of genius is annexed. In order to arrive at this knowledge, inquiry is made in the following chapter, what are the powers by which we are moved.

CHAP. V.

These powers are reduced to two: one communicated by the strong passions, and the other by an aversion to lassitude, or inaction. The effects of this last force are examined in this chapter.

CHAP. VI.

It is proved that the passions lead us to heroic actions, and enable us to acquire the most noble ideas.

CHAP. VII.

CHAP. VIII.

After having proved that the passions deliver us from incertitude and indolence, and endue us with that continuity of attention necessary to raise the mind to the most exalted ideas, it is proper to examine at length whether all men are susceptible of passions, and whether they are so to that degree proper to endue them with this species of attention. In order to discover this, it is proper to ascend to their origin.

CHAP. IX.

The design of this chapter is to shew that all our passions have their source in the love of pleasure, or in the fear of pain; consequently in natural sensibility. For examples of this kind, choice is made of the passions that appear most independent of this sensibility, that is, avarice, ambition, pride, and friendship.

CHAP. X.

It is proved that this passion is founded on the love of pleasure and the fear of pain; and it is shewn how avarice, by kindling in us the thirst of pleasure, may always deprive us of it.

CHAP. XI.

The application of the same principles, which prove that the same motives that make us desire riches make us seek for grandeur.

CHAP. XII.

This objection is answered, and it is proved that, in this respect, it is with ambition as with avarice.

CHAP. XIII.

The subject of this chapter is to shew that people desire to be worthy of esteem only that they may be esteemed; and for no other reason than to enjoy the advantages which esteem procures: advantages that are always reduced to natural pleasures.

CHAP. XIV.

Another application of the same principles.

CHAP. XV.

After having proved, in the preceding chapters, that all our passions receive their origin from natural sensibility; to confirm this truth, it is proved, in this chapter, that, by the assistance of natural pleasures, legislators may fill the heart with all the passions. But granting that all men are susceptible of passions, as it may be supposed they are not less so of the degree of passion necessary to raise them to the most exalted ideas, and that there might be brought, as an example of this opinion, the insensibility of certain nations to the love of glory and virtue; it is proved that the indifference of these nations, in this respect, depends only on accidental causes, such as the different forms of governments.

CHAP. XVI.

In order to solve this question, inquiry is made into man, in relation to the mixture of his vices and his virtues, the sport of his passions, and the idea that ought to be annexed to the word virtuous; and it is discovered that it is not to nature, but to the particular legislation of some empires, that we ought to attribute the indifference of certain nations to virtue. In order to cast a greater light on this subject, inquiry is particularly made into despotic governments and free states, and into the different effects produced by the different forms of these governments. The author begins with despotic power; and, the better to know its nature examines what motive inflames man with an unbridled desire of arbitrary power.

CHAP. XVII.

CHAP. XVIII.

It is proved in this chapter, that the viziers have no interest in obtaining instruction, or supporting censure; that, being taken from the body of the citizens, they, on entering into place, have no principles of justice or skill in the art of government; and that they cannot form clear ideas of virtue.

CHAP. XIX.

CHAP. XX.

It is proved, that, in despotic empires, people have really a contempt for virtue, and that they only honour the name.

CHAP. XXI.

After having shewn, in the stupidity and baseness of most of the people subject to arbitrary power, the cause of the overthrow of despotic empires, it is concluded, from what has been said on this subject, that the indifference of certain nations to virtue, depends solely on the particular form of government: and, that nothing may be left that might be wished for on this subject, an inquiry is made, in the following chapters, into the causes of the contrary effects.

CHAP. XXII.

It is shewn in this chapter, that this love of glory and virtue depend, in every empire, on the address with which the legislator unites private interest with that of the public; an union more easily formed in some countries than in others.

CHAP. XXIII.

It is proved in this chapter, that the production of great men is in all countries the necessary effect of the rewards assigned to great abilities and distinguished virtue; and that the virtues and talents are no where so well rewarded as in poor and warlike republics.

CHAP. XXIV.

This chapter contains the proof of the proposition laid down in the preceding chapter. From it is drawn this conclusion, that we may apply to every species of the passions what is said in the same chapter, of the love or indifference of certain nations for glory and virtue; whence it is concluded, that we ought not to attribute to nature that unequal degree of the passions, of which certain nations appear susceptible. This truth is confirmed by proving, in the following chapters, that the force of men's passions is always proportioned to the force of the means made use of to excite them.

CHAP. XXV.

After having shewn the exactness of this connection, it is examined, to what degree of warmth the enthusiasm of the passions may be carried.

CHAP. XXVI.

It is proved, in this chapter, that the passions may be carried to an incredible height, and that all men are consequently capable of a degree of passion more than sufficient to make them triumph over their indolence, and to endue them with that continued attention to which superiority of mind is annexed: that thus the great inequality of genius, perceivable among mankind, depends on the different education they receive, and the unknown chain of different circumstances in which they are placed. In the following chapters is examined, whether these principles are agreeable to facts.

The first design of this chapter is to shew, that the numerous circumstances, the concourse of which is absolutely necessary to form illustrious men, are so seldom found united, that, on supposing all men have equal mental faculties, those who have a genius of the first rank would be as uncommon as they are found to be. It is moreover proved in this chapter, that in morality alone we ought to seek for the true cause of the inequality of genius; that in vain we should attribute it to the different temperature of climates; and in vain endeavour to explain, from physical causes, an infinite number of political phenomena, that are very naturally explained by moral causes. Such are the conquests of the northern nations, the slavery and allegorical genius of the orientals, and, in short, the superiority of different nations in different arts and sciences.

In this chapter is shewn, that, to moral causes alone we ought to attribute the conquests of the northern nations.

The application of the same principles.

The nations who are the most illustrious in the arts and sciences, are those among whom the same arts and sciences have been most honoured: it is not then from the different temperature of climates, but from moral causes that we ought to search for the reason of the inequality of genius.

The general conclusion of this discourse is, that all men well-organized, have the natural power of acquiring the most exalted ideas, and that the difference of genius observable in them, depends on the various circumstances in which they are placed, and on the different education they receive. This conclusion discovers the full importance of education.

ESSAY IV.

OF THE DIFFERENT FACULTIES OF THE MIND.

To convey an exact knowledge of the nature of the mind, it is proposed, in this discourse, to give clear ideas of its several faculties.

CHAP. I.

CHAP. II.

CHAP. III.

CHAP. IV.

CHAP. V.

CHAP. VI.

CHAP. VII.

CHAP. VIII.

It is proved, in this chapter, that in complicated questions, judgment is not sufficient to obtain a clear view of things; but that an extensive mind is necessary for that purpose; that, in general, men are liable to be puffed up with an opinion of their own judgment, and to prefer it to genius: that consequently they pretend to be superior to men of abilities, and believe, that by acknowledging this, they really do themselves but justice; and do not perceive that they are drawn into this error by a mistake, common to almost all mankind: a mistake of which it is, doubtless, useful to discover the cause.

CHAP. IX.

This chapter is properly only an exposition of the two following. There is here shewn only the difficulty of knowing ourselves.

CHAP. X.

An explication of the preceding chapter.

CHAP. XI.

Enquiry is made in this chapter, why we are so prodigal of advice, and so blind to the motives that determine us to give it; and into what errors ignorance of ourselves may, in this respect, sometimes precipitate others. At the conclusion of this chapter are pointed out some of the means proper to facilitate the knowledge of ourselves.

CHAP. XII.

CHAP. XIII.

CHAP. XIV.

After having endeavoured, in the preceding chapter, to annex clear ideas to several of the mental powers and faculties, it is of use to know what are the abilities of mind, which, in their own nature, must reciprocally exclude each other; and the talents which, from contrary habits, are rendered in a manner incompatible. This is the subject to be examined both in this chapter and the following, in which is more particularly shewn the injustice of the public, in this respect, in relation to men of genius.

CHAP. XV.

Attention is paid in this chapter to the consideration of qualities that must reciprocally exclude each other; this is done in order to enlighten mankind with regard to the means of reaping the best advantage possible from their mental abilities.

CHAP. XVI.

This method being pointed out, it seems that the plan of an excellent education ought necessarily to conclude this work; but this plan, though it might, perhaps, appear easy to sketch out, would be, as will be seen in the following chapter, very difficult to execute.

CHAP. XVII.

It is here proved, that it would, doubtless, be extremely useful to perfect the public education; but that nothing could be more difficult: that our manners here actually oppose every kind of reformation; that in vast and powerful empires they have not always an urgent necessity for great men; and that, consequently, the government cannot apply much attention to that part of the administration. It is, however, observed, that in monarchies, such as ours, it would not be impossible to give the plan of an excellent education; but that this attempt would be absolutely vain in empires subject to despotic power, such as those of the east.

DE L'ESPRIT;

OR,

ESSAYS ON THE MIND.

ESSAY I.

CHAP. I.

OF THE MIND CONSIDERED IN ITSELF.

WE hear every day disputes with regard to what ought to be called the Mind; each person delivers his thoughts, but annexes different ideas to the word; and thus the debate is continued, without understanding each other.

In order therefore to enable us to give a just and precise idea of the word Mind, and its different acceptations, it is necessary first to consider the Mind in itself.

We consider the Mind either as the effect of the faculty of thinking, and in this sense the Mind is no more than an assemblage of our thoughts; or, we consider it as the very faculty of thinking.

But, in order to understand what is meant by the Mind, in the latter acceptation, we ought previously to know the productive causes of our ideas.

Man has two faculties; or, if I may be allowed the expression, two passive powers, whose existence is generally and distinctly acknowledged.

The one is the faculty of receiving the different impressions caused by external objects, and is called Physical Sensibility.

B

The other is the faculty of preserving the impressions caused by these objects, called Memory ; and Memory is nothing more than a continued, but weakened, sensation.

Those faculties which I consider as the productive causes of our thoughts, and which we have in common with beasts, would produce but a very small number of ideas, if they were not assisted by certain external organisations.

If Nature, instead of hands and flexible fingers, had terminated our wrist with the foot of a horse, mankind would doubtless have been totally destitute of art, habitation, and defence, against other animals. Wholly employed in the care of procuring food, and avoiding the beasts of prey, they would have still continued wandering in the forests, like fugitive flocks*.

---

* Many pieces have been written on the souls of beasts. They have been alternately denied and allowed the faculty of thinking. And, perhaps, a research sufficiently accurate has not yet been made into the difference between the nature of man and that of other animals, from whence the cause of the inferiority of what is called the soul of the latter may be derived.

1. All the feet of animals terminate either in horn, as those of the ox and the deer; or in nails, as those of the dog and the wolf; or in claws, as those of the lion and the cat. Now this different organisation of our hands, from that of the feet of animals, deprives them, as Mr. Buffon asserts, not only of all claim to the sense of the touch; but also of the dexterity requisite in handling an instrument, in order to make any of the discoveries which suppose the use of hands.

2. The life of animals, in general, being of a shorter duration than that of man, neither permits them to make so many observations, nor consequently to acquire so many ideas.

3. Animals, being better armed and better clothed by nature than the human species, have fewer wants, and consequently ought to have less invention. If the voracious animals are more cunning than others, it is because hunger, ever inventive, inspires them with the art of forming stratagems to surprise their prey.

4. The animals compose only a society that flies from man, who, by the assistance of weapons, made by himself, is become formidable to the strongest among them.

Besides, man is the most fruitful animal upon earth. He is born,

It is therefore evident, that, according to this supposition, the police would never have been carried in any society to that degree of perfection, to which it is now arrived. There is not a nation now existing, but, with regard to the action of the mind, must not have continued very inferior to certain savage nations,

---

and lives in every climate ; while many of the other animals, as the lion, the elephant, and the rhinoceros, are found only in a certain latitude.

And the more a species of animals, capable of making observations, is multiplied, the more ideas and genius it possesses.

But some may ask why monkeys, whose paws are nearly as dexterous as our hands, do not make a progress equal to that of man ? Because they are inferior to him in several respects ; because men are more multiplied upon the earth ; because among tho different species of monkeys, there are but few whose strength can be compared to that of man ; because the monkeys, being frugivorous, have fewer wants, and therefore less invention, than man ; because their life is shorter, and they form only a fugitive society with regard to man, and such animals as the tiger, the lion, &c. and, finally, because the organical disposition of their body keeps them, like children, in perpetual motion, even after their desires are satisfied. Monkeys are not susceptible of lassitude, which ought to be considered, as I shall prove in the third essay, as one of the principles of the perfection of the human mind.

By combining all these differences between the nature of man and beast, we may understand, why sensibility and memory, though faculties common to man and other animals, are in the latter only sterile faculties.

It may perhaps be objected, that God, agreeable to his justice, cannot have subjected to pain and death innocent creatures ; and consequently that beasts are mere machines. But, in answer to this objection, I must observe, that, as neither the scripture, nor the church, has any where declared, that animals are mere machines, we are doubtless ignorant of the motives for God's conduct towards animals, though we ought to suppose them just. There is no necessity for having recourse to Malebranche's jocular reply to a person, who, maintaining to him that animals were sensible of pain, said, They have then probably eaten forbidden hay

who have not two hundred different ideas*, nor two hundred
words to express those ideas ; and whose language must consequently be reduced, like that of animals, to five or six different
sounds or cries†, if we take from it the words bow, arrow, nets,
&c. which suppose the use of hands.   From whence I conclude,
that, without a certain exterior organisation, sensibility and memory in us would prove two sterile faculties.   We ought to examine if these two faculties, by the assistance of this organisation, have in reality produced all our thoughts.

But, before we examine this subject, I may possibly be asked,
whether these two faculties are modifications of a spiritual or a
material substance ? This question, which has formerly been so
often debated by philosophers ‡, and by some persons revived

---

* The ideas of numbers, so simple, so easily acquired, and to which
our wants often refer us, are so prodigiously limited in certain nations,
that they cannot reckon more than three, expressing all numbers
above three by the vague expression, A great many.

† Of this kind were the people Dampier found in an island producing neither tree nor shrub, and who lived on the fish which the
waves drove into their creeks ; nor was their language any more than
a sort of clucking noise, resembling that of a turkey-cock.

‡ Whatever may have been affirmed by the stoics, Seneca was not
fully convinced of the spirituality of the soul : " Your letter (says he
to one of his friends) came at an improper time, being delivered to
me, when I was taking a delicious walk in the temple of Hope. There
I freed myself from all doubts with regard to my soul's immortality :
my imagination, gently warmed by the reasoning of some great men,
firmly believed in that immortality, which they promise more than
they prove. I began to be displeased with my existence, and to despise the remains of an unhappy life, when I had opened to myself
with delight the gates of eternity ; but your letter awakened me, and
of so pleasing a dream left me only the regret of knowing it was a
dream."

A proof, says Mr. Deslandes, in his critical history of philosophy,
that formerly neither the immortality, nor the immateriality, of the
soul was believed, is, that, in the time of Nero, the people of Rome
complained, that the introduction of the new-fangled doctrine of the
other world enervated the courage of the soldiers, and rendered them

in our time, does not necessarily fall within the limits of my work. What I have to offer, with regard to the mind, is equally conformable to either of these hypotheses. I shall therefore only observe, that, if the church had not fixed our belief in respect to this particular, and we had been obliged by the light of reason alone, to acquire a knowledge of the thinking principle, we must have granted, that neither opinion is capable of demonstration; and, consequently, that, by weighing the reasons on both sides, balancing the difficulties, and determining in favour of the greater number of probabilities, we should form only conditional judgments. It would be the fate of this problem, as it hath been of many others, to be resolvable only by the assistance of the calculation of probabilities *.

----

timorous; that it deprived the unhappy of their principal consolation, and added double terror to death, by threatening them with new sufferings after this life.

* It would be impossible to observe the axiom of Descartes, and to acquiesce in evidence only. This axiom is repeated in the schools, because it is not sufficiently understood. For Descartes, not having placed a sign; if I may be allowed the expression, at the inn of evidence, every one thinks he has a right of lodging there his opinion. Whoever will be satisfied with evidence only can hardly be sure of any thing, except his own existence. How could he, for example, be convinced of that of other bodies? For cannot God, by his omnipotence, make the same impressions on our senses, as the presence of the objects would excite? And if we grant, that the Deity can do this, how can it be affirmed, that he does not employ his power in this manner, and that the whole universe is nothing more than a mere phænomenon? Besides, as we are affected in our dreams by the same sensation we should feel were the object present, how can it be proved, that our life is not one continued dream? I would not be understood from hence, to deny the existence of bodies, but only to shew that we have less assurance of it than of our own existence. And, as truth is an indivisible point, we cannot say of a certain fact, that it is more or less true; it is therefore evident, that, if we are more certain of our own existence than of that of other bodies, the existence of the latter is no more than a probability. It is, indeed, a very great probability, and, with regard to the conduct of life, equivalent to evidence; notwith-

I shall therefore dwell no longer on this question, but proceed to my subject.   I say, then, that the Physical Sensibility and

---

standing which, it is only a probability.   If then almost all our truths may be reduced to probabilities, we could not too highly express our gratitude to the man of genius, who would undertake to construct physical, metaphysical, moral, and political, tables, in which should be precisely marked all the different degrees of probability, and consequently of belief, assignable to each opinion.

The existence of bodies, for example, would be placed in the physical tables, as the first degree of certainty in the following would be determined what wagers may be laid, that the sun will rise to-morrow; that he will rise in ten, in twenty years, &c.   In like manner, there would be placed in the moral and political tables, as the first degree of certainty, the existence of Rome or of London; then that of the heroes, as Cæsar or William the Conqueror; and in this manner, we should descend, by the scale of probability, to the facts of the least certainty; and finally, from the pretended miracles of Mahomet, even down to the prodigies attested by so many Arabians, but whose falsity is nevertheless highly probable here below, where liars are so common, and prodigies so rare.

It would then follow, that men, who differ in sentiments generally from the impossibility of finding proper signs to express the different degrees of belief they annex to their opinion, would communicate their ideas to each other with more facility; because they might always, if I may so express myself, refer their several opinions to some particular number in the tables of probabilities.

As the progress of the Mind is always slow, and the several discoveries in the sciences have been made at great distances of time from one another, it must be granted, that, if tables of probability were once formed, there would be only slight alterations made afterwards, and even those successively, which would relate, in consequence of the discoveries made, to the manner of increasing or diminishing the probability of certain propositions, which we call truths; but, in reality, only probabilities more or less accumulated.   By this means the state of doubting, always insupportable to the far greater part of mankind, would be more easily endured.   Doubts, then, would no longer continue vague, because subject to calculation, and consequently capable of valuation; they would be converted into affirmative propositions. Then the sect of Carneades, whose doctrine was formerly esteemed tho

Memory, or, to speak more exactly, that Sensibility alone, produceth all our ideas, and in effect Memory can be nothing more than one of the organs of Physical Sensibility. The principle that feels in us must necessarily be the principle that remembers: since to remember, as I shall prove hereafter, is properly nothing more than to feel.

When, in consequence of a series of ideas, or of the concussion caused in my organ of hearing by certain sounds, I recollect the appearance of an oak, my interior organs must necessarily at that time be in the same situation in which they were when I saw that oak. That situation of the organs must therefore incontestibly excite a sensation; whence it is evident, that to remember is to feel.

This principle being laid down, I farther say, that all the operations of the Mind consist in the power we have of perceiving the resemblance and difference, the agreement or disagreement, of various objects among themselves. And this power, being the Physical Sensibility itself, every thing is reducible to feeling.

---

philosophy of excellence, being called by the name of elective, would be purged of all those slight errors, for which wrangling ignorance has with too much harshness reproached a philosophical sect, whose dogmas were equally adapted to improve the Mind and polish the manners.

Though this sect, agreeable to their principles, admitted no truths, yet they admitted at least appearances, and would have us regulate life by those appearances; and that we should rather act when it appeared more eligible, than waste our time in examination; that we ought to deliberate maturely, when we had time sufficient for that purpose, that the determination might consequently be more certain; and that a free passage might thence be opened in the soul for all new truth; an advantage refused by the dogmatics. They farther intended, that we should be less tenacious of our own opinions; less ready to condemn those of others, and consequently become more sociable; and, in fine, that the habit of doubting, having rendered us less irritable by contradiction, should stifle in us the most fertile seeds of hatred amongst men. We do not here glance at revealed truth; these are truths of another order.

In order to be convinced of this truth, let us consider Nature. She presents objects to us; those objects have relations both with regard to us and themselves; the knowledge of those relations constitute what we call the Mind, which is more or less extensive as our knowledge in this particular is more or less diffusive. The human Mind ascends to the knowledge of those relations; but cannot pass these bounds. All the words therefore of which the various languages are composed, and which may be considered as a collection of the signs of all the thoughts of man, recal to us either objects, as the words Oak, Ocean, Sun; or represent ideas, namely, the different relations which objects bear to one another; and these are either simple, as the words, Greatness, Littleness, or compounded, as Vice, Virtue; or, finally, they express the different relations which objects have with ourselves, that is, our action upon them, as in the words, I break, I dig, I raise; or their impression upon us, as, I am wounded, dazzled, terrified.

If I have before confined the signification of the word Idea, used in very different acceptations, since we equally say, the Idea of a tree, and the Idea of virtue, it is because an undetermined signification of the expression may sometimes cause us to commit those errors which always flow from an abuse of words.

The conclusion of what I have hitherto advanced is, that, if all the words of different languages were confined to objects, or the relation of those objects, with regard either to us or one another, the Mind would consequently consist in comparing our sensations and ideas; that is, in contemplating the resemblances and differences, the agreements and disagreements, that subsist among them. Judgment therefore is only this very faculty of perceiving, or at least the declaration of it; and, consequently, all the operations of the Mind are reducible to judgment.

The question being thus properly limited, I shall proceed to examine, if Judging be not Feeling. When I judge of the magnitude or the colour of objects presented to me, it is evident, that the judgment is formed from the different impressions made by those objects on my senses; and therefore may be said, with the greatest propriety, to be nothing more than a sensation. For I can equally say, I judge, or I feel, that of two objects, the one, which I call a fathom, makes a different impression on me, from that of the other, which I call Foot: also, that the colour which I call Red acts upon my eyes differently from that which I call Yellow: from whence I conclude, that in all parallel cases, Judging is the same with Feeling.

But some will say, let us suppose that we are desirous to know, whether the strength of the body be preferable to its magnitude; can it then be asserted, that judging is nothing more than feeling? I answer, Yes; because, to enable me to form a judgment on this subject, my momory must successively retrace to me the pictures of the different situations in which I have acted, during the whole course of my life. Consequently, Judging is seeing in those different pictures, that the strength of the body will be oftener of service to me, than its size or magnitude. Others may reply, if a judgment is to be formed, whether justice is preferable to goodness in a king, can it be imagined, that such a judgment is only a sensation?

This opinion hath, doubtless, at first the appearance of a paradox; yet, to prove the truth of it, let us suppose, that a man has the knowledge of what is called Good and Evil; and that he also knows what evil is, more or less so, according as it is more or less pernicious to the welfare of society. According to this supposition, what art must a poet or orator employ, to make him perceive, in a more lively manner, that justice, preferable in a king to goodness, preserves more citizens for the state?

The orator will present three pictures to his imagination; in one he will paint the just king, who condemns a criminal, and orders him to execution. In the second, he will exhibit the good king opening the same criminal's prison, and taking off his fetters. In the third, he will represent this very criminal arming himself with a poniard, as he quits the prison, and hastening to massacre fifty citizens. Now, what man, at the sight of these three pictures, will not be convinced, that justice, which by the death of one has prevented the death of fifty, is in a king preferable to goodness? This judgment, however, is really no more than a sensation. In effect, if from a habitude of uniting certain ideas to certain words, we can, as experience proves, by striking the ear with certain sounds, excite in us nearly the same sensations that would be excited by the very presence of the objects; it is evident, that, from the display of those three pictures, to judge, that, in a king justice is preferable to goodness, is feeling and seeing; that, in the first picture, only one citizen is immolated, and in the third, fifty are massacred; from whence I conclude, that every judgment is nothing more than a sensation.

But should this question be started, must we also rank in the class of Sensations, judgments formed; for example, on the greater or less degree of the excellence of certain methods; such as, that proper for fixing a great number of objects in our memory, that of abstraction, or that of analysis?

In order to answer this question, we must begin by determining the signification of this word Method. A method is nothing more than the means we employ to attain some end proposed. Let us suppose, a person intends to place certain objects, or certain ideas, in his memory; and that chance should have so arranged them there, that the remembrance of one fact, or of one idea, makes him recollect an infinity of other facts, or of other ideas; and that he may from hence have certain objects more readily and deeply engraved in his memory. To infer from thence a judgment, that this order is the best, and, to give it the name of Method, signifies, that he has exerted less efforts of attention, and suffered a less painful sensation, by studying in that order, than in any other. But, to remember a painful sensation, is to feel; it is therefore evident that, in this case, Judging is Feeling.

Let us farther suppose, that, in order to prove the truth of certain propositions in geometry, and to make them more easily conceived by his pupils, a geometrician had determined to make them consider the lines independently of their breadth and thickness; to judge, therefore, that this means or method of abstraction, is more proper to convey to his scholars the knowledge of certain geometrical propositions, signifies, that less efforts of attention will be necessary; and that his scholars will undergo a less painful sensation in using this method than any other.

Let us suppose, for a final example, that, by separately examining each truth contained in a complicated proposition, the understanding of that proposition is sooner attained. Therefore, to judge that the means or method of analysis is the best, is saying also, that less powerful efforts of attention have been made; and consequently, that a less painful sensation hath been sufficient, by particularly considering each truth contained in this complicated proposition, than would have been requisite, had it been attempted to understand them all at once.

The result of what I have said, is, that the judgments formed on the means and methods which chance presents to us, in order to attain a certain end, are, in the strictest propriety, nothing more than sensations. Therefore, in man, all is reducible to feeling.

But how did it happen, some may ask, that hitherto there has been supposed in us a faculty of judging, distinct from the faculty of feeling? My answer is, that we are indebted for that supposition to a belief, which has hitherto prevailed, of its being impossible to explain, in any other manner, certain errors of the Mind.

But entirely to remove this difficulty, I am going to shew, in the following chapters, that all our false judgments and errors have their source from two causes, which suppose in us only the faculty of feeling; and, consequently, that it would be of no utility, or rather absurd, to admit a faculty of judging, which could only explain, what might as well be done without its assistance. I shall, therefore, proceed with the subject; and I say, that all our erroneous judgments are either the effect of our passions, or our ignorance.

CHAP. II.

OF THE ERRORS OCCASIONED BY OUR PASSIONS.

THE passions lead us into error, because they fix our attention to that particular part of the object they present to us, not al-

lowing us to view it on every side. A king passionately affects the title of Conqueror. Victory, says he, calls me to the
remotest part of the earth: I shall fight; I shall gain the victory; I shall load mine enemy with chains, and the terror of
my name, like an impenetrable rampart, will defend the
entrance of my empire. Inebriated with this hope, he forgets
that fortune is inconstant; and, that the victor shares the load of
misery almost equally with the vanquished. He does not
perceive, that the welfare of his subjects is only a pretence
for his martial frenzy; and that pride alone forges his arms,
and displays his ensigns: his whole attention is fixed on the
pomp of the triumph.

Fear, equally powerful with pride, will produce the same
effect; it will raise ghosts and phantoms, and disperse them
among the tombs, and in the darkness of the woods, present
them to the eyes of the affrighted traveller, seize on all the faculties of his soul, without leaving any one at liberty to reflect
on the absurdity of the motives for such a ridiculous terror.

The passions not only fix the attention on particular sides of
the objects they present to us; but they also deceives us, by
exhibiting the same objects, when they do not really exist.
The story of a country clergyman and an amorous lady is well
known. They had heard, and concluded, that the moon was
peopled, and were looking for the inhabitants through their
telescopes. If I am not mistaken, said the lady, I perceive two
shadows; they mutually incline towards each other: doubtless
they are two happy lovers.——O fie! madam, replied the
clergyman, these two shadows are the two steeples of a cathe-
dral. This tale is our history, it being common for us to see in
things what we are desirous of finding there: on the earth, as
in the moon, different passions will cause us to see either lovers
or steeples. Illusion is a necessary effect of the passions, the
strength or force of which is generally measured by the degree of obscurity into which they lead us. This was well
known to a certain lady, who being caught by her lover in the
arms of his rival, obstinately denied the fact of which he had
been a witness. How! said he, have you the assurance——Ah!
perfidious creature, cried the lady, it is plain you no longer

love me; for you believe your eyes, before all I can say. This
is equally applicable to all the passions, as well as to love. All
strike us with the most perfect blindness. When ambition has
kindled a war between two nations, and the anxious citizens
ask one another the news, what readiness appears, on one side,
to give credit to the good; and, on the other, what incredulity,
with regard to the bad? How often have christians, from placing a ridiculous confidence in monks, denied the possibility of
the antipodes. There is no century which has not, by some
ridiculous affirmation or negation, afforded matter of laughter
to the following age. A past folly is seldom sufficient to shew
mankind their present folly.

The same passions, however, which are the germ of an infinity of errors, are also the sources of our knowledge. If they
mislead us, they, at the same time, impart to us the strength
necessary for walking. It is they alone that can rouze us from
that sluggishness and torpor always ready to seize on the faculties of our soul.

But, as this is not the place for examining the truth of this
proposition, I shall pass to the second cause of our errors.

CHAP. III.

OF IGNORANCE.

WE deceive ourselves when we pretend to judge of an
object from one side only, to which our attention has been
fixed by our passions. We also deceive ourselves, when we
pretend to judge of a subject, when our memory does not contain all the facts, on a comparison of which the propriety of
our decisions depend. Not that any person is destitute of a
just perception : all have an idea of what they see; but by not
mistrusting our ignorance, we are too apt to believe that what
we see in an object is all that is perceivable in it.

In questions of any difficulty, we are to consider ignorance
as the principal cause of our errors. To shew how easily we
are, in this case, deceived, and how by drawing from their

principles consequences always just, men arrive at conclusions directly opposite. I shall give, as an instance, a question a little complicated: such is that of Luxury, which has occasioned very different judgments according to the light in which it has been considered.

The word Luxury, being a vague term, without any fixed meaning, and generally no more than a relative expression, we must previously fix an adequate idea to the word Luxury, taken in a strict sense; after which, a definition must be given of Luxury, both with regard to a nation and an individual.

By the word Luxury, we are, in a strict sense, to understand all kinds of superfluities. That is, whatever is not necessary to a person's subsistence. When the question relates to a policed people, and the individuals of which it is composed, the word Luxury has a very different meaning; it becomes absolutely relative. The Luxury of a policed nation, is the expending its Wealth on what is called superfluities, by a people with which this nation is compared. This is the case of England, with regard to Switzerland.

Luxury, in an individual, is also the employment of his riches on what should be called superfluities, considering his station, and the country in which he lives. Such was the Luxury of Bourvalais.

Having given this definition of the word, let us see under what different appearances national Luxury has been considered; since some have accounted it useful, and others detrimental, to a state. The former have confined their attention to the manufactures, which owe their origin to Luxury, and induce a foreign nation eagerly to exchange its treasures for the industry of the other. They see the increase of riches bring in its train the increase of Luxury, and the perfection of arts proper to gratify it. With them, the age of Luxury is the æra of the grandeur and power of a state. The plenty of money, say they, which it supposes, and brings into the nation, renders it happy at home and formidable abroad. By money, numerous forces are maintained; magazines erected; arsenals filled with stores; and alliances formed and supported with powerful princes: in fine, it is by money, that a nation cannot only resist, but even rule over others more populous, and consequently of more real power than itself. As luxury renders a nation formidable abroad, so it procures every kind of felicity at home. It softens the manners, creates new diversions, and thus furnishes a comfortable subsistence to a competent number of artists and labourers. It excites a salutary cupidity, which rouses man from that indolence, that lassitude, which should be considered as one of the most cruel diseases of human nature. It diffuses through the whole, a vivifying heat : causes life to circulate through all the members of a state ; rouzes industry ; opens the harbours ; builds ships ; conveys them over the ocean ; and makes common to all mankind those productions and riches which covetous nature has concealed in the deep recesses of the sea, and the bowels of the earth ; or keeps separate in a thousand different climates. This, I believe, is nearly the point of view in which luxury presents itself to those who consider it as useful to states.

Let us now examine the appearance under which it presents itself to those philosophers who look on it as the bane of nations.

The happiness of a people depends upon the national felicity, and the respect they inspire in others. With regard to the first, it is our opinion these philosophers will say, that luxury, and the wealth it produces in a state, will render the subjects happier only in proportion as this wealth is equally divided; so that every one may procure those conveniences of which he sees himself abridged by indigence.

Luxury is not therefore injurious as luxury, but as the effect of a great disparity in the wealth of individuals*. Ac-

---

* Luxury causes a circulation of money; it draws it from the coffers where avarice would hoard it : it is luxury, therefore, say some, that restores the equilibre between the fortunes of individuals. But, I answer, that it does not produce this effect. Luxury always supposes a cause of inequality of wealth among individuals. And this cause, which makes the first rich men, must, when these are ruined by luxury, be re-producing others. Take away this cause of the inequality of riches, and luxury will disappear with it. Nothing of

cordingly, luxury is never carried to excess, when there is not
too great inequality in the distribution of riches; it increases
in proportion, as these are confined to fewer individuals, and
arrives at its utmost height when a nation divides itself into
two classes, one abounding in superfluities, the other wanting necessaries.

When it is arrived at this height, the state of a nation is
the more melancholy, as it is incurable. How shall then any
equality be re-established in the fortunes of individuals? The
rich man will have purchased extensive lordships; and being
able to take advantage of the necessities of his neighbours, he
will, in a short time, have annexed an infinite number of small
farms to his estate. A diminution of the number of proprietors
increases the number of labourers. When these are multiplied,
so that there are more labourers than work, it will be with the
workmen as with all kinds of merchandize, which becomes of
less value in proportion as it becomes more common. Besides,
the rich man, whose luxury even exceeds his wealth, is under
a necessity of lowering the price of labour, and giving the
workman no more than is absolutely necessary for a bare sub-

---

what is called luxury can be seen in countries where the fortunes of
individuals are nearly equal. I add, that this inequality of riches,
being once founded, luxury itself is partly the cause of the reproduction of luxury: for whoever ruins himself by his luxury, transfers the
greatest part of his wealth to those artificers who administer to luxury;
and these, enriched with the spoils of an infinite number of pro-
digals, become rich in their turn, and afterwards ruin themselves in
the same manner. Now that wealth, which from the wrecks of so
many fortunes spreads itself over the country, can be only the least
part; as the productions of the earth adapted to the common use of
mankind, can never exceed a certain price.

It is otherwise with regard to those products when they have been
manufactured by industry; for their value is then whatever fancy
pleases, and the price becomes excessive. Thus luxury necessarily
keeps money in the hands of its artizans, causes a perpetual circulation of it in that class of men; and, consequently, must support an
inequality of riches among individuals.

sistence*. The latter is obliged, through necessity, to accept of it; but in case of sickness, or an increase of his family, for want of a sufficiency of wholesome food, he dies, and incumbers the state with an indigent and destitute family. To prevent such calamities, recourse must be had to a new distribution of lands; a distribution always unjust and impracticable. Hence it is evident, that luxury, when it is arrived to a certain pitch, renders it impossible to restore an equality between the fortunes of individuals. Then the rich, with their wealth, flock to the capitals, as the seats of diversion, and the arts of luxury; while the country remains desolated, poor, and uncultivated. Seven or eight millions of people languish in misery†,

---

* It is commonly thought, that the country is ruined by services, imposts, and especially the poll-tax. These I shall readily allow to be very burdensome; yet it must not be imagined, that the suppression of this impost alone would render the condition of the peasants entirely happy. In most provinces the price of a day's labour is only eight sols. Now if from these eight sols I deduct the imposition of the church, that is, near ninety Sundays and holy-days, and perhaps thirty-five days in the year, when the husbandman is ill, without work, or employed in his lord's services; all that remains to him is no more than six sols per day. While he is single, I will suppose that these six sols are sufficient to answer all his expences of food, cloathing, and lodging; on his marrying, these six sols will be deficient, as during the first years after marriage, his wife will be too much taken up in looking after the children, to assist him: let us suppose, that his poll-tax is then entirely remitted, which amounts to five or six francs; and thus he gains about a farthing a-day more. Now certainly this farthing would make very little alteration in his condition. What then must be done to render his condition happy? Make a considerable addition to the price of a day's labour. In order to this, the proprietors must constantly reside on their estates: then, like their ancestors, they would reward the services of their domestics, by bestowing on them some acres of land. The number of proprietors would insensibly multiply; that of day-labourers decrease; and the latter, by becoming more scarce, would set a higher value upon their work.

† It is very strange that the nations most celebrated for their luxury and *police*, should be the very countries where the majority of

and five or six thousand riot in an opulence which renders them odious, without augmenting their happiness.

What indeed can the profuse variety of a table add to a person's happiness? Is it not sufficient for him to wait the call of

---

the inhabitants are more unhappy than the savage nations, which are held in such contempt by the civilized. It is a question, whether the condition of a savage be not preferable to that of a peasant? The savage has no prison, no increase of imposts, to fear; no oppressive lord, no tyrannical sub-delegate; he is not perpetually mortified and debased, by daily seeing persons infinitely above him in riches and power; without superior, without servitude, more healthy and vigourous than the peasant, because happier; he enjoys the satisfaction of equality, especially of that inestimable privilege, liberty, so vainly claimed by most nations.

In policed countries, the whole art of government has often consisted in making an infinite number of men subservient to the happiness of a few; in keeping, for this purpose, the multitude under oppression, and in violating all the privileges of humanity they have a right to demand.

But the true end of the legislative office, is the general happiness. Possibly this happiness could not be procured but by again introducing the pastoral life; and possibly the discoveries in legislation bring us back, in this respect, to the point from whence government had its rise. Not that I pretend to decide so nice a question, and which requires the most careful examination: but I own, to me it is very astonishing, that so many forms of government, established at least on a pretence of the public good; that so many laws, so many regulations, should, in most kingdoms, have proved only the instrument of oppression and calamity. Possibly this misfortune can be removed only by returning to manners infinitely more simple. I am well aware, that many attractive pleasures must be then renounced: but if the general good require it, this sacrifice would become a duty. May we not even apprehend that the extreme felicity of some individuals always flows from the calamities of the majority? A truth not unhappily expressed in the two following lines on the savages:

Chez eux tout est commun, chez eux tout est égal;
Comme ils sont sans palais, ils sont sans hôpital.

With them all common is, and equal all;
No palace have they, nor a hospital.

hunger; but he must proportion his exercises, or the length of his airings, to the bad taste of his cook, that he may relish as delicious every food that is not detestable? Besides, does he not, by frugality and exercise, avoid that train of distempers occasioned by gluttony, irritated by the variety and delicacy of the dishes. Happiness, therefore, does not depend on the elegance of the table.

Neither does it consist in the richness of dress, or the splendour of equipage. A person of quality appearing in public, dressed in an embroidered suit, and leaning in a brilliant chariot, feels no physical pleasures, and these only are real. At most, he is only affected with the pleasure of vanity, of which the privation would possibly be insupportable; though the enjoyment be flat and insipid. Without any addition to his own happiness, the rich man, by displaying his luxury, shocks humanity; and the wretch who, by comparing the rags of poverty to the robe of opulence, imagines that there is the same difference between their happiness as their dress, recals, on this occasion, the painful remembrance of the distresses he endures; and thus deprives himself of the wretch's only comfort, a momentary forgetfulness of his misery.

It is therefore certain, continue these philosophers, that luxury is not productive of the happiness of any; and that too great an inequality of riches among the members of a state implies, that the greatest part of them are wretched. Thus a nation, where luxury has been introduced, is not very happy in itself; let us now see whether it be respected abroad.

The plenty of money which luxury produces in a state, at first dazzles the imagination. This state is for a time very powerful; but this advantage, if there can be any advantage independent of the happiness of its members, is, as Mr. Hume observes, only transitory. Riches, like those seas which successively forsake and overflow a thousand different tracts of land, must successively travel through a thousand climates. When, by the beauty of its manufactures, and the perfection of the arts of luxury, a nation has drawn into it the riches of its neighbours, it is evident that the price of goods, workmanship, and labour, will necessarily fall among these impoverished people; and thence, by clandestinely procuring some manufacturers out of this rich nation, may, by degrees, in their turn, impoverish it, by supplying themselves at a lower price with those goods which they before imported from their rich neighbours*. And no sooner is the want of money per-

---

* What I mention of the commerce of the goods for luxury must not be applied to all kinds of commerce. The riches brought into a state by the perfection of the manufactures and the arts of luxury, are only temporary, and do not increase the happiness of individuals. But it is very different with regard to the wealth flowing in from the commerce of goods immediately necessary. This commerce suppose an excellent cultivation of the lands, a subdivision of these lands into an infinity of small demesnes, and consequently a nearer equality in the partition of riches. I well know that this commerce of necessaries will, in process of time, occasion a great disproportion in the fortunes of individuals, and introduce luxury. But it will not be impossible, in such a case, to check the progress of luxury. This is certain, that the concentration of riches in a small number of hands proceeds much more slowly, both because the proprietors are at once both cultivators and traders, and because the number of proprietors being greater, and that of day-labourers smaller, these, by reason of their paucity, are, as I have already observed in a preceding note, able to prescribe laws for fixing the value of their day's work, and require such wages as will procure a comfortable subsistence for themselves and families. Thus every person has a share of the riches accruing to a state by the traffic of provisions. Nor is this commerce subject to the same vicissitudes as that of the manufactures of luxury. An art or a manufacture easily passes from one country to another; but to overcome the ignorance and sloth of peasants, and prevail on them to undertake the culture of a new commodity, is a work of time. To naturalize this new commodity in a country is attended with great trouble and expence, by which the advantages of trade will almost ever incline to that country which produces this commodity naturally; and where it has for a long time been cultivated.

There is, however, a case, perhaps imaginary, when the establishment of manufactures and the commerce of the arts of luxury might be esteemed highly useful. This is, when the extent and fertility of a country are not proportionate to the number of its inhabitants. That is, when a state is not able to maintain all its people. In this

ceived in a state accustomed to luxury, than it becomes contemptible.

In order to surmount these difficulties, the only method is to return to a simple life; but this both the customs and laws oppose. Accordingly, the epocha of the greatest luxury of a nation is generally the epocha preceding its fall and debasement. The happiness and apparent power which luxury for a time imparts to nations, may be compared to those violent fevers, from which, during the paroxisms, the patient derives an astonishing strength, and which seem to augment his powers only to deprive him at once, when the fit is over, both of this strength and his life.

In order to be convinced of this truth, say these philosophers, let us consider what renders a nation truly respectable to its neighbours. Doubtless the number and vigour of its members, their love for their country, and their courage and virtue.

If we survey the numbers of the inhabitants of different nations, we shall find that the most luxurious countries are not the most populous. It is well known that Switzerland, in proportion to its extent, is better peopled than Spain, France, or even England.

The expence of men necessarily occasioned by an extensive trade* is not in those countries the sole cause of depopulation;

---

case, a nation, not having the advantage of sending its people to such a country as America, must either send colonies to ravage the neighbouring countries, and, as others have done before them, settle themselves in more fertile countries, where they may procure a subsistence, or erect manufactures, compel the neighbouring nations to trade with them, and give them in exchange the provisions necessary for the subsistence of a certain number of inhabitants. The last is doubtless the most humane; for whatever the chance of war may be, every colony, whether victor or vanquished, entering a country in a hostilely manner, certainly occasions more desolation, calamities, and evils, than can possibly flow from raising a kind of tribute, exacted rather by humanity than force.

* This expence of men is, however, so great, that the number de-

luxury creates a thousand others, drawing the riches of a nation to the capital, leaving the country in want, favouring arbitrary power, and consequently the augmentation of subsidies; it also affords opulent nations an easy method of contracting debts*, which cannot be discharged but by loading the people with taxes. Now these different causes of depopulation, by plunging a whole country into misery, must necessarily impair the constitution of the body. When was it ever known that a people given to luxury were robust? One part are enervated by pleasure, and the other emaciated by want.

If a poor or savage nation, as the Chevalier de Folard observes, have in this respect a great superiority over nations addicted to luxury, it is because a labourer is generally richer in a poor than in a wealthy nation; it is because a Swiss peasant is in easier circumstances than a French peasant†.

---

stroyed by our American commerce cannot be thought of without horror. Humanity, which inspires us with a love for all our fellow-creatures, requires that, with regard to the trade for negroes, I should place in the account of misfortunes both the death of my countrymen and that of so many Africans, stimulated to battle by the hope of making prisoners to give in exchange for our goods. If to the number of men slain in the wars and dying in their passage from Africa to America, be added that of the negroes, who after they are sold become victims to the caprices and tyranny of a cruel master; and if to this sum we join the number of those who perish by fire, shipwreck, or the scurvy; and lastly, the number of sailors who die during their stay at St. Domingo, either from distempers common to the climate, or the consequences of debauchery, which is no where more dangerous, every hogshead of sugar landed in Europe must be allowed to be dyed with human blood. Now, from a view of the miseries occasioned by the culture and exportation of this commodity, who would not refuse to deprive himself of the use of it, and renounce a pleasure which must be purchased by the tears and destruction of so many of our fellow-creatures? But let us remove our eyes from so melancholy a spectacle, so disgraceful to human nature, and which fills a generous mind with horror.

* Holland, England, and France, are overwhelmed with debts, while Switzerland does not owe a penny.

† It is not sufficient, says Grotius, that the people be provided with

Robust bodies are formed only by a sufficiency of simple and wholesome food, manly exercise, not carried to excess, and a constant habit of bearing the inclemencies of the weather; this the peasants are inured to, and consequently infinitely more proper to bear the fatigues of war than manufacturers, most of whom are used to a sedentary life. It is also in poor nations that these indefatigable armies are formed, which give a turn to the fate of empires.

What opposition can be made against such armies, by a country abandoned to luxury and indolence? Neither the number nor strength of its inhabitants can intimidate them. It will perhaps be said, that the love of one's country will supply the want of numbers and strength. But among such a people, what can produce this love for their country? The labouring people, which makes two thirds of every nation, are wretched: the artificers are without property, and having been taken from the villages, and placed in some manufacture or shop, and from thence to others of the same kind, roving is become familiar to them; and they cannot contract an attachment for any place: and being certain of getting a livelihood any where, they consider themselves not as the members of any country, but as citizens of the world.

Such a people, therefore, will not be long able to distinguish themselves by their courage; because courage is generally the effect of the vigour of the body, that blind reliance on our own strength which conceals from men half the danger to which they expose themselves: or it flows from a strong patriotic zeal, which despises dangers when employed in the service of its country. But luxury, in process of time, dries up these two sources of courage*. Possibly avarice might open a third, had

---

things absolutely necessary to their preservation and life; it must be rendered easy and pleasant to them.

* In consequence of this a military genius has always been considered as incompatible with a commercial: not that they are absolutely irreconcileable, but that this is one of the most difficult problems in politics. Those who have hitherto written on trade have treated it as an abstracted question: they did not sufficiently perceive

the barbarous customs of former ages been still continued, when the vanquished were carried into slavery, and cities abandoned to pillage.

But the soldier being no longer stimulated by this motive, he can now act only from a principle of honour. Now the desire of honour is extinguished when the people become inflamed with the love of riches*. It is to no purpose to say, that what opulent nations lose in virtue and courage they gain in happiness and pleasures. A Spartan† was equally happy with a Persian, and the first Romans, whose only reward for courage was a donation of some provisions, would not have envied the splendour of Crassus.

Caius Duillius, who, by an act of the senate, was every evening conducted back to his house by a company of men carrying flambeaux, and playing on flutes, was as well pleased with this simple concert as we are with the finest sonata. But granting that opulent nations may procure themselves some conveniencies unknown to those of a poor state, who will enjoy those conveniencies? A handful of men of wealth and power, who, considering themselves as the whole nation, con-

---

that every thing has its relatives, and that in government there can properly be no abstracted question; that here the merit of an author consists in connecting together all the parts of the administration; and that a state is a machine moved by different springs, the force of which is to be increased or diminished, according to the reciprocal action of those springs, and the effect intended to be produced.

* There is no necessity for observing that, in this respect, luxury is more dangerous to a continental than an insular nation; ships being their ramparts, and seamen their soldiers.

† When the valour of the Spartans was once mentioned with great applause, in presence of Alcibiades, " I see nothing remarkable in this," said he; " for, considering the wretched life they lead, it should be their peculiar business to die." This sarcasm fell from the mouth of a young man brought up in luxury; but he was mistaken; Lacedemon did not in the least envy the happiness of Athens; which made an ancient say, it was better to live like the Spartans, under good laws, than like the Sybarites, under fragrant bowers.

clude, from their private ease, that the peasants are happy.
But should these conveniencies be diffused among a greater
number of the inhabitants, is this an advantage to be compared
with these accruing to a poor state, from the courage, hardi-
ness, temperance, and an abhorrence of slavery in its inhabitants? Nations among whom luxury have got footing, fall,
sooner or later, victims to despotism. They offer their faint
and trembling hands to the chains which tyranny has forged
for them. How shall they avoid it? In such nations, some
live in voluptuousness, and voluptuousness is destitute both of
thought and foresight; others languish in penury and pinch-
ing want; and entirely absorbed in finding methods for its relief, never look so high as liberty. In a despotic government
the riches of the nation are at the disposal of its master; in a
republic they are the property of men of power, or of their
brave neighbours. " Bring us your treasures," might the
Romans have said to the Carthaginians, " they belong to us:
Rome and Carthage both aimed at riches, but pursued different methods to attain their ends. While you encouraged the
industry of your people, erected manufactures, covered the
sea with your ships, attempted the discovery of uninhabited
countries, and brought to Carthage the gold of Spain and
Africa, we were, more wisely, promoting courage and hardi-
ness, inuring our soldiers to the fatigues of war, well knowing
that the industrious man labours only for the brave. The time
for entering on possession is now arrived: deliver up to us
those treasures you are not able to defend." The Romans did
not indeed speak in this manner, but their conduct sufficiently
proved that they were animated with the same sentiments.
Why should not the poverty of Rome have been superior to
the opulence of Carthage, and in this respect maintained the
advantage which almost all poor nations have had over the
wealthy? Did not the frugal Lacedemon triumph over the
wealthy and commercial Athens? Did not the frugal Romans
trample on the golden sceptres of Asia? Were not Egypt,
Phœnicia, Tyre, Rhodes, Genoa, and Venice, either subdued or humbled by nations whom they termed Barbarians?
And who knows but one day the flourishing state of Holland,

actually less happy than Switzerland, will oppose an invader with a less obstinate resistance? Such is the point of light in which luxury is seen by those philosophers who have considered it as the bane of nations.

The conclusion of the premises is, that men, though they have a clear view of the objects before them, and draw just consequences from their principles, yet their results are often contradictory; because they do not contain in their memory all the objects, on a comparison of which the truths they seek must depend.

It is, I think, needless to say, that in stating the question of luxury under two different aspects, I do not pretend to determine whether luxury be useful or detrimental to states; an accurate solution of this moral problem would require details foreign to my intended purpose. All I intended by this instance was to shew that in complicated questions, when our judgments are not biassed by our passions, ignorance alone is the cause of our errors: that is, by imagining that the side we view of an object is all that can be seen in that object.

CHAP. VII.

OF THE ABUSE OF WORDS.

ANOTHER cause of error, and which is also a branch of ignorance, is the abuse of words, and the want of clearness in the ideas annexed to them. This subject has been so happily discussed by Mr. Locke, that, if I undertake to examine it, the conveniency of those readers who are not sufficiently acquainted with the work of that philosopher is my only motive.

Descartes had before Locke observed that the Peripateticks, intrenching themselves behind the obscurity of words, were not unlike a blind man, who, in order to be a match for his clear-sighted antagonist, should draw him into a dark cavern. "Now," added he, "if this man can introduce light into the cavern, and compel the Peripateticks to fix clear ideas to their words, the victory is his own. In imitation of Descartes and Locke, I shall shew that, both in metaphysics and morality, the abuse of words, and the ignorance of their true import, is a labyrinth in which the greatest geniuses have lost themselves; and, in order to set this particular in a clear light, instance, in some of those words which have given rise to the longest and sharpest disputes among philosophers: such, in metaphysics, are Matter, Space, and Infinite.

It has at all times been alternately asserted that Matter felt, or did not feel, and given rise to disputes equally loud and vague. It was very late before it came into the disputants' heads, to ask one another, what they were disputing about, and to annex a precise idea to the word Matter? Had they at first fixed the meaning of it, they would have perceived, if I may use the expression, that men were the creators of Matter; that Matter was not a being; that in nature there were only individuals to which the name of Body had been given; and that this word Matter could import no more than the collection of properties common to all bodies. The meaning of this word being determined, all that remained was to know, whether extent, solidity, and impenetrability, were the only properties common to all bodies; and whether the discovery of a power, such for instance as attraction, might not give rise to a conjecture that bodies had some properties hitherto unknown, such as that of sensation, which though evident only in the organized members of animals, might yet be common to all individuals? The question being reduced to this, it would have appeared, that, if strictly speaking, it is impossible to demonstrate that all bodies are absolutely insensible, no man, unless instructed by a particular revelation, can decide the question otherwise than by calculating and comparing the verisimilitude of this opinion with that of the contrary.

To bring therefore this dispute to an issue, there was no necessity for erecting different systems of the world, of losing one's self in the combination of possibilities, and exhausting the genius in those prodigious efforts which have terminated, and in reality could not but have terminated in errors, more or less ingenious. Indeed (let me be allowed this reflection) if we are to avail ourselves as much as possible from observation, we must walk only by its side, stop at the very instant when it leaves us, and nobly dare to be ignorant of what is not yet to be known.

Instructed by the errors of great men who have gone before us, we should be sensible, that our observations, however multiplied and concentrated, are scarce sufficient to form one of those partial systems comprehended in the general system; and that it is from the depths of imagination, that the several systems of the universe have hitherto been drawn; and, as our informations of remote countries are always imperfect, so the informations philosophers have of the system of the world are also defective. With a great genius and a multitude of combinations, the products of their labours will be only fictions, till time and chance shall furnish them with a general fact, to which all others may be referred.

What I have said of the word Matter, I say also of Space. Most of the philosophers have made a being of it; and the ignorance of the true sense of the word has occasioned long disputes *. They would have been greatly shortened by annexing a clear idea to this word; for then the sages would have agreed, that Space, considered in bodies, is what we call extension; that we owe the idea of a void, which partly composes the idea of Space, to the interval seen betwixt two lofty mountains; an interval which being filled only by air, that is, by a body which at a certain distance makes no sensible impression on us, must have given us an idea of a vacuum; being nothing more than a power of representing to ourselves mountains separated from each other, and the intervening distances not being filled by other bodies.

With regard to the idea of Infinite, comprehended also within the idea of Space, I say that we owe this idea of Infinite only to the power which a man standing on a plain has of continually extending its limits, the boundary of his imagination not being determinable: the absence of limits is therefore the only idea

---

* See the dispute between Leibnitz and Clarke.

we can form of infinite. Had philosophers, previously to their giving any opinion on this subject, determined the signification of the word Infinite, I am inclined to believe, they would have adopted the above definition, and not spent their time in frivo-lous disputes. To the false philosophy of former ages, our gross ignorance of the true signification of words is principally owing; as the art of abusing them made up the greatest part of that philosophy. This art, in which the whole science of the schools consisted, confounded all ideas; and the obscurity it threw on the expressions, generally diffused itself over all the sciences, especially morality.

When the famous M. de la Rochefoucault said that Self-love is the principle of all our actions, what invectives, occasioned by the ignorance of the word Self-love, were thrown out against that illustrious author! Self-love was considered as pride and vanity; and therefore M. Rochefoucault was said to consider vice as the source of all the virtues. Yet it was easy to per-ceive, that Self-love was nothing more than a sentiment im-planted in us by nature; that in every individual this senti-ment became vice or virtue, according to his dispositions and passions; and that Self-love, differently modified, was equally productive of pride and modesty.

The knowledge of these ideas would have secured M. de la Rochefoucault from the reproach so often thrown upon him, that he saw human nature through too gloomy a medium. He saw it in its true light. I own that a clear view of the indif-ference of almost all men concerning us is a mortifying spec-tacle to our vanity: but, after all, men must be considered as they are. To be offended at the effects of their Self-love is to complain of the showers of spring, the heats of summer, the rains of autumn, and the frosts of winter.

In order to love mankind, little must be expected from them. In order to view their faults without asperity, we must accus-tom ourselves to forgiveness; to a sense that indulgence is a justice which frail humanity has a right to require from wis-dom. Now nothing has a greater tendency to dispose us to indulgence, to close our hearts against hatred, and open them to the principles of a humane and mild morality, than a pro-

found knowledge of the human heart; and this knowledge
Mr. Rochefoucault possessed. Accordingly, the wisest men
have always been the most indulgent. What beautiful maxims
of humanity are scattered through their works! It was the
saying of Plato, Live with your inferiors and domestics as with
unfortunate friends. " Must I always," said an Indian philosopher, " hear the rich crying out, Lord destroy all who take
from us the least parcel of our possessions; while the poor
man, with plaintive voice and eyes lifted up to heaven, cries,
Lord give me a part of the goods thou dealest out in such pro-
fusion to the rich; and if others less happy deprive me of a
part, instead of imprecating thy vengeance, I shall consider
these thefts in the same manner as in seed-time we see the
doves ranging over the fields in quest of their food."

However, if the word Self-love, by being misunderstood,
raised such an opposition to M. Rochefoucault, what disputes,
and of much greater importance, have not been occasioned by
the word Liberty! Disputes which might have been easily
decided, had all men been such friends to truth as father Malebranche, and agreed with that able divine in his Premotion
Physique, that Liberty is a mystery. When urged on this
question, he used to say, I am forced instantly to stop short.
Not that it is impossible to form an adequate idea of the word
Liberty, taken in the common acceptation. A man at liberty
is a person neither in chains, under confinement, nor intimi-
dated like a slave by the fear of punishment. In this sense,
the liberty of man consists in the free exercise of his power.
I say of his power, because, to consider our inability of soaring
to the clouds like the eagle, of living under the water like the
whale, of making ourselves king or pope, as a want of liberty,
would be ridiculous. Thus we have an adequate idea of the
word Liberty, in a common acceptation. But not when the word
Liberty is applied to the will. What then is Liberty? Nothing
more can be understood by it than the free power of willing, or
not willing a thing. But this power would suppose that there
could be wills without a motive, and consequently effects without
a cause. And it would follow, that we could equally wish ourselves good and evil; a supposition absolutely impossible. In fact,

if the desire of pleasure be the true principle of all our thoughts, and of all our actions; if all men really tend towards their true or apparent happiness, it will follow that all our wills are no more than the effect of this tendency. In this sense, therefore, no adequate idea can be annexed to this word Liberty. But it will be said, If we are under a necessity of pursuing happiness wherever we discern it, we are at least at liberty in making choice of the means for procuring our happiness*. Yes, I answer; but then Liberty is only a synonimous term for Knowledge. The more or less a person understands of the law, or the more or less able the counsellor is by whom he is directed in his affairs, the more or less eligible will be his measures. But whatever his conduct be, the desire of happiness will always induce him to take those measures which appear to him the best calculated to promote his interest, his dispositions, his passions, and in fine, whatever he accounts his happiness.

How can the problem of liberty be philosophically solved, if, as Mr. Locke has proved, we are the disciples of friends, parents, books, and, in fine, all the objects that surrounded us? All our thoughts and wills must then be either the immediate effects, or necessary consequences, of the impressions we have received.

Thus no idea can be formed of the word Liberty, when applied to the will †. It must be considered as a mystery; and

---

* There are still some who consider the suspension of the mind as a proof of Liberty. They are not aware, that in volition suspension is no less necessary than precipitancy. When, for want of consideration, we have drawn on ourselves some misfortune, Self-love renders suspension absolutely necessary. The word deliberation is equally mistaken. We conceive, for instance, that while we are chusing between two pleasures nearly equal, that we are deliberating. But what we consider as Deliberation is only the slowness with which the heavier of two weights nearly equal, makes one of the scales of a balance subside.

† "Liberty," say the Stoics, "is a chimera. For want of knowing the motives, collecting the circumstances, by which we are determined to act in a certain manner, we think ourselves free. Can it be thought, that man has a self-determining power? Is he not rather impelled and

we may well cry out with St. Paul, O the depth! and allow
that it is a subject only proper for theology ; and that a philosophical treatise on Liberty would be a treatise on effects without causes:

Thus we see, that an ignorance of the true signification of
words often proves an eternal source of disputes and calamities.
Not to mention the effusion of blood which theological feuds
and disputes have caused—disputes almost always founded on
the abuse of words; what calamities and misfortunes have not
this ignorance been productive of, and into what errors has it
not plunged nations !

These errors are multiplied beyond what is commonly
thought: The story of a Swiss * is well known. He was
posted at one of the doors of the Thuilleries, with strict orders
not to suffer any person to come in.   A citizen comes up, and
offers to enter. " There is no going in;" says the Swiss. " I do
not want to go in," answers the citizen ; " but only to go out
over the Pont-royal." " If you desire only to go out," replied the
Swiss, you may pass on†."   Could it be thought, that this tale

---

determined by external objects, and their infinite combinations? Is
his will a vague and independent faculty, acting arbitrarily and without choice? It acts either in consequence of judgment, an act of the
understanding, representing to him that such a thing is more advantageous to his interest than any other ; or, independently of this act,
the circumstances in which a person finds himself, incline and force
the will to take a certain direction; and he then flatters himself that
he turned that way freely, though he could not well turn any other
way."—Histoire critique de la Philosophie.

   * The guards of the king of France are all Switzers.

   † " If," says Montagne, " at seeing a chancellor in his robe, his ample
wig, and sedate countenance, we can hardly form a more diverting
image to the fancy, than this same chancellor consummating marriage ;
possibly something, not less a subject of laughter, is the solicitous air,
the important and solemn gravity with which certain great men sit in
the divan only to deliberate like the Swiss. ' If you desire only to go
out, you may pass on.' The application of these words are so easy
and frequent, that the sagacity of the reader in this particular may be
depended on, and he may depend on finding every where Swiss cen-
tinels.

is the history of the people of Rome? Cæsar appears in the Forum, with an intention of being crowned; and the Romans, for want of annexing precise ideas to the word Royalty, made no difficulty of granting him, under the title of Imperator, what they would not hear of under that of Rex.

What I have said of the Romans is, in general, applicable to all divans and councils of princes. Among nations, as among sovereigns, there is not one which the abuse of words has not plunged into some gross error. To avoid this snare, Leibnitz directs a philosophical language to be formed, determining the precise signification of every word. We should then understand one another, and communicate our ideas with precision; disputes which are rendered perpetual by the abuse of words would be brought to an issue; and, in all sciences, men would soon be obliged to adopt the same principles.

But the execution of so desirable a scheme is, perhaps, impossible. Languages owe their origin to necessity, not to philosophers; and necessity here is easily satisfied. Afterwards some false ideas were annexed to certain words; then these ideas and words were combined and compared with one another. Every new combination has produced a new error; these errors have increased, and in their increase become so complicated, that now, without infinite labour and application, the source of them cannot be traced. It is with languages as with an algebraic calculation: at first some errors creep into it; these are

---

I cannot here forbear relating a pleasant particular, being the answer of an English nobleman to a minister of state. The minister was saying to some courtier, "There can be nothing more ridiculous than the manner in which the council of state assemble in some Negro nations. In the council-chamber are placed twelve large jars, half full of water. Twelve counsellors of state enter naked; and stalking along with great gravity, each leaps into his jar, and immerses himself up to his chin; and, in this pretty attitude, they deliberate on the national affairs. You do not smile," continued the minister, addressing himself to a noble lord who sat next him. "Smile! no," answered his lordship; "I see every day things more ridiculous than that." "Pray what?" returned the minister. "A country," replied the nobleman, "where the jars alone sit in council."

not perceived; the calculation is continued from step to step, till we arrive at consequences absolutely ridiculous. The absurdity is perceived; but how shall we find the place of the first error? This requires the repetition and proofs of a great variety of calculations. Unhappily, there are few capable of undertaking it, and still fewer who will submit to the drudgery, especially when the authority of men in power opposes this verification.

Thus have I shewn the true causes of our erroneous judgments. I have demonstrated, that all the errors of the mind have their source, either in the passions, or in ignorance either of certain facts, or the true import of words. Error, therefore, is not essentially annexed to the human mind; our false judgments are the effects of accidental causes, which do not suppose in us a faculty of perception. Error, therefore, is only an accident; and therefore it follows, that all men have a sound understanding.

These principles being admitted, nothing will oppose my asserting, that to judge, as I have already proved, is properly nothing more than to perceive. And the general conclusion of this discourse is, that the Mind may be considered either as the faculty productive of our thoughts, and in this sense it is nothing more than sensibility and memory; or the Mind may be considered as an effect of these faculties; and, in this sense, the mind is only an assemblage of thoughts, and in every person may be subdivided into as many parts as he has ideas.

These are the true aspects under which the mind appears, considered in itself. Let us now consider the Mind relatively to society.

ESSAY II.

CHAP. I.

OF THE MIND RELATIVELY TO SOCIETY.

Science is only the remembrance of the facts or ideas of others. The Mind, as distinguished from Science, is therefore an assemblage of new ideas of whatever kind.

This definition of the Mind is precise. It is even very instructive to a philosopher, but cannot be generally adopted: a definition for the public must be such as will enable them to compare different understandings, and to judge of their force and comprehension. But, if the above definition were admitted, how would the public measure the extent of a person's understanding? Who could lay before them an exact list of his ideas? and how shall science and understanding be distinguished?

Suppose I claim the discovery of an idea already known; the public, to be convinced whether the title of second inventor belongs to me, must previously know what I have read, seen, and heard; a knowledge, which it neither can nor will acquire. Besides, according to this impossible hypothesis, that the public could have an exact enumeration of the quantity and quality of a person's ideas; I say, that, in consequence of this enumeration, the public would be often obliged to class among geniuses, persons whom it denies to be men of wit; and such in general are all artificers.

However frivolous an art may appear, yet it is susceptible of infinite combinations. When Marcel, with his hand placed on his forehead, his eyes fixed, his body without motion, and in the attitude of profound meditation, on seeing a young lady dance, cries out, " What variety in a minute!" doubtless, this dancing-master then perceived in the manner of bending, rising, and performing the steps, elegancies invisible to com-

mon eyes *; and therefore his exclamation is no farther ridiculous than in the too great importance it places on trifles.
Now if the art of dancing includes so great a number of ideas
and combinations, who knows, whether the art of declamation
does not suppose in the actress, who excels in it, as many ideas
as a politician employs in forming a system of government?

If we consult our best romances, who will affirm, that, in the
gestures, dress, and studied speeches, of a perfect coquet, there
are not as many combinations and ideas as any system of the
world requires; and that Le Couvreur and Ninon de l'Enclos
were not, though of very different kinds, as great geniuses as
Aristotle and Solon?

I do not pretend to give a strict demonstration of this proposition. I only intend to shew, that, however ridiculous it may
appear, no person living can solve it. Deceived by our ignorance, we too often consider the boundaries which that ignorance gives to an art, as its Ne plus ultra. But supposing that,
in this respect, the public could be undeceived; I say, that the
clearest evidence will never alter its manner of judgment. It
will never measure its esteem for an art by the greater or
smaller number of combinations necessary for proceeding in it.
1. Because there is no such thing as enumerating these combinations. 2. Because it will consider the Mind only in that
light in which it is of importance to know it, viz. as relating to
society. Now, considered in this point of light, I say, that the
Mind is no more than an assemblage, more or less numerous,
not only of new ideas, but also of such as are interesting to the
public; and that the reputation of a man of wit does not so
much depend upon the number and delicacy of his ideas, as on
the happy choice of them.

---

* This dancing-master pretends to know a person's temper from his
gait and air. A foreigner coming once into his dancing-school, Marcel
asked him, "What countryman are you?" "I am an Englishman."—
"You an Englishman!" replied Marcel; "You a native of that island
where the people share in the public administration, and make a part
of the supreme power! No, sir; that down look, that air of timidity,
that effeminate gait, tell me you are only the titled slave of some
elector."

In effect, if the combinations of chess be infinite, and there is no excelling in it without forming a great number; why are not the distinguished players at chess honoured by the public with the title of great geniuses? Because their ideas are of no use to it, either with regard to entertainment or instruction, and, consequently, that it has no interest to esteem them; and interest * presides over all our decisions.

If the public has overlooked those errors, the invention of which sometimes implies more combinations and genius than the discovery of a truth; and if it esteems Locke more than Mallebranche, it is because it always measures its esteem by its interest. In what other balance should it weigh the merit of men's ideas? Every individual judges of things and persons, by the agreeable or disagreeable impressions he receives from them; and the public is no more than an assemblage of all the individuals; therefore it cannot fail of making its interest the rule of its decisions.

This point of view, in which I examine the understanding, is, I believe, the only one wherein it should be considered.— There is no other method of valuing each idea, of fixing the uncertainty of our judgments on this point, and, in fine, of discovering the cause of the amazing diversity of men's opinions with regard to the mind; a diversity absolutely depending on the difference of the passions and ideas, their prejudices and inclinations, and consequently of their interests.

It would, indeed, be very strange, that the general interest† should fix a value on the different actions of men, and give the appellations of vicious or lawful as they were useful, detrimental, or indifferent, to the public, and that this same interest should not have been the sole dispenser of the esteem or contempt annexed to the ideas of men.

---

* The word interest is generally confined to the love of money; but the intelligent reader will perceive that I use it in a more extensive sense; and that I apply it in general to whatever may procure us pleasure, or exempt us from pain.

† It is, perhaps, needless to observe, that I here speak as a politician, not as a divine.

Ideas, like actions, may be divided into three different classes.

Useful ideas: and, taking this expression in its most extensive sense, I understand by it, every idea adapted to our instruction or entertainment.

Detrimental ideas are those which make a contrary impression on us.

Indifferent ideas: by these I mean all which, for want of an intrinsic agreeableness, or by being rendered too familiar, make very little impression on us. Such ideas have hardly any existence; and can only, if I may use the expression, be termed indifferent for an instant. Their duration, or succession, by which they become tedious, soon reduces them to the class of detrimental ideas.

In order to shew how pregnant with truth this method of considering the mind is, I shall apply successively the foregoing principles to the actions and ideas of men; and prove that, at all times, and in all countries, both with regard to morality and genius, personal interest alone dictates the judgment of individuals; while general interest dictates that of nations; and consequently that, in the public as in individuals, it is always love and gratitude that praises, and hatred and revenge that depreciates.

In order to demonstrate this truth, and clearly shew the exact and perpetual similarity in our manner of judging either the actions or ideas of men, I shall consider Probity, and the Mind, or Understanding, in different respects, and relatively; 1. To an individual. 2. To a small society. 3. To a nation. 4. To different ages and countries. 5. To the whole universe: and in these inquiries, always taking experience for my guide, shall prove that, in every point of view, interest is the only judge of Probity and the Understanding.

CHAP II.

OF PROBITY RELATIVELY TO AN INDIVIDUAL.

IT is not real Probity; that is Probity, with regard to the public, that I consider in this chapter; but merely Probity, considered relatively to each individual.

In this point of view, I say, that each individual calls Probity in another only the habitude of actions which are useful to him: I say habitude, because it is not one single honest action, more than one single ingenious idea, that will gain us the title of virtuous and witty. There is not that penurious wretch on earth which has not once behaved with generosity; nor a liberal person who has not once been parsimonious; no villain who has not done a good action; no person so stupid who has not uttered one smart sentence; and, in fine, no man who, on inspecting certain actions of his life, will not seem possessed of all the opposite virtues and vices. A greater uniformity in the behaviour of men would suppose in them a continuity of attention which they are incapable of; differing from one another only more or less. The man of absolute uniformity has no existence; for that no perfection, either with regard to vice or virtue, is to be found on the earth.

It is therefore to the habitude of actions advantageous to him, that an individual gives the name of Probity: I say of actions, because we cannot judge of intentions. How is it possible? It is seldom or never that action is the effect of a sentiment; we ourselves are often ignorant of the motives by which we are determined. A rich man bestows a comfortable subsistence on a worthy man reduced to poverty. Doubtless he does a good action; but is this action simply the effect of a desire of rendering a man happy? Pity, the hopes of gratitude, vanity itself, all these different motives, separately or aggregately, may they not, unknown to himself, have determined him, to that commendable action? Now if a man be, in general, ignorant himself of the motives of his generous action, how can the public be acquainted with them? Thus it is only from the actions of men, that the public can judge of their probity. A

man, for instance, has twenty degrees of passion for virtue;
but he has thirty degrees of love for a woman; and this woman
would instigate him to be guilty of murder. Upon this supposition, it is certain, that this person is nearer guilt than he,
who, with only ten degrees of passion for virtue, has only five
degrees of love for so wicked a woman. Hence I conclude,
that of two men, the more honest in his actions has sometimes
the less passion for virtue.

Every philosopher also agrees, that the virtue of men greatly
depends on the circumstances in which they are placed. Virtuous men have too often sunk under a strange series of unhappy events.

He who will warrant his virtue in every possible situation,
is either an impostor or a fool; characters equally to be mistrusted.

After determining the idea I affix to this word Probity, considered in relation to every individual, we must, to assure ourselves of the propriety of this definition, have recourse to observation; and this will inform us, that there are men whom
a happy disposition, a strong desire of glory and esteem, inspire with the same love for justice and virtue, which men in
general have for riches and honours.

The actions personally advantageous to these virtuous men
are so truly just, that they tend to promote the general welfare, or, at least, not to lessen it.

But the number of these men is so small, that I only mention them in honour of humanity. And the most numerous
class, which alone comprehends the far greater part of mankind, is that of men so entirely devoted to their own interest,
that they never consider the welfare of the whole. Concentrated, if I may be allowed the expression, in their own happiness*; these men call those actions only honest, which are

---

* Our hatred or love is an effect of the good or harm we have received. "Among the savages," says Hobbes, "the only wicked man
is the robust; and, in a civilized state, the man in power." The
strong man, however, considered in these two senses, is not more
wicked than weak. This Hobbes was aware of: but he knew that the

advantageous to themselves. A judge acquits a criminal, a minister prefers an unworthy person; yet both are just, if those they have favoured may be credited. But should the judge punish, and the minister refuse, the criminal, and the party denied, will always consider them as unjust.

If the monks, who, during the first dynasty, were entrusted to write the lives of our kings, have only given those of their benefactors, indicating the other reigns only with these words, NIHIL FECIT; and if they have given the name of slothful kings to some princes, truly worthy of esteem ; it is because a monk is a man, and every man, in his judgment, consults only his own interest.

The Christians, who justly branded with the name of barbarity and guilt the cruelties inflicted on them by the Pagans, did not they give the name of zeal to the cruelties they, in their turn, inflicted on those same Pagans? It will, on examination, be found, that there is not a crime but is placed among honest actions, by the societies to which this crime is advantageous; nor an action of public benefit that is not censured by some particular society to which it is detrimental.

In effect, what man, if he sacrifices the pride of stiling himself more virtuous than others, to the pride of being more sincere ; and if, with a scrupulous attention, he searches all the recesses of his soul ; will not perceive that his virtues and vices are wholly owing to the different modifications of personal interest* ; that all equally tend to their happiness ; that

---

epithet of Wicked is applied only to those whose wickedness is formidable. The anger and blows of a child are often thought engaging in him ; but those of a strong man provoke; his blows hurt, and he is called a brute.

* The humane man is he to whom the sight of another's misfortunes is insupportable, and who, to remove this afflicting spectacle, is, as it were, forced to relieve the wretched. The cruel man, on the contrary, is he to whom the sight of another's misfortunes gives a secret pleasure; and it is to prolong that pleasure, that he refuses all relief to the wretched. Now these two persons, so very opposite, both equally tend to their pleasures, and are actuated by the same spring. But it will be said, if a man does every thing for himself, no grati-

it is the diversity of the passions and tastes, of which some are agreeable, and others contrary to the public interest, which terms our actions either virtues or vices? Instead of despising the vicious man, we should pity him, rejoice in our own happy disposition, thank heaven for not having given us any of those tastes and passions, which would have forced us to have sought our happiness in the misery of another. For, after all, interest is always obeyed; hence the injustice of all our judgments, and the appellations of just and unjust are lavished on the same actions, according to the advantage resulting from them to particulars.

If the physical universe be subject to the laws of motion, the moral universe is equally so to those of interest. Interest is, on earth, the mighty magician, which to the eyes of every creature changes the appearance of all objects. The innocent sheep, which feeds in our fields, is it not an object of dread and horror to those imperceptible insects which live upon the leaves of herbs? " Let us," say they, " hasten from hence: that voracious and cruel animal is coming, whose enormous throat swallows at once both us and our cities. Why does not he act like the lion and tyger? Those benign animals do not destroy our habitations; they do not feed on our blood; but, as just avengers of guilt, punish in the sheep the cruelties it inflicts on us." Thus different interests metamorphose objects: we consider the lion as a cruel animal, whereas, among the insects, it is the sheep; and what Leibnitz said of the physical universe may be applied to the moral. That this world, being constantly in motion, every instant offered a new and different phænomenon to each of its inhabitants.

This principle is so agreeable to experience, that, without

---

tude is due to benefactors? I answer, the benefactor has at least no right to require any; for, otherwise, instead of bestowing a gift, he has only made a contract. The Germans, (says Tacitus,) make and receive presents, without any reciprocations of gratitude; it is in favour of the unfortunate, and to multiply the number of benefactors; and therefore the public, with very good reason, imposes on the obliged the duty of gratitude.

entering into a farther discussion, I think myself warranted to conclude, that personal interest is the only and universal estimator of the merit of human actions; and therefore, that Probity, with regard to an individual is, according to my definition, nothing more than the habitude of actions personally advantageous to this individual.

CHAP. III.

OF THE MIND, OR UNDERSTANDING, WITH REGARD TO AN INDIVIDUAL.

LET us now transfer to ideas the principles I have above applied to actions; and it must be aknowledged, that each individual gives the name of Understanding only to the habitude of those ideas which are useful to him, either with regard to instruction or entertainment; and that, in this respect also, personal interest is still the only judge of the merit of men.

Every idea offered to us has always some regard to our station, passions, or opinions. Now in all these several cases we value an idea in proportion to its use. The pilot, the physician, and the engineer, will have more regard for a shipwright, a botanist, and a mechanic, than a bookseller, a goldsmith, and a mason, will have for the same persons; they always preferring to them the novelist, the designer, and the architect.

With regard to ideas proper for opposing or countenancing our passions or our taste, we shall doubtless account those the most valuable, which most flatter those passions or tastes*. A woman of an amorous complexion will place a greater value on

---

* In order to deceive a woman, who was remarkable for a volubility of tongue, but otherwise did not want wit, a person was introduced to her as one that had a remarkable share of it. The lady received him with the greatest joy and civility; but, through eagerness of rendering herself agreeable to him, she asked him a hundred questions, without perceiving that he returned no answer. At the conclusion of the visit, she was asked how she liked the person? "He is a delightful man, indeed," answered she, "his wit is so ready, and of

a romance than on a metaphysical treatise: a person of the character of Charles XII. will prefer the history of Alexander to every other work: and, certainly, the miser will perceive understanding only in those who shall inform him where to place his money at the highest interest.

In opinions, as in passions, to esteem the ideas of others, it must be our interest to esteem them; and here I cannot help observing, that, with respect to the latter, men may be moved by two kinds of interest. There are not wanting men, who are animated with a noble and judicious pride; who, friends to truth, attached to their opinions without obstinacy, preserve their minds in that state of suspension which leaves a free passage for new truths: of this number are some philosophic minds, and some persons who, too young to have established opinions, do not blush to change them; these two classes of men will always esteem in others true and adequate ideas, and such as are proper. for gratifying their passion for truth, produced by a judicious pride.

There are others, and in this number I comprehend the far greatest part, who are animated by a less noble vanity. These can esteem in others such ideas only as are conformable to their own*, and proper for justifying the high opinion they all entertain of the precision of their understanding. On this analogy of ideas is founded their hatred or their love.—

so exquisite a turn'!" This exclamation excited in the whole company a burst of laughter; for this charming companion, this remarkable wit, was dumb.

* All who are of a limited understanding, are continually depreciating, or decrying, those whose understanding is equally solid and comprehensive. They accuse them of too much refinement; and of thinking, with regard to every particular, in too abstracted a manner. " We will never," says Mr. Hume, " allow that a thing is just when it is beyond our weak comprehension. The difference," adds that illustrious philosopher, " between the common person and the person of genius, is chiefly seen in the more or less depth of the principles on which they found their ideas. With most men every judgment is particular; they do not extend their views to the universal propositions; to them every general idea is obscure."

Hence that sure and ready instinct in almost all common persons, for knowing and avoiding persons of merit*; hence the strong attraction between persons of genius; that attraction, which, as it were, forces them to seek the acquaintance of each other, notwithstanding the danger that often attends their intercourse, from their common thirst of glory: hence that sure way of judging of a person's temper and understanding by his choice of books and friends. The fool has only fools for his companions: every connection of friendship, when not founded on an interest of decency, love, protection, avarice, ambition, or some other similar motive, always supposes between men some resemblance of ideas, or sentiments. It is this that brings together persons of a very different condition†. On this account it was that Augustus, Mæcenas, Scipio, Julian, Richelieu and Condé, lived familiarly with men of genius; and hence the well-known proverb, the truth of which is confirmed by its frequent use, "Shew me your company, I will shew you the man."

Thus the analogy or conformity of ideas is to be considered as the attractive and repulsive force which separates men, or draws them nearer to one another‡. Place in Constantinople a philosopher, who, being a stranger to the lights of revelation, could follow only those of reason. Let this philosopher deny Mahomet's mission, the visions and pretended miracles of that prophet; who doubts but those who are called true Musselmans would conceive an aversion to this philosopher, look upon him with horror, call him madman, impious wretch, and sometimes even a dishonest man. It would be to little purpose for him to say, that in such a religion it is absurd for him to be-

---

* Fools, were it in their power, would gladly banish all men of genius; and, like the Ephesians, would be always crying out, "If any among us excel, let him go and excel elsewhere."

† At court, the more wit a great man has, the more countenance he shews to the men of wit.

‡ There are very few men who, had they the power, would not make use of tortures to cause their opinions to be adopted. Have not we, in our days, seen persons of so little sense, and such an ex-

lieve miracles of which he was not himself a witness; and as it is more probable that they are lies than miracles*, to give too easy credit to them, is rather believing in impostors than God. It would be equally vain for him to represent, that, had God been willing to confirm Mahomet's mission, he would never have made use of miracles that appear ridiculous to the eyes of a reason the least reflective. Whatever arguments the philosopher might use to support his incredulity, he would never obtain, among those good Musselmans, the character of wise and honest, till he became so weak as to believe absurdities, or so false as to pretend a belief of them. So true is it, that men judge of the opinions of others by the conformity of them with their own; and it is only by fooleries that fools are persuaded.

If the savage of Canada prefers us to the other nations of Europe, it is because we approach nearer to his manners, and

---

cessive pride, as to desire that the civil power would punish a writer, because he was of a different opinion from them, in preferring the Italian music to the French. If it is only in religious disputes that men generally proceed to extremities, it is because other disputes do not afford the same pretences, nor the same means, for being cruel. It is only to impotence that a person generally owes his moderation. The humane and moderate man is rarely to be found. On his meeting with a person of a different religion, he says, " This man, indeed, entertains different opinions from me; but why should I persecute him? The gospel has no where enjoined us to use tortures and prisons for making converts. True religion never built scaffolds; yet its ministers have sometimes been seen, in order to avenge their pride, offended by opinions different from theirs, to arm in their behalf the stupid credulity of people and princes. Few men have deserved the panegyric of the Egyptian priests in Sethos, on queen Nephte. " So far from exciting animosity, molestation, persecution, through the suggestion of a mistaken piety; she, say these priests, has drawn from religion only maxims of lenity: she never believed that it was lawful to torture men, in order to honour the Gods."

* Why, in such a religion, should not the witness of a miracle be suspected? " We are," says M. de Fontenelle, "in order to relate a fact precisely as we have seen it, that is, without addition or diminution, to keep so strict a watch over ourselves, that he, who pretends he has never caught himself in a lie in this respect, may be concluded a liar."

way of living. It is to this complaisance we owe the grand eulogium he thinks he makes on a Frenchman, in saying, "He is a man like me."

Thus it appears, that, in manners, opinions, and ideas, it is always ourselves we esteem in others; and this is the reason why the Cæsars, the Alexanders, and in general all great men, have constantly had other great men under them.

A prince of capacity grasps the sceptre, and is scarce seated on the throne, before all the posts are filled by superior men. The prince did not form them such, he seems even to have taken them at random; but, forced to esteem and prefer persons only of a genius similar to his own, his choice must of necessity be good. On the other hand, a weak prince is, by the same reason, compelled to entertain such as resemble him; and thus he generally makes a bad choice. It is from a succession of such princes, that the highest employments have been, for several ages, filled by a succession of weak men — Accordingly the people, who cannot personally know their master, judge of him only from the talents of those he employs, and is esteemed for entertaining men of merit. Queen Christina used to say, that, under a stupid monarch, the whole court is, or will become, such.

But it will be said, men are sometimes seen to admire in others ideas which they never would have produced, and which have no similarity with their own. The following saying of a Cardinal is generally known. On the nomination of a pope, he went up to him, and accosted him in this manner: "You are now pope, and this is the last time you will hear truth; seduced by flattery, you will soon fancy yourself a great man; but remember, that before your exaltation you were both ignorant and obstinate; farewell, I am now to adore you." Few courtiers have wit and resolution to talk in such a manner; most of them, like those people who both worship and scourge their idol, tacitly rejoice at the fall of the master to whom they are subject. Their vindictive temper inspires them to commend such sarcasms; and revenge is an interest. Whoever is not animated by an interest of this kind, esteems and feels only such ideas as are analogous to his own; accordingly, the wand for discovering a recent and unknown merit is, and indeed can only be, in the hands of men of genius; for the lapidary alone is skilful in rough diamonds, and genius only perceives genius. It was the eye of a Turenne alone that in young Churchill could discern the famous Marlborough.

Every idea too foreign to our manner of seeing or reflecting will always appear ridiculous to us. The execution of a project, though vast and elevated, will appear easy to a great minister; while an ordinary minister will consider it as senseless and chimerical; and this project, according to a phrase common among fools, will be referred to Plato's republic. This is the reason why, in certain countries, where the minds are enervated with superstition, sluggish, and little capable of noble enterprises, the greatest ridicule that can be thrown on a person, is to say of him, he endeavours to reform the state. A ridicule which, from the indigence, the depopulation of these countries, and consequently the necessity of a reformation, in the eyes of foreigners, reflects on the authors of it. It is with such people as with those mean buffoons* who think they severely expose a person, when they say, with a sneering and malicious accent, " He is a Roman! he is a wit!" A kind of raillery, which, taken in its true sense, signifies that this man is not like them; that is, he is neither a fool nor dishonest.— How many of these weak acknowledgments and absurd phrases does an attentive mind hear in different companies; which, reduced to their precise meaning, would sufficiently confound those who use them. The man of merit, therefore, should be indifferent with regard to the esteem or contempt of an individual, as each signifies nothing more than that he does not think or

---

* The wealthy citizens add, in derision, that the wit is often seen at the rich man's door, but the rich man never at the door of the wit; that is, answers the poet Saadi, " Because the man of wit knows the value of riches, and the rich man is ignorant of the value of knowledge. Besides, how should riches esteem knowledge? The man of learning can set a value upon ignorance, having known it in his childhood; but the ignorant man cannot estimate learning, because he never knew it."

act like him. I might, by an infinity of other facts, farther prove, that we esteem only such ideas as are analogous to our own; but, to ascertain this truth, it must be supported by proofs drawn from just reasoning.

CHAP. IV.

OF THE NECESSITY WE ARE UNDER OF ESTEEMING IN OTHERS ONLY OURSELVES.

Two causes equally powerful determine to this action, vanity and indolence. I say vanity, because the desire of esteem is common to all men; though some, to the pleasure of being admired, will add the merit of contemning admiration; but this contempt is not real, the person admired never thinking the admirer stupid: Now, if all men are fond of esteem, every one, knowing, from experience, that his ideas will appear esteemable, or contemptible to others, only as they agree or clash with their own, the consequence is, that, swayed by vanity, every one cannot help esteeming in others a conformity of ideas, which assure him of their esteem; and to hate in them an opposition of ideas, as a certain indication of their hatred; or, at least, of their contempt, which is to be considered as a corrective of hatred. But even suppose a person should sacrifice his vanity to the love of truth, if this person be not animated with the keenest desire of information, I say, that his indolence will allow him to have, for those opinions opposite to his own, only an esteem upon trust. In order to explain what I mean by an esteem upon trust, I shall distinguish esteem into two kinds, one, which may be considered as the effect, either of deference to public opinion*, or of confidence in the judgment of certain

---

* M. de la Fontaine had only such an esteem for Plato's philosophy. M. de Fontinelle relates on this head, that la Fontaine one day said to him: " This Plato was certainly a great philosopher." " Do you find any remarkable clearness of ideas in him ?" answered Fontinelle. " Oh! no: he is impenetrably obscure." " Do not you find

persons; and this I call esteem upon trust. Such is that of certain persons for very indifferent novels, merely because they imagine them to come from the pens of our famous writers. Such is even the general admiration of Descartes and Newton; an admiration which, in most men, is the more enthusiastic, as it is founded on the less knowledge. Whether, after forming to ourselves a vague idea of the merit of those great geniuses, their admirers, in this idea, respect the work of their own admiration; or whether, in pretending to be judges of such a man as Newton, they think to share in the eulogiums they so profusely bestow on him. This kind of esteem, which our ignorance often obliges us to use, is, from that very circumstance, the most general. Nothing is so uncommon as to judge according to our own sentiments.

The other kind of esteem is that which, independently of the opinions of others, is produced solely by the impression made on us by certain ideas; and therefore I call it Felt-esteem, being the only real esteem, and that which is here meant. Now, in order to prove, that indolence allows us to grant this kind of esteem only to ideas analogous to our own, it will be sufficient to observe that, as geometry sensibly proves, by the analogy and secret relations which ideas already known have with unknown ideas, we obtain a knowledge of the latter; and that, by following the progression of these analogies, we may attain the utmost perfection of a science; it follows, that ideas of no analogy with our own, would be to us unintelligible ideas. But it will be said, there are no ideas which have not necessarily some relation, as they would otherwise be universally unknown. Yes; but this relation may be either immediate or remote: when immediate, the faint desire every one has of information, renders him capable of the attention which the intelligence of

---

that he contradicts himself?" "Indeed," replied Fontaine, " he is nothing more than a sophist." Then at once forgetting the acknowledgments he had just made, " Plato," says he, " places his characters so properly! Socrates was on the Pyream, when Alcibiades, with a garland of flowers round his head. What an admirable philosopher this Plato was!"

such ideas supposes: but, when remote, as it generally is in those opinions which are the result of a great number of ideas and various sentiments, it is evident, that, without being animated by a very keen desire for information, and also a situation proper for gratifying that desire, indolence will never allow us to conceive, nor consequently to acquire, any Felt-esteem contrary to our own.

Few have leisure sufficient for information. The poor man, for instance, can neither reflect nor examine; he receives truth or error only by prejudice: employed in daily labour, he cannot rise to a certain sphere of ideas. Accordingly he prefers the blue library *, to the writings of St. Real, Roche-foucault, and cardinal de Retz. Also, on those days of public rejoicings, when there is free admittance to the playhouses, the actors, sensible what audience they have to entertain, will rather act Don Japhet and Pourceaugnac, than Heraclius and the Misantrope. What I say of the populace, may be applied to all the classes of mankind. The men of the world are distracted by a thousand affairs and pleasures. With their taste, philosophical works have as little analogy, as the Misantrope with that of the populace. Accordingly, they will, in general, prefer a romance to Locke. It is from the same principle of analogies, that we explain why the learned, and even men of wit, have preferred authors less esteemed, to those of a superior reputation. Why did Malherbe prefer Statius to every other poet? Why did Heinsius † and Corneille value Lucan beyond Virgil? How came Adrian to prefer the eloquence of Cato to that of Cicero? For what reason did Scaliger ‡ consider Homer and Horace as far beneath Virgil and Juvenal? Because, the

---

* Small books stitched in blue paper.

† " Lucan," said Heinsius, in comparison of the other poets, " is what a fiery horse, proudly neighing, is to a drove of asses, whose ignoble voice betrays their servile disposition."

‡ Scaliger quotes the seventeenth Ode of the fourth book of Horace as execrable; and Heinsius quotes it as one of the master-pieces of antiquity.

esteem we have for an author, is proportional to the analogy between his ideas and those of his reader.

Let a manuscript work be put into the hands of seven men of genius, equally free from prepossessions or prejudice, and let them be separately desired to mark the most striking passages: each of them will underline different places; and if, afterwards, the approved passages be compared with the genius and temper of the approver, each will be found to have praised only the ideas analogous to his manner of seeing and perceiving; and that understanding is, if I may be allowed the expression, a string that vibrates only with the unison.

If the Abbé de Longuerue, as he himself used to say, of all the works of St. Augustine, remembered only, that the Trojan horse was a military machine; and, in the romance of Cleopatra, a famous counsellor could see nothing interesting, except the dissolution of the marriage of Eliza with Artabanes; it must be acknowledged, that the only difference, in this respect, between the learned, or men of wit, and the common, is, that the former having a greater number of ideas, their sphere of analogies is much more extensive. If the question relates to species of wit, very different from what he is master of, the man of genius, who is, in all respects, like other men, esteems only those ideas that are analogous to his own. Let a Newton, a Quinaut, a Machiavel, be brought together; let them not be named; let no opportunity be given them for conceiving for each other that kind of esteem which I call esteem on trust; it will be found that, after having reciprocally, but to no purpose, endeavoured to communicate their ideas to one another, Newton will look upon Quinaut as an insupportable, paltry rhimer; Newton will seem to him a maker of Almanacks; and both will consider Machiavel as a coffee-house politician; and, in fine, all three, by calling each other men of very little genius, will revenge, by a reciprocal contempt, the mutual uneasiness they gave each other.

Now, if superior men, entirely absorbed in their respective kinds of study, are not susceptible of a Felt-esteem, for a species of genius too different from their own, every author who abounds with new ideas can only expect esteem from two sorts of men; either young persons, who, by not previously adopting any opinion, have still the desire and leisure of informing themselves; or of those whose minds, being desirous of truth, and analogous to that of the author, had previously some glimpse of the existence of these ideas. But the number of such men has always been very small. This retards the progress of the human mind: and hence the extreme slowness with which every truth becomes displayed to the eyes of all the world.

From what has been said, it follows, that most men, submitting to indolence, conceive those ideas only which are analogous to their own.

It appears, from what has been just said, that most men, subject to indolence, form a perfect conception only of those ideas that are analogous to their own; that they have only a Felt-esteem for no other than this kind of ideas: and hence proceeds that high opinion which every one is, in a manner, forced to have of himself; an opinion which the moralists would not, perhaps, have attributed to pride, had they been more thoroughly acquainted with the principles just laid down. They would then have been sensible, that the sacred respect and the profound admiration, which, when alone, they often feel for themselves, can be nothing more than the effect of the necessity we were under of having an higher esteem of ourselves than for others.

How can we forbear having the highest ideas of ourselves? Every man changes his opinions, as soon as he believes that those opinions are false. Every one, therefore, believes, that he thinks justly, and consequently, much better than those whose ideas are contrary to his own. Now, if there are not two men who think exactly alike, it must necessarily follow, that each in particular believes, that his sentiments are more just than those entertained by all the rest of mankind*. The

---

* Experience informs us, that every one places in the rank of dunces, and of bad books, every man and every work that contradicts his opinions; that he would impose silence on the man, and suppress

duchess de la Ferte said, one day, to madam de Stahl, " I must confess, my dear friend, that I find no body always in the right but myself*. Let us hear the Talopoins, the Bonzes, the Bramins, the Guebres, the Imans, and the Marabouts, when they preach against each other in the assembly of the multitude, does not each of them say, like the duchess de la Ferte? ' Ye people, I assure you, that I alone am always in the right.' Each then believes that he has a superior understanding, and the fools are not the persons who are the least sensible of it †. This gave room for the fable of the four merchants, who went to the fair to sell beauty, birth, dignity, and wit; all of whom disposed of their merchandize, except the last, who returned without even taking handsel.

" But," say they, " we find some men acknowledge that others have greater mental abilities than themselves." " Yes," I reply; " we do find people who confess it; and this confession springs from a delicacy of soul; in the mean time, they have only an esteem upon trust, for those whom they acknowledge their superior; they only join in the public opinion, in giving them this preference, and confess that these persons

the work. Thus the orthodox, who are deficient in understanding, have sometimes given heretics an advantage over them. " If, in a trial at the bar," say these last, " one party should forbid the other to exhibit his proofs in support of his right; would not this act of violence in one of the parties be considered as a proof of the injustice of his cause?"

* See the entertaining Memoirs of madam de Stahl, which has been lately translated into English.

† " What presumption," say the persons of mean abilities, " is there in those called men of genius? How superior do they think themselves to the rest of mankind?" But the others reply, " the stag who boasted of being the swiftest of all stags, must, doubtless, be puffed up with pride; but, without wounding his modesty, he may safely say, that he runs better than a tortoise. You are the tortoise; you have neither read nor spent your hours in meditation : how then can you have a mind cultivated like his, who has taken great pains in acquiring knowledge? You accuse him with presumption; and you, without study and reflection, would be upon an equal footing with him." Which then of the two is the more presumptuous?

are esteemed, without being inwardly convinced, that they are more worthy of esteem than themselves.*

A man will confess, without difficulty, that in geometry he is much inferior to Fontaine, d'Alembert, Clairaut, and Euler; that in poetry he is excelled by Moliere, Racine, and Voltaire; but I say, that this man will set so much the less value on that perfection in proportion as he acknowledges he has superiors in it; and that, besides, he will think himself so greatly recompensed for the superiority the persons above-mentioned have over him, either by finding that those sciences are of no consequence, or by the variety of his knowledge, his good sense, his acquaintance with the world, or by some other of the like advantages; that, every thing properly considered, he will think himself as worthy of esteem as any other person whatever.†

But how, say they, can it be imagined, that a man, who, for example, executes the subordinate offices of the magistrate, can believe that he has a genius equal to Corneille? 'Tis true,

---

* Fontenelle would readily have agreed that Corneille had a superior genius in poetry to him; but he would not have been sensible of it. Suppose, in order to be convinced of this truth, that Fontenelle had been desired to give the ideas he had entertained of the perfection of poetry: it is certain that he would here have proposed no other excellent rules than such as he himself had observed as well as Corneille; he must therefore have secretly entertained the belief that he himself was as great a poet as any other whatever; and that, in confessing himself inferior to Corneille, he consequently did no more than sacrifice his opinion to that of the public. Few men have the courage to confess, that they have what I call a greater Felt-esteem for themselves, than for any body else; but whether they deny or confess it, it does not alter the existence of this sentiment in their minds.

† We praise ourselves for every thing we possess: some boast of their stupidity under the name of good sense; others praise their beauty; some, puffed up with their riches, place these gifts of fortune to the account of judgement and prudence; the woman who spends the evening with her cook, thinks herself as worthy of esteem as a person of learning. One who prints a work in folio, despises the writer of a romance, and fancies himself as superior to the latter, as a folio is bigger than a pamphlet.

I reply, that here he will make no body his confidant: however, when by a scrupulous examination, we have discovered
how much we are daily affected by sentiments of pride, without our perceiving it, and what eulogiums are necessary to
embolden us so far as to make us confess to ourselves and to
others the profound esteem we have for our own abilities, we
shall perceive that the silence of pride is no proof of its absence.
Let us suppose, to follow the above example, that three counsellors leaving the play-house, accidentally meet, and begin to
talk of Corneille; all three perhaps cry out at once, that Corneille was the greatest genius in the world: however, if, to
disburden himself of this intolerable weight of esteem, one of
them adds, that Corneille was indeed a great man, but he excelled in what is of a very frivolous nature; it is certain, if we
may judge from the contempt which certain people affect to
entertain for poetry, the two other counsellors will be of the
same opinion with the first: then, from confidence to confidence
they come to compare the quibbles of law with poetry: the
art of pleading, says another, has its plots, its delicacies, and
its combinations, like all other arts. Really, replies the third,
there is no art more difficult. Now, from an hypothesis very
easily admitted, that, in this difficult art, each of these counsellors thinks himself the most able of the three, the result
of this conference will be, that each of them fancies he has
as great a genius as Corneille. We are, through vanity, and
above all, through ignorance, so necessitated to esteem ourselves preferably to others, that the greatest man in every art,
is he whom each artist places in the first rank after himself.
In the time of Themistocles, when pride was only different
from the pride of the present age, in its being more disguised,
all the captains, after the battle of Salamis, were obliged, by
notes laid upon the altar of Neptune, to declare who had the
greatest share in obtaining the victory; each gave that honour
to himself, and adjudged the second place to Themistocles: upon
which, the discerning people gave the greatest reward to him,
whom each captain had considered as the most worthy except
himself.

It is then certain, that every person has necessarily the

highest idea of himself; and that he consequently never esteems in another any thing but his own image and resemblance.

The general conclusion of what I have said on the capacity of the mind, considered in relation to the individual, is, that it is only the assemblage of interesting ideas to that individual, whether as agreeable or instructive: whence it follows, that personal interest, as I had proposed to shew, is in this respect the only judge of the merit of mankind.

CHAP. V.

OF PROBITY IN RELATION TO PRIVATE SOCIETIES.

UNDER this point of view, I say, that probity is only a more or less distinguished habit of performing actions particularly useful to this little society. Certain virtuous societies indeed frequently appear to lay aside their own interest to judge the actions of men, in conformity to the interest of the public; but in this they only gratify the passion which an enlightened pride gives them for virtue; and consequently, like all other societies, obey the law of personal interest. What other motive can determine men to generous actions? It is as impossible to love virtue for the sake of virtue as to love vice for the sake of vice.*

Brutus sacrificed his son to the safety of Rome, only because the paternal love he felt for him was less powerful than his

---

* The continual declamations of moralists against the malignity of mankind are a proof of their knowing but little of human nature. Men are not cruel and perfidious, but carried away by their own interest. The declamations of the moralist will certainly make no change in this moral spring of the universe. They ought not therefore to complain of the wickedness of mankind, but of the ignorance of the legislators, who have always placed private interest in opposition to the general interest. If the Scythians were more virtuous than we, it is because their legislators, and their manner of life, inspired more probity.

I

love for his country: in this instance he only yielded to the stronger passion; a passion which, animating him for the public interest, made him perceive, in a severity to his own child, so generous, so proper to revive the love of liberty, the only resource that could save Rome, and prevent her falling again under the tyranny of the Tarquins. In the critical circumstances in which Rome was then placed, such an action was necessary to serve as a foundation to the vast power to which afterwards the love of liberty and the public welfare arose.

But, as there are few Brutuses, and fewer societies composed of such men, I shall take my examples from the common order, to prove that in each society private interest is the only distributer of the esteem bestowed on account of human actions.

To be convinced of this, let us cast our eyes upon a man who sacrifices all his fortune to save a relation, who is an assassin, from undergoing the severity of the law. This man will certainly be considered by his family as extremely virtuous, though he is really extremely unjust. I say extremely unjust; because, if the hope of impunity multiplies crimes, and the certainty of punishment is absolutely necessary to preserve order in any nation, it is evident, that a pardon granted to a criminal is injustice to the public, of which he renders himself an accomplice who solicits for such a pardon.*

When a minister, deaf to the solicitations of his relations and friends, believes that he ought to raise none to the highest

---

* I have been guilty, said Chilo, when dying. but of one crime, that of having, during my magistracy, saved from the rigour of the laws a criminal, my best friend.

I shall also cite on this subject a fact related in Gulistan. An Arab going to complain to the sultan of the violences committed by two unknown persons in his house, the sultan went thither; caused the lights to be put out; seized the criminals; had their heads wrapped up in a cloke, and ordered that they should be stabbed. The execution being thus performed, he ordered the flambeaux brought with him to be again lighted; and, having examined the bodies of the criminals, lifted up his hands, and returned thanks to God. "What favour," said the vizier "have you then received from heaven?"—"Vizier," reposts in the state, but men of the greatest merit; so just a minister will certainly pass in society for a man useless, void of friendship, and perhaps even void of honesty. It may be said, to the disgrace of the present age, that it is almost always to injustice that a man in a high post owes the titles of a good friend, of a good relation, of a virtuous and beneficent man, lavishly bestowed upon him by the society in which he lives.

When a father, by his intrigues, obtains the post of general for a son incapable of commanding, that father shall be mentioned by his family as a worthy and beneficent man: yet what can be more abominable, than to expose a nation, or at least several provinces, to the ravages which follow a defeat, only to gratify the ambition of a family?

What can be more worthy of punishment than the solicitations, against which it is impossible for a sovereign to be always on his guard? Such solicitations, that have but too often plunged nations in the greatest misfortunes, are the inexhaustible sources of calamities: calamities from which, perhaps, the people can be no otherwise delivered, than by breaking the bonds of affinity that unite mankind, and declaring every citizen a child of the state. This is the only means of stifling the vices authorised by an appearance of virtue, of hindering the subdivision of a people into an infinite number of families or little societies, whose interests are almost always opposite to that of the public, and at length extinguish in the mind all kind of love for our country.

What I have said sufficiently proves, that, before the tribunal of a small society, interest is the only judge of the merit of men's actions: I should, therefore, have added nothing to what I have said, had I not proposed the public utility as the principal end of this work. Now I am sensible that an honest

---

plied the sultan, " I thought my son had been the author of these crimes; therefore, I ordered the lights to be put out, and the faces of these unhappy wretches to be covered with a cloke. I was afraid lest paternal tenderness should make me fail in the justice which I owe my subjects. Judge whether I ought not to thank heaven, when I find myself just, without having taken away the life of my son!"

man, apprehensive of the ascendency the opinion of the society in which he lives may have over him, may justly be afraid of being frequently turned from the path of virtue.

I shall not, therefore, quit this subject without pointing out the means of escaping the seductions and avoiding the snares that private societies lay for the probity of honest men, and into which they are but too often surprised.

CHAP. VI.

OF THE MEANS OF SECURING VIRTUE.

A MAN is just when all his actions tend to the public welfare. Doing well is not all that is requisite to merit the title of virtuous. A prince has a thousand places to bestow; he must fill them up; and he cannot avoid rendering a thousand people happy. Here then his virtue depends only on the justice and injustice of his choice*. If, when a place of importance is vacant, he gives it from friendship, from weakness, from solicitation, or from indolence, to a man of moderate abilities, in preference to another of superior talents, he ought to be considered as unjust, whatever praises others may bestow on his probity.

In the affair of probity, he ought only to consult and listen to the public interest, and not to the men by whom he is surrounded; for personal interest too often leads him into an illusion.

In courts, this interest gives to falsehood the name of prudence, and that of stupidity to truth, which is there considered at least as a folly, and must ever be considered as such.

It is there dangerous; and offensive virtues will always be considered in the rank of faults. Truth meets with favour only from humane and good princes, such as Lewis XII. and

---

* In certain countries the placemen are covered with the skin of an ass, to let them know that they are not indebted for it to what is called decency or favour, but only to justice.

Lewis XV. The players having represented the first on the stage, his courtiers persuaded him to punish them: " No," said he, " they do me justice; they believe me worthy of hearing the truth." An example of moderation since imitated by the Duke d'————. The above prince, being forced to lay some impositions on a province, was wearied out by the remonstrances of a deputy from the states of that province, and at length replied, with vivacity, " And what are your forces that you would bring to oppose my will? What can you do?" —" Obey and hate," replied the deputy. A noble answer, that did equal honour to the deputy and the prince. It was almost as difficult for the one to hear as for the other to make it. The same prince had a mistress, who was carried off by a gentleman. He was exasperated, and his favourites incited him to revenge. " Punish," said they, " an insolent——"— " I know," he replied, " that it is easy for me to revenge it; a word would be sufficient to rid me of a rival, and that is the very reason that hinders my pronouncing it."

Such moderation is very rare; truth commonly meets with too bad a reception from princes and the great, to stay long in courts. How can she dwell in a country where most of those who are stiled men of probity, habituated to baseness and flattery, give, and really ought to give, to those vices the name of the customs of the world? It is difficult to perceive that to be criminal which they find to be useful. Who doubts, however, that there is not a kind of flattery more dangerous, and consequently more criminal, in the eyes of a prince animated with a love of true glory, than the libels wrote against him? Not that I here vindicate libels; but flattery may lead a prince from the way of virtue, while a libel may sometimes bring a tyrant into it. It is not often that by the freedom of speech the complaints of the oppressed can reach the throne* : but interest will always hide such truths from the private connections of the court; and perhaps there is no other method of

---

* " It is not," says the poet Saadi, " the timid voice of ministers that ought to bring to the ears of kings the lamentations of the miserable; the cries of the people should pierce directly to the throne."

defending ourselves from the seducing illusions that prevail there, than by keeping at a distance from those connections. It is at least certain that there can be no method of preserving there a virtue constantly firm and uncorrupt, without having habitually present to the mind a principle of public utility*; without being thoroughly acquainted with the true interest of the public, and consequently without moral and political knowledge. Perfect probity never falls to the lot of the stupid; for probity without knowledge is only probity of intention, for which the public neither have nor can have any real regard; both because they cannot judge of the intention, and because in the judgment they form, they consult nothing but their own interest.

If he is saved from death who has the misfortune to kill his friend in the chace, this favour is not merely shewn to the innocence of his intentions, since the law capitally condemns the sentinel who involuntarily suffers himself to be surprised by sleep. The public, in the first case, only pardons, that the loss of one citizen may not be added to the loss of another; in the second, he is punished in order to prevent their being surprised, and the misfortunes to which they might be exposed by such want of vigilance.

We ought then, in order to be virtuous, to blend the light of knowledge with greatness of soul. Whoever assembles within himself these different gifts of nature, always directs

---

* In consequence of this principle, Fontenelle has defined a lie, the concealing what truth ought to divulge. A man, leaving a woman's bed, meets her husband, who cries—" Where have you been?" What shall he answer? Shall he tell the truth? " No," says Fontenelle, " because the truth would then be of no use to any one. Now, Truth herself is subject to the public utility. She should preside in the composition of history, and in the study of arts and sciences: she ought to be present with the great, and even to snatch from them the veil that hides the faults prejudicial to the public; but she ought never to reveal those that injure none but the man himself. It is afflicting him to no purpose; under the pretence of speaking truth, it is being cruel and brutal; instead of shewing a love of truth, it is glorying in another's humiliation."

his course by the compass of the public utility. This utility is the principle on which all human virtues are founded, and the basis of all legislations. It ought to inspire the legislator with the resolution to force the people to submit to his laws.; to this principle, in short, he ought to sacrifice all his sentiments, and even those of humanity itself.

Public humanity is sometimes void of pity for individuals*. When a vessel is surprised by long calms, and famine has, with an imperious voice, commanded the mariners to draw lots for the unfortunate victim who is to serve as a repast to his companions, they kill him without remorse: this vessel is the emblem of a nation; every thing becomes lawful, and even virtuous, that procures the public safety.

The conclusion of what I have just said is, that in the case of probity counsel is not to be taken from private connections, but only from the interest of the public: he who constantly consults it will have all his actions directed either immediately to the public utility, or to the advantage of individuals, without their being detrimental to the state.

The person who succours merit in distress gives undoubtedly an example of beneficence conformable to the general interest: he pays the tax which probity imposes on riches.

Honest poverty has no other patrimony than the treasures of virtuous opulence.

Whoever conducts himself by this principle may give to his own mind an advantageous testimony of his probity, and prove that he really merits the title of a worthy man. I say

---

* This principle was among the Arabians consecrated by the example of severity given by the famous Ziad, governor of Basra. After having in vain endeavoured to purge that city from the assassins who infested it, he saw himself obliged to inflict the pains of death on every man who was found in the streets at night. They stopped a stranger; he is conducted to the governor's tribunal; he endeavours to move him by his tears. " Unhappy stranger," says Ziad, " I must appear to thee unjust, in punishing a breach of orders that thou were ignorant of; but the safety of Basra depends on thy death: I lament and condemn thee."

merits; for to obtain a singular reputation of this kind, it is not enough to be virtuous; it is necessary he should, like Codrus and Regulus, be happily placed in times, in circumstances, and in a station, that will allow his actions to have a sufficient influence on the welfare of the public. In any other situation the probity of a citizen unknown to the public is, if I may so express myself, only a virtuous accomplishment in private society, of singular benefit to those with whom he is connected.

A private man can only by his abilities render himself useful and praiseworthy to a nation. Of what service is the probity of an individual to the public? It is comparatively of little use*. Thus the living are judged as posterity judges the dead: they do not inquire in what degree Juvenal was wicked, Ovid debauched, Hannibal cruel, Lucretia impious, how far Horace was a libertine, Augustus guilty of dissimulation, and Cæsar the husband of every wife, and the wife of every husband: posterity is only employed in forming a judgment of their respective talents.

Upon which I shall remark that most of those who warmly exclaim against the domestic vices of illustrious men do not give so great a proof of their love for the public welfare as of their envying their abilities: this, in their eyes, frequently wears the mask of a virtue, but is commonly no more than a disguised envy, since in general they have not the same horror for the vices of a man destitute of merit. Without making an apology for vices, we may safely say, that worthy men would have cause to blush at the sentiments on which they pride themselves, did they discover the baseness of the principles upon which they are founded.

Perhaps the public shew too great an indifference for virtue; perhaps our authors are sometimes more careful in the correction of their works than in that of their manners, and follow the example of Averroes, a philosopher, who, it is

---

* It is allowable to praise his heart, but not his mind; because the first is of no great consequence, and envy fancies that such an eulogium will obtain but a small degree of admiration from the public.

said, allowed himself to commit knavish actions, which he regarded not only as hardly injurious, but even of use to his reputation. By this means, say they, he put his rivals on a different scent, and turned those criticisms on his manners that would have been employed against his works, and doubtless have given a more dangerous shock to his glory.

I have in this chapter pointed out the means of escaping the seductions of private connections, of preserving our virtue unshaken amidst the shock of a thousand private and different interests, by having a regard, in all our steps, to the interest of the public.

CHAP. VII.

OF THE UNDERSTANDING IN RELATION TO PARTICULAR SOCIETIES.

WHAT I have here said of understanding in relation to a single man, I shall here say of it with respect to particular societies, but not repeat on this subject a tedious enumeration of the same proofs; I shall only shew, by new applications of the same principle, that every society, like every individual, looks with esteem or contempt on the ideas of other societies only according to their agreement or disagreement with the ideas, passions, genius, and station in life, of the persons who compose that society.

Suppose a Fakir was to appear in a circle of Sybarites, would he not be regarded with that contemptuous pity which sensual and soft minds feel for a man who loses real pleasures to pursue an imaginary good? Should a conqueror enter the retreat of the philosophers, who can doubt but that he would treat their most profound speculations as things in themselves the most vain and frivolous; that he would consider these men with that contemptuous disdain which a mind, filled with its own greatness, has for those whom it little esteems, and with that superiority with which power looks down upon weakness. But if I transport this conqueror to the portico—" Proud

K

mortal," says the offended stoic, " who despisest souls more
lofty than thine own, learn that the object of thy desires is
that of our contempt; and that nothing appears great on
earth when contemplated by an elevated mind. In an antient
forest sits a traveller at the foot of the cedar, which to him
seems to touch the heavens: above the clouds, where the
eagle soars, the lofty trees creep above the ground, like the
humble broom, and present to the eye of the king of birds
only a verdant carpet spread over the plains." Thus the
stoic filled with pride is revenged for the disdain shewn by the
ambitious, and thus, in general, all treat each other who are
animated by different passions.

Let a woman, young, beautiful, and full of gallantry, such
as history has painted the celebrated Cleopatra, who, by the
multiplicity of her charms, the attractions of her wit, the variety of her caresses, makes her lover daily taste all the delights that could be found in inconstancy, and in short, whose
first enjoyment was, as Echard says, only the first favour; let
such a woman appear in an assembly of prudes, whose age and
deformity secured their chastity, they would there despise her
charms and her talents; sheltered from seduction by the Me-
dusean shield of deformity, these prudes form no conception
of the pleasure arising from the infatuation of a lover; and do
not perceive the difficulty a beautiful woman finds in resisting
the desire of making him the confidant of all her secret
charms: they therefore fall with fury upon this lovely woman, and place her weakness among crimes of the blackest
die; but let one of these prudes, in her turn, appear in a
circle of coquets, she will there be treated with as little respect as youth and beauty shew to old age and deformity. To
be revenged on her prudery, they will tell her, that the fair
who yields to love, and the disagreeable who resist that passion, are both prompted by vanity; that, in case of a lover,
one seeks an admirer of her charms, and the other flies on him
who proclaims her disgrace; and that both being animated by
the same motive, there is no other difference but that of
beauty between the prude and the woman of gallantry.

Thus the different passions reciprocally insult over each other; the ostentatious man, who will not know merit in a mean situation, and would see it creep at his feet, is in his turn despised by men of sense and learning. " Foolish mortal," cry they, " on what dost thou pride thyself? Dost thou glory in the honours that are paid thee? This homage is not paid to thy merit, but to thy splendor and thy power. Thou art nothing of thyself: if thou shinest, the lustre is reflected on thee by the favour of thy sovereign. Behold the vapours that arise from the mud of those marshes; sustained in the air, they are changed into gaudy clouds; they shine like thee, with a splendour borrowed from the sun; but that star sets, and the glowing brightness of the cloud disappears."

As contrary passions excite a reciprocal contempt in those who are animated by them, so too much opposition in the mind produces nearly the same effect.

Being necessitated (as I have already proved in chapter iv.) to relish no ideas but those that are analogous to our own, how is it possible for us to admire a turn of mind very different from ours? As the study of a science or an art makes us perceive an infinite number of beauties and difficulties in it, of which we could have formed no conception without our having engaged in such study, we have therefore necessarily more of what I call felt-esteem for that science or art which we thus cultivate.

Our esteem for the other arts and sciences is always more or less proportionable to their connection with the other arts to which we apply ourselves. For this reason, the geometrician has commonly a greater esteem for the philosopher than for the poet, and the latter has an higher opinion of the orator than of the geometrician.

Thus, with the best intentions, illustrious men of different tastes set very little value on each other. To be convinced of the reality of the contempt, which on their part is always reciprocal (for there is no debt more faithfully paid than contempt), let us listen to the discourses of men of genius.

Like several empirics dispersed in a market-place, each calls admirers to himself, and thinks that he alone can deserve them. The writer of romances is persuaded that his work supposes the most invention and delicacy of mind ; the metaphysician fancies that he is the source of evidence, and the confidant of nature. " I alone," says he, " can generalize ideas, and discover the seeds of the events that daily unfold themselves in the physical and moral world, and by me alone man is enlightened." The poet, who considers the metaphysicians as grave formal fools, assures them, that if they would search for Truth in the well in which she has hid herself, they need have nothing to draw her from thence but the sieve of the Danaides; that the discoveries of their art are doubtful, but that the charms of his are certain.

By such discourses, these three men reciprocally prove the little esteem they have for each other ; and if in such a dispute they take a politician for their arbitrator, he will say, " You must know that the arts and sciences are only serious trifles and frivolous difficulties. We may apply ourselves to them in our infancy, in order to exercise the mind, but it is only the knowledge of the people's interest that ought to fill the heads of persons of sense arrived at the years of discretion. Every other object is little, and whatever is little is despicable :" whence he concludes, that he alone is worthy of universal admiration.

Now, to close this article with another example, let us suppose a natural philosopher has listened to this conclusion : he will immediately reply to the politician, " You deceive yourself. If we measure greatness of mind by the greatness of the objects about which we are conversant, it is I alone who am really worthy of esteem. A single discovery of mine changes the interest of nations. I rub a needle upon the loadstone, and inclose it within the compass; upon which America is discovered; they dig mines; a thousand vessels, loaded with gold, divide the waves of the sea, empty their treasures in Europe ; and the face of the political world is changed. Always employed on grand objects, if I retire to silence and solitude, it is not to study the little revolutions of governments, but those of the universe; it is not to penetrate into the trifling secrets of courts, but into those of nature; I discover how the sea has formed mountains, and how it has encroached upon the earth; I measure both the force which moves the stars, and the extent of the luminous circles they describe in the azure vault of heaven; I calculate their magnitude, compare it with that of the earth, and blush at the smallness of this globe. As I am so ashamed of the hive, judge of the contempt I must feel for the insects who inhabit it: the greatest legislator is no more in my eye than the king of bees."

Thus we see by what method of reasoning each proves, that he himself is the possessor of the most noble endowments of the mind; and how excited, by the desire of proving it to others, the men of genius and learning, reciprocally depreciate each other, without perceiving that each of them, being involved in the contempt he inspires for his equals, becomes the sport and derision of the public, whose admiration he is ambitious of obtaining.

In vain would he endeavour to diminish the prepossession each has entertained in favour of his own turn of mind. We laugh at a florist standing immoveably fixed over a bed of tulips; he has his eyes continually upon them, and sees nothing around him worthy of his admiration, but the fine mixture of the colours, which, by cultivation, he has forced nature to paint: every man is this florist, if he forms a judgment of the minds of men only from their knowledge of flowers; we also measure our esteem for them only from the conformity of their ideas with our own.

Our esteem is so dependant on this conformity of ideas, that no body can attentively examine themselves, without perceiving, that, in all the minutes of a day, they do not afford the same person exactly the same degree of esteem; and it is always to some one or other of these contradictions, inevitable in the intimate and daily commerce with mankind, that we ought to attribute the perpetual variation of the thermometer of our esteem; thus every man whose ideas are not analogous to those of the people with whom he converses, is always despised by them.

The philosopher, who lives among a set of coxcombs, will be the jest and ridicule of the company. He will find himself

played upon by the greatest fool amongst them, whose insipid
jokes will pass for excellent turns of wit; for the success of the
raillery depends less on the delicacy of the author's wit, than
on his attention to ridicule none but those ideas that are disagreeable to the company. It is in pleasantry as in pieces
wrote with a party spirit, which are always admired by the
cabal.

The unjust contempt of particular classes of men for each
other is, therefore, like the contempt of an individual for an
individual, only the effect of ignorance and pride : a pride that
is, doubtless, censurable, though it is necessary, and inherent
in human nature. Pride is the seed of so many virtues and
qualifications, that we ought neither to hope its destruction nor
attempt to weaken it; but only to direct it to worthy purposes.
If I here ridicule the pride of certain persons, I doubtless do
this only from another kind of pride, perhaps better intended
than their's in this particular instance, as being more conformable to the general interest; for justice in judgment and actions is never any thing more than the happy union between
our interest and that of the public *.

If the esteem different societies entertain for certain sentiments and sciences is different according to the diversity of
passions, and the mental pursuits of those who compose such
societies; who can doubt, but that the different situations of
men produce the same effect; and that ideas, agreeable to
persons of a certain rank, are disagreeable to those in a different
station? When a warrior, or a merchant, expatiates before the

---

* Interest presents objects to us only with such aspects as appear
useful to us on our perceiving them. When we judge of them as
conformable to the public interest, we are not so properly to do
honour to a just manner of thinking, or to our love of justice, as to
being accidentally placed in such a situation as makes it our interest
to see objects in the same light as the public. Whoever thoroughly
examines his own mind will find so many errors, that they will force
him to be modest; and, instead of being puffed up with his own abilities, he will be ignorant of his superiority. Good sense, like health,
when we have it, we do not perceive it.

gentlemen of the law, one on the art of sieges, encampments, and military evolutions, and the other on the trade of indigo, sugar, silk, and cacaos, they will be heard with less pleasure and avidity than the man who lays open the intrigues of the judges, the prerogatives of magistracy, and the manner of conducting a particular suit; for he will talk of the objects which their turn of mind, or their vanity, renders more particularly interesting to them.

In general, people consider, with contempt, the mind of a man who is in a station inferior to theirs. Whatever merit a citizen may have, he will always be despised by a man who enjoys a high post, if that placeman has a weak understanding; " Though there is," as Domat says, " but one civil distinction between a citizen and a great lord, and one natural distinction between a man of sense and a stupid nobleman."

It is always, then, personal interest, modified according to the difference of our wants, our passions, our genius, and our conditions, which, combining in various societies, in an infinite number of ways, produces such an astonishing diversity of opinions.

It is in consequence of this variety of interests, that each society have their genius, their particular manner of judging, and their favourite spirit, which they would freely deify, if the fear of the censures of the public did not oppose such an apotheosis.

Thus we see the reason why people form themselves into different societies. There is scarcely a man so stupid, but, if he pays a certain attention to the choice of his company, may spend his life amidst a concert of praises, uttered by sincere admirers; while there is not a man of sense, who, if he promiscuously joins in different companies, will not be successively treated as a fool, and a wise man, as agreeable and tiresome, as stupid and a man of genius.

The general conclusion of what I have just said is, that personal interest in each society is the only appraiser of the merit of persons and things. It only remains to shew, why men the most generally admired and sought after by particular societies, such as those, of which the superior stations are composed, are not always esteemed by the public.

CHAP. VII.

OF THE DIFFERENCE BETWEEN THE JUDGMENTS OF THE PUBLIC AND THOSE OF PRIVATE SOCIETIES.

To discover the cause of the difference between the judgments formed by the public and by private societies, it must be observed, that a nation is only an assemblage of the citizens of which it is composed: that the interest of each citizen is always, by some ties, attached to the public interest: that, like the stars, which suspended in the deserts of space, are there moved by two principal motions, the first slow*, in common with the whole universe, and the second more rapid, and peculiar to those bodies: so each society is moved by two different kinds of interest.

The first and weaker is in common with the whole society in general, that is, with the nation; and the second, more powerful, is absolutely peculiar to the individual.

Consequently from these two kinds of interest arise two kinds of ideas, adapted to please private societies.

One, which more immediately relates to the public interest, and has for its object laws, politics, commerce, war, arts, and sciences: in this species of ideas, every individual is interested; this species is consequently the more generally, and, at the same time, the more weakly esteemed by most private societies. I say by most, because there are societies, such as those of the academical kind, where the ideas, most generally useful, are such as are the most particularly agreeable, and where personal interest is, by that means, confounded with the public interest.

The other species of ideas has an immediate relation to the private interest of each little society; that is, to the tastes and aversions, to the projects and pleasures of its members. It is, therefore, more interesting and more agreeable, in the eyes of those of this society, who are commonly indifferent enough with respect to the public interest.

---

* According to the system of the antient philosophers.

This distinction being admitted, whoever acquires a very great number of ideas of this last kind, that is, of those ideas that are particularly interesting to the society in which he lives, will, consequently, be regarded by them as a man of abilities: but, if this man appears in a public light, either by writing a work, or by being raised to a high post, he will frequently appear in a very mean light. Thus a voice appears charming in the chamber, that is too weak for the theatre.

When a man, on the contrary, is wholly possessed by ideas, in which the whole community in general are interested, he will be less agreeable to the societies among whom he spends his time. To them he will sometimes appear insipid, and out of his sphere; but, if he is placed in a public light, either by writing a new work, or being raised to an eminent post, his genius will then shine, and he will merit the title of a man of superior abilities. He is a large Colossal statue that appears disagreeable in the sculptor's workshop, but, being raised in a public square, becomes the admiration of the citizens.

But why do not people unite in their own minds both these kinds of ideas, and obtain at once the esteem both of the nation in general, and of the individuals? "This is," I reply, "because the kind of study to which a man must apply himself, in order to acquire ideas wherein the public is concerned, and to obtain those that relate to the private societies and classes among mankind, are absolutely different."

If we would please the world, we must not dive too deep into any subject, but skim incessantly from one subject to another. Our knowledge should be various, and for that reason it must be superficial; we should know every thing without losing our time in learning to know every thing perfectly; and consequently give our knowledge more surface than depth.

Now the public has no interest in esteeming men who are universally superficial; they, perhaps, do not even do them strict justice, and never give themselves the trouble to measure the abilities of a mind filled with too many different kinds of knowledge. It being only for their interest to esteem those who render themselves superior in one kind, and, by that means, improve the sum of human knowledge; the public ought,

therefore, to set but little value on the superficial attainments
of the multitude.

We ought then, in order to obtain a general esteem, to give
our knowledge more depth than surface; and to concentre, if I
may so express myself, as in the focus of a burning glass, all the
heat and rays of the mind.   How then is it possible to divide
our application to these two kinds of study, since the life we
must lead, to follow either the one or the other, is entirely different?   We can have, therefore, only one of these species of
knowledge without the other.

If, in order to acquire those ideas in which the public are
interested, it is necessary, as I shall prove in the following
chapters, to have recourse to silence and solitude; it is, on the
contrary, necessary, in order to present before private societies
such ideas as are most agreeable to them, to mix entirely with
the multitude, with whom it is impossible to live without filling our heads with false and puerile ideas: I say false, because
every man who is acquainted with only one settled manner of
thought, necessarily considers those of the class with whom he
converses as the most excellent society in the universe; he is
led to imitate the different nations in the contempt they mutually shew for the manners, religion, and even the different
dresses of each other; where every thing appears ridiculous,
that does not resemble what they have been accustomed to
behold; and consequently they fall into errors of the grossest
kind.   Whoever warmly engages himself in the little interests
of private societies must necessarily place too great an esteem
on trifles.

Therefore, who can flatter himself with here escaping the
snares of self-love, when he sees that there is no attorney in his
office, no counseller in his chamber, no merchant in his compt-
ing-house, no officer in his garrison, who does not believe, that
the attention of mankind is fixed on him?*

---

* What pleader is there, who is not in an ecstasy at the reading of
his factum, and does not consider it as a more serious and important
affair than the works, not only of Fontenelle, but of all the philosophers
who have written on the knowledge of the heart, and of the human

Every one may apply to himself this tale of a mother in one of the convents, who, being witness of a dispute between the assistant and her superior, asked the first she found in the parlour, " Do you know that mother Cecilia and mother Theresa have just been quarrelling? But you are surprised?—Bless me! is it possible that you can be really ignorant of their quarrel? Where do you come from?" We are all of us more or less this mother: that in which we and our companions are employed, must be the employment of all mankind; what we think, believe, and say, must be thought, believed, and said by the whole universe.

How a courtier who lives amidst a variety of company, where nothing is talked of but the cabals and intrigues of the court, of those who rise into credit, or fall into disgrace, and who, in the extensive circle of his acquaintance, sees nobody who is not more or less affected with the same subjects; how, I say, can this courtier avoid persuading himself, that the intrigues of the court are the objects most worthy of meditation, and such as are the most generally interesting to the human mind? Can he imagine that at the shop next to his own house, the people neither know him, nor any of those who are the subjects of his

---

understanding? " The works of the latter," says he, " are amusing, but frivolous, and by no means worthy of being the object of study."

To shew in a clear light the importance which every person gives to his own employments, I shall here quote some lines from the preface of a book intitled, A treatise on the Nightingale: " I have," says the author, " employed twenty years in composing this work. Men of reflection have always maintained, that the greatest and the most refined pleasure we are capable of tasting in this world, is that which results from our being sensible that we are of some use to society: this we ought to have in view in all our actions; and he who does not thus employ himself in doing all he can to promote the general good of mankind, seems to be ignorant, that he is born as much for the advantage of others, as for his own. Such are the motives that have engaged me to present to the public, this Treatise on the Nightingale." Some lines after, the author adds: " That love of the public welfare which has induced me to publish this work, has not suffered me to forget, that it ought to be written with frankness and sincerity."

conversation; that they do not even suspect the existence of the things that so warmly affect his imagination; that in a corner of his garret, there lives a philosopher, to whom the intrigues and cabals formed by an ambitious man to obtain the ribbons of all the orders of knighthood in Europe, appear as puerile, and even less rational, than a plot formed by some school-boys, to steal a box of sugar-plums; and in whose opinion the ambitious are only old children, who think themselves men?

A courtier could never imagine, that any person living had such sentiments; if he came to suspect it, he would be like the king of Pegu, who, having asked some Venetians the name of their sovereign, and they answering, that they were not governed by kings, thought this answer so ridiculous, that he burst into laughter.

The great, 'tis true, are in general not subject to his suspicions; every one of them believes, that he fills a large and conspicuous space on this globe; and imagines that there is only one turn of thought, which ought to be the standard of thinking among mankind; and that this manner of thinking is that of all those with whom he converses. If from time to time he hears, that there are opinions different from his own, he perceives them only at a distance, where the objects are confused, and imagines them confined to the heads of a small number of stupid mortals. He is, in this respect, as silly as the Chinese geographer, who, filled with an extravagant love for his native country, drew a map of the world, that was almost entirely covered by the empire of China, on the confines of which could just be perceived Asia, Africa, Europe, and America. Each is to himself the whole universe, and the others are nothing.

We see, then, that a man being forced to render himself agreeable to the little society in which he is placed; to apply himself to trifling concerns, and to adopt a thousand prejudices, he must insensibly crowd his brain with an infinite number of ideas that will appear absurd and ridiculous, when exposed to the public observation.

I however, with great pleasure observe, that by these courtiers I do not mean all in high stations : a Turenne, a Richelieu, a Luxembourg, a Ruchefoucault, a Retz, and many others prove, that folly is not the necessary lot of all in an elevated rank; and that by the above we are to understand only those who never move, but in their own vortices.

These are the men whom the public have, with such good reason, considered as absolutely void of sense. I shall bring, as a proof of it, their ridiculous and exclusive pretensions to an elegant manner of speaking, and a polite behaviour. These pretentions I the more freely choose as an example, because the young men, the dupes of the jargon of the world, too often take affectation for wit, and good sense for folly.

CHAP. IX.

OF AN ELEGANT MANNER OF SPEAKING, AND A POLITE BEHAVIOUR.

EVERY little society, divided by taste and interest, respectively accuse each other with having a bad manner of speech; that of the young men displeases the old, that of the passionate man he who is of a phlegmatic disposition, and that of the monk the man of the world.

If they understand by a good, or elegant manner, that proper to please equally in all companies; there is no man who has a good manner. For, in order to be possessed of this qualification, he ought to be acquainted with all kinds of knowledge, all kinds of wit, and perhaps all the different jargons; which is absolutely impossible. We can then only understand by the words Elegant Manner, that kind of conversation where both the ideas and the expressions in which they are clothed ought to be the most generally adapted to please. Now the elegant manner thus defined, belongs to no one class of men in particular, but only to those who employ themselves upon grand and important subjects; and, being versed in the arts and sciences, as morality, metaphysics, war, commerce, and politics, constantly present to the mind objects that are of the utmost importance to human beings. This kind of conversation is doubtless the most generally interesting; but it is not, as I have already observed, the most agreeable to some particular societies. Every one of these societies regards their manner of speaking as superior to that of the men of wit, and that of the men of wit as simply superior to that of every other kind.

Little societies are, in this respect, like the peasants of different provinces, who speak more readily the jargon of their own village than the language of the nation; but prefer the national language to the dialect of any of the other provinces. A good manner of speaking is what each society considers as the best except his own, and that this manner is that of the men of wit.

I however confess, that were it necessary to chuse to which manner we ought to give the preference, it would, beyond all contradiction, fall to that of the courtiers. Not but that a citizen has as many ideas: both frequently talk without a meaning; and with respect to ideas, neither has any advantage over the other; but the former, from the advantages of his situation, obtains those ideas that are more generally interesting.

In fact, if the manners, the inclinations, the prejudices, and the character of kings, have a considerable influence on the happiness or unhappiness of the public, every circumstance relating to them must be highly interesting. The conversation of a man attached to the court, who cannot speak of his own employments, without frequently mentioning his master, is therefore not so insipid as that of a citizen. Besides, persons of high rank, being generally raised greatly above want, and having scarcely any thing else to do but to render themselves agreeable, it is certain that their conversation must, in this respect also, receive great advantages from their station; this generally renders the ladies of the court so superior to other women in graces, in wit, vivacity; and for this reason the women of genius are almost entirely composed of the ladies of the court.

But though the manner of speaking at court is superior to

that of the citizen, the great, not having always curious anecdotes to repeat, of the private life of kings, their conversation
most commonly turns on the privileges of their employments,
on those of their birth, on their adventures of gallantry, and
on the ridiculous incidents of an evening; conversations that
must appear insipid to most other societies.

Courtiers are then exactly in the same case as persons closely
employed in any business or mechanic art; they make them
the only and perpetual subject of conversation: in consequence
of this, they are taxed with a bad manner of speaking; because those who are disgusted always revenge themselves by
giving a contemptuous word to those who fill them with
disgust.

It will be replied, perhaps, That no society accuses the great
of having a bad manner of expression; but if most societies are
silent in this respect, it is because it is imposed upon them by
birth and titles, which prevent their discovering their sentiments, and frequently hinders their countenancing them, even
in their own minds. To be convinced of this, let us examine
a man of good sense on this subject. The manner in which
the great express themselves, he will say, is very frequently
full of affectation. This manner, used at court, was doubtless
introduced there by some person engaged in intrigues; who, to
throw a veil over his designs, resolved to talk without saying
any thing: the dupes of this affectation followed his example,
without having any thing to conceal. They borrowed the jargon of the first, and fancied they uttered something very fine,
when they pronounced words so melodiously arrayed. The
men in place, in order to divert the great from attending to
affairs of an important nature, and to render them incapable
of applying to them, applauded this manner of speaking, allowed it to be termed wit, and were the first in giving it that
name. But whatever eulogiums are given to this jargon, if we
estimate the merit of the pretty turns and phrases so admired
in polite companies, by translating them into another language, the translation will remove our prejudices in their
favour, and most of the phrases will be found void of sense.

Therefore, many people have the greatest contempt for these shining geniuses, and frequently repeat this verse of the play :

"" When a good manner appears, good sense retires."

The true elegant manner of speaking, is, therefore, that of the man of sense, in whatsoever station he is placed.

I will add, that the courtiers, applying themselves to very few ideas, are in this respect inferior to men of genius, but are superior to them in the manner of expressing their ideas; and their pretensions here appear beyond all contradiction to be well founded. Though words, in themselves, are neither noble nor mean, and in a country where the people are respected, as in England, they neither do, nor ought to, make this distinction; yet in a monarchy, where the people are held in no esteem, it is certain, that words ought to take either the one or the other of these denominations, according as they are used or rejected at court; and thus the expressions of the courtiers must always be elegant; but most courtiers, employing themselves only about trifles, the dictionary of the noble language is for this reason very short, and is not sufficient even for a romance, in which these of high rank, who attempt to write, often find themselves much inferior to men of letters*.

With respect to those subjects that are considered as serious, and at the same time connected with philosophy and the arts, experience informs us, that the great can here scarcely stam-

---

* What creates the greatest prejudice in favour of the great, is the easy air, and the pleasing gestures that accompany their discourse, which ought to be considered as the effect of the confidence necessarily inspired by the advantage of their rank ; and, in this respect, they are therefore commonly much superior to men of learning. Now, as declamation is, according to Aristotle, the first part of eloquence, they may, in conversing on trifles, have, on this account, the advantage over men of letters. An advantage which they lose in writing, not only because they are not then supported by the delusive arts of declamation, but because their writings are only in the style of their conversations; and we commonly write ill, when we write as we speak.

mer out their meaning*: whence it follows, that, in regard to expression, they are not superior to men of learning; and that, in this respect, they have no advantage over common men, except in trifling, which they have made their study, and in a manner formed into a particular art; but this superiority is not yet well established, and yet almost all men exaggerate it, from a mechanical respect they shew to birth and titles.

But ridiculous as this exclusive privilege of having a good manner of speaking may appear in the great, it is less a ridicule peculiar to their station than to human nature. Why should not pride persuade the great that they, and those of their class, are endued with minds more adapted to please in conversation, when the same pride has fully persuaded nearly all men in general, that nature has lighted the sun, only to give fertility to this little point called the earth, and disseminated the firmament with stars, only to enlighten it during the night.

Men are vain, full of contempt, and consequently unjust, whenever they can be so with impunity. For which reason, all men imagine, that on this globe there is no part of it; in this part of the earth, no nation; in the nation, no province; in the province, no city; in the city, no society comparable to ours; we think ourselves superior to all our acquaintance; and, step by step, surprise ourselves into a secret persuasion that we are the first persons in the universe†. Thus, foolish as the exclusive pretensions to an elegant manner of speaking may be, and how ridiculous soever the public may represent the great in this respect, this folly will always meet with favour from an indulgent and sound philosophy, which ought to spare them the mortification of tasting the bitterness of useless remedies.

If an oister, confined with his shell, is acquainted with no more of the universe than the rock on which it is fixed; and, therefore, cannot judge of its extent; how can the courtier, involved in the midst of a little society, always surrounded by

---

* I only speak, in this chapter, of those of the great who have never exerted and improved the powers of the mind.

† See the Mock Pedant, a comedy by Cyrano de Bergerac.

the same objects, and acquainted with only one train of thoughts, be able to judge of the merit of things?

Truth is never engendered and perceived, but in the fermentation of contrary opinions. The universe is only known to us in proportion as we become acquainted with it. Whoever confines himself to conversing with one set of companions, cannot avoid adopting their prejudices, especially if they flatter his pride?

Who can separate himself from an error, when vanity, the companion of ignorance, has tied him to it, and rendered it dear to him?

Through an effect of the same vanity, the courtiers imagine themselves the sole possessors of a polite behaviour; which, according to them, is the highest merit, and without which no such thing as merit can subsist. They do not perceive that this behaviour, which they call the custom of the world, by way of excellence, is only the custom of those with whom they converse. At Monomotapa, when the king sneezes, all the courtiers are obliged, through politeness, to sneeze also; and the sneezing, spreading from the court to the city, and from the city to the provinces, the whole empire seems to have gotten a cold. Who can doubt, but that there are some courtiers who value themselves in sneezing in a more noble manner than other men, who do not consider themselves, as in this respect, the only possessors of the polite behaviour; and treat as bad company, or as barbarians, every individual, and all the nations whose sneezing appears to them less harmonious?

Do not the inhabitants of the Marian islands pretend that civility consists in taking hold of the foot of him to whom they would do honour, in gently stroking the face, and in never spitting before a superior?

Do not the Chiriguanes maintain, that it is proper they should have breeches; but that the politest manner of wearing them is under the arm, as we do our hats?

Do not the inhabitants of the Philippines say, that it is not the business of the husband to make his wife taste the first pleasures of love? that this is a trouble which he hires another to discharge? Do not they add, That a girl who is a maid at the time of her marriage is void of merit, and only worthy of contempt?

Do they not maintain at Pegu, that it is the most polite and decent behaviour for the king to advance into the audience-chamber, with a fan in his hand, preceded by four of the most beautiful young men of the court, who are destined to his pleasures, and are, at the same time, his interpreters, and the heralds who declare his will?

Were I to run through all the nations, I should every where find a different behaviour*; and each people, in particular, would necessarily think themselves in the possession of that which is the most polite. Now, if there be nothing more ridiculous than such pretensions, even in the eyes of our courtiers; if they do but return from these to themselves; they will see that, under different names, they ridicule their own conduct.

To prove that what they here call, "The custom of the world," is so far from being universally pleasing, that it must generally displease, let us transport successively, the petit maitre most learned in the gestures, attitudes, and behaviour,

---

* In the kingdom of Juida, when the inhabitants meet, they throw themselves down from the hammocks in which they are, place themselves on their knees over against each other, kiss the ground, clap their hands, make their compliments, and rise. The people in this country certainly believe that their manner of saluting is the most polite.

The inhabitants of the Manillas say, that politeness requires that they should bow their bodies very low, put each of their hands on their cheeks, and raise up one foot from the ground, keeping the knees bent.

The savage of New Orleans maintained, that we failed in politeness towards our kings. " When I present myself," said he, " to the great chief, I salute him with a howl; then I run to the bottom of the cabin, without casting a single glance to the right side, when the chief is seated. There I renew my salutation, raising my hands upon my head, and howling three times. The chief invites me to sit, by a low sigh: upon which I thank him with another howl. At every question the chief asks me, I howl once before I answer him; and I take leave of him by drawling out a howl until I am out of his presence."

called the custom of the world, to China, Holland, and England; and with him send a man of sense, whose ignorance in these particulars has occasioned his being treated as stupid, or as bad company; it is certain, that the latter will pass among these several people as better instructed in the true behaviour of the world than the former?

But whence would they form such a judgment? It is, because reason, independent of the modes and customs of a country, is no where a stranger, and no where ridiculous; but on the contrary, the customs of a country where they are unknown, always render him who observes them ridiculous, in proportion as he is more attentive to fulfil what he believes to be polite behaviour?

If, to avoid the dull and methodical air that is held in abhorrence by good company, our young men often play the fool, who can doubt but that, in the eyes of the English, the Germans, and the Spaniards, our petit maitre will not appear the more ridiculous, as they are more attentive to perform what they believe to be polite behaviour?

It is therefore certain, at least if we may judge from the reception given to our persons of distinction in foreign countries, that what they call the usage of the world, is so far from pleasing universally, that it must be more generally displeasing; and that it is as different from the true custom of the world, which is always founded on reason, as civility is from true politeness.

The one only supposes manners; the other a refined, delicate, and habitual, benevolence to mankind.

However, though there is nothing more ridiculous than these exclusive pretensions to an elegant manner of expression and a polite behaviour, it is so difficult, as I have observed above, to live in the societies of the great, without adopting some of their errors, that men of sense, who are most on their guard, are not always sure of keeping clear of them. Hence, errors of this kind are extremely multiplied, which has determined the public to place the agreeable in the rank of the false and little geniuses: I say little, because the mind, which is neither great nor little in itself, always borrows one or other of these denominations from the grandeur or the smallness of the objects it considers; and the courtiers can scarcely apply themselves to any other but little objects.

It follows, from the two preceding chapters, that the public interest is almost always different from that of private societies; and that, in consequence of this, the men most esteemed in these societies, are not always, in the opinion of the public, most worthy of esteem.

I shall now shew, that those, who merit the greatest esteem from the public, must, by their manner of living and turn of thought, be most disagreeable to private societies.

CHAP. X.

WHY MEN ADMIRED BY THE PUBLIC ARE NOT ALWAYS ESTEEMED BY MEN OF THE WORLD.

In order to please private societies, it is not necessary the horizon of our ideas should be very capacious; but we ought to engage in conversation, and to study and know the world: on the contrary, to obtain a great reputation in any art or science whatsoever, and by that means to obtain the public esteem, requires, as I have said above, a very different kind of study.

Suppose men desirous of studying moral philosophy; it is only by the assistance of history, and the wings of meditation, that they can, according to the different powers of their minds, raise themselves to different heights; whence one discovers cities, another nations, this one part of the world, and the other the whole universe. It is only by contemplating the earth in this point of view, all raising it to this height, that it insensibly diminishes, under the eye of a philosopher, to a small space; and to his view takes the form of a village, inhabited by different families, that bear the name of Chinese, English, French, Italian, and in short, all those we give to the different nations. Thus, bringing before him the manners, laws, customs, religious, and the different passions that actuate mankind, he be-

comes almost insensible, both to the praise and the satire of nations, can break all the chains of prejudice, examine with a
tranquil eye the contrary opinions that divide the human
species; pass, without astonishment, from a seraglio to a
chartreuse, contemplate with pleasure the extent of human
folly, and see, with the same eye, Alcibiades cut off the
tail of his dog, and Mahomet shut himself up in a cavern,
the one to ridicule the folly of the Athenians, and the other to
enjoy the adoration of the world.

Now such ideas never present themselves but in silence
and solitude. If the muses, say the poets, love the woods,
meadows, and fountains, it is because they enjoy there the
tranquillity that flies from cities. The reflections made there
on himself, by a man detached from the little interests of
society, are the reflections made on man in general: they
therefore belong to, and please, human nature. Now, in
this solitude, where we are, in a manner, in spite of ourselves,
led to the study of arts and sciences; how then can we
employ ourselves in the little affairs that are the daily entertainment of the men of the world?

Hence our Corneille and La Fontaine have sometimes appeared insipid amidst the sprightly mirth of good company;
their merit itself has contributed to make them be thought so.
How can the men of the world discover the illustrious man
under the cloke of modesty? There are few men skilled in
true merit. If most of the Romans, as Tacitus says, deceived,
by the mildness and simplicity of Agricola, sought for the great
man under his exterior modesty, without being able to find
him; we must be sensible that, happy in escaping the contempt of private societies, the great man, especially if he be
modest, must renounce a felt-esteem for most of them. He is,
therefore, but feebly moved by the desire of pleasing them.—
He has a confused idea, that the esteem of these societies can
only prove the analogy between his ideas and theirs; that this
analogy would often be of little advantage to his reputation, and
that the public esteem is the only one worthy of envy; the
only one desirable; since it is always a testimony of public
gratitude, and consequently a proof of real merit. The great

man, therefore, incapable of any of the efforts necessary to please private societies, finds every thing possible in his endeavours to merit the general esteem. As the pride of commanding kings recompensed the Romans for enduring the severity of military discipline, so the noble pleasure of being esteemed comforts the illustrious man, even under the unjust frowns of fortune; and, if he have obtained this esteem, he thinks himself the possessor of the most desirable wealth. In fact, whatsoever indifference we affect to shew for the public opinion, every one seeks for self-esteem, and believes that he is more worthy of it, in proportion as he finds himself more generally esteemed.

As our wants, our passions, and, above all our indolence, do not stifle in our minds this desire of esteem, there is no person who does not strive to deserve it, and does not desire the public suffrage as a surety for the high opinion he has of himself. Therefore, a contempt for reputation, and the sacrifice said to be made of it to fortune and reflection, is always inspired by the despair of rendering ourselves illustrious.

We boast of what we have, and despise what we have not. This is a necessary effect of pride ; and we should rebel against it, were we not its dupes. It would, in this case, be too cruel to inform a man of the true motives of his contempt, and merit is never led to commit so barbarous an action. Every man, (let me be permitted to observe by the way,) when he is not born wicked, and when his passions do not extinguish the light of reason, will be always more indulgent, in proportion as he is more enlightened. That this is a truth, I shall the more readily prove, as, by doing justice in this respect to the man of merit, I shall be able, even from the motives of his indulgence, the more plainly to shew the cause of the little value he sets on the esteem of particular societies, and, consequently, the little success he can have in obtaining it.

If the great man is always the most indulgent ; if he considers, as a benefit, all the evil that is not done him, and, as a gift, all that the wickedness of mankind suffer him to enjoy ; if he pours over the faults of others the lenient balm of pity, and is slow in discovering them; it is because the elevation of his mind will not permit him to expatiate upon the vices and follies of single persons, but upon those of mankind in general.   If he considers their faults, it is not with the malevolent eye of envy, which is always unjust, but with the serenity wherewith two men, desirous of knowing the human heart, and of obtaining a knowledge of the mind, reciprocally examine each other as two subjects of instruction, and two living streams of moral experience; very different, in this respect, from the half wits; who, ambitious of a reputation that flies from them, bloated with the poison of jealousy, and incessantly upon the watch for the faults of others, lose all their little merit, if men cease to become ridiculous.   The knowledge of the human mind is not to be obtained by such men as these: they are formed only to extinguish noble talents by the efforts they make to stifle them.   Merit is like gunpowder, the strength of whose explosion is in proportion to the degree in which it is compressed.   But, what hatred soever we bear to these envious persons, they are more to be pitied than blamed.   The presence of merit gives them pain: if they attack it as an enemy, and if they are wicked, it is because they are unhappy; it is because they endeavour to punish the offence merit has given to their vanity: their crimes are only acts of revenge.

Another motion of the indulgence granted by the man of merit springs from the knowledge of the human mind.   He has so often experienced its weakness, in the midst of the applauses of an Areopagus, that he is frequently tempted, like Phocion, to return to his friend, to ask him if he had not uttered something very foolish; and, being always on his guard against vanity, he freely excuses in others the errors into which he himself has sometimes fallen.   He perceives that it is to the multitude of fools we owe the expression " a man of genius;" and that, in gratitude, he ought to bear, without being offended, the abuse thrown upon him by men of mean abilities.   He knows, that if these last secretly boast among themselves of their rendering merit ridiculous, and of the contempt they pretend to feel for it, they are like those bullies in impiety who blaspheme with trembling.

The last cause I shall mention of the indulgence shewn by

men of merit, springs from the clear views of the necessity of human decisions. They know that our ideas, if I may thus venture to express myself, so necessarily proceed from the company we keep, the books we read, and the objects presented to our sight, that a superior intelligence might equally divine our thoughts, from the objects presented before us; and, from our thoughts, divine the number and nature of the objects offered to the mind.

The person of discernment knows that men are what they were designed to be; and that all hatred against them is, therefore, unjust; that a fool bears follies as a wild stock bears bitter fruit; that to insult him, is to reproach the oak for bearing acorns, and not olives; that if the man of mean abilities appears stupid to him, he in return appears a fool to the man of abilities: for as all fools are void of understanding, a man of genius will always appear a fool to a man of mean intellects. Indulgence then is always the effect of superior light, when it is not intercepted by the passions. But that indulgence, principally founded on the elevation of soul inspired by the love of glory, renders the man of abilities very different with respect to the esteem of private societies. Now this indifference, joined to a different kind of life, and to studies very unlike those that are necessary to please either the public, or, what is called good company, will almost always render a man of merit disagreeable to the men of the world.

The general conclusion of what I have said on the mind, in regard to particular societies, is, that solely employed about their own interest, each society measures on the scale of the same interest the degree of esteem it grants to different kinds of understandings and ideas. It is with very small societies, as with a single person, who, if he has a suit at law of great consequence, will receive his advocate with more complaisance, and with greater testimonies of respect and esteem, than he would receive Descartes, Locke, or Corneille: but the suit being ended, he would shew an higher respect for the latter. Thus the difference of his situation determines the reception he gives to each.

I would, in finishing this chapter, endeavour to encourage

the small number of modest men, who, distracted by business, or the care of their fortunes, can make no trial of their great talents; and consequently cannot, on the principles above established, know whether, with respect to genius, they are really worthy of esteem. But, whatever desire I have to do them justice in this respect, it must be confessed, that a man who declares that he has a great genius, without giving any proof of his abilities, is exactly in the case of a man who pretends to be noble, without having any titles of nobility. The public can neither know nor esteem any merit, that is not proved by facts. Are they to judge of men of different ranks, they ask the military man, " What victory have you obtained?" The man in place, " What relief have you afforded to the miseries of the people?" To a private person, " By what work have you enlightened the human mind?" And whoever can make no answer to these questions, is neither known, nor esteemed by the public.

I am sensible that, seduced by the delusions of power, by the surrounding pomp of grandeur, and the hope of the favours distributed by a person in an important place, a great number of men mechanically acknowledge great merit, wherever they perceive great power. But their eulogiums, as fleeting as the credit of those on whom they are bestowed, cannot impose on the sensible part of the public. Sheltered from influence, exempt from all private interest, the public judge as the stranger; who acknowledges for a man of merit, only him who is distinguished by his talents; it is he alone whom the stranger seeks with eagerness: an eagerness that is always pleasing to him who is the object of it*. When we are not adorned with dignities, this is a certain sign of real merit.

He who would exactly know his own value, can then only

---

* Fontenelle was never better pleased with any eulogium than with the question of a Swede, who, entering Paris, asked the officers of the barrier, where M. de Fontenelle lived? And they not being able to inform him, " How," said he, " are you Frenchmen, ignorant of the abode of your most illustrious citizens? You are unworthy of such a man."

learn it from the public, and ought therefore to expose himself to its judgment. We know the ridicule affected to be thrown on those who attempt to obtain the esteem of the nation by being authors: but this ridicule makes no impression on the man of merit; he will consider them as an effect of the jealousy of those little minds, who imagining, that if no body gives a proof of merit, they themselves might the more easily arrive at it: this, however, is the only means by which a person can either merit, or obtain the esteem of the public.

If we cast our eyes on all those great wits so much boasted of in particular companies, we shall see that, being placed by the public in the rank of men of abilities, they owe the reputation for wit with which some have decorated them, only to their being incapable of proving their folly, even by a bad work. Thus, among these prodigies, those who promise most, if I may dare to use the expression, are, with respect to genius, neither more nor less than a Perhaps.

Thus truth, however certain it may be, and what reason soever modest men have to doubt the reality of the merit that has often passed the crucible of the public, yet, with respect to genius, a man may believe himself really worthy of the general esteem; first, when he feels the highest regard for such men as are most esteemed by the public, and by foreign nations; secondly, when he is praised *, as Cicero says, by a man already praised; and, lastly, when he obtains the esteem of those who, in their works, or in posts of eminence, have already discovered great abilities: their esteem for him supposes a great analogy between his ideas and theirs; and that analogy may be considered, if not as a complete proof, at least, as a very high probability, that if he was, like them, exposed to public notice, he would, like them, have a share in the public esteem.

---

* The degree of genius necessary to please us, is pretty nearly the same proportion that we ourselves have.

N 2

CHAP. XI.

OF PROBITY IN RELATION TO THE PUBLIC.

I SHALL not in this chapter treat of Probity, with respect to a particular person, or a private society; but of true probity; of probity considered in relation to the public. This kind of probity is the only one that really merits, and has in general obtained the name. It is only considering it in this point of view, that we can form clear ideas of honesty, and discover a guide to virtue.

Now, under this aspect, I say that the public, like particular societies, is only determined in its judgments by motives of interest; that it does not give the name of noble to great and heroic actions, but to those that are of public use; and that the esteem of the public, for such and such an action, is not proportioned to the degree of strength, courage, or generosity, necessary to execute it, but to the importance of that action, and the public advantage derived from it.

In fact, when encouraged by the presence of an army, one man alone fights three men who are wounded: this is doubtless a brave action; but it is what a thousand of our grenadiers are capable of, and for which they will never be mentioned in history; but when the safety of an empire formed to subdue the universe, depends on the success of this battle, Horatius is an hero, he is the admiration of his fellow-citizens, and his name, celebrated in history, is handed down to the most distant ages.

Two persons threw themselves into a gulf; this was an action common to Sapho and Curtius; but the first did it to put an end to the torments of love, and the other to save Rome; Sapho was therefore a fool, and Curtius a hero. In vain have some philosophers given the name of folly to each of these actions; the public see clearer than they, and never gives the name of fool to those from whom it receives advantage.

CHAP. XII.

OF GENIUS IN RELATION TO THE PUBLIC.

LET us apply to Genius what I have said on Probity, and we shall see that the public is invariable in its decisions, and never consults any thing but its interest; that it does not proportion its esteem to the different species of genius, or to the unequal difficulty of those species; that is, to the number and delicacy of the ideas necessary to succeed; but only to the greater or lesser advantage derived from it.

If an ignorant general gains three battles over a general still more ignorant than himself, he will, at least, during life, be invested with a glory that is never granted to the most excellent painter in the world. The latter has, however, merited the title of a great painter, by a remarkable superiority over other great masters, and excelling in an art without doubt less necessary, but perhaps more difficult than that of war. I say more difficult, because, on opening history, we see an infinite number of men, as Epaminondas, Lucullus, Alexander, Mahomet, Spinola, Cromwell, and Charles XII. in an instant obtain the reputation of great generals, and the first day they took the command, defeated armies; but no painter, how happy soever the genius he has received from nature, is cited among the illustrious painters, who has not at least spent ten or twelve years of his life in the preliminary studies of that art. Why, then, is a greater esteem granted to an ignorant general than to an able painter?

This unequal distribution of glory, so unjust in appearance, proceeds from the inequality of the advantages these two men procure to the nation. If it be still demanded why the public ascribes that superior genius to an able negotiator, which it refuses to allow to a celebrated advocate? Does the importance of the affairs with which the first is entrusted prove that he has a genius superior to that of the second? Does it not frequently require as much sagacity and art to discuss the interests and terminate the suit of two lords in a parish, as to pacify two nations? Why, then, is the public so avaricious of its

esteem to the advocate, and so prodigal of it to the negotiator?
It is because the public, whenever it is not blinded by prejudice or superstition, is capable of very refined reasonings on
its own concerns. The instinct that makes it refer every thing
to its interest is like the æther, which penetrates all bodies,
without making any sensible impression upon them. The
public has less need of painters and celebrated advocates than
of able generals and negotiators; it attaches therefore to the
talents of these last the esteem always necessary to engage
some citizen to acquire them.

On which side soever we turn our eyes, we shall always see
interest preside in the distribution the public makes of its
esteem.

When the Dutch erected a statue to William Buckelst, who
had taught them the secret of salting and barreling herrings,
they did not confer this honour upon him on account of the
extent of genius necessary for that discovery, but from the
importance of the secret, and the advantage it procured to
the nation.

When the petty Augustins sent a deputation to Rome, to
obtain the permission of the holy see to cut their beards, who
knows but that father Eustacius employed in that negotiation
as much genius and refinement as the president Jeannin in his
negotiation in Holland? Nothing can be affirmed on this subject. To what then do we attribute the sensation of laughter, or the esteem excited by these two different negotiations,
if it be not to the difference of their objects? We always
suppose that great effects spring from great causes. A man
enjoys a high post, and by the position in which he is placed,
he performs great things with very small abilities : this man
will pass with the multitude, as far superior to him who, in
an inferior post, and in less happy circumstances, can scarcely,
with great abilities, execute little things. These two men are
like unequal weights, applied to the different ends of a long
lever, where the lightest weight, placed at one of the extremities, raises up a weight ten times heavier, placed nearer the
point of support.

Now if the public, as I have proved, always judges according to its own interest, and is entirely indifferent with respect to all other considerations; and, being an enthusiastic admirer of the arts from which it receives advantage, it ought not to require of the artists, who cultivate them, that high degree of perfection which is absolutely necessary for those who attach themselves to the arts less useful, and in which it is frequently more difficult to succeed. Therefore men, according as they apply themselves to arts, more or less useful, may be compared to tools and jewels: the first are always esteemed good, when the steel is well tempered, and the second are valued only according as they are perfect. Hence our vanity is always the more flattered with our success, when we obtain it in a way less useful to the public, where we with greater difficulty merit its approbation, and where the success necessarily supposes more genius and personal merit.

By what different prejudices is the public affected, when it judges of the merit of an author, or of a general? Does it form a judgment of the first? It compares him with all those who have excelled in that kind of writing, and grants him its esteem only as he surpasses, or at least equals, those who have preceded him. Does it judge of the merit of a general? It makes no enquiry, before it bestows its praises, whether he equals in ability a Cæsar, a Scipio, or a Sertorius. If a dramatic poet writes a good tragedy upon a plot already known, he is called a despicable plagiary; but if a general, in a campaign, draws up his troops in the same order of battle, and makes use of the same stratagems that have been practised by a former general, he is frequently the more esteemed for it.

If an author gains the prize over sixty competitors, yet, if the public does not acknowledge the merit of those competitors, or if their works are too insignificant, the author and his success are soon forgotten.

But when a general has triumphed, has the public, before his being crowned, ever stated the ability and valour of the conquered? Is the general required to have that refined and delicate sentiment of military glory which, at the death of M. de Turenne, determined M. de Montecuculi to quit the command of the army? " They can no longer," said he, " oppose against me an enemy worthy of me."

The public then weighs in very different scales the merit of an author and that of a general. Now why does it contemn in the one the mediocrity it frequently admires in the other? It is because it derives no advantage from the mediocrity of a writer, and may derive very great ones from that of a general, where ignorance is sometimes crowned with success. Its interest therefore requires that he should prize in the one what it despises in the other.

Besides, if the public happiness depends on the merit of men in great employments, and if great posts are seldom filled by great men, in order to induce men of moderate abilities to perform their enterprizes with all the prudence and activity of which they are capable, it is necessary to flatter them with the hopes of great glory. This hope alone may elevate, even to moderate abilities, those who would never have had them, if the public was a too severe judge of their merit, and had given them a disgust for its esteem, from the difficulty of obtaining it.

This is the cause of the secret indulgence with which the public forms a judgment of men in great employments; an indulgence that is sometimes blind in the people, but always attended with discernment in the man enlightened with knowledge. The latter knows that men are influenced by objects that surround them; that flattery, assiduous with the great, is mixed with all the instructions that are given them; and therefore, that we cannot, without injustice, demand from them as many virtues and abilities as are required from a private person.

If a judicious spectator hisses at the French theatre what he applauds in the Italian; if in a fine woman, and a pretty child, every thing is graceful, witty, and genteel, why should the great be treated with less indulgence? We may lawfully admire in them the abilities commonly found among private obscure persons; because it is more difficult for them to acquire them. Spoiled by flattery, like handsome women by their admirers; engaged in a thousand pleasures, and distracted with a thousand cares, they have not, like a philosopher, leisure for thought to acquire a great number of ideas*, or to enlarge the bounds of their own genius, and that of the human mind. It is not to the great that we owe discoveries in the arts and sciences; their hand has not formed a plan of the heavens and earth; has not built ships, erected palaces, forged plow-shares, nor even written the first laws: it was the philosophers who polished mankind, and from societies of savages raised societies to the degrees of perfection, to which they are now arrived. If we had been only assisted by the knowledge of men in power, perhaps we might yet have had neither corn for food, nor scissars to cut our nails.

Superiority of understanding principally depends, as I shall prove in the following discourse, on a certain concourse of circumstances, wherein those of the common class are rarely placed, and which it is almost impossible the great should ever meet with: we ought, therefore, to judge the great with indulgence, and to be sensible that it is very uncommon to have a man of tolerable abilities in an important post.

Thus the public, especially in times of calamity, is profuse of eulogiums. What praises were given to Varro for not despairing of the safety of the republic! In such circumstances as those in which the Romans were then involved, a man of real merit is a god.

If Camillus had foreseen the misfortunes to which he put a stop; if that hero, when chosen general at the battle of

---

* This was it that probably made M. Nicole assert, that God has given genius to men of the common class, to recompense them for the other advantages the great have over them. Though he adds— " I don't believe that God has condemned the great to have mean abilities: but if most of them have but a small degree of understanding, it is because they are ignorant, and have not contracted a habit of reflection. I shall, however, add, that it is not for the interest of the lower part of mankind that the great should be thus void of understanding."

Allia, had there defeated the Gauls he conquered at the foot of the capitol; Camillus, like an hundred other captains, would not have acquired the title of the second founder of Rome. If in times of prosperity M. de Villars had fought in Italy the battle of Denain, and if he had obtained that victory at a time when France did not lie open to the enemy, the action would have been less important, the gratitude of the public less lively, and the general's glory not so great.

The conclusion of what I have said is, that the public always judges according to the public interest; and if it has lost sight of this, it can form no idea of either probity or genius.

If the nations enslaved by despotic power are the contempt of other nations, if in the empires of Mogul and Morocco we discover very few illustrious men, it is because the mind, as I have already observed, being in itself neither great nor little, borrows either of these denominations from the grandeur or the smallness of the objects it contemplates. Now, in most arbitrary governments, the citizens cannot, without displeasing a despotic prince, employ themselves in the study of the law of nature, or in that of the public, moral, and political. They dare not ascend to the first principles of those sciences, nor form grand ideas; they cannot therefore merit the title of great geniuses. But if all the decisions of the public are subject to the law of the public interest, we ought, it is said, to find in this principle of the general interest, all the contradictions we, in this respect, imagine to be evident in the ideas of the public. For this purpose, I shall pursue the parallel begun between the general and the author, and propose this question:—If the military art is, of all others, the most useful, why have there been so many generals whose glory is more eclipsed in their life-time, and so many illustrious men of all kinds, whose memory and exploits are buried in the same tomb, when the glory of the authors and their contemporaries is still preserved in its first state? The answer to this question is, that if we except the captains who have really improved the military art, as Pyrrhus, Hannibal, Gustavus, Condé, and Turenne, who in this particular may be placed in the rank of models and inventors, all the generals who were of an inferior class to these, ceasing at their death to be of service to their country, have no longer a right to its acknowledgements, and consequently to its esteem. On the contrary, the authors, in ceasing to live, do not cease to be of use to the public; they have left in its hands the works that had already merited its esteem. Now, as the gratitude ought to subsist as long as the benefit, their glory cannot be eclipsed till the time comes, when their works will cease to be of use to their country. It is then only to the different and unequal use the author and the general appear to be of to the public after their death, that we ought to attribute that successive superiority of glory, which at different times they by turns obtain over each other.

Hence we see the reason why so many kings have been deified on the throne, and forgotten immediately after their death; why the names of illustrious writers, who, when living, were so rarely mentioned with princes, are, after their death, so often joined to those of kings; why the name of Confucius is more known, and more respected in Europe, than that of any of the emperors of China; and why we place the names of Horace and Virgil by the side of that of Augustus.

If we apply to distance of place, what I here say of distance of time; if we demand, why the illustrious learned is less esteemed by his own country than an able minister; and for what reason a Rosny, who is more honoured amongst us than a Descartes, is less esteemed by the stranger? It is, I reply, because a great minister is scarcely of any use but to his country: and that, in improving the instruments proper for the cultivation of the arts and sciences, in habituating the human mind to more order and justness, Descartes has rendered himself more useful to the world, and ought, consequently, to be more respected by it.

But, say they, if nations, in all their judgments, never consult any thing but their own interests, why are the husbandman and the vine-dresser, who are doubtless more useful than the poet and the geometrician, less esteemed?

It is because the public has a confused sensation that esteem is in its hands an imaginary treasure of no real value, without

a wise and prudent distribution be made of it; that consequently esteem ought not to be attached to labours of which
all men are capable: for esteem, then, by becoming too common, would lose, in a manner, all its virtue; it would no longer
fertilize the seeds of genius and probity, placed in all minds,
and would no longer produce those illustrious men of all kinds,
whom it animates to the pursuit of glory, by the difficulty of
obtaining it. The public perceives, then, that it is the art, and
not the artist, which ought to be honoured; and that if formerly
the first who cultivated the earth, were deified under the names
of Ceres and Bacchus, this honour, so justly granted to the
inventors of agriculture, ought not to be lavished on labourers.

In all countries where the peasant is not overloaded with
taxes, the hope of gain, united to that of the harvest, is sufficient to engage him to cultivate the earth; and I conclude
from it, that, in certain cases, as has been shewn by the celebrated M. Duclos,* it is the interest of nations to proportion
their esteem not only to the utility of an art, but also to its
difficulty.

Who doubts but that a collection of facts, such as that of
the Bibliotheque Orientale, is not as instructive, as agreeable,
and consequently as useful, as an excellent tragedy? Why,
then, has the public a greater esteem for the tragic poet than
for the learned compiler? It is because being convinced, by
the great number of attempts, and the few who have succeeded,
of the difficulty of dramatic poetry, the public is sensible, that,
to form such geniuses as those of Corneille, Racine, Crebillon,
and Voltaire, the success ought to be attended with infinitely
more glory; and that it is sufficient that the compilers be
honoured by a smaller share of esteem, in order to be abundantly supplied with those works of which all men are capable,
and which are properly only works of time and patience.

Among the learned, all those who, deprived of the lights of
philosophy, only form into collections facts scattered in the ruins

---

* See his excellent work entitled, " Considerations on the Manners
of the Age."

of antiquity, are, in relation to the man of genius, what the hewer of stones is to the architect; these are they who furnish the materials for the edifice; and without them the architect would be useless.   But few men can become good architects, and all men are capable of cutting stones; the interest of the public therefore requires, that the first should be paid with an esteem proportionable to the difficulty of their art.   From the same motive, and because a systematical and inventive genius is not commonly acquired without long and painful meditations, more esteem is granted to this kind of genius than to any other; and, in short, in all the kinds where the utility is nearly equal, the public always proportions its esteems to the unequal difficulty of the several kinds.

I say, an utility nearly equal; because, if it were possible to imagine a kind of abilities absolutely useless, whatsoever difficulty there might be in excelling in it, the public would grant no esteem to such a talent: he who had acquired it would be treated as Alexander treated the man who, in his presence, darted, it is said, with wonderful address, grains of millet-seed through the eye of a needle, and obtained nothing from the equity of that prince but a bushel of millet-seed for his reward.

The contradiction that sometimes seems observeable between the interest and the judgment of the public, is then only apparent; and the public interest, as I had proposed to prove, is therefore the sole distributor of the esteem granted to different kinds of genius.

CHAP. XIII.

OF PROBITY IN RELATION TO VARIOUS AGES AND NATIONS.

In all ages and nations, probity can be only an habit of performing actions that are of use to our country. However certain this proposition may be, to render this truth the more evident, I shall endeavour to give a clear and full idea of this virtue.

To this purpose, I shall examine two sentiments on this subject, that have hitherto divided the moralists.

Some maintain, that we have an idea of virtue absolutely independent of different ages and governments; and that virtue is always one and the same. The others maintain, on the contrary, that every nation forms a different idea of it.

The first bring, in proof of their opinions, the ingenious, but unintelligible dreams of the Platonists. Virtue, according to them, is nothing but the idea of order, harmony, and essential beauty. But this beauty is a mystery of which they can convey no fixed ideas: they therefore do not establish their system on the knowledge which history affords us of the human heart, and the powers of the mind.

The second, and amongst them Montaigne, with arms more strangely tempered than those of reasoning, that is, with facts, attack the opinion of the first; prove that an action virtuous in the north, is vicious in the south ; and from thence conclude, that the ideas of virtue is merely arbitrary.

Such are the opinions of these two sects of philosophers. Those, from their not having consulted history err, in a metaphysical labyrinth of words: these, from their not having examined with sufficient depth the facts presented by history, have thought that caprice alone decided the goodness or turpitude of human actions. These two philosophical sects are deceived; but they would both have escaped error, had they, with an attentive eye, considered the history of the world. They would then have perceived, that time must necessarily produce, in the physical and moral world, revolutions that change the face of empires; that, in the great catastrophes of kingdoms, the people always experience great changes; that the same actions may successively become useful and prejudicial, and consequently, by turns, assume the name of virtuous and vicious.

If, in consequence of this observation, they would have been willing to form a mere abstract idea of virtue, independent of practice, they would have acknowledged, that, by the word Virtue can only be understood, a desire of the general happiness; that, consequently, the public welfare is the object of virtue; and that the actions it enjoins, are the means it makes use of to accomplish that end; that, therefore, the idea of virtue is not arbitrary; that, in different ages and countries, all men, at least those who live in society, ought to form the same idea of it; and, in short, if the people represent it under different forms, it is because they take for virtue the various means they employ to accomplish the end.

This definition of virtue, I think, gives an idea of it that is at once clear, simple, and conformable to experience; a con＋formity that alone can establish the truth of an opinion.

The pyramid of Venus-Urania, whose top was lost in the clouds, and whose base was fixed on the earth, is the emblem of all systems, which crumble to pieces as fast as they are built, if they are not founded on the steady basis of facts and experience. It is therefore on facts, that is, on the hitherto inexplicable folly and fantasticalness of the various laws and customs, that I establish the proof of my opinion.

However stupid we suppose mankind, it is certain that, enlightened by their own interest, they have not, without mo-tives, adopted the ridiculous customs we find established amongst some of them; the fantasticalness of these customs proceed, then, from the diversity of the interests of different nations; and, in fact, if they have always, though confusedly, understood by the word virtue the desire of the public happiness; if they have consequently given the name of honesty only to actions useful to the nation; and if the idea of utility has always been secretly connected with the idea of virtue, we may assert, that the most ridiculous, and even the most cruel customs, have always had, for their foundation, as I am going to shew by some examples, either a real or apparent utility with respect to the public welfare.

Theft was permitted at Sparta; they only punished the aukwardness of the thief who was surprised*: could any thing

---

* Robbery is also honoured in the kingdom of Congo: but no theft is to be performed, nor any thing taken, without the knowledge of the possessor of the thing stolen: every thing is to be taken by force. "This custom," say they, "keeps up the courage of the people."

be more absurd than this custom? However, if we call to mind the laws of Lycurgus, and the contempt shewn for gold and silver, in a country where the laws allowed the circulation of no other money than that of a kind of heavy brittle iron, it will appear that poultry and pulse were almost the only things that could be stolen. These thefts being always performed with address, and frequently denied with firmness†, they enured the Lacedemonians to a habit of courage and vigilance: the law then which allowed of stealing, might be very useful to that people, who had as much reason to be afraid of the treachery of the Ilotes, as of the ambition of the Persians; and could only oppose against the attempts of the one, and the innumerable armies of the other, the bulwark of these two virtues. It is therefore certain, that theft, which is always prejudicial to a rich people, was of use to Sparta, and there‐ fore properly honoured.

At the end of winter, when the scarcity of provisions obliges the savage to quit his cabin, and hunger calls him to go to the chase, in search of provisions; some of the savage nations assem‐ ble before their departure, when making their old men mount the oaks, they shake the boughs with great violence, on which most of the old men falling, they are in a moment massacred. This fact is well known; and nothing can at first appear more abominable. However, what room for surprize is there, when, after having examined its origin, we find that the savage con‐ siders the fall of these unhappy old men, as a proof of their

---

On the contrary, among the Scythians, no crime was greater than that of robbery; and their manner of living required that it should be severely punished: their flocks wandered here and there in the plains; with what ease might they then have been stolen; and what disorders would the toleration of robbery have occasioned? "Therefore," says Aristotle, "have they established amongst them this law, as the guardian of their flocks."

† Every body knows the circumstance related of the young Spartan, who, rather than discover his theft, suffered, without crying out, his bowels to be devoured by a young fox that he had stolen, and con‐ cealed under his robe.

inability to sustain the fatigues of hunting! Were they left in their cabins, or in the forests, they would fall a prey to hunger, or the wild beasts; they therefore choose rather to preserve them from the long duration, and the violence of pain; and, by a speedy and necessary parricide, save their fathers from a slow and cruel death. This is the principle on which so execrable a custom is founded; that erratic people, whom hunting, and the necessity of procuring provisions, detains for six months together, in immense forests, are thus, in a manner, necessitated to this barbarity; and, in those countries, parricide is inspired and committed from the same principle of humanity, that makes us to look upon it with horror *.

But, without having recourse to savage nations, let us cast our eyes on polite countries, such as China: if it be demanded, why an absolute authority is there given to fathers over the lives of their children, we find, that the lands of that empire, how extensive soever they are, cannot sometimes furnish subsistence for the numerous inhabitants; now, as the too great disproportion between the multiplicity of men, and the fertility of the lands, would necessarily occasion wars, fatal to that empire, and, perhaps, to the whole world; we see that, in a time of famine, and to prevent an infinite number of murders and unnecessary misfortunes, the Chinese nation, humane in its intentions, but barbarous in the choice of the means, has, through a sentiment of humanity, though a mistaken one, considered the permission to murder their infants, as necessary to the repose of the world. " We sacrifice," say they, "for this purpose, some unfortunate victims, to whom infancy and ignorance conceal

---

* In the kingdom of Juida, in Africa, the people give no assistance to the sick; they cure themselves as well as they can, and when they are recovered, live in the same cordiality with those who had thus abandoned them.

The inhabitants of Congo kill those whom they imagine past recovery, to shorten their pains and agonies.

In the isle of Formosa, when a man is dangerously ill, they put a slip knot about his neck, and strangle him, to save him from the pain of a lingering death.

the knowledge and the horrors of death, in which, perhaps, consists its most formidable terrors*.

It is doubtless from the desire of preventing the too great multiplication of the human species, and consequently from the same origin, that certain nations in Africa still preserve a ridiculous veneration for anchorets, who deny themselves that commerce with women, which they allow themselves with the brutes.

It was equally a motive of public interest, and the desire of protecting modest beauty against the attempts of incontinence, that formerly engaged the Swiss to publish an edict, by which it was not only permitted, but even ordained, that each priest should provide himself a concubine †.

On the coast of Coromandel, where the women freed themselves by poison from the troublesome yoke of marriage, this was at length the motive which, by a remedy as odious as the evil, engaged the legislature to provide for the safety of husbands, by forcing the women to burn themselves on their husband's pile ‡.

In conformity with my reasonings, all the facts I have just cited concur to prove, that the customs, even the most foolish

---

* The manner of dispatching girls in Catholic countries, is forcing them to take the veil, any many thus pass an unhappy life; a prey to depair; perhaps our custom, in this respect, is more barbarous than that of the Chinese.

† Zeuinglius, in writing to the Swiss Cantons, repeats the edict made by their ancestors, that enjoined every priest to have his concubine, for fear he should attempt his neighbour's chastity. See Father Paul's history of the council of Trent, book I.

It is said, in the seventeenth canon of the council of Toledo, that, " he who is contented with one woman, by the title of wife or concubine, according to his choice, shall not be debarred from the communion." The chur chthen probably tolerated concubinage, to secure the married women from insult.

‡ The women of Mezurado are burnt with the bodies of their husbands. They themselves demand the honour of being led to the pile; but, at the same time, use all their endeavours to prevent it.

and the most cruel, have always their source in the real, or apparent, utility of the public.

But it is said that these customs are not, on this account, the less odious or ridiculous. It is true. But it is only because we are ignorant of the motives of their establishment; and because these customs, consecrated by antiquity and superstition, sub-sisted here by negligence, or the weakness of government, long after the causes of their establishment were removed.

When France was, in a manner, only a vast forest, who doubts that those donations of uncultivated lands made to the religious orders, ought then to have been permitted: and that the pro-longation of such a permission would not now be as absure and injurious to the state, as it might be wise and useful, when France was uncultivated? All the customs that procure only transient advantages are like scaffolds, that should be pulled down, when the palaces are raised.

Nothing could be a greater proof of wisdom in the founder of the empire of the Incas, than his representing to the Peru-vians that he was the offspring of the sun; and had brought them the laws dictated to him by the God his father. This falshood impressed on the minds of the savages an higher re-spect for the laws of that legislator: this falshood was there-fore of such use to the rising state, as to deserve to be con-sidered as virtuous; but, after having established the founda-tions of a good legislation; after being assured, by the form of the government itself, of the exactness with which the laws would be always observed, this legislator ought to have become less proud, or still more judicious; he should have foreseen the rovolutions that might have happened in the manners and inte-rests of his people, and the changes that, in consequence of them, ought to be made in the laws; he should therefore have declared to the people, by himself or his successor, that he had made use of a necessary falshood only to render them happy; by which confession he would have stripped the laws of the marks of divinity, which rendered them sacred and inviolable, which would have opposed all reformation, and might at last have rendered them prejudicial to the state, if by the landing of the Europeans that empire had not been destroyed, almost as soon as it had been formed.

The interest of states, like all human things, is subject to a thousand revolutions. The same laws and the same customs become successively useful and prejudicial to the same people; whence, I conclude, that these laws ought by turns to be adopted and rejected, and that the same actions ought successively to bear the names of virtuous and vicious; a proposition that cannot be denied without confessing, that there are actions, which at one and the same time, are virtuous and prejudicial to the state, and consequently without sapping the foundations of all government, and all society.

The general conclusion of all I have just said is, that virtue is only the desire of the happiness of mankind; and that probity, which I consider as virtue put into action, is among all people, and in all the various governments of the world, only the habit of performing actions useful to our country *.

However evident this conclusion may be, as there is no nation that does not know, and confound together two different kinds of virtue, the one what I shall call Prejudicial Virtue, and the other, True Virtue; I believe, that, in order to render nothing more to be desired on this subject, I ought to examine the nature of these different kinds of virtue.

CHAP. XIV.

OF VIRTUES, PREJUDICIAL AND TRUE.

I give the name of Prejudicial Virtues to all those where an exact observance of them does not in the least contribute to the public happiness, such as the austerities of those senseless Fakirs

---

* I believe it is not necessary to observe, that I treat only of political, and not of religious probity, which proposes other ends, prescribes duties of a different nature, and has a relation to more sublime objects.

with which the Indies are peopled; virtues that, being often indifferent, and even prejudicial to the state, are the punishment of those who make vows for the performance of them. These false virtues are, in most nations, more honoured than the true virtues, and those that practise them held in greater veneration than good citizens.

No body is more honoured at Indostan than the Bramins* : the people adore even their nudities† : and pay the greatest respect to their penances, which are really frightful‡ : some remain all their lives tied to a tree; others hang scorching over a fire; some are loaded with heavy chains; others take no nourishment but mere liquids; some shut up their mouths with a padlock, and others fasten to it a little bell; and it is an honour to parents to prostitute their daughters to the Fakirs.

Among the actions or customs, to which superstition has united the name of sacred, one of the most pleasant is undoubtedly that of Juibus's priestesses, of the island of Formosa. " To officiate worthily, and to merit the veneration of the people, they ought, after the sermons, contorsions, and howlings, are ended, to cry out that they see their gods; this being done, they roll on the earth, mount to the roof of the pagod, discover their nakedness, slap their posteriors, scatter about

---

* The Bramins have the exclusive privilege of begging alms : they exhort the people to give them, and give none themselves.

† " Why, when we are men," say these Bramins, " should we be ashamed of going naked, when we came naked, and without shame, out of our mother's womb ?"
The Cirabees are no less ashamed of being seen clothed, than we of being caught naked. If most savages cover certain parts of their bodies, it is less on account of their modesty than from the tenderness and sensibility of certain parts, and the fear of wounding them in traversing the woods and thickets.

‡ In the kingdom of Pegu are a kind of anchorets named Santons; they never beg for any thing, though dying with hunger. Indeed, care is taken to anticipate all their desires. Whoever confesses to them cannot be punished, whatever crime he may have committed.— The Santons lodge in the country, and dwell in the trunks of hollow trees; after their death they are honoured as gods.

their urine, come down naked, and then wash in the presence of the assembly *."

Happy the people among whom the prejudicial virtues are only ridiculous; they are frequently extremely barbarous †. In the capital of Cochin, they bring up crocodiles; and whoever exposes himself to the fury of one of these animals, and is devoured, is reckoned among the elect. In the kingdom of Martemban, it is an act of virtue, on the day when the idol is brought out, for the people to throw themselves under the wheels of his chariot, or to cut their throats as he passes by; and whoever offers himself to this death, is reputed a saint, and his name is on that account registered in a book.

As there are prejudicial virtues, there are also crimes of prejudice. It is one for a Bramin to marry a virgin. If, during the three months in which the people of the island of Formosa are ordered to go naked, a man fastens upon him the smallest

---

* " Voyages of the Dutch East-India company."

† The women of Madagascar believe, that there are fortunate and unfortunate days and hours; and it is a duty of their religion, when any of them are delivered in an unfortunate day or hour, to expose the infants to be devoured by the wild beasts, to bury them alive, or to strangle them.

In one of the temples in the empire of Pegu, they educate their virgins. Every year, at the festival of the idol, they sacrifice one of these unhappy creatures. The priest, in his sacerdotal habits, strips her naked, strangles her, plucks out her heart, and throws it in the idol's face. The sacrifice being ended, the priest dines, dresses himself in a habit of a horrible form, and dances before the people. In other temples, in the same country, men only are sacrificed. For this purpose they buy a handsome well-made slave: this slave is dressed in a white robe, and being washed three successive mornings, is at length shewn to the people. The fourth day the priest opens his breast, plucks out his heart, sprinkles the idol with his blood, and eats his flesh as sacred food. " Innocent blood," say the priests, " ought to flow to expiate the sins of the nation: besides, it is necessary that some should go to the great God, to put him in mind of his people." It is, however, proper to remark, that the priests never charge themselves with this commission.

piece of linen; he wears, say they, a cloathing unworthy of a man. In the same island, it is a crime for a woman with child to be brought to bed before the thirty-fifth year of her age. Are they pregnant, they extend themselves at the foot of the priestess, who, in execution of the law, tramples upon them, till she causes a miscarriage.

When the priests or magicians of Pegu have foretold the recovery or death of the sick *, it is a crime for the sick person condemned to recover. While he is on his recovery, every one flies from, and abuses him. " If he had been good," say the priests, " God would have received him into his company."

There is, perhaps, no country where the people have not a greater abhorrence for some of these crimes of prejudice, than for villanies the most atrocious, and the most injurious to society.

Among the Giagues, a people who devour their conquered enemies, " They are allowed," says Father Cavazi, " to pound their children in a mortar, with roots, oil, and leaves; to boil them, and form the whole into a paste, with which they rub their bodies, to render them invulnerable; it would be an abominable sacrilege not to massacre, with the blows of a spade, a young man and woman in the month of March, before the queen of the country. When the corn is ripe, the queen, surrounded by her courtiers, leaves the palace, and cutting the throats of those she finds in her way, gives them her retinue to eat. These sacrifices, she pretends, are necessary to appease the ghosts of her ancestors, who see with regret, the common people enjoy a life of which they are deprived; this poor consolation they imagine may be sufficient to prevail on them to bless the harvest.

In the kingdoms of Congo, Angola, and Matamba, the husband may, without disgrace, sell his wife; the father his son;

---

* A Giague, after his death, is asked, " Why he left this life?" When a priest, counterfeiting the voice of the deceased, answers, " that he has not made a sufficient number of sacrifices to his ancestors." These sacrifices are a considerable part of the revenues of the priests.

and the son his father; in these countries, they know only one
crime *, that of refusing the first fruits of the harvest to Chitombe, who is the high-priest of the nation. "These people,"
says Father Labat, " so destitute of all true virtue, are very
scrupulous observers of this custom." A person solely employed in the augmentation of his revenues has the best title
with them to be the Chitombe : he has not the least desire to
instruct the ignorant; he is even afraid lest too just an idea of
virtue should diminish their superstition, and the tribute they
pay him.

What I have said of prejudicial virtues, and vicious prejudices, is sufficient to shew the difference between those virtues and true virtue; that is, with those which incessantly add
to the public felicity, and without which society could not
subsist.

In consequence of these two different kinds of virtue, I
shall distinguish two different kinds of the corruption of manners; Religious and Political Corruption †. But, before I enter
into this discussion, I declare that I write in the character of a
philosopher, and not of a divine; and, therefore, in this and
the following chapters, I shall not pretend to treat of any other
virtues but those that are merely human. This information

---

* In the kingdom of Lao, the Talopoins, who are the priests of the
country, can only be judged by the king himself. They go to confession every month; and, being faithful observers of that custom,
may commit a thousand abominations with impunity. They so far
blind their princes, that a Talopoin, convicted of using false money,
was sent back acquitted by the king; who only replied, " That the
seculars ought to make him greater presents." The most considerable
persons in the country think it a great honour to perform the meanest
offices for the Talopoins, and none of them will wear a habit that has
not been for some time worn by a Talopoin.

† This distinction is necessary, first, because I consider probity in
a philosophical light, and independently of the obligations of religion,
with respect to society, which I beg the reader to keep in view,
through the whole course of this work; and secondly, to avoid the
perpetual confusion found among idolatrous nations, between the
principles of religion and those of a political and moral nature.

being given, I enter upon the subject, and say, that with respect to corruption of manners, the name of religious corruption is given to all kinds of libertinism, and principally to that of men with women. This species of corruption, for which I am not an advocate, and which is doubtless criminal, since it is offensive to God, is not, however, incompatible with the happiness of a nation. The people of different countries have believed, and believe still, that this corruption is not criminal: but it is doubtless so in France, since it is contrary to the laws of the country; but it would not be so if women were in common, and their offspring declared the children of the state: this crime would then, in a political view, be attended with no danger. In fact, if we take a survey of the earth, we shall see different nations of people, among whom what we call libertinism is not only considered as no corruption of manners, but is found authorized by the laws, and even consecrated by religion.

Without reckoning the seraglios in the East, which are under the protection of the laws, at Tonquin, where fruitfulness is honoured, the pain imposed by the law on barren women is to search for agreeable girls, and to bring them to their husbands. In consequence of this political institution, the Tonquinese think the Europeans ridiculous in having only one wife; and cannot conceive why, among us, rational beings can think of honouring God by a vow of chastity. They maintain that, when there is an opportunity, it is as criminal not to give life to what has is not, as to take it from those who already have it*.

It is also under the protection of the laws, that the Siamese women, with their bosoms and thighs half naked, are carried into the streets in palanquins, where they shew shemselves in the most lascivious attitudes. This law was established by one of their queens named Tirada, who, in order to disgust the

---

* Among the Giagues, when a girl has the signs of her being capable of bearing children, they make a feast; but, when these signs disappear, they put those women to death, as unworthy of life, when they can no longer communicate it.

men against a more shameful passion, thought herself obliged
to use all the power of beauty. " This project," say the
Siamese, " succeeded." They add, " That it is besides a wise
law, since it is agreeable to the men to have desires, and to
the women to excite them. Thus it is the happiness of both
sexes, and the only blessing heaven has mingled with the evils
by which we are afflicted, and what soul can be so barbarous
as to desire to deprive us of it * ?

In the kingdom of Batimena†, every woman, of what condition soever, is obliged by the law, upon pain of death, to
yield to the embraces of whoever desires it ; a refusal is a sentence of death.

I should never have done, were I to endeavour to give a
list of all the nations that have not the same ideas as we of
this kind of corruption of manners ; I shall content myself
then, after having mentioned some of the countries where libertinism is authorised by law, to cite some of those where the
same libertinism forms a part of religious worship.

In the island of Formosa, drunkenness and lewdness are acts
of religion. " Delights," say those people, " are the daughters
of heaven, the gifts of its goodness ; to enjoy them is to honour
the Deity; it is answering his kindness. Can it be questioned,
that the sight of the caresses and enjoyments of love is not
pleasing to the Gods? The Gods are good, and there is no
offering of our gratitude more acceptable to them than our
pleasures; and, in consequence of this reasoning, they publicly
give themselves up to every kind of prostitution ‡.

---

* A very sensible writer says, on this subject, " It is beyond contradiction, that all pleasures, contrary to the general good, ought to
be prohibited; but, before this prohibition, it is proper that, by a
thousand efforts of the mind, endeavours be used to reconcile this
pleasure with the general happiness. Men," he adds, " are so unhappy, that one pleasure more is well worth the pains of an attempt
to separate from this whatever may be dangerous with respect to society; and, perhaps, it might be easy to succeed, were we with this
view to examine the laws of those countries where these pleasures are
permitted."

† " Christianity in the Indies, book iv. page 308.

‡ In the kingdom of Thibet, the young women near about their

It is also, in order to obtain the favour of the Gods, that the queen of the Giagues, before declaring war, orders the most beautiful women, and the handsomest of her warriors, to appear before her; where, in different attitudes, they enjoy the pleasures of love. " In how many countries," says Cicero, " are temples erected to debauchery? how many altars have been raised to prostituted women * ?" Besides the antient worship of Venus, do not the Banians, under the name of the goddess Banani, adore one of their queens, who, according to Gamelli Carreri, " exposed all her beauties to the sight of her whole court, and successively lavished her favours to several lovers, and even to two at the same time ?"

I shall close my quotations on this head with a passage from Julius Firmicus Maternus, a father of the second century, in his Treatise de Errore Profanarum Religionum. " Assyria, together with a part of Africa," says this father, " worship the air by the name of Juno, or the virgin Venus. This goddess presides over the elements: she has her temples, where

---

necks the gifts of lewdness; that is, the rings of their gallants; and the more they have, with the greater splendor and rejoicings are their nuptials celebrated.

* At Babylon, all the women were to encamp near the temple of Venus, and once in their life, by an expiatory prostitution, obtain the remission of their sins: they were not to deny the desire of the first stranger, who was for purifying their soul, by the enjoyment of their bodies. The pretty and handsome had, doubtless, soon discharged their penance; but they, whom nature had not favoured with an inviting person, may be generally supposed to have waited a long time, till some charitable stranger had restored them to a state of peace.

The convents of the Bonzes are full of idolatrous nuns as concubines. When tired of them, they are dismissed and replaced by others; the gates of these convents are crowded by votaries, and it is generally by presents to the Bonzes, that they obtain the high favour of being admitted. In the kingdom of Cochin, the Bramins, being desirous of giving the first taste of the joys of love to brides, make both the sovereign and people tell them this holy work is to be committed to them: wherever they go, fathers leave them with their daughters, as husbands do with their wives.

priests officiate dressed and painted like women; they perform their devotions in languid effeminate accents; provoke men's desires, gratify them, and glory in their lewdness; and, after these preparatory pleasures, call on the goddess with vehement vociferations and instrumental music, pretending to be under a divine inspiration, and to utter prophecies."

Thus there are many countries where that corruption of manners, which I call religious, is authorised by the laws; or consecrated by the religion.

What innumerable evils, will it be said, are annexed to this kind of corruption? May it not be answered, that dissoluteness is then only politically dangerous in a state, when it counter-venes the law of the country, or is blended with some other defect of the government? It is in vain to add, that the nations There such dissoluteness prevails are the contempt of the whole world. But, without mentioning the eastern nations and others, either savage or martial, who, though given up to vo-luptuousness of every kind, are happy at home, and formidable abroad; what nation ever excelled the Greeks! a people which, to this day, is the admiration and honour of human nature. Before the Peleponesian war, an æra fatal to their virtue, what nation, what country, produced so many virtuous and great men? Yet the taste of the Greeks, for the most indecent love, is well known: so general was it, that Aristides, surnamed the Just, that Aristides, with whose praises, said the Athenians, our ears are perpetually filled, loved Themistocles. It was the beauty of the young Stesileus, which, kindling violent desires in the heart of both, at the same time inflamed it with impla-cable hatred against each other. Plato was sensual; Socrates himself, whom the oracle of Apollo declared to be the wisest of men, besides having two wives, and frequenting courtesans, loved Alcibiades and Archelaus. Thus it is certain, that, ac-cording to our idea of morality, the most virtuous of the Greeks would have been looked upon in Europe as debauchees. Now this kind of corruption of manners was in Greece carried to the utmost excess, when at the same time this country produced such great men of every kind, that it made Persia tremble; consequently, that corruption of manners which I call religious does not seem incompatible with the greatness and felicity of a state.

There is another kind of corruption of manners, which is preparative of the fall of an empire, and presages its ruin; this I shall distinguish by the name of political corruption. With this a people is infected when the bulk of the individuals separate their interest from that of the public. This kind of corruption, which sometimes is blended with the preceding, has led many moralists to confound them: if the question be only of the political interest of a state, the latter would, perhaps, be the most dangerous. A people, however pure its first manners might have been, when this corruption gets footing, must necessarily be unhappy at home, and little feared abroad: the duration of such an empire is precarious; it is chance which either delays or hastens the fall of it.

To evince how dangerous this anarchy of the several interests is in a state, let us consider the evils arising only from the opposition of the interests of one body to those of the commonwealth. We will allow the Bonzes, the Talopoins, all the virtues of ourselves: yet, if the interests of the body of the Bonzes be not connected with the public interest; if, for instance, the Bonze's authority depends on the people's blindness, the Bonze will necessarily be an enemy to the nation which maintains him; will be to that nation what the Romans were to the world, honest among themselves, robbers with regard to the universe. Were every Bonze in himself greatly averse to dignities and high stations, the body will not be the less ambitious; all its members will labour for its aggrandizement often without knowing it: they will even think themselves authorised so to do from a principle of virtue * ; therefore in a state there is nothing more dangerous than a body whose interest is not connected with the general interest.

If the Pagan priests caused Socrates to be put to death, and were ever opposing eminent persons, it was owing to the oppo-

---

* In the true religion, priests have been found, who, in the times of ignorance, have abused the devotion of the people for arrogating to themselves the rights of sovereignty.

sition of their private interest to that of the public; it was because the priests of a false religion find their account in keeping
the people in blindness, and for this purpose persecute and remove out of the way all who may open their eyes: an example
which has sometimes been copied by the ministers of the true
religion, who, without the same necessity, have practised the
same cruelties, have persecuted, have oppressed, great men;
have lavished their panegyrics on works of little merit, and
have virulently criticised others very excellent; but in both
have been disowned by more candid or more knowing divines*.

---

* Father Millot, in a discourse which obtained the prize of the academy at Dijon, on the question, " Whether it is most useful to study
men or books?" expresses himself in the following manner, concerning M. de Montesquieu. " Those rules of conduct, those maxims of
government, which should be engraved on the thrones of kings, and
on the hearts of every one invested with authority; is it not to a close
study of men that we owe them? Witness that illustrious patriot, that
interpreter, that judge, of the laws, on whose tomb France and all Europe shed tears; but whose genius will ever be seen to instruct nations,
tracing the plan of public happiness; that immortal writer, who
abridged every thing, because he saw every thing, who was for putting
us on thinking, as what we stand more in need of than reading.
With what sagacity had he studied human nature! Travelling like
Solon, meditating like Pythagoras, conversing like Plato, reading like
Cicero, writing like Tacitus, his continual object was man; men he
studied, and knew them. The fertile seeds already are seen to germi-
nate, which he cast into the minds of the chiefs of nations and the
rulers of empires. Let us gratefully reap the fruits, &c." Father
Millot adds in a note, " When an author of confessed probity, a free-
thinker, who, always expressing himself as he imagines, formally says,
Christianity, the sole view of which seems to be the happiness of the
other life, also constitutes our happiness in this," and after refuting a
dangerous paradox of Bayle, he adds, " The principles of Christianity,
well engraved in the heart, would be infinitely stronger than this false
honour of monarchies, these human virtues of republics, and this servile fear of despotic states, which is stronger than the three principles
of political government, laid down in the Spirit of Laws: can such an
author, by any one who has read his work, be accused of designing to
strike at Christianity?"

For instance, can there be any thing more ridiculous than the prohibition in some countries against bringing into it a single copy of the Spirit of Laws? a work which more than one prince takes care that his son shall read over and over. May we not here use the expression of a man of wit, that the monks, in soliciting this prohibition, acted as the Scythians did with their slaves, putting out their eyes that they might turn the mill with less distraction.

Thus it is clear, that the public happiness, or calamity, depends solely on the agreement or opposition of the interest of individuals with the general interest; and that the religious corruption of manners may, as history abundantly proves, be often joined with magnanimity, elevation of soul, wisdom, abilities; in fine, with all the qualities which form great men.

That citizens, infected with this kind of corruption of manners, have often rendered more important services to their country than the most austere anchorites, is undeniable: how happy have been the consequences of the amorous Circassian's care, either for her own or her daughter's beauty, who first ventured on innoculation? what numbers of children have, by this method, been saved from an early death? Possibly there is not a foundress of any order of nuns to whom the world owes such an extensive and important benefit, and who, consequently, is entitled to so much of its acknowledgment.

Let me be allowed once more, for a conclusion of this chapter, to declare, that it has by no means been my intention to vindicate debauchery. All I meant was only to impart clear ideas of these two different kinds of corruption of manners, which have been too often confounded, and the general ideas of which seemed to have been dark and perplexed; because, on a more explicit information of the true scope of the question, the importance of it may be better known, the degree of contempt assignable to these two different sorts of corruption may be better determined, and we shall better perceive that there are two different species of bad actions; some vicious in every form of government, others which in a state are pernicious, and consequently criminal, only as those actions are contradictory to the laws of those countries.

Moralists, by a clearer insight into the evil, will naturally acquire a greater skill in the cure. They may now view morality in a new point of light, and, from a vain science, improve it to a science of universal utility.

CHAP. XV.

OF THE USE ACCRUING TO MORALITY, FROM THE KNOWLEDGE OF THE PRINCIPLES LAID DOWN IN THE PRECEDING CHAPTERS.

If morality hitherto has little contributed to the happiness of mankind, it is not owing to any want of perspicuity or beauty of stile, or propriety and loftiness of sentiment, in the moralists: but amidst all their superior talents, it must be owned, that they have not often enough considered the different vices of nations as necessarily resulting from the different form of their government; yet, it is only by considering morality in this point of light, that it can become of any real use to men. What have hitherto been the effects of all the splendid maxims of morality? If some individuals have been corrected by them of faults which perhaps they reproached themselves with, no change in the manners of nations have been produced. What is this to be imputed to? It is because the vices of a people, if I may presume to say so, always lie at the bottom of its legislation. There he must search, who would pluck up the root whence its vices arise. He who wants either penetration, or courage, for such an undertaking, is, in this respect, of little or no use to the universe. To attempt extinguishing the vices annexed to the legislation of a people, without making any change in this legislation, is no less than rejecting the just consequence after admitting the principles.

What can be hoped for from so many declamations against the falsity of women, if this vice be the necessary effect of an opposition betwixt the desires of nature and the sentiments which, by the law of decency, women are forced to affect? In Malabar and Madagascar, all women are faithful, because they have gallants without number, and they never pitch on a husband till after repeated trials: it is the same with the savages of New Orleans, and of those people where the relations of the Great Sun, the princess of the blood, may, on any disgust taken at their husbands, dismiss them and marry others. In such countries, no unfaithful wives are heard of, because they have no manner of interest to be so.

Very far am I from inferring that, from these examples, the same manners should be introduced among us; I only say, that women cannot reasonably be reproached with a breach of faith which decency and the laws, as it were, imposed on them as a necessity; and that whilst the causes are suffered to subsist the effects will continue.

For a second instance, we shall take defamation. This is a vice, but a necessary vice, because in every country where the people have no share in the administration of public affairs, and being thus little concerned about mental improvement, must stagnate in a scandalous sloth. Now, if in this country it be the fashion to contract a numerous acquaintance, and to frequent public places, and loquacity is accounted the mark of breeding and spirit, he who is ignorant, and not able to discourse of things, must necessarily make persons the subject of his talk; and panegyric being insupportable, and satire entertaining, the ignorant, to avoid being insupportable, are obliged to talk scandal: thus this vice cannot be suppressed without abolishing the productive cause, without delivering the citizens from idleness, and consequently without altering the form of government. Why is the man of sense generally less a busy body in private companies than the man of fashion? It is because the former, taken up with greater objects, speaks of persons only as they have, like great men, an immediate relation with great things; likewise the man of sense, as he never defames but by way of revenge, it is very rarely he defames; whereas the man of the world must either defame or be mute.

What I say of defaming, I likewise say of debauchery, against which the moralists have always so violently inveighed: debauchery is so generally allowed to be a necessary consequence of luxury, that any farther proof of it would be superfluous. Now if luxury, which I am very far from thinking, but which is commonly believed, be very useful to the state, if, as may be easily shewn, the taste for it cannot be extinguished, and citizens brought to the observance of sumptuary laws, without altering the form of government, then some alterations of this kind must take place, antecedently to any hopes of abolishing debauchery. Every harangue on this head is good divinity, but not policy; the object of policy and legislation is the opulency, power, and happiness of a people : now, with regard to this, I say, that if luxury be really useful to France, it would be ridiculous to attempt to introduce there an austerity of manners incompatible with a taste for luxury. There is no proportion between the advantages which commerce and luxury procure to a state in its present constitution, (advantages which to suppress debauchery it must forego) and the infinitely small evil occasioned by the love of women. This is to complain of finding in a rich mine some sparks of copper intermixed with veins of gold. Wherever luxury is necessary, it is a solecism in politics to account intriguing a moral vice; and if it must be called a moral vice, the consequence is, that, in some countries and some ages, there are useful vices, and that it is to the mud of the Nile Egypt owes its fertility. In effect, on a political examination of the behaviour of intriguing women, it will be found that, though in certain respects blameable, they are, in others, of great use to the public ; that, for instance, in the use they make of their money, they are more advantageous to the state than the most virtuous of their sex. By the desire of pleasing, which sends an intriguing woman to the mercer and milliner, she not only saves an infinite number of workmen from the indigence into which sumptuary laws at once would plunge them, but the same desire puts her upon acts of the most judicious charity. If luxury be supposed useful to a nation, is it not the women of dress, who, by exciting the industry of the artists of luxury, continually improve their usefulness to the state? Virtuous women, therefore, are not so well advised by their directors in bestowing on beggars and criminals, as intriguing women by the desire of pleasing: these support useful members of society, the others nuisances, even the enemies of mankind.

From what I have said, it follows that no change in the ideas of a people is to be hoped for, till after a change in its legislation; that the reformation of manners is to be begun by the reformation of laws, and declamations against a vice useful in the present form of government, would politically be detrimental, were they not found fruitless. But so they will always be, for it is only the force of the laws that can ever act on the bulk of a nation. Besides, let me be allowed cursorily to observe, that, among the moralists there are very few who, by setting our passions at variance, know how to avail themselves of them, so as to procure their opinions to be adopted. Most of their admonitions are too dogmatical and imperious; yet they should be sensible that invectives will never prevail against sentiments; that it is only a passion which can get the better of a passion; for instance, to bring a gay woman to more reserve and modesty in public, her vanity must be contrasted with her coquetry, and it must be urged to her that modesty is an invention of love and of refined delight*; that

---

* It is by considering modesty in this light that we may answer the arguments of the Stoics and Cynics, who affirmed that the virtuous man did nothing in private which he should not do in public, and who consequently believed that they might publicly act the pleasures of love. If most legislators have censured these cynical principles, and classed modesty among the virtues, it is, will it be answered, because they apprehended that the frequent sight of enjoyment might cast some disgust on a pleasure on which depends the conservation of the species, and the continuance of the world? They were likewise aware that dress, concealing some female charms, decked a woman with all the beauties which a lively imagination could suggest; that this dress inflamed curiosity; heightened the joys of female caresses, rendered their favours more extatic, and multiplied the delights of our afflictive state. If Lycurgus had banished from Sparta a certain kind of modesty, and if the young women, in presence of a whole people, wrestled naked with the youth of the other sex, the legislator's intention herein was, that being made stronger by such exercise,

it is to the gauze which covers a woman's beauties, that
the world owes most of its pleasures; that at Malabar, where
the young beauties appear in company half naked; that in
certain parts of America, where the women wear no covering,
the desires have nothing of that ardour and vivacity which curiosity would impart to them; that in those countries beauty
serves only for the call of necessity; and that, on the contrary, among those nations where modesty has placed a veil
between desires and nudities, this mysterious veil is the talisman which holds the lover at his charmer's feet; that, in fine,
modesty puts into beauty's weak hands the sceptre to which
power submits. Besides, they will say to the woman of gallantry—" You must know that the wretched are very numerous; that the unfortunate born enemies to the happy man
make a crime of his happiness; that they hate in him a felicity
too independent of them; that the subject of your amusements
is to be concealed from their sight; and that levity and indecency, by betraying the secrets of your pleasures, exposes you
to all the strokes of their revenge.

By thus substituting the soft language of interest, instead of
the peremptory clamour of invective, the moralists may establish their maxims. I shall not enlarge farther on this head,
but return to my subject; and I say, that all men tend only
towards their happiness; that it is a tendency from which they
cannot be diverted; that the attempt would be fruitless, and
even the success dangerous; consequently, it is only by incor-
porating personal and general interest, that they can be rendered virtuous. This being granted, morality is evidently no

---

their children might be more robust and fitter for the constitution of
that state, which was purely military. He knew that however the
custom of seeing naked women might cool the desire of seeing their
hidden beauties, the desire itself was unextinguishable, especially in a
country where it was only in secret and by stealth that husbands were
admitted to the embraces of their wives. Besides, Lycurgus, as he
made love one of the principal springs of his legislative system, intended it for the recompence, and not the occupation, of the Spartans

more than a frivolous science, unless blended with policy and legislation: whence I conclude that, if philosophers would be of use to the world, they should survey objects from the same point of view as the legislator. Though not invested with the same power, they are to be actuated by the same principle. The moralist is to indicate the laws, of which the legislator insures the execution, by stamping them with the seal of his authority.

Among the moralists, there are doubtless but few duly impressed with this truth, even of those whose minds are capable of the most exalted ideas; many in the study of morality and the portraits of vices are animated only by personal interest and private contentions; consequently they confine themselves only to the representation of such vices as molest society; and their mind gradually contracting itself within the narrow circle of their interest, soon loses the force necessary for soaring to sublime ideas. In the science of morality, the elevation of the thought often depends on the elevation of the soul. To fix on such moral truths as are of real advantage to men, there must be a warm passion for the general good; and unhappily morality, like religion, is not without hypocrites.

CHAP. XVI.

OF HYPOCRITICAL MORALISTS.

By a hypocrite, I mean him who, in the study of morality, is not animated by a desire of procuring the happiness of mankind, being too much taken up with himself: this is a numerous class, and known on one hand by the coldness with which they discuss those vices big with the fall of empires; and on the other by their impotent invectives against private vices. It is in vain for such to say that they have the public welfare at heart. " Were you really animated with such a generous passion," it will be said to them, " your hatred to every vice would be always proportionate to the mischief it does in society; and if you are irritated at such faults as are least detri-

mental to a state, with what eye should you look on the ignorance of the proper means for forming valiant and magnanimous patriots?   How extreme would be your concern at perceiving some faults in the administration of justice, or the as-
sessment of taxes; or how would you glow with indignation at
a fault in military discipline, which so often decides the fate of
battles and the devastations of provinces?   Were such your
temper, overcome by excess of grief, you would, like Nerva,
detesting life, by which you are a spectator of the calamities
of your country, terminate its course; or at least you would
imitate that heroic Chinese who, justly provoked at the op-
pressions of the great, boldly entered the emperor's presence
with his complaints.   " I come," says he, " to offer myself to
that punishment which, on account of such representations,
six hundred of my fellow-subjects have already suffered.   I
give you notice to prepare for further execution; China has
still eighteen thousand firm patriots, who, for the same information, will be coming to ask of you the same reward."   At
these words he ceased speaking; but the emperor, astonished
at his firmness, rewarded it in the manner most acceptable to
a virtuous man, the punishment of the guilty, and the suppression of oppressive imposts.   In this manner the love of
the public welfare declares itself.   If you are really animated
by these passions, I would say to these censors—" Your hatred
to every vice will be proportioned to its detriment to the state :
if it be only the offences injuring yourselves, which excite
your anger, the name of moralist does not belong to you; you
are no more than mere egotists."   Thus it is only by an absolute detachment from personal interest, by a profound study of
the science of legislation, that a moralist can become service-
able to his country.   He is then able to weigh the advantages
or disadvantages of a law or custom, and to judge whether it
should be abolished or continued.

We are too often obliged to comply with errors, or even
barbarous customs; if, in Europe, duels have been so long tolerated, it is because, in nations void of a Roman love for their
country, and where courage is not exercised by continual
wars, moralists probably could think of no other way of sup-

porting courage, that the state might not be destitute of valiant defenders; and, by this toleration, they hoped to have purchased a great good at the expence of a small evil. They were extremely deceived with regard to the particular case of duelling; but there are a thousand others where this must be complied with, and it is often in the choice of two evils that the man of genius distinguishes himself. Away with those pedants, enamoured with a false idea of perfection! nothing is more dangerous in a state than these senseless moral declaimers, who, concentered within a small sphere of ideas, are continually repeating what they have heard from their nurses, incessantly recommending moderation in our desires, and an universal extinction of the passions; not aware that their precepts, though useful to a few individuals in certain circumstances, would prove the ruin of the nations that should adopt them.

In fact, if, as history informs us, strong passions, such as pride and patriotism among the Greeks and Romans, fanaticism among the Arabs, and avarice among freebooters, always produce the most formidable wars; whatever general leads men without passions against such soldiers, will oppose only fearful lambs to the fury of wolves. Wise Nature has, therefore, always placed in the heart of man a preservative against the reasonings of such philosophers. Thus the nations who subject their intentions to these precepts, always find themselves feeble in action; and without this happy weakness, the people scrupulously attached to their maxims would become the contempt and the slaves of other nations.

It requires those vast geniuses that embrace all the parts of a government to determine how far the fire of the passions ought to be exalted or moderated. Whoever is endowed with these abilities is, in a manner, designed by Nature to fulfil, with respect to the legislature, the part of a thinking minister*; and, to justify the observation of Cicero, that a man of genius is never a mere citizen, but a true magistrate.

---

* In China they distinguish two kinds of ministers; the one are the Signing ministers, who grant audiences, and add their signatures;

Before we shew the advantages the universe would receive from more extensive and more sound ideas of morality, I think I ought to remark, by the way, that these ideas throw great light upon all the sciences, especially upon history, whose progress is at the same time the cause and effect of the progress of morality.

Were writers better instructed in the true objects of history, they would praise nothing in the private life of a king but such particulars as were proper to represent his character; they would not so curiously describe his manners, and his domestic virtues and vices; they would be sensible that the public demands from sovereigns an account of their edicts, and not of their suppers; that the public love to know the man in the prince, only so far as the man has a share in the deliberations of the prince; and that, instead of puerile anecdotes, they ought, in order to instruct and please, substitute the agreeable or dreadful picture of the public felicity or misery, and the causes that produce them. From the mere exhibition of such a picture, would arise an infinite number of reflections and useful regulations.

What I say of history, I also say of metaphysics and civil law. There are few sciences but what have a relation to that of morality. The chain which connects them together is more extensive than we are apt to imagine; it surrounds the whole universe.

CHAP. XVII.

OF THE ADVANTAGES THAT RESULT FROM THE PRINCIPLES ABOVE ESTABLISHED.

I PASS with rapidity over the advantages that would be obtained by individuals; these would consist in their having

---

the others bear the name of Thinking ministers, and have the care of forming projects, examining those who present them, and proposing such changes as times and circumstances require to be made in the administration.

clear ideas of morality; the principles of which have been hitherto so ambiguous and contradictory, that they permitted the most senseless persons constantly to justify the folly of their conduct by some of its maxims.

Besides, the individual being better informed of his duties, would be less dependent on the opinion of his friends. Sheltered from the injustice wherein, unknown to himself, he might be frequently involved by those with whom he converses, he would be freed from the puerile fear of ridicule; a phantom that banishes reason, and is the terror of those timid and ignorant souls who sacrifice their inclinations, their pleasures, their repose, and sometimes even their virtues, to the humour and caprice of those splenetic mortals whose criticism we cannot escape, when we have the misfortune to be known.

A person solely subject to reason and virtue might then brave every prejudice, and arm himself with those manly and courageous sentiments that form the distinguishing character of a virtuous man; sentiments desirable in every citizen, and which we have a right to expect from the great. How shall the person, raised to the highest posts, remove the obstacles to the general welfare, which certain prejudices raise against it, and resist the menaces and cabals of men in power, often interested in the public misfortune, if his soul is not inaccessible to all kinds of solicitations, fears, and prejudices?

It appears then that the knowledge of the above principles procures at least these advantages to the individual; it gives him a clear and certain idea of honesty; saves him from all inquietude on this subject, secures the peace of his conscience, and consequently procures him the inward secret pleasure blended with the practice of virtue.

As to the advantages the public would derive from it, they would doubtless be more considerable. In consequence of these principles, we might, if I may venture to use the expression, compose a catechism of probity, the maxims of which being simple, true, and level to all understandings, would teach the people that virtue, though invariable in the object it proposes, is not so in the means it makes use of:

that, consequently, we ought to consider actions as indifferent in themselves; to be sensible, that it is the business of the state to determine those that are worthy of esteem or contempt; and, in fine, that it is the office of the legislator to fix, from his knowledge of the public interest, the instant when an action ceases to be virtuous, and becomes vicious.

These principles being once received, with what facility would the legislator extinguish the torches of fanaticism and superstition, suppress abuses, reform barbarous customs, perhaps useful at their establishment, but since become fatal to the world? Customs that subsist only from the fear of not being able to abolish them, without causing an insurrection among people, who are always accustomed to take the practice of certain actions for virtue itself, without kindling long and bloody wars; and in short, without occasioning those seditions which are always dangerous to the common-people, and can really be neither foreseen nor subdued but by men of firmness and great abilities.

It is then by weakening the stupid veneration of the people for ancient laws and customs, that sovereigns would be enabled to purge the earth of most of the evils that lay it waste, and be furnished with the means of securing the possession of their crowns.

At present, when the interest of a state is changed, and the laws which at their first foundation were useful, are became prejudicial; those very laws, by the respect constantly preserved for them, must necessarily draw the state to its ruin. Who doubts that the destruction of the Roman republic was the effect of a ridiculous veneration for the ancient laws, and that this blind respect forged the fetters with which Cæsar loaded his country? After the destruction of Carthage, when Rome attained the summit of her glory, the Romans, from the opposition they then found between their interests, their manners, and their laws, ought to have foreseen the revolution with which the empire was threatened; and to have been sensible that, to save the state, the republic in a body ought to have pressed the making those reformations which the times and circumstances required, and above all to hasten the prevention of those changes that personal ambition, the most dangerous to the legislature, might introduce. The Romans would have had recourse to this remedy, had they had clearer ideas of morality. Instructed by the history of all nations, they would have perceived, that the same laws which had raised them to the highest elevation, could not support them in that state; that an empire is like a vessel which the winds have driven to a certain latitude, where, being opposed by other winds, it is in danger of being lost, if to avoid shipwreck the pilot does not speedily change his course: this political truth was well known to Mr. Locke, who, on the establishment of the legislature of Carolina, proposed that his laws should be in force only during one century; and, that time being expired, they should become void, if they were not a-fresh examined and confirmed by the English. He was sensible that a military or commercial government supposed very different laws; and that a legislation proper to favour commerce and industry might one day become fatal to that colony, if its neighbours entered into a war amongst themselves, and circumstances made it necessary for that people to become more warlike than commercial.

If we apply Mr. Locke's idea to the false religions, we shall be soon convinced of the folly of their inventors and their followers. Whoever, in fact, examines the religions, (all of which, except ours, are formed by the hand of man,) must perceive, that none of them was ever contrived by the great genius of legislature, but by the narrow mind of an ordinary person; that consequently a false religion was never founded on the basis of the laws, and a principle of public utility, a principle always invariable, but pliable in its application to all the various situations in which a people can successively be placed. This is the only principle that ought to be admitted by those, who, after the example of Anastasius, Ripperda, Thamas Kouli-Kan, and Gehan-Guir, would trace the plan of a new religion, and render it of use to mankind. If in the composition of false religions, this plan had been always followed, they would have preserved, in these religions, whatever is of use; they would neither have destroyed Elysium nor Tartarus; and the legislator might at his pleasure have given pictures of them more or less pleasing or

terrible, according to the greater or less strength of his imagination. These religions, merely stripped of what is hurtful
in them, could not have laid the mind under the shameful
yoke of a foolish credulity. What crimes and superstitions
would then have vanished from the earth! We should not have
seen an inhabitant of Java*, persuaded by the slightest incon-
venience that the fatal hour was come, make haste to rejoin
the god of his fathers, implore death, and consent to receive it;
the priests would have endeavoured, in vain, to obtain his consent to be strangled by their hands, and to suffer them to regale
themselves with his flesh. The Persians would have never
nourished that abominable sect of dervises, who demand alms
sword in hand; who kill with impunity whoever does not admit
their principles to be true; who raise a murdering hand against
a Sophi, and plunge the poniard into the breast of an Amurath.
The Romans, who were as superstitious as the Negroes†, would
not have regulated the exertion of their courage by the appetite of the sacred chickens. In short, the religions of the
East could not have produced those long and bloody wars‡, first
made by the Saracens agains the Christians; and afterwards,
under the standards of Omar and Hali, continued by the same
Saracens against each other; and this doubtless gave birth to

---

* To the east of Sumatra.

† When the warriors of Congo advance towards an enemy, if they
meet in their way a hare, a crow, or some other fearful animal, they
say it is the genius of the enemy, come to inform them of their fear,
and then fight with intrepidity. But if they hear the crowing of a cock,
at any other hour than is usual, they say, it is a certain presage of a
defeat; and therefore they always resolve not to expose themselves
to it. If the crowing of a cock is at the same time heard by both
armies, no courage can detain them, for, being equally frighted at the
fatal omen, they instantly disband themseves, and both sides retire.
When the savage of New Orleans marches against the enemy with
most intrepidity, a dream, or the barking of a dog, is sufficient to
make him return home.

‡ The human passions have sometimes kindled the like wars
among the Christians themselves; but nothing can be more contrary

the fable made use of by the prince of Indostan, to suppress the indiscreet zeal of an Iman.

" Submit thyself, said the Iman, to the order of the most high. The earth is going to receive his holy law; victory every where marches before Omar. Thou seest Arabia, Persia, Syria, and all Asia, subdued: the Roman eagle is trampled under the feet of the faithful, and the sword of terror is restored to the hand of Khaled. For these certain signs, acknowledge the truth of my religion, the sublimity of the Koran, the simplicity of its doctrines, and the mildness of our law. Our God is not cruel; he is honoured by our very pleasures; and, as Mohammed says, by breathing the odour of perfumes, and by tasting the voluptuous caresses of love, my soul is kindled with new fervour, and springs with greater rapidity up towards heaven. Crowned insect, how long wilt thou wrestle against thy God? Open thine eyes, see the superstitions and vices with which thy people are infected: wilt thou for ever deprive thyself of the light of the Koran?"

" Iman, replied the prince, there was a time when the republic of beavers, as in my empire, complained of a few robberies, and even of some assassinations: to prevent these crimes, nothing more was necessary than to open some public treasuries, where the rich might deposit their wealth; to enlarge the high roads, and to erect a few prisons. The senate of beavers were ready to come to this resolution, when one who was advanced in years, lifting up his eyes to the azure firmament, suddenly cried out, Let us take example from man. He believes that the palace in the air is built, inhabited, and governed, by a more powerful Being than himself: this Being is named Michapour. Let us publish this doctrine, that the nation of the beavers may submit to it. Let us persuade them that an ethereal spirit is, by order of this God, placed as a centinel on

to the spirit of their religion, which is a spirit of disinterestedness and peace; to its morals, which breath nothing but mildness and indulgence; to its maxims, which every where prescribe beneficence and charity; to the spirituality of the objects it presents to the mind; to the sublimity of its motives; and, in short, to the grandeur and the nature of the rewards it proposes.

each planet; that, from thence contemplating our actions, he may be employed in dispensing happiness to the good, and misery to the wicked: this creed being once believed, guilt will fly far from us. He was silent; they enter into a consultation; they deliberate on the affair; the idea pleases on account of its novelty, and is adopted: this becomes the established religion, and the beavers at first live like brethren. Soon after, however, a great controversy arises. One says that it is the otter, and another says that it is the musk-rat, who first presented to Michapour the grains of sand with which he formed the earth. The dispute grows warm; the people divide into parties; they abuse each other; from abuse they come to blows, and Fanaticism sounds her charge. Before that religion some robberies and assassinations had been committed; but now a civil war is kindled, and half the nation expires. Be instructed by this fable, and pretend not, O cruel Iman, added this Indian prince, to prove to me the truth and utility of a religion that spreads desolation through the universe."

It follows from what has been said in this chapter, that, if the legislature were authorized, in consequence of the principles above established, to make such changes in the laws, customs, and false religions, as the times and circumstances required, they might drain the source of an infinite number of evils, and doubtless secure the repose of nations, by extending the duration of empires.

Besides, what light would these principles spread over morality, in making us sensible of the necessary dependence there is between manners and the laws of a country; and by informing us that the science of morality is nothing more than the science of the legislature? Who doubts that the moralists, being more assiduous at this study, would then carry the science to that high degree of perfection which good minds can now have only a glimpse of, and to which perhaps they do not imagine it can ever arrive*?

---

* It is in vain to say, that this great work of an excellent legislation is not to be performed by human wisdom, and therefore no better than a mere chimera. I would suppose that a long and blind

If, in almost every government, all the laws, being incoherent and inconsistent with each other, seem to be the work of mere chance, it is because, guided by different views and interests, those who formed them gave themselves little trouble about the connection and agreement that subsisted between them. It is with respect to the formation of these entire bodies of laws, as with the formation of certain islands. The peasants resolved to clear the fields of the useless woods, stones, herbs, and mud; for that purpose they let in a river, when those materials, driven by the currents, were collected into a heap about some reeds; they hardened, and at length formed a piece of dry land.

It is, however, on the uniformity of the legislator's views, and the dependence of these laws on each other, that their excellence consists. But, in order to establish this dependence, it would be necessary to refer them all to one simple principle, such as that of the public utility; or, that of the greatest number of men, subject to the same form of government: a principle more extensive and more fruitful than imagination can conceive: a principle that includes all the morality and all the legislations, of which many men discourse without understanding them, and of which the legislators themselves have yet but a very superficial idea, at least if we may judge from the unhappiness of almost all the nations upon earth*.

---

series of events following each other, the first buds of which were unfolded at the creation, is the universal cause of all that has been or shall be. On admitting this principle, I add, that if in this long chain of events is necessarily comprehended the wise men and the fools, the cowards and the heroes, that have governed the world, why may there not also be comprehended in it the discovery of the true principles of government, to which that science owes its perfection, and the world its happiness?

* In most of the empires of the East, they have not even the least idea of the laws of nature and nations. Whoever should endeavour to enlighten the people in this respect, would almost constantly expose himself to the fury of the tyrants who lay waste those unhappy countries. In order to violate with the greater impunity the laws of humanity, they will have their subjects ignorant of what, as

CHAP. XVIII.

OF THE MIND, CONSIDERED WITH RESPECT TO DIFFERENT AGES AND COUNTRIES.

I HAVE proved, that the same actions, successively useful and prejudicial in various ages and countries, were alternately esteemed and despised. It is with ideas as with actions. The diversity of the people's interests, and the changes produced in those interests, produced revolutions in their tastes, occasioned the sudden creation or entire annihilation of certain kinds of genius, and the unjust or proper, though always reciprocal, contempt which different geniuses, ages, and countries, have always felt for each other.

The truth of this proposition I am going to prove in the two following chapters, by several examples.

CHAP. XIX.

THE ESTEEM FOR DIFFERENT KINDS OF GENIUS IS IN EVERY AGE PROPORTIONED TO THE INTEREST THE PEOPLE HAVE IN ESTEEMING THEM.

To shew the perfect justness of this proposition, let us first take romances for an example. From the publication of Amadis to the romances of the present age, that kind of writing has successively experienced a thousand vicissitudes. Would we know the cause? If it be asked, why the romances that have been held in esteem during three hundred years now appear tedious and ridiculous, we shall find that the principal merit of most of these works depends on the exactness with which,

---

men, they have a right to expect from the prince, and of the tacit contract by which he binds himself to his people. What reason soever these princes give for their conduct, it can only be founded on a perverse desire of tyrannizing over their subjects.

in these performances, the virtues and vices, the passions, customs, and follies, of a nation are painted.

Now the manners of a nation generally change every age; this change must then occasion a revolution in taste, and consequently in romances: one nation is therefore constantly forced by the very desire of amusement to despise in one age what it admired in that which preceded it*. What I have said of romances may be applied to almost all other works. But, to shew this truth in a stronger light, it may perhaps be proper to compare the genius of the ages of ignorance with that of the present age. Let us stop a moment to make this inquiry.

As the ecclesiastics were then the only persons who were able to write, I can only draw my observations from their works and sermons. Whoever reads them will perceive no less difference between those of Menot† and father Bourdaloue, than between the knight of the sun and the princess of Cleves. Our manners being changed, and our knowledge increased, we now laugh at what we formerly admired. Who does not smile at the sermon delivered by a preacher at Bourdeaux, who, to shew the gratitude of the deceased, for all who cause prayers to be offered for them, and give for that purpose money to the monks, gravely

---

* Not but that these ancient romances are still agreeable to some philosophers, who look upon them as the true history of the manners of the people, considered in a certain age, and under a certain form of government. These philosophers, convinced that there is a great difference between two romances, the one written by a Sibarite, and the other by a Crotoniate, choose to form a judgment of the character and genius of a nation from the kind of romance with which they are most charmed. These sorts of judgments are commonly very just: an able politician may, by these helps, determine pretty exactly what enterprizes it would be prudent or rash to attempt against a nation. But common people, who read romances less for instruction than amusement, do not consider them in this point of view; and, consequently, cannot form the same judgment from them.

† In one of Menot's sermons, he treats of the promise of the Messiah, and says, " God had from all eternity pre-ordained the incarnation, and the salvation of the human race; but he resolved that some great personages, such as the holy fathers, should entreat for it. Adam,

T

cried out in the pulpit that, " at the mere sound of the money, which fell into a box or plate, and sounded tin, tin, tin, all the souls in purgatory were seized with such joy, that they could not forbear laughing out ha, ha, ha *."

Enos, Enoch, Methusalah, Lamech, and Noah, after having in vain besought him for that purpose, agreed among themselves to send ambassadors to him; the first was Moses, the second David, the third Isaiah, and the last the church; but these ambassadors having no better success than the patriarchs, they thought it advisable to send some women. Madam Eve presented herself first, to whom God made answer, ' Eve, thou hast sinned, thou art not worthy of my son.' Afterwards they sent madam Sarah, who cried, ' O God, do thou help us;' but God said, ' Thou hast rendered thyself unworthy of it by the incredulity thou shewedst when I informed thee, that thou shouldst be the mother of Isaac.' The third was madam Rebecca, to whom God said, ' Thou hast done a great injury to Esau, in favour of Jacob.' The fourth was madam Judith, to whom God said, ' Thou art an assassin.' The fifth was madam Esther, to whom he said, ' Thou hast been too great a coquette; thou hast spent thy time in dressing thyself to please Ahasuerus. At length they sent the chamber-maid, who was fourteen years of age. She cast down her eyes, and, with a bashful countenance, kneeled and said, ' Let my beloved come into my garden, and eat of the fruit of his apples; and the garden was the virgin's womb.' Now the son having heard these words, said, ' Father, I have loved her from my youth, and will have her for my mother.' At that instant God called Gabriel, and said, ' O Gabriel, go to Nazareth, and present these letters from me to Mary:' and the son added, ' Take mine, and tell her, that I have chosen her to be my mother.' ' Assure her,' said the Holy Ghost, ' that I will dwell within her; let her know that she shall be my temple, and deliver to her these letters.' All Menot's other sermons are nearly in the same taste.

* In those times such ignorance prevailed, that an incumbent having a trial with his parishioners about who should pave the church, the priest, when the judge was ready to give the cause against him, thought proper to quote this passage from the prophet Jeremiah, " Paveant illi, & ego non paveam;" when the judge, not knowing what to answer, ordered that the church should be paved at the expence of the parishioners.

In the simplicity of the ages of ignorance, objects presented themselves under a very different aspect from that in which they appear to enlightened eyes. The tragedies of our Saviour's passion, edifying as they were to our ancestors, appear to us as scandalous. It seems the same with respect to almost all the subtle questions then debated in the divinity-schools. Nothing can appear more indecent than disputes in form, whether God is naked or clothed in the host? whether, if God be omnipotent, he has the power of sinning? whether God could assume the nature of a woman, a devil, an ass, a rock, a gourd, and a thousand other questions still more extravagant * ?

Every thing, even miracles themselves, bore in those times of ignorance, the marks of the bad taste of the age †.

There was a time, when the arts and sciences were considered by the church as earthly things unworthy of a Christian. It is even said on this subject, that an angel whipped St. Jerome for endeavouring to imitate Cicero's style. The abbé Cartaut pretends, that this was for imitating him but badly.

* Utrum Deus potuerit suppositare mulierem, vel diabolum, vel asinum, vel silicem, vel cucurbitam: &, si suppositasset cucurbitam, quemadmodum fuerit concionatura, editura miracula, & quonammodo fuisset fixa cruci. Apolog. p. Herodot. vol. iii. p. 127.

† Whatever may be said in vindication of the ages of ignorance, it can never be proved that they were favourable to religion, though they were to superstition. Therefore nothing can be more ridiculous than the declamations uttered against philosophers, or against the academies in the country. Those who compose them, it is said, cannot enlighten the earth; they would therefore do better to cultivate it. Such men, it may be replied, are not in a condition to labour at that employment. Besides, would it be of any advantage to agriculture, to register them in the list of labourers, while we entertain so many mendicants, soldiers, artists in points of luxury, and domestics: this would be to recover the finances of a state, by saving the ends of candles. I shall even add, that, supposing these country academies make but few discoveries, we may at least consider them as the canals by which the knowledge of the capital is communicated to the provinces. Nothing can be of greater use than enlightening the minds of mankind: " Philosophical knowledge," says the abbé de Fleury, " can never be prejudicial." " It is only by improving human reason,"

Among many of those pretended miracles mentioned in the memoirs of the academy of inscriptions and belles-lettres*, I shall choose one wrought in favour of a monk. " This monk, returning from a house into which he was introduced every night, had a river to pass : but, Satan oversetting the boat, the monk was drowned, as he was beginning the invitatory of the matins to the Virgin Mary. Two devils seized his soul, but were stopped by two angels, who claimed him on account of his being a Christian. ' My Lords,' said the devils to the angels, ' it is true, God died for his friends, and that is no fable; but this man was one of God's enemies: and since we have found him in the filth of sin, we shall go and cast him into the mire of hell, and shall be well rewarded by our provost.' After many altercations, the angels proposed to refer the dispute to the Virgin's tribunal. The devils replied, ' that they would freely take God for judge ; because his judgment was always agree-able to the laws: but, as for the Virgin, said they, we cannot hope for justice from her ; for she would break all the gates of hell rather than leave there for a single day the person who, while living, performed some reverences to her image. God

adds Mr. Hume, " that nations can hope to improve their laws and politics." The mind is like fire, its effects are every where seen: there are few great politicians and great captains in a country, where there are no men distinguished by their skill in literature and the sciences. How can it be imagined, that a people, who know neither the art of writing nor that of reasoning, can form good laws, and free themselves from that yoke of superstition which spread desolation through the ages of ignorance ? Solon, Lycurgus, and that Pythagoras who formed so many legislators, prove how far the progress of reason may contribute to the public happiness. We ought, therefore, to consider these country academies as very useful. I even say, that, if we consider the learned merely as traders, and compare the hundred thousand livres the king distributes among the academies and the men of learning, with the produce of the sale of our books to foreigners, we may assert, that this kind of commerce gained a thousand per cent. to the state.

* " History of the Academy of Inscriptions and Belles Lettres, tome xviii."

contradicts her in nothing. She may say, that the magpie is black, and that troubled waters are clear: he agrees to every thing. We no longer know what we are about: of a duce she will make a tre, of two duces two cinqs; she holds both the dice and the chance. The day when God made her mother was very fatal to us."

People must, doubtless, be but little edified by such a miracle; and the following is equally ridiculous. It is taken from Letters edifying and curious on the visit of the bishop of Halicarnassus; and appears to me so very extravagant, that I cannot resist the desire of placing it here.

To prove the excellence of baptism, the author relates, that " formerly in the kingdom of Armenia was a king who had a great aversion to the Christians; and therefore persecuted those of that religion in a very cruel manner. He well deserved to be punished by the Almighty; but God, who is infinitely good, and who opened the heart of St. Paul to convert him when persecuting the faithful, opened also the heart of this monarch, and made him know his holy religion: for it happened, as the king was holding a council in the palace with the Mandarins, to deliberate on the means of abolishing entirely the Christian religion throughout his dominions, that the king and Mandarins were immediately changed into swine. At the grunting of these hogs, the people flocked thither, without knowing the cause of such an extraordinary change. Among them was a Christian named Gregory, who had been put to the torture the day before; and, running at the noise occasioned by this event, reproached the king for his cruelty to those of his religion. At Gregory's discourse, the swine put a stop to their noise, became silent, and lifted up their snouts to hear him, while Gregory examined them in these terms: ' Are you from this time forward resolved to amend your lives?' At this demand, all the swine bowed their heads, and cried, ' Ouen, ouen, ouen,' as if they would have said *oui*, (or yes). Then Gregory thus resumed his discourse. ' If you are resolved to amend; if you repent of your sins, and consent to be baptized, in order that you may perfectly observe the holy religion; the Lord will look upon you with pity; if not, you will be miserable, both in this world and the next. All the swine bowed their heads, and cried, ' ouen, ouen, ouen,' as if they would have said, ' they desired to do so.' Gregory seeing the swine thus humbled, took holy water, and baptized them all : and there immediately happened a great miracle ; for, as he baptized each hog, he instantly changed into a more beautiful person than he was before."

These miracles, sermons, tragedies, and theological questions, that appear so ridiculous to us, were, and must have been, admired in the ages of ignorance ; because they were suited to the genius of the times, and men always admire ideas analogous to their own. The gross stupidity of most of them would not permit them to form any conception of the holiness and grandeur of religion; for with almost every body religion was, in a manner, nothing more than superstition and idolatry. But, thanks to philosophy, we may now say, that we have more elevated sentiments. Whatever injustice has been done to the sciences, whatever corruptions they are accused of introducing into our manners, it is certain that most of our clergy are now as pure as they were then depraved ; at least, if we give any credit to history and ancient preachers. Maillard and Menot, the most celebrated among them, have always these words in their mouths : Sacerdotes religiosi, concubinarii. " Damned infamous wretches," cries Maillard, " whose names are written in the registers of the devil, thieves and robbers, as St. Bernard says, can you think that the founders of your benefices gave you them to do nothing but to live luxuriously and play with the girls ? And you, gentlemen, the fat abbots, with your benefices, who keep horses, dogs, and wenches, ask St. Stephen if he obtained paradise by leading such a life as this, making good cheer, being always at feasts and banquets, giving wealth to the church, and the crucifix to the ladies of pleasure * ?"

* This Maillard, who, with such vehemence declaimed against the clergy, was not himself exempt from the vices with which he provoked his brethren. He was called the Gomorreen Doctor ; and the following epigram was made on him, which appears tolerably well turned for the time :

Nostre maistre Maillard tout par tout met le nez,
Tantost va chez le roy, tantost va chez la royne ;
Il fait tout, il scait tout, & à rien n'est idoine ;

I shall stop no longer to consider those stupid ages in which all men, the superstitious and the brave, amused themselves with nothing but the tales of the monks and extravagant feats of chivalry. Ignorance and folly always prevail together: before the revival of philosophy, authors, though born in different ages, wrote all in the same strain. What is called taste supposes knowledge: but there is no taste, and consequently no revolutions of taste among the people who continue barbarous; for these are only to be found in enlightened ages. Now these kinds of revolutions are always preceded by some change in the form of government, the manners, laws, and situation, of a people. There is then a secret dependence established between the taste of a nation and its interest.

To illustrate this principle by some applications. If it be asked, why the most memorable tragic paintings of revenge, such as that of Atrides, does not kindle in us the same transports as those with which they filled the Greeks? we shall find that this difference of impression is occasioned by the difference between our religion and polity, and the religion and polity of the Greeks.

The ancients raised temples to revenge: that passion, now placed among the vices, was then reckoned among the virtues. The antient polity favoured this worship. In an age too warlike not to be a little savage, the only means of putting a restraint upon rage, fury, and treachery, was making it dishonourable to forget an injury, and to place the picture of revenge

---

Il est grand orateur, poëte de mieux nés,
Juge si bon qu'au feu mille en a condamnés,
Sophiste aussy aigu que les fesses d'un moine.
Mais il est si meschant, pour n'estre pas chanoine,
Qu'auprès de lui son saincts le diable & les damnés.
Si se fourrer par tout à gloire il le répute,
Pourquoy dedans Poissi n'est il à la dispute?
Il dit qu'à grand regret il en est eloigné;
Car Beze il eut vaincu, tant il est habile homme.
Pourquoi donc n'y est-il? Il est embesoigné,
Après les fondemens pour rebastir Sodome.

by the side of that of an affront: thus they kept up in the hearts of the citizens a respectful and salutary fear, that supplied the defects of the government. The painting of that passion was so very analogous to the ancient prejudices of the people, that it could not fail of being examined with pleasure.

But in the age in which we live, at a time when the police is much improved, and in which we are no longer subject to the same prejudices, it is evident, that, from consulting in the same manner our own interest, we must see with indifference the painting of a passion, which, far from maintaining peace and harmony in society, produces nothing but disorders and useless cruelties. Why do the tragedies, full of those brave and manly sentiments that inspire a love of our country, now make so slight an impression upon us? Because it is very uncommon for people to unite a certain degree of courage and virtue with an extreme submission: thus the Romans became base and vile as soon as they had obtained a master; and, as Homer says, " The dreadful instant that puts the freeman in irons snatches from him half his primeval virtue." Whence I conclude, that the ages of liberty, which produce great men and great passions, are the only times wherein people are really admirers of brave and noble sentiments.

Why was Corneille's manner so much admired, while that great poet was living, and so little relished at present? It is because, being just escaped from those troublesome times, when minds, heated by the fire of sedition, are more daring, fonder of bold sentiments, and more susceptible of ambition; it is because the characters Corneille gives his heroes, and the projects he makes the ambitious form, were consequently more analogous to the spirit of the age, than they are now, at a time when we have few heroes *, few true citizens, and few men inflamed by ambition, since a happy calm has succeeded so many storms, and the volcanos of sedition are extinct.

How can an artist, accustomed to groan under the weight of indigence and contempt; a rich man, and even a great lord

---

* Civil wars are a misfortune, to which we frequently owe great men.

accustomed to cringe to a man in a high post, and to regard him with that sacred respect which the Egyptian feels for his gods, and the negro for his idol, be struck with the verse, where Corneille says,

" Pour être plus qu'un roi, tu te crois quelque chose ?"

That is,

" To be more than a king, thou thinkest thyself something."

Such sentiments must appear to them foolish and gigantic. They cannot admire elevation of mind without frequently blushing at the abject state of their own; therefore, if we except a small number of wits, and men of elevated genius, who still preserve a rational and felt-esteem for Corneille, the other admirers of that great poet esteem him less from their own judgment and taste, than from hearsay, and a favourable prepossession.

Every change in government, or the manners of a people, must necessarily introduce a revolution in taste. From age to age, people are differently struck with the same objects, according to the different passions by which they are animated.

It is with respect to the sentiments of men as with their ideas; if we only conceive in others the ideas analogous to our own, " we can only," says Sallust, " be affected by those passions which strongly affect ourselves *."

To be touched with the painting of some passion, we must have felt it ourselves.

Let us suppose that the shepherd Tircis meets with Cataline, and that they reciprocally make each other the confident of the sentiments of love and ambition, with which they are agitated ; they certainly can only communicate to each other an impression of the passions that animate them, but very different from what they feel themselves. The first cannot conceive that there is any thing so captivating in supreme power ;

---

* At seeing an account of an heroic action, the reader believes nothing that he is not capable of doing himself: he rejects the rest as mere invention.

and the second, that there is such a charm in the tender smile of a woman beloved. Now, to apply the different kinds of tragedy to this principle, I say, that in every country where the inhabitants have no share in the management of public affairs; where the words country and citizen are seldom mentioned, the public can be only pleased by representing on the stage, passions suited to the people; such, for instance, as love. Not that all men are equally sensible of this: it is certain that fierce and bold minds, the ambitious, politicians, misers, and men involved in important affairs, are but slightly touched with the painting of that passion: and this is the very reason why dramatic pieces have not such great success as in republican states, where the hatred of tyrants, the love of liberty and of our country, are the points for engaging the public esteem.

In any other government, the citizens, not being united by a common interest, the diversity of personal interests must necessarily oppose the universality of the applause. In these countries we can only pretend to a greater or lesser success, by painting such passions as are more or less generally interesting to individuals. Now, among the passions of this kind, there is no doubt but that of love, which is in part founded on a necessity of nature, is the most universally felt. Thus we now prefer, in France, Racine to Corneille, who, in another age, or perhaps in a different country, such as England, would probably have the preference.

This proceeds from weakness, that is a necessary consequence of luxury, and a change of manners; which, depriving us of all strength and elevation of mind, makes us already prefer comedies to tragedies, which are now nothing but comedies in an elevated style, where the action is performed in a king's palace.

The happy increase of sovereign authority, which disarming sedition, and degrading the condition of tradesmen, has almost entirely banished them from the comic scene; where we no longer see any but men of a good air and in high life, who really fill the place that was formerly possessed by men of the common rank, and are properly the bourgeois of the age.

We see then, that, at different times, certain kinds of genius made very different impressions on the public; but that these were always proportioned to their interest in approving them. Now, this public interest is sometimes so very different in one age from what it is in the next, as to occasion the sudden creation or annihilation of certain kinds of ideas and works; such are all those of controversy, which are now as unknown as they were, and ought to have been, formerly known and admired.

In fact, at a time when the people, being divided about their creed, were animated by a spirit of intemperate zeal; when those of each sect, ardent to maintain their opinions, would take up either the sword or arguments to declare, prove and cause them to be adopted, by the whole world; works of controversy were, on account of the subjects, too generally interesting not to be universally esteemed; besides, these works were wrote, at least on the part of certain heretics, with all the address and spirit imaginable, to persuade a person of the truth of the tale of an ass's skin; or that of Blue beard, which resemble some heresies *. The controversial writers were obliged to employ, in their writings, all the art, the force, and the resources of logic, that their works might be master-pieces of subtilty, and perhaps, in this particular, the greatest efforts of the human mind. It is therefore certain, both from the importance of the subject, and from the manner of treating it, that the controvertists must have then been considered as the writers most worthy of esteem.

But, in an age when the spirit of fanatacism has almost entirely fled; when both the king and people, instructed by past misfortunes, no longer employ themselves in theological disputes; and when the principles of the true religion are daily more and more confirmed, these writers ought no longer to make the same impression on the minds of the people. Thus a person now reads those writings with the same disgust that he would find in perusing a Peruvian controversy, in which is debated, whether Mancocapac is, or is not, the son of the sun. To confirm what I have just said, by a fact that has fallen

---

* See the History of Heresies, by St. Epiphanius.

within our own observation, let us call to mind the heat with which the dispute was carried on, in relation to the superiority of the antients over the moderns. This fanaticism gave reputation to several indifferent dissertations composed on this subject; and yet the indifference with which it has been since considered, has suffered to be lost in oblivion the dissertations of the celebrated de la Motte, and the learned Abbé Terrasson; dissertations which, notwithstanding their having a just title to be considered as master-pieces and models in this kind of writing, are almost unknown to all but men of learning.

These examples are sufficient to prove, that, to the public interest differently modified, according to the different ages, we ought to attribute the creation and annihilation of certain kinds of ideas and works.

Nothing now remains but to shew how this public interest, in spite of the changes that daily happen in the manners, passions, and tastes of a people, may however secure to certain works the constant esteem of all ages.

For this purpose we must remember, that the manner of writing in most esteem in one age and country, is often the most despised in another age and in another country; and, consequently, that this is not what is strictly called genius. Now, among the sentiments entertained of these pieces, some are fleeting and others durable. We may then reduce to two kinds, all the different species of genius: the one, where a momentary utility is dependent on the changes that happen in commerce, government, the passions, employments, and prejudices of a people, which may be termed, the spirit of the mode *: the other, whose utility is eternal, unalterable, independent of the various manners and governments, confined to the very nature of man, and consequently always invariable.

---

* I understand, by this word, whatever belongs to the nature of man and of things: I consequently comprehend, under the same word, the works that appear to us more durable: such are the false religions which successively take place of each other, and, in relation to the revolutions of ages, may be reckoned among the works of the mode.

This may perhaps be considered as the true genius, or that most desirable.

All kinds of genius being thus reduced to these two, I shall consequently distinguish the works produced by them into two sorts.

The one is designed to have a glorious and rapid success; the other, a success more extensive and durable. A satirical romance, for instance, in which is painted, in a true but severe light, the follies of the great, will certainly have a run among the common people. Nature, who has engraven on all hearts the sensation of primitive equality, has placed an eternal seed of hatred between the great and the little: these last, therefore, seize, with all the pleasure and sagacity possible, the finest strokes of these ridiculous pictures, wherever the great appear unworthy of their superiority. Such works must then have a rapid, though not an extensive and durable success: not extensive, because it is necessarily confined to the country where these follies took their birth; and not durable, because the mode, by introducing new follies, displaces the old ones, and thus soon effaces the remembrance of the follies of the men, and of the authors who have exhibited them; and because, weary of contemplating the same follies, the malignity of the common people makes them search for fresh faults, from new motives of justifying their contempt for the great. Their impatience, in this respect, still hastens the fall of these works, and their fame is frequently shorter than the duration of the ridicule.

Such is the success that necessarily attends a satyrical romance. In regard to a work on morality or metaphysics, it cannot succeed in the same manner; the desire of instruction, which is always more uncommon, and less lively, than that of censure, cannot furnish, in one nation, either so great a number of readers, or of such passionate admirers. Besides, the principles of these sciences, with whatever clearness they are represented, always require from the readers a degree of attention that must necessarily diminish their number very considerably.

But if the merit of this moral or metaphysical work is not so speedily known as those of a satyrical kind, it is more gene-

rally acknowleged; because treatises, such as those of Locke
or Nicole, which treat neither of an Italian, a Frenchman, nor
an Englishman, but of man in general, must necessarily find
readers among all civilized nations, and even continue to do so
in every age. Whatever work derives its merit from the
elegance of the observations made on the nature of man and
things, cannot cease to please at any time.

I have said enough to shew the true cause of the different
kinds of esteem, united to the exertion of different kinds of
genius; if any doubts still remained on this subject, I might,
by making fresh applications of the principles above established,
obtain fresh proofs of their truth.

Would we know, for example, what would be the different
success of two writers, one of whom distinguished himself by
the depth of his thoughts, and the other by the elegance of
his language? In consequence of what I have said, the success of the first will be slower; because many more are judges
of the delicacy, the graces, the pleasing turn of an expression;
and, in fine, of all the beauties of style, than of the beauty and
justness of ideas. A polite writer, like Malherbe, must then have a
success more rapid than extended, and more shining than durable.
There are two reasons for this; the first is, that a work translated
from one language to another, always loses in the translation
the freshness and strength of its colouring; and consequently
passes to strangers, stripped of the charms of style, which,
upon my supposition, is its principal excellence; the second is,
that the language insensibly grows old; the most happy turns
of expression become, at length, more common; and, in short,
the work being thus, in the very country where it was composed, deprived of the beauties that rendered it agreeable, can
at most preserve for the author only the esteem of tradition.

In order to obtain an entire success, it is necessary, that fine
ideas should be dressed in the beauties of language. Without
this happy choice, a work cannot stand the test of time, and
especially of a translation, which may be considered as the
most proper crucible for separating the pure gold from the
tinsel. Thus we ought to attribute to this defect of ideas,
too common to our antient poets, the unjust contempt which
many judicious persons have conceived against poetry.

I shall only add one word to what I have said, namely, that, among the works deserving to be celebrated through all ages and countries, there are some which, being in a peculiar manner more generally interesting to human nature, must have a speedier and more extensive success. To be convinced of this, it is sufficient to recollect, that among men there are few who have not experienced some passion : that most of them are less pleased with the depth of an idea, than with the beauty of a description; that, as experience proves, almost all of them have felt more than they have seen, but have seen more than they have reflected * ; so, the paintings of the passions must be more generally agreeable than those of natural objects; and a poetical description of the same objects must find more admirers than philosophical works.   Even with regard to these last works, men being less desirous of understanding botany, geography, and the fine arts, than of knowing the human heart; the excellent philosophers of this last kind must be more generally known and esteemed than botanists, geographers, and great critics.   Thus, M. de la Motte, (if I may be allowed to mention him as an example) would have been doubtless more generally known and esteemed, had he treated more interesting subjects with the same delicacy, elegance, and judgment, he has shewn in his discourses on the ode, fable, and tragedy.

The public, satisfied with admiring the most finished pieces of celebrated poets, set little value on great critics, whose works are only read, judged, and valued, by persons versed in that art, to whom they are of use.   This is the true cause of the small proportion observed between the reputation and merit of M. de la Motte.

Let us now see what are the works that ought to have a rapid, as well as an extensive and durable success.

The several kinds of success are to be obtained at once, only

---

* This is the reason why, in Greece, Rome, and almost all countries, the poetical age has always foretold and preceded that of philosophy.

in the works where, according to my principles, the authors
have joined a momentary and durable utility; as in certain
poems, romances, theatrical pieces, and moral and political
writings: on which it is proper to observe, that these works,
soon stripped of the beauties that depend on the manners and
prejudices of the times and countries where they are written,
preserve nothing for posterity but the beauties common to all
ages and countries; and, for this reason, Homer must now appear
less agreeable than he did to the Greeks of his time. But this
loss; or, if I may presume to say so, this diminution of merit,
is more or less great, according as the durable beauties which
enter into the composition of a work, and are always unequally
mixed with those of a day, have a greater or less ascendency
over these last. Why is the Learned Women of the celebrated
Moliere already less esteemed than his Miser, his Tartuffe, and
his Misanthrope? People have not calculated the number of
ideas contained in each of these pieces, and consequently they
have not determined the degree of esteem due to them; but
they have found, by experience, that a comedy, such as the
Miser, where the success is founded on the painting of a vice
that ever subsists, and is always prejudicial to mankind, necessarily includes an infinite number of beauties, that flow from
the happy choice of the subject, which renders them durable:
on the contrary, a comedy, such as that of the Learned Women,
whose success was only supported by a fashionable and transient folly, could only sparkle with those momentous beauties
that arise from the subject; and though once, perhaps, more
proper to make a lively impression on the public, could not
make those that are so durable. Hence we seldom see, among
different nations, celebrated pieces pass with success from one
theatre to another.

The conclusion of this chapter is, that the esteem granted to
all works of genius is, in every age, always proportionable to
the interest people have in esteeming them.

CHAP. XX.

OF GENIUS CONSIDERED IN RELATION TO DIFFERENT COUNTRIES.

WHAT I have said on the different ages, I apply to different countries; and prove that the esteem or contempt affixed to the same kind of genius among different people, are always the effect of the different forms of their governments, and consequently, of the diversity of their interests.

Why is eloquence held in such esteem in republics? It is because, by the form of their government, eloquence opens a way to riches and grandeur. Now the fondness and regard all men entertain for wealth and honour must necessarily make them reflect on the proper means of acquiring them. In republics, honour is paid, not only to eloquence, but to all the sciences, which, like politics, civil law, morality, poetry, or philosophy, may serve to form orators.

In despotic countries, on the contrary, they set but little value on the same kind of eloquence; because it does not lead to fortune. In those countries it is scarcely of any use, because men do not give themselves the trouble to persuade when they can command.

Why did the Spartans affect to shew great contempt for that kind of genius proper to carry to perfection works of luxury? It was, because a poor little republic, that could only oppose the virtue and valour of its citizens against the formidable power of Persia, ought to despise all the arts adapted to enervate the brave, which were perhaps with reason deified at Tyre, or at Sidon.

Why have the people of England less esteem for the art of war, than the ancient Romans and Greeks? It is because the English, having now more of the Carthagenian than the Roman, are, by the form of their government, and their natural situation, less in need of great generals than of able merchants; it is because the spirit of trade, which necessarily leads in its

train a taste for luxury and effeminacy, must every day
increase, in their esteem, the value of gold, and industry must
daily diminish their regard for the military art, and even for
courage: a virtue which, among a free people, for a long time
supported the national pride; but nevertheless, growing daily
weaker and weaker, may, perhaps, be the distant cause of the
fall, or subjection, of that nation. If, on the contrary, celebrated writers, as, for example, a Locke, and a Addison, have
been hitherto more honoured in England than in any other
country, it is from its being impossible that a high value
should not be set on merit, in a country where every citizen
has a share in the management of affairs in general, and where
every man of abilities may enlighten the public with respect
to its true interest. For this reason, we so commonly meet in
London with knowing men, who are with much more difficulty found in France: not that the climate of England, as has
been pretended, is more favourable to genius than ours; the
list of our celebrated men, in war, politics, and the arts and
sciences, is perhaps more numerous than theirs. If the English nobility are in general more learned than ours, it is because
they are forced to acquire knowledge to recompence them for
the advantages the form of our government may have over
theirs; they have therefore, in this respect, a very considerable one over ours; an advantage which they will preserve,
till luxury has entirely corrupted the principles of their government, till it has made them insensibly bend their necks to servitude, and has taught them to prefer riches to talents. It is
a merit at London to have learning; but at Paris it is ridiculous.
This is sufficient to justify the answer made by a foreigner to
the Duke of Orleans, regent of France, who examined him
with respect to the character and different genius of the
several nations of Europe. " The only manner of replying
to your royal highness's question," said the foreigner,
" is to repeat the first questions that among the different
nations is most commonly asked on the appearance of a person
among them." " In Spain," added he, " they ask, Is he a
grandee of the first quality? In Germany, Is he admitted into
the chapters? In France, Is he respected at court? In Holland,

How much money is he worth? In England, What sort of a man is he?"

The same general interest which, in republican states, and those of a mixed government, presides in the distribution of esteem, is also in empires subject to despotic power, the sole distributer of that esteem. If in those governments little regard is shewn to genius; and if, at Ispahan and Constantinople, they have more respect for the eunuch, the icoglan, and the pascha, than for men of merit; it is because the people there have no interest in esteeming great men : not that these great men are in those countries useless and displeasing; but none of the individuals of whom the public is composed, have any interest in becoming so, and every person has always little esteem for what he has no ambition to obtain.

Who in those empires can engage a single person to support the fatigues of study, and the meditations necessary to carry his abilities to perfection? Great talents are always suspected in unjust governments; and abilities can neither procure dignities nor riches. Riches and dignities are however the only advantages visible to all eyes, the only ones reputed real blessings, and as such are universally desired. In vain, is it said, that they are insipid to the possessor; they are, if you will, decorations that are sometimes disagreeable in the eyes of the actor; but nevertheless, they always appear admirable in the point of view from whence they are contemplated by the spectator; and therefore people make the greatest efforts to obtain them. Thus illustrious men only increase in countries where honour and riches are purchased by great abilities; and thus despotic states are, from a contrary reason, always barren of great men. Upon which I shall observe, that gold is now of such great value in the eyes of all nations, that, in governments infinitely more wise and learned, the possession of that metal is almost always considered as the first merit. How many rich men are there, who, elated by universal homage, think themselves superior to* men of

---

* Seduced by their own vanity, and the praises of a thousand flatterers, the most moderate among them believe themselves at least

abilities; felicitate themselves in a tone superbly modest, for having preferred the useful to the agreeable; and having, in the want of genius, say they, made a purchase of good sense, which, according to the signification they affix to the word, is the true, the good, and the supreme genius! Such men must always take philosophers for visionary speculatists, their writings for works seriously frivolous, and ignorance for merit.

Riches and honours are too much coveted, for any one to honour talents in the people, where the pretensions to merit are exclusive of the pretensions to fortune. Where is the country in which, to make a fortune, a man of genius is not obliged to lose, in the antichamber of a protector, the time which, to excel in any manner, he ought to employ in close and continual studies? To what flattery, to what meannesses, must he stoop to obtain the favour of the great! If he is born in Turkey, he must expose himself to the disdain of a mufti, or a sultana; in France, to the affrontive goodness of a great lord*, or a placeman, who, despising in him a kind of genius too different from his own, considers him as a man useless to the state, incapable of serious affairs, and, like a pretty child, entirely taken up with ingenious trifles. Besides, being strictly jealous of the reputation of men of merit†, and afraid of their censure, the

---

superior to every one who is not above them in this respect. They do not perceive that it is with men of genius as with those who run a race: "Such a one," say they to each other, "does not run at all." Yet, it is neither the impotent, nor the man of the ordinary capacity, who gains the prize.

If people are silent with respect to the poor abilities of most of the men so vain of their riches, it is because they do not even think of mentioning them. People's silence, with respect to us, is always a bad sign; it proceeds from their being unable to be revenged on us for our superiority. They say little that is bad of those who do not deserve praise.

* They sometimes counterfeit good men; but through their goodness, as through the rents in Diogenes' cloak, we may perceive their vanity.

† "On my entering into the world," said the president de Montesquieu, one day, "I was introduced as a man of genius, and was re-

placeman receives them less from taste than from ostentation, only to shew that he has people of all kinds at his house. Now, how can it be imagined that a man, animated by a passion for glory, which makes him desire the sweets of pleasure, will debar himself so far? Whoever is born to do honour to the age in which he lives, is always on his guard against the great; he enters into connections with none but persons whose genius and character are calculated to make him esteem people of abilities, and to be disgusted in most companies; seeks for, and meets a man of genius, with the same pleasure that two Frenchmen find in meeting with each other in China, where they become friends at first sight.

The character therefore proper to form illustrious men necessarily exposes them to the hatred, or at least the indifference of the great, and of men in place, especially among people like the Orientals, who, being rendered stupid by the form of their government, and their religion, remain in a shameful ignorance, and hold, if I may presume to say so, the middle rank between men and brutes.

After having proved that the want of esteem for merit is, in the East, founded on the small interest people have in esteeming men of genius, the better to shew the power of that interest, let us apply to this principle things that are more familiar to us. Let us examine why the public interest, modified according to the form of our government, gives us, for instance, such a disgust for that kind of dispensations that appear to us insupportable; and we shall find that these dissertations are heavy and tiresome; that the citizens having, by the form of our government, less occasion for instruction than amusement,

---

ceived favourably enough by the men in place; but when, by the success of the Persian Letters, I had perhaps proved that this character was just, and that I had obtained some esteem from the public, that of the placemen grew cold, and I suffered a thousand mortifications. You must imagine," added he, " that, secretly hurt by the reputation of a man who had obtained some applause, they humbled him, out of revenge; and that a man himself ought to merit many praises, to enable him to support patiently the praises of another."

they generally desire only those works that can render them agreeable in company : they must consequently set little value on close reasoning; and must more or less resemble that courtier who, being less tired than perplexed by the reasons a wise man brought in proof of his opinion, cried out, hastily—" Oh, sir! I would not have it proved to me."

Every thing among us yields to laziness. If, in conversation, we only make use of loose and hyperbolical phrases; if exaggeration is become the peculiar eloquence of our age and nation; and if we set no value on the justness and precision of our ideas and expressions, it is because we are no ways interested to esteem them. It is out of respect to this laziness that we consider taste as a gift of nature, an instinct superior to all the rational knowledge, and, in short, as a quick and lively sensation of good and evil; a sensation that dispenses us from all examination, and reduces all the rules of criticism to two single words, delightful and detestable. To the same laziness we also owe some of the advantages we enjoy above other nations. Our little propensity to application, which will soon render us incapable of it, makes us desire a clearness in all works, to supply this incapacity for attention : we are children, who, in our reading, must be supported by the leading-string of order. An author must therefore then take all the pains imaginable to prevent his readers taking any; and should often repeat, after Alexander—" O Athenians ! how much has it cost me to obtain your praises !" Now the necessity of being clear, in order to be read, renders us, in this respect, superior to the English, who give themselves the less trouble about being extremely clear, because their readers pay less regard to it; for their minds being more used to close application, they can the more easily supply this defect. This, in a science like metaphysics, may give us some advantage over our neighbours. If people have always applied to this science the proverb—" There is no wonder without a veil ;" and if its darkness has long caused it to be treated with respect, our laziness now no longer endeavours to pierce through it, its obscurity renders it contemptible : people would have it stripped of the unintelligible language in which it has been hitherto clothed, and separated from the clouds of mystery wherein it was involved. Now this desire, which is solely owing to our laziness, is the only means of rendering metaphysics, that has been hitherto only a science of words, a science of things. But, to satisfy the taste of the public on this point, as the illustrious historiographer of the academy of Berlin remarks, " it is necessary that minds should break the shackles of superstitious respect, know the limits which ought eternally to separate reason and religion, that enquirers, foolishly averse to every work founded on argumentation, may no longer be condemned as a nation of triflers."

What I have said is, I think, sufficient to discover at the same time the cause of our fondness for tales and romances, our superiority in the frivolous, and yet difficult art of talking and saying nothing, and of the preference we give to a sprightly wit, above any other kind of genius; a preference that accustoms us to consider the wit as a diverting creature, and to disgrace him, by confounding him with a harlequin; and a preference, in fine, that renders us the most gallant, the most amiable, and the most frivolous people in Europe.

It necessarily follows, from our manners, that we ought to be so. The path to ambition is, by the form of our government, that against most of the citizens, and nothing remains for them but pleasure. Among the pleasures, that of love is the most lively; in order to enjoy it, we must render ourselves agreeable to the women; as soon as love is felt, that of pleasing ought to kindle in our breasts. Unhappily, it is with lovers as with those winged insects that take the colour of the herb to which they attach themselves; it is only by borrowing the resemblance of the object beloved, that a lover is enabled to please. Now if the women, by education, acquire rather trifling endowments and graces, then strength and justness of ideas, (our minds being modelled by theirs,) must consequently catch the same defects.

There are only two ways of securing ourselves from them. The first is improving the education of women; giving them more elevation of soul, and more extent to their minds.

There is no doubt but we should be enabled to perform great things, if we had a love for our preceptor, and the hand of beauty was to cast into our minds the seeds of wit and virtue. The second means (and this is what I certainly cannot advise), would be to disencumber the women of those remains of modesty which, before it can be sacrificed, gives them a right to require the perpetual worship and adoration of their lovers. The favours of women would then become more common, and appear less precious; and the men becoming more independent and more wise, would lose in their company only the hours consecrated to love, and consequently they might enlarge and strengthen their minds by study and meditation. Among all nations, and in all countries devoted to the idolatry of women, there is a necessity of making them Roman ladies, or sultanas; the middle way between these two is the most dangerous.

What I have said above proves that it is to the diversity of governments, and consequently to the interest of the people, that we must attribute the astonishing variety of their characters, genius, and taste. If we imagine that we sometimes perceive a point to which the general esteem radiates; if, for example, the art of war is among almost all nations, considered as the principal; it is because a great general will be in a manner every where considered as the most useful man, at least, till the conclusion of an universal and unalterable peace: but that peace being once confirmed, people will, without dispute, give the men celebrated in the sciences, laws, literature, and the polite arts, the preference to the greatest generals upon earth: whence I conclude, that the general interest is, in every nation, the only dispenser of its esteem.

It is to this cause, as I am going to prove, that we ought to attribute the unjust or rational, but always reciprocal, contempt, which nations shew for their different manners, customs, and characters.

CHAP. XXI.

OF THE RECIPROCAL CONTEMPT OF NATIONS, PROCEED-ING FROM THEIR VANITY.

It is with nations as with individuals: if every one of us believes himself infallible, places contradiction in the rank of offences, and can neither esteem nor admire any thing in another but what resembles something in himself; so every nation, in like manner, never esteems in others, any ideas that are not analogous to its own, and every contrary opinion is a seed of contempt.

Let us cast our eyes with rapidity over the universe: there are the English, who take us for giddy-headed mortals, while we say that their brains are disordered. There is the Arab, who, persuaded of the infallibility of his Khalif, laughs at the credulity of the Tartar, who believes the Great Lama immortal. In Africa is the negro, who, paying his adorations to a root, the claw of a lobster, or the horn of an animal, sees nothing on the earth but an immense mass of deities, and laughs at the scarcity of gods among us; while the ill-informed musselman accuses us with acknowledging three. Farther still are the inhabitants of the mountain of Bata, who are persuaded that every man who eats a roasted cuckoo before his death is a saint; they consequently make a mock of the Indian. " What can be more ridiculous," say they, " than to bring a cow to the bed of the sick, and to imagine that if the cow whom they draw along by the tail, happens to piss, and some drops of her urine fall upon the dying, this renders him a saint? What more absurd in the bramins, than to require of their new converts to eat no other food for six months than cow's dung* ?"

---

* " Theatre of Idolatry, by Abraham Roger."

The cow, according to Vincent le Blanc, is reputed holy and venerable at Calicut. There is nothing that has in general a greater reputation for sanctity: it seems that the custom of eating cow's dung by way of penance, is very ancient in the East.

The reciprocal contempt of nations is always founded on some difference of manners and customs. From this motive*, the inhabitant of Antioch formerly despised, in the emperor Julian, that simplicity of manners, and that frugality which justly obtained the admiration of the Gauls. The difference of religion, and consequently of opinion, induced at the same time the Christians, more zealous than just, to blacken with the most infamous calumnies, the memory of a prince who, by diminishing the taxes, restoring military discipline, and reviving the expiring virtue of the Romans, so justly deserved to be placed in the rank of the greatest emperors†.

If we cast our eyes on all sides, we see every place thus unjust. Each nation, convinced that she is the sole possessor of wisdom, takes all others for fools, and nearly resembles the inhabitants of the Marian Islands‡, who, being thence persuaded that theirs was the only language in the universe, concluded from thence that all other men knew not how to speak.

If a sage descended from heaven, and in his conduct consulted only the light of reason, he would universally pass for a fool. He would be, as Socrates says, like a physician, whom the pastry-cooks accused before a tribunal composed of children, for having prohibited the eating of pies and tarts; and would certainly be condemned. In vain would this sage support his opinions, by the strongest demonstrations; all the nations would be with respect to him, as the nation of humpbacked people, among whom, as the Indian fabulist say, came a god, beautiful, young, and well-proportioned. This god, they add, entered into the capital, where he was soon surrounded by a multitude of the inhabitants: his figure ap-

---

* One of the inhabitants of the Caribbee Islands, offended at our contempt, cried out—" I know no other savages but the Europeans, who adopt none of our customs."—Of the Origin and Manners of the Caribbees, by La Borde.

† There was engraven on the tomb of Julian, at Tarsus—" Here lies Julian, who lost his life on the banks of the Tigris. He was an excellent emperor, and a valiant warrior."

‡ " Voyages of the Dutch East India Company."

peared extraordinary; their laughter and taunts declared their astonishment; and they were going to carry their affronts still farther, if, to save him from danger, one of the inhabitants, who had doubtless seen other men that were not hump-backed, had not suddenly cried out—" O my friends! what are we going to do? Let us not insult this unhappy piece of deformity : if Heaven has granted to us all the gifts of beauty, if it has adorned our backs with a mountain of flesh, let us be filled with gratitude to the immortals, repair to the temple, and return thanks to the gods." This fable is the history of human vanity. All people admire their own defects, and de-spise the contrary qualities. To succeed in any country, we must carry the hump of the nation into which we travel.

There are in every country but few advocates who plead the cause of the neighbouring nations; few men who acknow-ledge in themselves the ridicule they cast upon strangers, and take example from I do not know what Tartar, who, on this subject, had the address to make the Great Lama himself blush at his injustice.

This Tartar had travelled through the North, visited the country of the Laplanders, and even purchased a wind of their sorcerers*. On his return to his native country, he re-lated his adventures; and the Great Lama resolving to hear him, was ready to burst his sides with laughing at his story. " Of what folly," cried he, " is the human mind capable! What fantastic customs! How credulous are the Laplanders! Are these men?"—" Yes, indeed," replied the Tartar: " I might inform you of something even still more surprising. These Laplanders, with their ridiculous wizards, laugh no less at our credulity than thou dost at theirs."—" Impious!" cried the Great Lama: " darest thou pronounce this blas-phemy, and compare my religion with theirs?"—" Eternal Father!" replied the Tartar, " before the secret imposition

---

* The Laplanders have sorcerers, who sell to mariners pieces of cord with knots tied at certain distances, which are to give them a fa-vourable wind.

of thy hand on my head, had washed me from my sin, I would
have represented that thou oughtest not to have engaged thy
subjects to make a profane use of their reason. If the severe
eye of examination and doubt was spread over all the objects
of human belief, who knows whether thy worship itself would
be sheltered from the raillery of the incredulous? Perhaps
thy holy urine, and thy sacred excrements, which thou dost
distribute in presents to the princes of the earth, would appear
less precious; perhaps they would not find they had still the
same savour *: they would no longer put it powdered into
their ragouts, nor any longer mix it in their sauces. Already,
in China, does impiety deny the nine incarnations of Visthnou.
Thou, whose penetrating view comprehends the past, the present, and the future, hast often repeated it to us: it is to the
talisman of blind belief that thou owest thine immortality, and
thy power on earth: without this entire submission to thy
doctrines, thou wouldest be obliged to quit this abode of darkness, and ascend to heaven, thy native country. Thou knowest
that the Lamas, subject to thy power, are one day to raise
altars to thee in all the countries of the world. Who can assure
thee, that they will execute this project, without the assistance
of human credulity; and that without it, enquiry, which is always impious, will not take the Lamas for Lapland wizards,
who sell winds to the fools that buy them? Excuse then, O
living Fo, the discourse dictated by my regard for thy worship; and may the Tartar learn of thee to respect the ignorance and credulity which heaven, ever impenetrable in its
views, seems to ordain, in order to make the earth submit to
thee.

Few men perceive the ridicule of their own nation, which
they cover from the eye of reason, while under a foreign name
they laugh at their own folly: but there are still fewer nations
capable of improving by such advice. All are so scrupulously
attached to the interest of their own vanity, that in every

---

* They give the Grand Lama the name of Eternal Father. The
princes are very greedy of his excrements. General History of
Voyages, tome vii.

country they give the title of wise only to those who, as Fontenelle says, " Are the fools of the common folly." How fantastic soever a fable is, it is in some nations believed, and whoever doubts of its truth, is treated by that nation as a fool. In the kingdom of Juida, where they adore the serpent, what man dare deny the tale which the Marabouts tell of a hog, which, say they, insulted the divinity of the serpent *, and eat him up. " An holy Marabout," they add, " perceived it, and carried his complaints to the king. In an instant, sentence of death was passed upon all the swine: the execution followed, and the whole race was going to be extirpated, when the people represented to his majesty, that it was not just to punish so many innocent swine for one guilty hog. These remonstrances suspended the prince's wrath : they appeased the grand Marabout, the massacre ceased, and the hogs were ordered to behave with more respect to the deity, for the future. " Thus," cry the Marabouts, " the serpent, to be revenged on the impious, kindled the wrath of kings, that the whole universe might acknowledge his divinity, his temple, and his high priest, at the order of the Marabout appointed to serve him, and of the virgins consecrated to his worship. If, retired at the bottom of his sanctuary, the serpent-god, invisible to the sight even of the king himself, receives not his questions, and makes no answer to his requests, but by the mouth of the priest; it is not for mortals to pry into these mysteries with a profane eye: their duty is to believe, to prostrate themselves, and to adore."

In Asia, on the contrary, when the Persians †, stained with the blood of the serpents, sacrificed to the God of goodness, ran to the temple of the Magi, to boast of this act of piety, can it be thought, that if a man had stopped them in order to prove the ridiculousness of their opinion, he would have been well received ? The more foolish an opinion is, the more it is praiseworthy, and the more dangerous it is to prove its folly.

Thus, Fontenelle was accustomed to say, that, " If he held

* Voyages to Guinea and Cayen, by Father Labat.
† Beausobre's History of Manicheism.

every truth in his hand, he would take great care not to open
it to shew them to men." In fact, if the discovery of one truth
alone, even in Europe, threw Galileo into the prisons of the
inquisition, to what punishment would he be condemned who
revealed them all *?

Among the rational part of my readers, who at this instant
laugh at the folly of the human mind, and are filled with indignation at the treatment of Galileo, perhaps there is not one,
who, in the age of that philosopher, would not have solicited
for his death. They would then have been of different sentiments, and in what cruelties are we involved when barbarity
and fanaticism are united to our opinions? How has this union
deluged the earth with the most dreadful evils! and yet it is
an union that it must be equally just, useful, and easy to
dissolve.

In order to learn to doubt of our opinions, it is sufficient
that we examine the powers of our minds, consider the picture of human follies, and recollect that six hundred years after
the establishment of universities, there arose an extraordinary
man †, who was persecuted by the age in which he lived, and
at length placed in the rank of demi-gods, for having taught
men to admit nothing for truth of which they had not clear
ideas: few men were capable of knowing the extent of this
principle, for among the greatest part of mankind principles
include no consequences.

However great the vanity of mankind may be, it is certain
that, if they frequently call to mind such facts: if, like Fontenelle, they often say to themselves, " Nobody escapes from
error, and am I alone infallible? May I not be deceived in
those very things which I maintain with the greatest fanaticism?" If men had this idea habitually present to their minds,

---

* " To think," says Aristippus, " is to draw upon ourselves the irreconcileable hatred of the ignorant, the weak, the superstitious, and
the corrupt, who all loudly declare themselves against those who
would take hold of truth, and in every thing seize whatever is essentially necessary to be known.

† Descartes.

they would be more on their guard against vanity, more attentive to the objections of their adversaries, and better prepared to perceive the force of truth : they would be more mild; more inclined to toleration, and doubtless would have a less high opinion of their own wisdom. Socrates frequently repeated, " All that I know is, that I know nothing." In our age we know every thing except what Socrates knew. Men would not be so often surprised into error, were it not for their ignorance; and their folly is in general the more incurable, from their believing themselves wise.

This folly, which is common to all nations, and is in part produced by their vanity, makes them not only despise the manners and customs that are different from their own, but makes them also regard, as a gift of nature, that superiority which some of them have over others: a superiority that is solely owing to the political constitution of their nation.

CHAP. XXII.

WHY NATIONS CONSIDER AS GIFTS OF NATURE THE QUALITIES SOLELY OWING TO THE FORM OF THEIR GOVERNMENT.

This error is likewise founded on vanity, and what nation can triumph in such an error ?   Let us suppose, for example, that a Frenchman, accustomed to speak freely, and here and there to converse with some good citizens, leaves Paris, and lands at Constantinople : what idea would he form of a country subject to despotic power, on his considering the disgrace to which he saw human nature reduced ?   On his every where perceiving the print of slavery ?   On his seeing tyranny infect, with her pestilential breath, the buds of every talent and every virtue ; spreading stupidity, servile fear, and depopulation, from Caucasus to Egypt ?   And, in short, on his being informed, that the tranquil Sultan, who is shut up in his seraglio, while the Persian defeats his troops, and ravages his provinces, unmoved by the public calamities, drinks his sherbet, caresses his women, causes his bashaws to be strangled, and is wearied with his indolence? Struck with the cowardice and slavery of these people, and at once animated by the sensations of pride and indignation, what Frenchman would not think himself of a superior nature to a Turk? Are there many who are sensible, that contempt for a whole nation is always unjust? That the superiority of one country over another depends on the greater or lesser happiness of their forms of government? And that, in fine, a Turk might make him the same answer that was made by a Persian to a Spartan soldier, who reproached him with the cowardice of his country, " Why do you insult me?" said he. This is the case of every nation that acknowledges an absolute master. A king is the universal soul of a despotic state; and it is his courage or weakness that causes this empire to revive or to languish. If we were conquerors under Cyrus, and are now vanquished under Xerxes, it is because Cyrus was the founder of the throne on which Xerxes was seated by his birth; it is because Cyrus when born had his equals; because Xerxes was always surrounded by slaves; and thou knowest that the vilest of these inhabit the palaces of kings. It is then the dregs of the nation thou seest invested with the first employments; it is the foam of the sea which rises on its surface. Acknowledge the injustice of thy contempt; but if thou art still in doubt, give us the laws of Sparta, and take Xerxes for thy master: thou wilt then be the slave, and I the hero.

Let us now call to mind the time when the cry of war had awakened all the nations of Europe, and its thunder was heard from the north to the south of France *. Suppose that at this time a republican, animated by the spirit of liberty, arrived at Paris, and entered into the best company, how would he be surprised at seeing every one there treat public affairs with indifference, and warmly employ themselves about nothing but the fashion, a novel, or a little dog.

Struck with the difference that in this respect would be visible between our nation and his own, there is scarcely an English-

---

* In the last war, when the enemy entered Provence.

man who would not believe himself to be a Being of a superior nature; who would not take the French for a giddy-brained trifling people, and France for the kingdom of baubles: not but that he might easily perceive, that his fellow-countrymen owe their spirit of patriotism, and the elevation unknown to all but free countries, not merely to the form of their government, but to the situation of England.

In fact, to be sensible that this liberty, of which the English are so proud, and that really includes so many virtues, is less the reward of their courage than the gift of fortune, let us consider the infinite number of factions that have hitherto divided England; and we shall be convinced, that if the sea, by embracing that empire, had not rendered it inaccessible to the neighbouring nations, they would, by taking advantage of the divisions in England, either have subdued them, or at least have furnished their kings with the means of bringing them into subjection; and that, therefore, their liberty is not the fruit of their wisdom. If, as they pretend, it only depends on a firmness and prudence peculiar to their nation; after the frightful crime committed on the person of Charles I. would they not at least have drawn all the advantages they might have reaped from it? Would they have suffered that, by public services and processions, a prince should be placed in the rank of martyrs, whom it was their interest, say some of them, to have considered as a victim sacrificed to the public welfare, and whose punishment was necessary, to set an example to the world, and ought for ever to terrify any prince who should endeavour to make the people submit to an arbitrary and tyrannical authority? All the sensible part of England must then be convinced, that its government, in its present form, could not subsist on the continent without great improvements, and that the only subject of their pride is reduced to the happiness of being born in an island rather than on the continent.

A particular person may any where make a confession of this kind; but never the public. Never does a nation submit its vanity to the shackles of reason: more equity in its judgments would suppose a suspension of vanity, too seldom to be found in a single person, ever to appear in a whole nation.

z

Each country therefore always places among the gifts of nature, the virtues derived from the form of its government. Its vanity is influenced by the counsels of interest; and who can resist the counsel of interest?

The general conclusion of what I have said on the mind, considered in relation to various countries, is, that interest is the only dispenser of the esteem or contempt which nations feel for their different manners, customs, and turns of mind.

The only objection that can be brought against the above conclusion is this: " If interest," say they, " be the only dispenser of the esteem granted to different kinds of genius and learning, why is morality, though of use to all nations, no more honoured? Why are the names of Descartes and Newton more celebrated than those of Nicole, La Bruyere, and all the other moralists, who, perhaps, in their works gave as great a proof of genius? It is, I reply, because great natural philosophers have, by their discoveries, been sometimes of use to the whole human race, while most moralists have hitherto been of no service to mankind. To what purpose is it to repeat incessantly, that it is noble to die for one's country? An apothegm never makes a hero. To merit esteem, moralists ought to search for the proper means of forming brave and virtuous men ; and thus employ that time and those abilities they have lost, in composing maxims of virtue. When Omar wrote to the Syrians, " I send against you men as greedy of death as ye are of pleasures," the Saracens, deceived by the delusions of ambition and credulity, considered heaven as the reward of valour and victory, and hell as the punishment of cowardice and a defeat. They were then animated with the most violent fanaticism ; and these passions, not maxims of morality, form courageous men. The moralists ought to be sensible of this ; and to know, that, like a statuary, who, from the trunk of a tree, can make a God or a bench, the legislator forms, at his pleasure, heroes, great geniuses, and virtuous men. I call for witness the Moscovites, transformed into men by Peter the Great.

In vain do the people, foolishly enamoured with their own government, seek for the cause of their misfortunes in the laws not being put in execution. "The non-performance of the laws," says the sultan Mahmouth, " is always a proof of the ignorance of the legislator. Reward, punishment, glory, and infamy, subject to his will, are four divinities, with which he can always promote the public welfare, and create illustrious men of all kinds."

The whole study of the moralists consists in determining the use that ought to be made of these rewards and punishments, and the assistance that may be drawn from them, in order to connect the personal with the general interest. This union is the master-piece which moralists ought to propose to themselves. If citizens could not procure their own private happiness without promoting that of the public, there would then be none vicious but fools. All men would be under the necessity of being virtuous, and the felicity of nations would be of benefit to morality: now, who doubts but, on that supposition, this science would be greatly honoured ; and that the excellent writers of this kind would, at least by an equitable and grateful posterity, be placed in the same rank with Solon, Lycurgus, and Confucius ?

But, it is replied, that the imperfection of morality, and the slowness of its progress, can be only an effect of the small proportion to be found between the esteem granted to moralists, and the efforts of mind necessary to carry that science to perfection: therefore the general interest, they add, is not considered in the distribution of the public esteem ?

In reply to this objection, we must search for the insurmountable obstacles that have hitherto opposed the advancement of morality, among the causes of that indifference with which people have considered a science, the improvement whereof must always be accompanied with that of the legislation, and consequently it is for the interest of every nation to bring it to perfection.

CHAP. XXIII.

OF THE CAUSES THAT HAVE HITHERTO RETARDED THE PROGRESS OF MORALITY.

IF poetry, geometry, astronomy, and, in general, all the sciences, advance more or less rapidly towards perfection, while morality seems scarcely to have left its cradle, it is because men, being forced to unite in society, and to give themselves laws, were obliged to form a system of morality before they had learnt, from observation, its true principles. The system being formed, no farther notice was taken of it ; thus we have, in a manner, the morals of the world in its infancy, and how shall it be brought to perfection ?

The progress of a science does not solely depend on its being of use to the public : every citizen of which a nation is composed ought to reap some advantage from its improvement. Now in the revolutions that have taken place among all the nations of the earth, the public interest, which is that of the majority, among whom the principles of sound morality ought to find its support, not being always agreeable to the interest of those most in power, the latter being indifferent with respect to the progress of all sciences, must effectually oppose that of morality.

The ambitious man, who is raised above his fellow-citizens; the tyrant who tramples them under his feet; and the fanatic, who keeps them prostrate; all these several scourges of the human race, all these different kinds of flagitious men, forced by their private interest to establish laws contrary to the general good, have been very sensible, that their power had no other foundation than the ignorance and weakness of mankind : they have therefore imposed silence on whosoever, by discovering to the people the true principles of morality, would have opened their eyes with respect to their misfortunes and their rights, and have armed them against injustice.

But, it is replied, if in the first ages of the world, when despotic princes held the nations in subjection, and ruled them with a rod of iron, it was then their interest to conceal from the people the true principles of morality; principles, which by animating them against tyrants, would have made revenge the duty of each citizen; yet now, when the sceptre is not purchased with guilt, but placed by unanimous consent in the hand of a prince, and supported by the love of the people; when the glory and happiness of a nation, reflecting on the sovereign, adds to his grandeur and felicity; what enemies of the human race are there still to oppose the progress of morality?

This is no longer done by kings, but by two other sorts of men in power. The first are the fanatics, whom I shall not confound with the men truly pious. These last support the maxims of religion, and the others are their destroyers: the one are the friends of humanity*; the other, who are outwardly mild but within barbarous, have the voice of Jacob and the hands of Esau: they are indifferent with respect to worthy actions; they judge virtuous not what is done, but what is believed; and the credulity of men is, according to them, the only standard of their probity†. They mortally hate, said queen Christina, all who are not their dupes; and to this they are led by their interest. Being ambitious, hypocritical, and artful, they imagine that, to enslave the people they ought to put out their eyes: thus, these impious wretches are incessantly setting up the cry of impiety against every man born to enlighten the nations: every new truth is suspected by them, and they resemble infants that are terrified at every thing in the dark.

---

* They freely say to the persecutors what the Scythians said to Alexander: "Thou art not then a God, since thou dost evil to men." As the Christians exclaimed against Saturn or the Moloch of the Carthaginians, to whom men were offered in sacrifice, that such a religion was a proof of its falsehood, how often have our fanatical priests given room to the heretics to retort this argument against them? How many priests of Moloch are there among us?

† Thus they have all the reluctance in the world against acknowledging the probity of a heretic.

The second species of men in power who oppose the progress of morality are the half-politicians. Among these are some naturally disposed to truth, who are enemies to newly discovered truths only from their indolence, and their being unwilling to apply the attention necessary to examine them. There are others animated by dangerous motives, and these are most to be feared. These are the men whose minds are without abilities, and whose souls are destitute of virtues; they want not the courage of being greatly wicked ; and, incapable of new and elevated views, they believe that their importance demands a weak or dissembled respect for all the received opinions and errors countenanced by them. Furious against every man who would stagger the empire, they arm* against him even those passions and prejudices which they despise ; and, without ceasing, terrify weak minds with the cry of novelty.

----

* Interest is always the concealed motive of persecution. There is no doubt but a want of toleration is an evil contrary to Christianity and sound politics: but it would be none to repent of the revocation of the edict of Nantes. These disputes, say they, are dangerous. They are so when authority takes a part in them: then the want of toleration in one party sometimes forces the other to take up arms. When the magistrates do not interfere, the divines, after abusing each other, come to an accomodation. This fact is proved by the peace enjoyed in the countries where toleration is allowed. But this toleration, they reply, though it be agreeable to certain governments, would be perhaps fatal to ours. Are not the Turks, whose religion is a religion of blood, and whose government is tyranny, less averse to toleration than we? We see churches at Constantinople, but there are no mosques at Paris: they do not put the Greeks to the torture on account of their creed, and yet their toleration does not kindle the flames of war.

To consider it as a Christian, it is a crime. The gospel, the apostles, and fathers, almost constantly preach of mildness and toleration. St. Paul and St. Chrysostom say, that a bishop ought to gain men by persuasion, not by constraint. Bishops, they add, should only have authority over those who submit to their power; but instead of this they are kings, who reign over those who could not submit to their dominion.

As if all truths banish virtue from the earth, and every thing
relating to them was of such advantage to vice, that we cannot

---

In the East, the council was condemned that consented to have
Bogomilus burnt.

What an example of moderation did St. Basil give in the fourth
century, when the question relating to the divinity of the Holy Ghost
was debated!—a question that occasioned much disturbance. That
saint, says St. Gregory de Nazianzen, though firmly persuaded of the
truth of the doctrine of the divinity of the Holy Spirit, consented
that the title of God should not be given to the third person in the
Trinity.

Though this wise condescension was, according to M. de Tillemont,
condemned by some angry zealots, and though St. Basil was accused
of betraying the truth by his silence, that very condescension was
approved by the most celebrated and most pious men of that time,
and, among others, by the great St. Athanasius, who cannot be suspected of wanting firmness.

This fact is related in M. de Tillemont's Life of St. Basil, art. 63,
64, and 65. That author adds, that the Œcumenic council of Constantinople approved St. Basil's conduct by imitating it.

St. Augustin says, that we ought neither to condemn nor punish
him who has not the same idea of God as we have: at least, says he,
if it is not through hatred to God, which is impossible. St. Athanasius, in his epistles ad Solitarios, lib. I. page 855, says, that the persecutions of the Arians are a proof that they have neither piety nor
the fear of God. The property of piety, adds he, is to persuade, and
not to constrain; we ought to take example from our Saviour, who
left every one the liberty of following him. He before says, page 830,
that the devil, the father of lies, has need of hatchets and axes to
cause his opinions to be embraced; but our Saviour is mildness itself.
He knocks; if we open, he enters; if we refuse him, he retires. It is
not with swords, javelins, prisons, soldiers, and arms in our hands,
that we teach the truth, but by the voice of persuasion.

People have really recourse to force only for want of arguments.
If a man denies that the three angles of a triangle are equal two right
angles, he is laughed at, but not persecuted; but fire and gibbets are
often used as arguments by divines, who have in this respect given
heretics and unbelievers the advantage over them. Jesus Christ did
no violence to any man. He only said, Follow thou me: but interest
has not always permitted his ministers to imitate his moderation.

he virtuous without being void of understanding; as if morality shewed the necessity of it, and as if the study of that
science consequently became fatal to the universe; they are
resolved, that the people shall be kept as prostrate before the
received prejudices as before the sacred crocodile of Memphis.
Does any person make a discovery in morality? It is to us
alone say they, that it ought to be revealed: we alone, after
the example of those who were initiated into the sacred mysteries of Egypt, ought to be the depositories of them: the rest
of the human race should be involved in the darkness of prejudice, for the natural state of man is blindness.

Like those physicians, who, jealous of the discovery of
emetics, abused the credulity of some prelates, by engaging
them to excommunicate a remedy whose assistance was so speedy
and so salutary, they impose upon the credulity of honest men,
who are, however, so stupid, that, under a government less
wise, they would drag to punishment a man with the integrity
and understanding of a Socrates.

Such are the means employed by these two kinds of men, to
impose silence on those enlightened by knowledge. In vain
would they endeavour to resist them by leaning on the favour
of the public. When a citizen is animated by a love of truth
and the general welfare, I am sensible that he will always diffuse through his work the perfume of truth, which will render
it agreeable to the public, who will become his protector.
But, as, when under the buckler of gratitude and the public
esteem, they are not secure from the persecution of those fanatics, there are very few among the wise so virtuous as to dare
to brave their fury.

These are the insurmountable obstacles that have hitherto
opposed the progress of morality, and the reasons why that
science is almost always useless, and, in consequence of my
principles, still deserves little esteem.

But may we not make the nations sensible of the advantages
they would obtain from an excellent system of morality? and
might we not hasten the progress of that science, by conferring
greater honours on those who improve it? Considering the
importance of this subject, I shall run the hazard of a digres-
sion, in order to treat it more fully.

CHAP. XXIV.

OF THE MEANS OF PERFECTING MORALITY.

It would be sufficient for this purpose to remove the obstacles placed against its progress by the two kinds of men I have mentioned. The only means of succeeding in this, is to pull off their masks, and to shew that the protectors of ignorance are the most cruel enemies of human beings; to shew the nations, that men are in general more stupid than wicked; that, in curing them of their errors, we should cure them of most of their vices; and that opposing their cure is committing the crime of treason against human nature.

Every man, who considers the picture of public miseries exhibited in history, soon perceives that ignorance, which is still more barbarous than self-love, has caused most of the calamities that have overflowed the earth. Struck with this truth, we are ready to cry out, Happy the nation where the citizens are permitted to perpetrate only the crimes that flow from self-love! How are they multiplied by ignorance, and what blood has been spilt on its altars*! However, man is made to be vir-

---

* A king of Mexico, on the consecration of a temple, caused six thousand four hundred and eight men to be sacrificed in four days.— Gemelli Carreri, vol. vi. page 56.

In India, the Brachmans of the school of Niagam, taking advantage of the favour of the princes, massacred the Baudhists in several kingdoms. These Baudhists are atheists, and the others deists. Balta was the prince who caused most blood to be spilt. To purify himself from this crime, he afterwards burnt himself with great solemnity on the coast of Oricha. It is observable, that those were deists who caused such a torrent of human blood to be spilt. See the Letters of Father Pons, the Jesuit.

The priests of Meroe in Ethiopia dispatched, whenever they pleased, a courier to the king, to order him to die. See Diodorus.

Whoever kills the king of Sumatra is elected king in his room. By such an assassination, say the people, heaven declares its will. Cardin observes that he heard a preacher, who was declaiming against the So-

tuous; and, in fact, if force essentially reside in the greater number, and justice consist in the practice of actions useful to the greater number, it is evident that justice is in its own nature always armed with a power sufficient to suppress vice, and place men under the necessity of being virtuous.

If audacious and powerful wickedness so often puts justice and virtue in chains, and oppresses the nations, this is only done by the assistance of ignorance, which conceals from every nation its true interest, hinders the action and union of its strength, and by that means shields the guilty from the sword of justice.

To what contempt ought he to be condemned, who would hold the people in the darkness of ignorance? This truth has not hitherto been insisted upon with sufficient force: no, all the altars of error must one day be overthrown. I know with what precaution we ought to advance a new opinion. I know, that in destroying prejudices, we ought to treat them with respect; and that, before we attack an error generally received, we ought to send, like the doves from the ark, some truths on the discovery, to see if the deluge of prejudices does not yet cover the face of the earth; if error begins to subside, and if there can be perceived here and there some isles where virtue and truth may find rest for their feet, and communicate themselves to mankind.

But so many precautions are only to be taken with those prejudices that are not very dangerous. What respect do we

---

phis, say, that they were atheists, and deserved to be burnt; that he was astonished they should be suffered to live; and that the killing a Sophi was an action more pleasing to God than the preservation of the lives of ten worthy men. How often has the same manner of reasoning been used among us!

It was doubtless from the view of so much blood spilt by fanaticism, that the abbé Longuerue, who is profoundly versed in history, says, that, if we were to put into two scales the good and the evil done by religion, the evil will preponderate, vol. i. page 11.

" Take not a house," says a Persian proverb, alluding to this subject, " in a quarter where the lower people are ignorant and devout."

owe to the man who, jealous of dominion, would besot the people, in order to tyrannize over them? We must with a bold hand break the talisman of imbecility, to which is attached the power of these malevolent genii; to discover to nations the true principles of morality; to teach them that, being insensibly drawn towards happiness, either apparent or real, grief and pleasure are the only movers of the moral universe; and that the sensation of self love is the only basis on which we can place the foundations of an useful morality.

How can they flatter themselves with concealing from men the knowledge of this principle? In order to succeed in it they must forbid their penetrating into their own hearts, examining their conduct, opening those historical works where they perceive men, in all ages and in all countries, solely attentive to the voice of pleasure, sacrifice human beings like themselves, I will not say to great and important interests, but to their sensuality and amusement. I take to witness those fish-ponds where the barbarous gluttony of the Romans drowned the slaves, and gave them as food to their fishes, in order to render them more delicate eating; that isle of Tiber, whither the cruelty of the masters transported their old, infirm, and sick slaves, and left them to perish by the torments of hunger: I also call to witness the ruins of those vast and superb amphitheatres, where the most polite people in the universe sacrificed thousands of gladiators to the mere pleasure that arose from beholding their combats; where the women ran in crowds; where the tender sex, nourished in luxury, softness, and pleasure,—that sex made for the ornament and delight of the world, who seemed as if made to breathe only voluptuous endearments,—carried their barbarity so far as to desire the wounded gladiators to fall, when dying, in an agreeable attitude. These facts, and a thousand others of the like kind, are too well attested for them to flatter themselves with concealing their true cause from men. Every one knows that he is not of a different nature from the Romans; that the difference of his education produces the difference of his sentiments, and from thence he is shocked at the bare recital of a spectacle which custom would doubtless have rendered agree-able, had he been born on the banks of the Tiber. In vain do some men, the dupes of their laziness in examining, and of their vanity in thinking too well of, themselves, imagine, that they owe the sentiments of humanity, with which they would be affected at such a spectacle, to the particular excel-lence of their nature : the sensible man agrees, that nature, as Pascal says*, and as experience proves, is nothing but our first habit. It is therefore absurd to conceal from men the principle by which they are actuated.

But supposing they could succeed in this, what advantage would mankind receive from it? They would certainly only veil from the eyes of men of gross ideas the sensation of self-love. They would not hinder their being actuated by this sensation, nor would they change its effects: men would not be any other than they are, therefore this ignorance would be of no use to them. I proceed still farther, and say, it would be prejudicial. It is, in fact, to a consciousness of our being actuated by self-love, that society owes most of the advantages it enjoys: this consciousness, imperfect as it still is, has in-formed mankind of the necessity of arming the hand of ma-gistrates with power, and has made the legislator obtain a confused idea of the necessity of founding the principles of probity on the basis of personal interest. Indeed, upon what other basis could they rest it? Could it be placed on the prin-ciples of those false religions, which, notwithstanding their errors, it is said, might be rendered subservient to the tempo-ral happiness of mankind†? But most of these are too absurd to serve as supports to virtue; neither could it be rested on the principles of the true religion. Indeed the morals of this re-ligion are excellent; its maxims elevate the soul, fill it with an inward joy, and give it a foretaste of the transports of hea-

---

* Sextus Empiricus said before him, that our natural principles are perhaps nothing more than our customary principles.

† Cicero did not think so; for, notwithstanding his being a place-man, as he really was, he thought it his duty to shew the people the absurdity of the Pagan religion.

ven: but these principles would only be suited to a small number of Christians dispersed over the earth; and a philosopher, who, in his writings, is always supposed to be speaking to the universe, ought to give virtue a foundation on which all nations may equally build, and consequently erect it on the basis of personal interest. He should the more closely adhere to this principle, as the motions of temporal interest, managed with address by a skilful legislator, are alone sufficient to form virtuous men. The example of the Turks, who admit into their religion the doctrine of necessity, a principle destructive to all religion, and may consequently be considered as Deists; the example of the Chinese materalists*; that of the Sadducees, who denied the immortality of the soul, and yet received from the Jews the title of the Just, by way of excellence; in fine, the example of the Gymnosophists, who, notwithstanding their being constantly accused of Atheism, were always respected for their wisdom and gravity, discharged the duties of society with the utmost exactness: all these examples, and a thousand others of the like kind, prove, that the hope or fear of temporal rewards and punishments are as efficacious and as proper to form virtuous men as those pleasures and pains that are eternal, which, being considered in the perspective of futurity, commonly make too weak an impression to engage men to sacrifice to them their present criminal pleasures.

Why should they not give the preference to motives of temporal interest? They inspire none of those pious and holy cruelties, condemned by our religion†, that law of love and

---

* Father le Compte and most of the Jesuits agree, that all the men of letters are Atheists. The celebrated abbé Longuerue is of the same opinion.

† When Bayle said, that religion, which in the first ages was humble, patient, and beneficent, is since become ambitious and sanguinary; since it puts to the sword whoever resists it; since it calls for tormentors, invents new kinds of torture, sends bulls to excite the people to revolt, forms conspiracies, and, in fine, orders the murder of princes, he mistook the work of man for that of religion; and

humanity; but which its ministers have so often used;—cruelties that will for ever be the disgrace of former ages, and the horror and astonishment of the future.

With what surprise ought the virtuous citizen and the Christian, filled with that spirit of charity so often recommended in the Gospel, to be seized, when he casts his eye upon the past ages of the world! He there sees different religions invoke all the rage of fanaticism, and glut themselves with human blood*.

There the different sects of Christians, exasperated against each other, tear in pieces the empire of Constantinople: farther still arises in Arabia a new religion, which commands the Saracens to lay waste the earth with fire and sword. The irruption of these barbarians is succeeded by a war against the Infidels. Under the standard of the cross entire nations desert

---

Christians have too often been these men. When they were only a small number, they pleaded for toleration; but their number and credit being increased, they preached against it. Bellarmine said, on this subject, that, if the Christians did not dethrone Nero and Dioclesian, it was not because they had not a right to do it, but because they were not strong enough; and it must be confessed, that they made use of their strength as soon as they were able. The emperors destroyed Paganism with arms in their hand; and thus, by fighting against heresies, preached the Gospel to the Frieslanders, the Saxons, and throughout all the north.

All these facts prove, that the principles of our holy religion have been but too often abused.

* In the infancy of the world, the first use man made of his reason was to persuade himself that the Gods were cruel. They thought of rendering the Gods propitious by the effusion of human blood; and, in the quivering entrails of the vanquished, they strove to read the decrees of fate. After the German had with the most horrible imprecations devoted his enemies to death, his heart was no longer open to pity; commiseration appeared to him as sacrilege.

To calm the resentment of the Nereides, a polite people fastened Andromeda to a rock; to appease Diana, and open a way to the city of Troy, Agamemnon himself dragged Iphigenia to the altar, Calchas struck the blow, and believed that he did honour to the Gods.

Europe, and spread like an inundation over Asia; they commit on the road the most base and scandalous robberies, and are buried in the sands of Arabia and Egypt. At length fanaticism arms afresh the hand of Christian princes, and orders the Catholics to massacre the heretics: then again appears on the earth the tortures invented by the Phalarises, the Busirises, and the Neros; it prepares, it kindles, in Spain the flaming pile of the inquisition; while the pious Spaniards leave their ports, and traverse the seas, to plant the cross and desolation in America*. If we cast our eyes to the north, the south, the east, and the west, we every where see the sacred knife of religion held up to the breasts of women, children, and old men; the earth smoking with the blood of victims sacrificed to the false Gods or to the Supreme Being; every place offers nothing to the sight but the vast, the horrible, carnage caused by a want of toleration. What virtuous man, and what Christian, if his tender mind be filled with the divine love that exhales from the maxims of the Gospel, if he be capable of feeling the complaints of the miserable, and if he have sometimes dried up their tears, would not at this sight be touched with compassion for human nature†, and endeavour to

---

* Thus, in an epistle supposed to be addressed to Charles V. an American is represented speaking thus:

———— Ce n'est point nous qui sommes les barbares:
Ce sont, seigneur, ce sont vos Cortez, vos Pizarres,
Qui, pour nous mettre au fait d'un systeme nouveau,
Assemblent, contre nous, le prêtre & le bourreau.

     That is,
It is not we who are barbarians:
These, my lord, are your Cortezes, your Pizarros,
Who, to oblige us to receive a new religion,
Assemble against us priests and executioners.

† On account of this persecution, Themistius the senator, in a letter addressed to the emperor Valens, says—" Is it a crime to think differently from thee? If the Christians are divided among themselves, the philosophers are no less so. Truth has an infinite number

found probity, not on principles so venerable as those of religion, but on those that cannot be so easily abused, such as the
motives of personal interest?

These motives, without contradicting the principles of our
religion, would be sufficient to lay men under a necessity of
being virtuous. The Pagan religion, by peopling Olympus
with villains, was doubtless less adapted than ours to form just
men. Who, however, can doubt that the first Romans were
more virtuous than we? who can deny that prisons have disarmed more robbers than religion? that the Italian, more devout than the French, has not with his chaplet of beads in his
hand used the stiletto and poison? and that, at the time when
devotion was warmer, and policy more imperfect, they did
not commit infinitely more crimes* than in the ages when devotion grew cool, and policy was carried to perfection?

It is then only by good laws† that we can form virtuous men.

---

of faces, by which she may be seen. God has engraven in all hearts
a respect for his attributes; but every one has the liberty of shewing
that respect in the manner he thinks most agreeable to the Deity;
and no one here has a right to prevent him."

St. Gregory de Nazienzen had a great esteem for Themistius, to
whom he wrote—" Thou alone, O Themistius! strugglest against
the decline of literature; thou art at the head of the learned; thou
canst philosophize in high employments, join study to power, and
dignities to science."

* There are few men restrained by religion. What crimes have
been committed even by those entrusted to guide us in the ways of
salvation, St. Bartholomew's day, the assassination of Henry IV. the
massacre of the Templars, &c. &c. &c. sufficiently prove.

† Eusebius, in his Evangelical Preparation, lib. vi. cap. 10; mentions this remarkable fragment of a Syrian philosopher, named Bardezanes: " Apud Seras, lex est qua cædes, scortatio, furtum &
simulachrorum cultus omnis prohibetur; quare, in amplissima re-
gione, non templum videas, non lenam, non meretricem, non adul-
teram, non furem in jus raptum, non homicidam, non toxicum."—
" Among the Seres; the law prohibits murder; fornication, robbery,
and all kinds of religious worship; so that in this vast region we see
neither temple, nor adultery, nor bawds, nor whores, nor robber

All the art therefore of the legislator consists in forcing them by self-love to be always just to each other. Now, in order to compose such laws, it is necessary that the human heart should be known, and in the first place, that we should be convinced that men having sensibility for themselves, and indifference with respect to others, are neither good nor bad, but ready to be either, according as a common interest unites or divides them; that self-love, a sensation necessary to the preservation of the species, is engraven by Nature in a manner not

---

nor assassins, nor poisoners." A proof that the laws are sufficient to restrain men.

We should never have done, were we to attempt giving a list of all the people who, without the idea of a God, live in society more or less happily, according to the greater or less wisdom of their legislator. I shall mention only those that first occur to my memory.

" Before the Gospel was preached to the inhabitants of the Marian Islands," says Father Jobien, the Jesuit, " they had neither altars nor temples, nor sacrifices, nor priests: they had only some cheats, named Macanas, who preached to them. They, however, believed that there was a hell and a paradise: their hell was a furnace, where the devil beat souls with a hammer, like iron in a forge; their paradise was filled with cacao-trees, sugar-canes, and women. But it was neither their virtues nor vices that entitled them to a place either in paradise or in hell; for hell was allotted to those who died of a violent death, and the others were admitted into paradise. Father Jobien adds, that, " To the south of the Marian Isles, are thirty-two islands, inhabited by nations who are absolutely destitute of the knowledge of any religion, or of a Deity, and employ themselves solely in eating, drinking, &c."

The Caribbees, according to Le Borde, who was employed in their conversion, have neither priests, nor altars, nor sacrifices, nor any idea of the Deity; and will be well paid by those who would make them Christians. They believe that the first man, named Longuo, had a great navel, from whence came mankind. This Longuo was the first agent; he had made the earth without mountains, which, according to them, where produced by a deluge. Envy was one of the first creatures, and she soon overspread the earth with evils; she thought herself beautiful, but, having seen the sun, she went to hide herself, and ever since appears only in the night.

to be erazed * ; that a physical sensibility has produced in us a
love of pleasure and a hatred of pain ; that pleasure and pain
have at length produced and opened in all hearts the buds of
self-love, which by unfolding themselves give birth to the passions, whence spring all our virtues and vices.

By contemplating these preliminary ideas, we learn why
the passions, of which the forbidden tree is, according to some
Rabbins, only an ingenious image, bear equally on it branches
of good and evil fruit; we perceive the mechanism employed
by them in the production of our virtues and vices; and, in
short, a legislator discovers the means of laying men under a
necessity of being virtuous, and causing the passions to bear no
other fruit than probity and wisdom.

Now, if the examination of these ideas, so proper to render
men virtuous, be forbidden by the two species of men in
power above-mentioned, the only means of hastening the progress of morality will be, as I have already said, to shew that

---

The Chiriguanes do not acknowledge a God.   Letters édiff. 24.

The Giagues, according to Father Cavassy, acknowledge no being
distinct from matter, and have not even in their language a word
expressive of that idea: they worship only their ancestors, whom they
believe to be always living; and imagine that their prince has authority over the rain.

" At Indostan," says Father Pons, the Jesuit, " is a sect of Brachmans, who think that the mind is united to matter, and absorbed by
it; that the wisdom which purifies the soul, and is only the knowledge
of truth, produces the deliverance of the mind, by way of an analysis.
Now the mind, according to these Brachmans, disengages itself sometimes of a form, and sometimes of a quality, by these three truths:
" I am not in any thing, nothing is in me, I am not." When the
mind shall be delivered from all these forms, there will be an end of
the world. They add, that religion is so far from disengaging the mind
from these forms, that it only binds it the faster within the matter by
which it is absorbed.

* The soldier and the commander of a privateer desire war, and
nobody imputes it to them as a crime. It is visible that, in this respect, their interest is not sufficiently connected with the general interest.

these protectors of stupidity are the most cruel enemies of human nature, and to snatch from their hands the sceptre of ignorance, by which they are authorized to command a stupid people. Upon which I shall observe, that this, simple and easy as it appears in speculation, is extremely difficult in the execution. Indeed, there are men who have great and judicious minds, united to the virtue and strength of soul: there are men, who, being persuaded that a citizen without courage is also without virtue, are sensible that the fortune, and even the life of every individual is not his own, but is in a manner a deposit, which he ought always to be ready to deliver up when the safety of the public makes it necessary; but the number of such men is always too few for them to enlighten the public: besides, virtue must ever be of little weight, when the manners of an age fix upon it the rust of ridicule. Thus morality and the legislation, which I consider as one and the same science, can only make an insensible progress.

Nothing but the lapse of time can recal those happy ages, described under the names of Astrea and Rhea, which were only an ingenious emblem of the perfection of these sciences.

CHAP. XXV.

OF PROBITY, IN RELATION TO THE WORLD IN GENERAL.

If there was any such thing as probity in relation to all mankind, it would only consist in the habit of performing actions useful to all nations: now no action can have an immediate influence on the happiness or unhappiness of all mankind. To illustrate this by an example, the most generous action can produce in the moral world an effect no more sensible than a stone thrown into the ocean can produce in the seas, by raising the surface.

There is then no practical probity in relation to the universe. With respect to probity of intention, which is reduced to a constant and habitual desire of the happiness of mankind, and consequently to vague and inefficacious wishes for the universal felicity, I maintain that it is nothing but a platonic chimera. In fact, if the opposition of interests that subsists between different nations, with respect to each other, keeps them in a state of perpetual war; if a peace concluded between two nations is in truth merely a cessation, like that between two vessels, which, after a long fight, take time to repair their rigging and stop their leaks, only to renew the attack; if nations cannot extend their conquests and their commerce without doing it at the expence of their rivals; in fine, if the felicity and grandeur of one nation is almost always closely connected with the misfortunes and weakness of another, it is evident that a spirit of patriotism, a passion so desirable, so virtuous, and so worthy of esteem, in any citizen, is, as is proved by the example of the Greeks and Romans, absolutely exclusive of the love for all mankind.

It is necessary, in order to give existence to this kind of probity, that the nations, by reciprocal laws and conventions, should unite together as families composing one state; that the private interest of nations should submit to a more general interest; and that the love of our country, becoming extinguished in the heart, should give place to the more extended flame of universal love: a supposition that will not be realized for a long series of time. Whence I conclude, that there can be no such thing as practical nor even intentional probity, with respect to all mankind; and in this respect the mind is at variance with probity.

In fact, though the actions of a single person cannot at all contribute to the general happiness, and though the influences of his virtue cannot sensibly extend beyond the limits of an empire, it is not so with his ideas: if a man discovers a specific remedy, or if he invents a wind-mill, these productions of the mind may render him a benefactor to the world *.

---

* Thus reason is the greatest of our advantages, and perhaps infinitely more to the happiness of men than the virtue of any particular person. To this is reserved the power of forming the best legislation, and consequently of rendering men as happy as possible. It is true, the romance of this legislation is not yet completed, and that several

Besides, in affairs of genius, the love of our country is not, as in the case of probity, exclusive of a love of all mankind. A nation does not acquire knowledge at the expence of the neighbouring states: on the contrary, the more nations are enlightened, the more they reciprocally reflect ideas, and the more the force and activity of the universal genius is augmented. Whence I conclude, that, though there is no probity relative to the universe, there are at least certain kinds of genius that may be considered in this light.

CHAP. XXVI.

OF GENIUS, WITH RESPECT TO THE UNIVERSE.

GENIUS, considered in this point of view, will be, in conformity to the preceding definitions, the power of raising interesting ideas in the minds of all people, either as instructive or agreeable.

This kind of genius is, doubtless, the most desirable. There never was a time when that species of ideas, which was supposed by all nations to flow from genius, was not really worthy of that name. It is not the same with respect to the power of creating those kinds of ideas which one nation alone supposes to be derived from this source. Every nation has a time of stupidity and degradation, during which the people have no clear idea of genius; it then prodigally bestows the name on certain assemblages of ideas that are agreeable to the mode, and always ridiculous in the eyes of posterity. These ages of degradation are commonly those of despotic power; when, as

---

ages will slide away before the fiction be realized; but, arming ourselves with the patience of the Abbé de Saint Pierre, we may, after him, foretell, that every thing that is now a subject of the imagination will have existence.

Men must necessarily have a confused sensation, that reason is the principal of all our advantages, since envy will allow a man to mention his probity, but not his good sense.

a poet says, God deprives nations of one half of their understandings, that they may be enabled to bear the miseries and
punishments of slavery.

Among the ideas proper to please all people, are those that
are instructive, which are belonging to certain arts and sciences:
others are also agreeable, such as, first, the admired ideas and
sentiments in certain parts of Homer, Virgil, Corneille, Tasso,
and Milton; in which, as I have already observed, those illustrious writers do not confine themselves to the painting of a
particular nation or age, but to that of human nature; such
are, in the second place, the grand images with which these
poets enrich their works.

To prove that in every work of genius there are beauties
proper to please universally, I chose these images for an example; and say, that grandeur in poetic pictures is a source of
universal pleasure *. Not that all men are equally struck with

---

* If grand pictures do not always forcibly strike us, this want of
effect usually depends on a cause that has no relation to their grandeur.
It most commonly proceeds from being connected in our own minds
with some disagreeable object. Upon which I shall observe, that we
rarely, in reading a poetical description, receive only the pure impression that would have been made on us by an exact view of the
image. All objects participate of the ugliness, as well as of the beauty,
of those with which they are commonly connected; to this cause we
ought to attribute most of our disgusts, and our unjust fits of enthusiastic applause. A proverb used in the market, though ever so excellent, always appears low; because it is necessarily connected in our
memory with the image of those who make use of it.

Who can doubt of its being from the same reason that the tales of
spirits and apparitions recur in the night upon the mind of the wandering traveller, and double the horrors of a forest? That in the
Pyrenean mountains, in the midst of deserts, abysses, and rocks, the
imagination, struck with the idea of the war of the Titans, beholds
the mountains of Ossa and Pelion, and looks with fear on the field of
battle of these giants? Who doubts but that the remembrance of the
bower described by Camoens, where the nymphs, naked, flying, and
pursued by warm desires, fell at the feet of the Portuguese, where
love sparkled in their eyes, and circulated in their veins; where their

them: there are some as insensible to the beauties of description as to the charms of harmony, and whom it would be as unjust, as it would be useless, to attempt to disabuse. By their insensibility, they have acquired an unhappy right of disowning the pleasure they do not feel; but there are only a small number of these people.

In fact, whether it be the habitual or an impatient desire of felicity that makes us wish for all perfections as a means of increasing our happiness, and renders all those grand objects agreeable to us where their contemplation seems to give a greater extent of soul, and more strength and elevation of ideas; whether grand objects make a stronger, a more lasting, and more agreeable impression; or whether, in short, it is from some other cause, we find that we are offended at a confined view, and perceive ourselves confined in the narrow passages between mountains, or when inclosed by a great wall; while, on the contrary, the eye loves to extend its view over a vast plain, to take in the surface of the sea, or to lose itself in examining a distant horizon.

Every thing that is great is adapted to please the eye and imagination of mankind: this species of descriptive beauty has infinitely the advantage over all those that, depending on justness of proportions, can neither be so warmly nor so generally felt, since all nations have not the same ideas of proportions.

If we oppose to the cascades, subterranean caves, and terraces, proportioned by art, the cataracts of the river St. Laurence, the gaping caverns of Ætna, the enormous masses of rock heaped upon each other without order in the Alps, shall we not find that the pleasure produced by the prodigality and

---

words were lost, and nothing heard but the murmers of happy lovers; who doubts, I say, that the remembrance of so voluptuous a description has some time embellished every grove?

From this reason it is so difficult to separate entirely from the pleasure we receive at the presence of an object all the other pleasing sensations that seem in a manner reflected upon it, from other objects to which it happens to be connected.

rude magnificence visible in the works of nature is infinitely
superior to that resulting from justness of proportions.

To be convinced of this, let a person in the night ascend a
mountain, in order to contemplate the firmament. What is
the charm that draws him thither? Is it the agreeable sym-
etry in which the stars are ranged? Here, in the Via lactea,
are innumerable suns heaped up without order, some farther
distant than others; and there are vast deserts. What is then
the source of his pleasures? The immensity of heaven itself.
Indeed, what idea must he form of this immensity, when worlds
of fire appear but as luminous points scattered here and there
in the plains of æther? When suns, still farther involved in
the profound spaces of the firmament, can scarcely be perceived? The imagination, which launches forwards to these
last spheres, to comprehend all the worlds possible, is swallowed up in the vast and immeasurable concavity of the heavens,
and plunged in a ravishing delight, produced by the contemplation of an object that fills his whole soul. Thus the grandeur
of the decorations of this kind has occasioned the observation,
"That art is inferior to nature;" which means no more than
that great and noble pictures appear to us preferable to those
that are comparatively little and mean.

In the arts susceptible of this kind of beauty, such as sculpture, architecture, and poetry, it is the enormity of the masses
that places the Colossus of Rhodes and the Pyramids of Memphis, among the wonders of the world. It is the grandeur of
the descriptions that makes us admire Milton, for having the
most strong and sublime imagination. His subject too, though
little capable of beauties of another kind, was infinitely so of
the beauties of description. He was obliged, by his subject
on the terrestrial paradise, to assemble in the short compass of
the garden of Eden all the beauties nature has dispersed over
the earth, to adorn a thousand different climates. Carried by
the choice of the same subject to the unformed abyss of Chaos,
he was to draw from thence his primitive materials for erecting
the universe, to excavate the bed of the ocean, to crown the
earth with mountains, to cover it with verdure, to move and

kindle the sun and stars, to spread over them the pavilion of the heavens, to paint the beauties of the first day of the world, and that freshness of the opening spring with which his lively imagination embellished nature at her birth. He had then not only the most grand, but the most new and varied, pictures to paint, which, to the imagination of man, are two other universal sources of pleasure.

It is with the imagination as with reason: by contemplation, or the combination either of the pictures of nature or of philosophical ideas, poets and philosophers improve their imaginations and their reason; and thus are enabled to excel in different kinds, in which it is equally rare, and perhaps equally difficult, to succeed.

What man, indeed, does not perceive, that the progress of the human mind ought to be uniform to whatever science or art it applies? " If, to please the mind," says Fontenelle, " we must employ, without fatiguing it; if we cannot employ it, without offering those new, grand, and primitive truths, where their novelty, importance, and fertility, strongly fix the attention; if we avoid fatiguing only by presenting ideas ranged with order, expressed in the most proper words, in which the subject has an uniformity and simplicity that renders it easily comprehended, and where the variety is joined to simplicity *; it is equally to the combination of grandeur, novelty, variety, and simplicity, in the pictures, that is joined the greatest pleasure of the imagination. If, for example, the view or description of a great lake is agreeable, that of a calm and boundless sea is doubtless still more so: its immensity is a source of greater pleasure. However beautiful this prospect may be, its uniformity would soon render it tiresome. Therefore, if enveloped by black clouds, and carried by the north-wind, the tempest, personified by the poet's imagination, hastens to the south, rolling before him moveable mountains of water; who doubts but that the rapid, simple, and varied, succession of terrifying pictures, presented by the troubled sea, will every moment

---

* It is proper to remark, that the simplicity in subjects and images is a perfection relative to the weakness of our minds.

make new impressions on the imagination, strongly fix our attention, employ the mind without fatiguing it, and consequently please us more? But if the night happen to redouble the horrors of the same tempest, and the watery mountains where the chain terminates and encloses the horizon be instantly lighted by repeated and reflected flashes of lightning, who can doubt but that this dark sea, suddenly changed to a sea of fire, would form, by the united novelty of the grandeur and variety of the images, a picture more adapted to fill the imagination with astonishment? Thus the art of poetry, considered merely as descriptive, is to offer nothing to view but objects in motion, and, if possible, to strike several senses at once. May not the description of the roaring of the water, the howling of the winds, and the burst of rolling thunder, add still to the secret terror, and, consequently, to the pleasure we experience at the view of a tempestuous sea? At the return of spring, does not the descent of Aurora into the gardens of Marly, to open the buds of flowers; do not the perfumes she at that instant exhales, the warbling of a thousand birds, and the murmur of cascades, increase the charms of those delightful groves? All the senses are so many gates, by which agreeable impressions may enter our souls; and the more of them are opened at once, the higher does our pleasure arise.

We see then, that, as there are ideas generally used to nations from their being as instructive as those that immediately belong to the sciences, there are others also universally useful, as being agreeable; and that, differing in this particular from probity, the genius of a single person may have a relation to the whole universe.

The conclusion of this discourse is, that in affairs that relate to the mind, as well as in moral actions, it is in the nature of man to praise love or gratitude, and to despise hatred or revenge. Interest then is the only dispenser of his esteem: genius, under whatsoever point of view it is considered, is then never any thing more than a capacity for assembling ideas that are new and interesting; and consequently useful to mankind, either as being instructive or agreeable.

ESSAY III.

CHAP. I.

WHETHER GENIUS OUGHT TO BE CONSIDERED AS A NATURAL GIFT, OR AS AN EFFECT OF EDUCATION.

I AM going to examine in this discourse what the mind receives from nature and education; for which purpose it is necessary, first, to determine what is here meant by the word Nature.

This word may raise in our minds a confused idea of a being or a force that has endued us with all our senses: now the senses are the sources of all our ideas. Being deprived of our senses, we are deprived of all the ideas relative to them: a man born blind has for this reason no idea of colours; it is then evident, that, in this signification, genius ought to be considered as a gift of nature.

But, if the word be taken in a different acceptation, and we suppose that among the men well formed and endued with all their senses, without any perceivable defect of their organization, nature has made such a remarkable difference, and formed such an unequal distribution of the intellectual powers, that one shall be so organized as to be stupid, and the other be a man of genius, the question will become more delicate.

I confess, that, at first, we cannot consider the great inequality in the minds of men, without admitting that there is the same difference between them as between bodies, some of which are weak and delicate, while others are strong and robust. What can here occasion such variations from the uniform manner wherein nature operates?

This reasoning, it is true, is founded only on analogy. It is like that of the astronomers, who conclude that the moon is inhabited, because it is composed of nearly the same matter as our earth.

How weak soever this reasoning may be, it must yet appear demonstrative; for, say they, to what cause can be attributed the great disproportion of intellects observable between people who appear to have had the same education?

In order to reply to this objection, it is proper first to inquire, whether several men can, strictly speaking, have the same education; and for this purpose to fix the idea included in the word Education.

If by education we merely understand that received in the same places, and under the same masters; in this sense the education is the same with an infinite number of men.

But, if we give to this word a more true and extensive signification, and in general comprehend every thing that relates to our instruction; then, I say, that nobody receives the same education; because each individual has, for his preceptors, if I may be allowed to say so, the form of government under which he lives, his friends, his mistresses, the people about him, whatever he reads, and in short chance; that is, an infinite number of events, with respect to which our ignorance will not permit us to perceive their causes, and the chain that connects them together. Now, this chance has a greater share in our education than is imagined. It is this that places certain objects before us, and in consequence of this occasions more happy ideas, and sometimes leads to the greatest discoveries. To give some examples: it was chance that conducted Galileo into the gardens of Florence, when the gardeners were working the pumps: it was that which inspired those gardeners, when, not being able to raise the water above the height of thirty-two feet, to ask him the cause, and by that question piqued the vanity of the philosopher: it was at length his vanity, put in action by so casual a question, that obliged him to make this natural effect the subject of his thoughts, till, at last, by discovering the weight of the air, he found the solution of the problem.

In the moment when the peaceful soul of Newton was employed by no business, and agitated by no passion, it was also chance that, drawing him under an apple-tree, loosened some of the fruit from the branches, and gave that philosopher the

first idea of his system on gravitation: it was really this inci-
dent that afterwards made him turn his thoughts to inquire
whether the moon does not gravitate towards the earth with
the same force as that with which bodies fall on its surface?
It is then to chance that great geniuses are frequently obliged
for their most happy thoughts. How many great minds are
confounded among the people of moderate capacities for want
of a certain tranquillity of soul, the question of a gardener, or
the fail of an apple!

I am sensible, that we cannot at first, without some pain, attribute such great effects to causes so distant and so small in
appearance*. However, experience informs us, that, in the
physical as in the moral world, the greatest events are often
produced by almost imperceptible causes. Who doubts that
Alexander owed, in part, his conquest of Persia to the institutor
of the Macedonian phalanx? that the adventures of Achilles,
animating that prince with all the rage of glory, had a share
in the destruction of the empire of Darius, as Quintius Curtius
contributed to the victories of Charles XII.? Who can doubt
that the tears of Veturia, by disarming Coriolanus, confirmed
the power of Rome, which was ready to sink under the efforts
of the Volscii, and occasioned that long train of victories which
changed the face of the world; and that, consequently, it was
to the tears of Veturia that Europe owes its present situation?

---

* We read, in the Literary Year, that Boileau, when a child, playing in a yard, fell down. In his fall, his coats turned up, when a
turkey gave him several pecks on a very tender part. Boileau felt
the injury during his whole life; and perhaps from thence arose that
severity of manners, and that want of sensibility visible in all his
works; from thence his satire against women, against Lulli, Quinaut,
and all verses of gallantry.

Perhaps his antipathy against turkies might occasion that secret
aversion he always had to the Jesuits, who brought them into France.
To the same accident, perhaps, we owe his satire on double meanings,
his admiration of Mr. Arnaud. and his epistle on the Love of God;
so true it is, that imperceptible causes often determine the whole
conduct of life, and the whole series of our ideas.

What a number of facts of the like kind* might here be mentioned? " Gustavus," says the abbé de Vertot " proceeded in vain through all the provinces of Sweden; he wandered above a year in the mountains of Delecarlia. The mountaineers, though prepossessed by his good mien, the tallness of his stature, and the apparent strength of his body, were not however determined to join him, till on that very day, when the prince harangued the Delecarlians, the old men of the country remarked that the north wind had for some time constantly blowed. This wind appeared to them as a certain sign of the protection of heaven, and as an order to take up arms in favour of the hero. It was then that the north wind placed the crown of Sweden on the head of Gustavus.

Most events spring from causes equally small: we are unacquainted with them, because most historians have been themselves ignorant of them, or have not had eyes capable of perceiving them. It is true, that, in this respect, the mind may repair their omissions; for the knowledge of certain principles easily supplies the knowledge of certain facts. Thus, without staying any longer to prove that chance plays a greater part in the theatre of the world than is imagined, I shall conclude what I have just said with observing, that, if under the word Education be comprehended every thing in general that contributes to our instruction, this chance must necessarily have the greatest share in it; and that no person, being placed in exactly the same concourse of circumstances, can receive exactly the same education.

This fact being well weighed, who can be certain that a difference in education does not produce the difference observeable in minds? Who can assert, that men are not like those trees of the same species, whose seed, being absolutely the same, but

---

* In the minority of Louis XIV. when that prince was ready to retire into Burgundy, St. Evremond says, " that the advice of Turenne kept him at Paris, and saved France. However, that great general," he adds, " received less honour from that important counsel than from defeating five hundred horse." So true is it, that we with difficulty attribute great effects to causes that appear so small and distant.

never sown exactly in the same earth, nor exposed entirely to the same winds, the same sun, or the same rain, must in unfolding themselves necessarily produce an infinity of different forms. I may then conclude, that the inequality observable in the minds of men may be indifferently considered, either as the effect of nature or of education. But, whatever truth there may be in this conclusion, yet, as it is extremely vague, and may be reduced in a manner to a perhaps, I think I ought to consider this question in a new point of view, and return back to principles more certain and determinate. To this purpose, it will be proper to reduce the question to simple points; to ascend to the origin of our ideas, and to the opening of the mind; and to recollect that man can only make use of his senses, remember, and observe resemblances and differences, that is, the connection subsisting between the different objects that present themselves, either to him, or to his memory; that therefore nature can only give men more or fewer capacities of mind, by enduring some, preferably to others, with a little more delicacy of the senses, extent of memory, and capacity of attention.

CHAP. II.

OF THE DELICACY OF THE SENSES.

Can the greater or less perfection of the organs of sense, in which is necessarily included that of the interior organization, since I can here judge of the delicacy of the senses only by effects, be the cause of the inequality observeable in the minds of men?

In order to reason with some degree of justness on this subject, it is necessary to inquire, whether the greater or less delicacy of the senses gives the mind either more extent or more justness, which necessarily includes all the mental faculties.

The greater or less perfection of the organs of sense has no influence on justness of thinking, if men, whatever impression they receive from the same objects, must always perceive the same connections between those objects. Now, to prove that they perceive them, I shall choose the sense of sight for an example, as that to which we owe the greatest number of our ideas. And I say, with respect to the difference of eyes, that if a fathom appears to one man shorter, snow less white, and ebony not so black, as they appear to another, yet these two men always perceive the same relations between those objects; consequently, a fathom always appears longer than a foot ; the snow whiter than any other body, and ebony the blackest of all kinds of wood.

Now, as the justness of our thoughts always consists in a clear view of the true relations that subsist between objects, and as in repeating, with respect to the other senses, what I have here said on that of sight, we shall constantly come to the same conclusion; I infer, that the greater or less degree of perfection, either in the external or internal organization, can have no influence on the justness of our judgments.

Moreover, if extent be distinguished from justness of thought, the greater or less degree of delicacy of the senses will make no addition to that extent. If sight be again taken for an example, it is evident, that a mind, being more or less extensive, does not depend on the greater or less number of objects, to the exclusion of others which a man endued with very fine senses may place in his memory. There are very few objects so imperceptible by their smallness, that, considered exactly with the same attention by two eyes equally young, and as well employed, can be perceived by the one, and not by the other: but, were the difference in this respect made by nature between men whom I call well organized, that is, in whose organization there appears no defect*, infinitely more considerable than it is, I am able to shew that this difference does not produce any with respect to the extensiveness of the mind.

---

* I speak in this chapter only of those men who are well organized and deprived of none of the senses, and who besides are not afflicted either with the disease of folly or stupidity, which are commonly produced, the one by a defect of memory, and the other by a total want of that faculty.

Let us suppose two men endued with the same capacity for attention, the same extent of memory, and, in short, equal in every thing except the delicacy of the senses; upon this hypothesis, he who has the best sight may, beyond all contradiction, place in his memory, and combine many of these objects which by their smallness are concealed from him who, in this respect, has a less perfect organization; but these two men having upon my supposition a memory equally extensive, and capable, if they please, of containing two thousand objects, it is certain, that the second may supply by historical facts the objects which a smaller degree of delicacy of sight would not have permitted him to receive; and that he may complete, if he please, the number of two thousand objects, contained in the memory of the first. Now, if between these two men, he who has the sense of sight less perfect may yet deposit in the magazine of his memory as great a number of objects as the other; and if, besides, these men are equal in every thing else, they must consequently form as many combinations. The greater or less perfection of the organ of sight cannot however fail of having an influence on the genius or bent of their minds, and make one a painter, or a botanist, and the other an historian and a politician; but it can have no influence with respect to the extent of their minds. Thus, we do not observe a constant superiority of mind either among those who have a greater delicacy in the senses of seeing and hearing, or those who habitually use spectacles and ear-trumpets; these means make a greater difference between them and other men than in this respect nature herself has done. From whence I conclude, that, between the men whom I call well organized, the superiority of knowledge is not in proportion to the external or internal perfection of these organs; and that the great inequality subsisting between minds necessarily depends on some other cause.

CHAP. III.

OF THE EXTENT OF THE MEMORY.

THE conclusion of the preceding chapter leads to the inquiry whether the unequal extent of the memory be the cause of the great variety of mental faculties in mankind? The memory is the magazine in which are deposited the sensations, facts, and ideas, whose different combinations form what is called knowledge.

The sensations, facts, and ideas, must then be considered as the primary matter of knowledge. Now, the more spacious the magazine of the memory is, the more it contains of this primary matter; and the greater is the ability of obtaining knowledge.

Though this manner of reasoning may seem well founded, yet in searching it thoroughly it will appear to be only specious. To give it a complete answer, it is necessary first to examine whether the difference of extent in the memory of persons well organized be as remarkable in fact as it is in appearance; and supposing this difference real, it must secondly be considered, whether it ought to be regarded as the cause of the unequal distribution of mental abilities.

As to the first subject of inquiry, I say that attention alone may engrave in the memory the subjects that, without attention, would make only insensible impressions upon us; nearly resembling those a reader successively receives of each of the letters that compose a page in a book. It is then certain, that, to judge whether the defect of memory is in men an effect of their inattention, or of an imperfection in the organs, we must have recourse to experience. This teaches us that among men there are many, as St. Augustin and Montaigne say of themselves, who appear to be endued with only a very weak memory; and yet, from the desire of obtaining knowledge, acquire such a number of ideas, as to cause them to be placed in the rank of persons of an extraordinary memory. Now, if the desire of instruction be alone sufficient to enable us to know a great deal, I conclude, that the memory is almost entirely factitious. The extent of the memory therefore first depends on the daily use made of it: secondly, on the attention with which we consider the objects we would impress upon it, and which without attention, as I have just said, would leave only slight traces that would be easily effaced; and, thirdly, on the order in which we range our ideas. To this order we

owe all the prodigies of memory ; it consists in uniting together all our ideas, and consequently charging the memory only
with such objects as by their nature, or the manner in which
they are considered, preserve between them a connection sufficient to recal each other.

The frequent representations of the same objects to the memory are in a manner so many touches of the graver, which
cuts them deeper in proportion to the frequency with which
they are represented*. Besides, this order, so proper to recal
the same objects to our remembrance, not only gives us an explanation of all the phenomena of the memory, but teaches us,
that the sagacity of mind in one person, that is, the promptitude with which one man is struck with the force of truth,
frequently depends on the analogy of that truth with the objects about which he is employed. He cannot catch it by perceiving all its connections without rejecting all the ideas that
first presented themselves to his remembrance, and without
turning up-side down the whole magazine of his memory, to
search for the ideas connected with that truth.

This is the reason why so many men are insensible to the
exposition of certain facts, for those truths shake the whole
chain of their thoughts, by awakening a great number of ideas
in their minds : it is a flash of lightning, which spreads a rapid
light over the whole horizon of their ideas. It is then to order
that a person frequently owes the sagacity of his mind, and the
extent of his memory : thus it is a want of order, the effect of
the indifference a person entertains for a certain kind of studies,
which prevents all remembrances in those who, in all respects,
appear to have more extensive memories. This is the reason
why the learned in languages and history, who, by the assistance of a chronological order, easily impress and preserve the
remembrance of words, dates, and historical facts, cannot often
retain the proof of a moral truth, the demonstration of a geome-

---

* "Memory," says Mr. Locke, "is a table of brass, covered with
characters that become insensibly effaced by time, if they are not sometimes touched up by the graver."

trical problem, or the painting of a landscape, which they have long examined : in fact, these sorts of objects having no analogy with the rest of the facts or ideas with which their memories are filled, they cannot frequently renew the representation, or impress them more deeply, and consequently they are unable to preserve them long.

This is the productive cause of all the different kinds of memory, and the reason why those who know the least in one kind of knowledge, are commonly those who in that kind forget the most.

It appears then, that a great memory is a phænomenon of order; that it is almost always factitious; and that between those whom I call well organized, that great disproportion visible in point of memory is not so much the effect of the unequal perfection of the organs that supply it with materials as of an unequal attention to improve it.

But, supposing that the unequal extent of memory observable among mankind was entirely the work of nature, and was as considerable in reality as it is in appearance, I assert, that it could not have any influence on the extent of the mind; first, because a great genius, as I am going to shew, does not necessarily suppose a great memory; and, secondly, because every man is endued with a memory sufficient to raise him to the highest degree of mental abilities.

Before the first of these propositions is proved, it is proper to observe, that, as perfect ignorance constitutes perfect folly, the man of genius sometimes appears to want memory only from the too-confined signification given to the word memory, in restraining it to the remembrance of names, dates, places, and persons, for which the man of genius has no curiosity, and often finds that here his memory fails him. But, in comprehending in the signification of this word the remembrance of ideas, images, and reasonings, none of them is deficient; whence it follows, that there is no such thing as genius without memory.

This observation being made, I am to inquire what extent of memory is necessary to constitute a great genius. Let us choose, for example, two men illustrious in different kinds of genius, as Locke and Milton, and examine whether the greatness of their

talents ought to be considered as the effect of the extraordinary
extent of their memories.

If we first cast our eyes on Locke; and suppose that, struck
with a happy thought of his own, or obtained by reading Aristotle, Gassendi, or Montaigne, that philosopher perceived that
all our ideas are derived from the senses, it is evident that, to
deduce his whole system from this first idea, required less extent of memory than close application to reflections; that the
smallest memory is sufficient to retain all the subjects, from the
comparison of which he is to deduce the certainty of his principle, to enable him to unravel the chain, and consequently to
merit and obtain the title of a great genius.

With respect to Milton, if I consider him in the point of view
in which he is generally allowed to be infinitely superior to the
other poets ; if I consider only the strength, grandeur, variety,
and novelty, of his poetic images, I am obliged to confess, that
the superiority of his genius in these does not suppose a great
extent of memory. Whatever grandeur there may be in his
pictures, such as that where, uniting fire to solid terrestrial matter, he paints the ground of hell as burning with solid, as the
lake with liquid fire; but, grand as his compositions are, I say,
it is evident, that the number of bold images proper to form
such pictures ought to be confined within proper bounds: consequently, the grandeur of this poet's imagination is less the
effect of a great extent of memory, than of deep reflection upon his art. It was this reflection that made him search out the
source of the pleasures of the imagination; and made him discover, that they consisted in the assemblage of new images,
proper to form grand, true, and striking pictures, and in the
constant choice of those strong expressions are the colours of
poetry, and by which he has rendered his descriptions visible
to the eyes of the imagination.

As the last example of the small extent of memory, necessary
to a fine imagination, I give in a note the translation of a piece
of English poetry*. This translation and the preceding ex-

---

* A young virgin, awaked and guided by love, goes before the appearance of Aurora, to a valley, where she waits for the coming of

amples will, I believe, prove to those who would decompose the works of illustrious men, that a great genius does not neces-

---

her lover, who, at the rising of the sun, is to offer a sacrifice to the Gods. Her soul, in the soft situation in which she is placed, by the hopes of approaching happiness, indulges, while waiting for him, the pleasure of contemplating the beauties of nature, and the rising of the luminary that was to bring the object of her tenderness. She expresses herself thus:

" Already the sun gilds the tops of those antique oaks; and the waves of those falling torrents that roar among the rocks shine with his beams. Already I perceive the summit of those shaggy mountains, whence arise the vaults which, half concealed in the air, offer a formidable retreat to the solitary who there retire. Night folds up her veil. Ye wanton fires, that mislead the wandering traveller, retire to the quagmires and marshy fens: and thou, sun, lord of the heavens, who fillest the air with reviving heat, who sowest with dewy pearls the flowers of these meadows, and givest colours to the varied beauties of nature, receive my first homage, and hasten thy course: thy appearance proclaims that of my lover. Freed from the pious cares that detain him still at the foot of the altars, love will soon bring him to mine. Let all around me partake of my joy! Let all bless the rising of the luminary, by which we are enlightened! Ye flowers, that enclose in your bosoms the odours that cool night condenses there, open your buds, and exhale in the air your balmy vapours. I know not whether the delightful intoxication that possesses my soul does not embellish whatever I behold; but the rivulet, that in pleasing meanders winds along this valley, enchants me with its murmurs. Zephyrus caresses me with his breath. The fragrant plants, pressed under my feet, waft to my senses their perfumes. Oh! if felicity sometimes condescends to visit the abode of mortals, to these places she doubtless retires. But with what secret trouble am I agitated! Already impatience mingles its poison with the sweetness of my expectation: this valley has already lost its beauties. Is joy then so fleeting? Is it as easy to snatch it from us, as for the light down of these plants to be blown away by the breath of the zephyrs? In vain have I recourse to flattering hope; each moment increases my disturbance. He will come no more! Who keeps him at a distance from me? What duty more sacred than that of calming the inquietudes of love? But what do I say? Fly jealous suspicions, injurious to his fidelity, and formed

sarily suppose a great memory. I will even add, that the extraordinary extent of the one is absolutely exclusive of the extraordinary extent of the other. As ignorance causes the genius to languish for want of nourishment, so vast erudition frequently chokes it up by a super-abundance of aliment. To be convinced of this, it will be sufficient to examine into the different use two men must make of their time, who would render themselves superior to each other, the one in genius, and the other in memory.

---

to extinguish my tenderness. If jealousy grows by the side of love, it will stifle it, if not pulled up by the roots: it is the ivy which by a verdant chain embraces but dries up the trunk that serves for its support. 1 know my lover too well to doubt of his tenderness. He, like me, has, far from the pomp of courts, sought the tranquil asylum of the fields. Touched by the simplicity of my heart, and by my beauty, my sensual rivals call him in vain to their arms. Shall he be seduced by the advances of coquetry, which on the cheek of the young maid tarnishes the snow of innocence, and the carnation of modesty, and daubs it with the whiteness of art, and the paint of effrontery? What do I say? His contempt for her is, perhaps, only a snare for me. Can I be ignorant of the partiality of men, and the arts they employ to seduce us? Nourished in a contempt for our sex, it is not us, it is their pleasures, that they love. Cruel as they are, they have placed in the rank of the virtues the barbarous fury of revenge, and the mad love of their country; but never have they reckoned fidelity among the virtues! Without remorse they abuse innocence, and often their vanity contemplates our griefs with delight. But, no! fly far from me, ye odious thoughts; my lover will come! A thousand times have I experienced it: as soon as I perceive him, my agitated mind is calm; and I often forget the too just cause I have for complaint; for near him I can only know happiness.—Yet, if he is treacherous to me, if in the very moment when my love excuses him, he consummates the crime of infidelity in another's bosom, may all nature take up arms in revenge! may he perish!—What do I say? Ye elements be deaf to my cries! thou earth, open not thy profound abyss! let the monster walk the time prescribed him on thy splendid surface. Let him still commit new crimes, and still cause the tears of the too-credulous maids to flow; and, if heaven avenge them, and punish him, may it at least be the prayer of some other unfortunate woman, &c.

If a work of genius is an assemblage of new ideas, and if every new idea is only a relation newly perceived between certain objects, he who would distinguish himself by his genius must necessarily employ the far greatest part of his time in observing the various relations objects have to each other, and spend only the least part in placing facts or ideas in his memory. On the contrary, he who would surpass others in extent of memory must, without losing his time in contemplating and comparing objects with each other, employ whole days without ceasing in arranging new objects in his memory. Now, by so different a use of time, it is evident, that the first of these two men must be as inferior in memory to the second as he will be superior in genius: a truth which was probably perceived by Descartes, when he said, that, in order to improve the mind, we ought less to learn than to contemplate. Whence I conclude, not only that a very great genius does not suppose a very great memory, but that the extraordinary extensiveness of the one is always exclusive of the extraordinary extent of the other.

To conclude this chapter, and to prove that the inequality observable in the mental abilities is not to be attributed to the unequal extent of the memory, it only remains to shew, that men being commonly well organized are endued with an extent of memory sufficient to raise the most lofty ideas. Every man is, in this respect, so favoured by nature, that, if the magazine of his memory is capable of containing a number of ideas or facts, he may, by comparing them, always perceive some new relations, constantly increase the number of his ideas, and consequently be always enlarging his mind. Now, if thirty or forty objects, as geometry shews, may be compared with each other in such a number of ways, that, in the course of a long life, no body could observe all the relations, or deduce all the possible ideas, that might be drawn from them, and if, among the men whom I call well organized, there are none whose memory cannot contain not only all the words of one language, but also an infinite number of dates, facts, names, places, and persons, and, in short, a number of particulars far exceeding six or seven thousand, I may boldly conclude from thence, that every man well organized is endued with a capacity of memory much superior to what he can use for enlarging his ideas; that a great extent of memory would not give a more extensive genius; and that, therefore, we should be far from considering this inequality of memory among mankind as the cause of inequality of their mental faculties, since this last inequality is only the effect either of the greater or less attention with which they observe the connections between different objects, or of the bad choice of the objects with which they load their memories. There are, indeed, barren objects, such as dates, names of places, persons, or other things of the like kind, which hold a great place in the memory without being able to produce either new or interesting ideas with respect to the public. The inequality of minds depends in part then on the choice of the objects placed in the memory. If young men who obtained a great reputation in the colleges have not always supported it in a more advanced age, it is because the comparison and happy application of Despautere's rules, which make good scholars, are not the least proof that these young men carried their views to those objects of comparison from which result such ideas as those in which the public is interested; and therefore few great men have not courage to be ignorant of an infinite number of useless things.

CHAP. IV.

OF THE UNEQUAL CAPACITY OF ATTENTION.

I HAVE shewn, that these great inequalities of genius do not depend on the greater or less degree of perfection, either of the organs of sense, or of the organ of memory. Nothing now remains but to search for the cause of the unequal capacity for attention among men.

As it is the greater or the less degree of attention that engraves more or less deeply the objects in the memory, which makes us perceive, more or less perfectly, the relations that form most of our judgments, whether true or false; and, as to this attention, we owe almost all our ideas, it seems evident, say they, that the unequal powers in the minds of men are owing to their unequal capacity for attention.

If the slightest disease, to which we give the name of indisposition, is thought sufficient to render most men incapable of a continued attention, it is doubtless to diseases, in a manner insensible, and consequently to the inequality of power given by nature to different men, that we ought principally to attribute the total incapacity for attention, and the unequal proportion of mental abilities observable in most of them: from whence it is concluded that those abilities are merely gifts of nature.

But how plausible soever this reasoning may appear, it is not confirmed by experience.

If we except the men afflicted by habitual diseases, who, being compelled by pain to fix their whole attention on their condition, cannot place it on objects proper to improve their minds, and consequently cannot be included in the number of the men whom I call well organized, we shall see that all other men, and even those of weak and delicate constitutions, ought, according to the above manner of reasoning, to have fewer abilities than men of a strong and robust form, though in this respect they frequently appear more favoured by nature.

In men of healthy and strong constitutions, who apply themselves to the arts and sciences, it seems as if their strength and vigour, by giving them a greater propensity to pleasure, frequently diverts them from study and reflection; and that those of a weak and delicate constitution cannot be diverted from their studies by slight and frequent indispositions. All that we can be certain of is, that, among the men animated by nearly an equal love of study, our success in measuring the greatness of their mental abilities seems entirely to depend either on the greater or fewer distractions occasioned by a difference of tastes, fortunes, and stations, and on the happy or unhappy choice of subjects on which we treat, the more or less perfect method used in composing, the greater or less propensity to reflection, the books we read, the men of taste with whom we converse, and, in short, the objects which chance daily presents to our view. It seems as if, in the concourse of circumstances necessary to form a man of genius, the different capacity for attention that may be produced by a greater or less strength of constitution is of no moment. Thus the inequality of genius, occasioned merely by the different constitutions of men, is altogether insensible; and, as no exact observations have hitherto been made to determine what constitution is most proper to form men of genius, we cannot yet be certain, whether the tall or the short, the fat or the lean, the bilious or the sanguine, have the greatest aptitude of mind.

But, though this summary answer may be sufficient to refute a manner of reasoning founded only on probabilities; yet, as this question is of great importance, it is necessary to resolve it with precision, and to inquire whether this want of attention in men is either the effect of a natural incapacity for application, or of a too-languid desire of instruction.

All the men whom I call well organized are capable of attention, since all learn to read, obtain their mother-tongue, and are capable of understanding the first propositions of Euclid. Now all men capable of comprehending these first propositions have a physical power of understanding them all: in fact, both in geometry and in all the other sciences, the greater or less facility with which we discover truth depends on the number, either greater or less, of those antecedent propositions, which, in order to perceive it, must be presented to the memory. Now, if every man well organized, as I have proved in the preceding chapter, may place in his memory a number of ideas much superior to what is required for the demonstration of any proposition in geometry; and if, by the assistance of order, and the frequent representation of the same ideas, we may, as experience proves, render them so familiar, and so habitually present, as to recollect them without difficulty, it must follow that every one has a physical power of pursuing the demonstration of any geometrical truth; and that, after having ascended from proposition to proposition, and from analogous ideas to other analogous ideas, till a person has acquired the knowledge, for instance, of ninety-nine propositions, he may demonstrate the hundredth with the same ease that he did the second, which is as distant from the first as the hundredth is from the ninety-ninth.

It is proper now to examine, whether the degree of attention necessary to comprehend the demonstration of one geometrical truth, is not sufficient for the discovery of those truths that place a man in the rank of those of distinguished learning. In order to this, I desire the reader to observe with me the steps by which the human mind is led either to the discovery of truth, or in merely following demonstration. I shall not draw my example from geometry, because the greatest part of mankind are ignorant of that science; I shall therefore choose morality, and propose the following problem: " Why unjust conquests do not reflect as much dishonour on nations as robberies do on individuals?"

In resolving this moral problem, the ideas that would first present themselves to my mind are those of justice, which are the most familiar to me: I consider it then between individuals, and perceive that robbery, which disturbs and overthrows the orders of society, is justly considered as infamous.

But what advantage soever there may be in applying to nations my ideas of the justice that subsists between citizens; yet, at the sight of so many unjust wars, at all times undertaken by people who are the admiration of the world, I shall soon suspect that the ideas of justice, considered as relating to a private person, are not applicable to nations. This suspicion would be the the first step made by my mind to arrive at the discovery proposed. To clear up this suspicion, I first banish the ideas of justice most familiar to me: I recal to my memory and reject successively an infinite number of ideas, till I perceive, that, in order to resolve this question, it is necessary first to form clear and general ideas of justice; and that, for this purpose, it is necessary to ascend to the establishment of society, till I come to those distant times when we may better perceive its origin, and in which we may more easily discover the reason why the principles of justice considered in relation to citizens is not applicable to nations.

This I may call the second step. I may consequently represent to my mind men absolutely destitute of knowledge and arts, and nearly such as they must have been in the first age of the world. I then see them dispersed in the woods, like other voracious animals: I see, that, before the invention of arms, these first men, being too weak to oppose the wild beasts, and becoming instructed by danger, necessity, or fear, perceived that it was for their mutual interest to enter into society, and to form a league against the animals their common enemies. I at length perceive that these men, thus assembled, soon became enemies, from the desire of possessing the same things, and took up arms mutually to ravish them from each other; that the strongest at first frequently took them from those who had greater mental abilities, who invented arms and prepared ambuscades to recover them again, and that strength and dexterity were consequently the first titles to property: that the earth originally belonged to the strongest, and afterwards to the more ingenious; and that these two were the only titles by which every thing was possessed : but that at length, instructed by their common misfortunes, they perceived that their union could be of no advantage to them, and that society could not subsist without adding new conventions to the first, by which each individual person should renounce his right to make use of his own strength and dexterity, contrary to the interest of the whole, and all in general should reciprocally guarantee the preservation of the life and substance of each, and engage to take up arms against the person who should violate these conventions: that thus the interest of particular persons formed a common interest, that necessarily gave to different actions the names, just, lawful, and unjust, according as they were useful, indifferent, or prejudicial, to society.

Being once arrived at this truth, I easily discover the source of human virtues. I see that men, without a sensibility of pain and natural pleasure, without desires, without passions, and equally indifferent with respect to every thing, would not have known a personal interest : that without personal interest they would not have united in society, would not have entered into conventions among themselves, and would not have had a general interest; consequently there would have been no actions, either just or unjust; and that thus natural sensibility and personal interest have been the authors of all justice.[*]

---

[*] This proposition cannot be denied, without admitting innate ideas.

This truth, founded on the following axiom of the civil law, " that interest is the measure of human actions," and besides, confirmed by a thousand facts, proves to me that virtuous or vicious, according as our particular passions or tastes are conformable or contrary to the general interest, tends so necessarily to our particular welfare, that the Divine Legislator himself has thought proper to engage men to the practice of virtue, by promising an eternal happiness in exchange for the temporal pleasures they are sometimes obliged to sacrifice to it.

This principle being established, my mind draws several consequences from it ; and I perceive that every convention, where private interest is found to be opposite to the general interest, would always have been violated, had not the legislators constantly proposed great rewards as inducements to the practice of virtue; and if they had not incessantly opposed the bank of dishonour and punishment against that natural inclination that leads all men to usurpation. I see then that rewards and punishments are the only bands by which they have been able to bind the private to the general interest ; and I conclude, that laws made for the happiness of all would be observed by none, if the magistrates were not armed with the power necessary to put them in execution. Without this power, the laws, being violated by the majority, might with justice be infringed by each individual ; because, having no other foundation than the public advantage, as soon as by a general infraction they became useless, they would from thenceforward be void, and cease to be laws; each person would then resume his original natural rights; each would solely consult his private interest, which justly forbids his observing laws that would become prejudicial to him who should alone observe them. And therefore, if, for the safety of travelling on the high roads, all should be forbidden to carry arms, and yet for want of patroles the roads should be infested with robbers, that law would not consequently have answered its end : I therefore not only say, that a man might travel upon it with arms, and violate that convention, or that law, without injustice, but that he could not even observe it without folly.

After my mind has thus proceeded step by step, till it has

arrived at clear and general ideas of justice ; after having found that it consists in the exact observation of the laws which the common interest, that is, the assemblage of all the interests of the individuals has caused them to make, I have nothing farther to do than to apply these ideas of justice to nations. Instructed by the principles above established, I immediately perceive that all nations have not entered into conventions, by which they reciprocally guarantee the possession of the countries and effects of each other. If I would discover the cause, my memory, on my tracing the general map of the world, informs me, that different states have not made these kinds of conventions, because they have not been prompted to it by so pressing an interest as that of the individuals; because nations may subsist without any such conventions, though society cannot be supported without laws. Whence I conclude, that the ideas of justice considered between nation and nation, or individual and individual, ought to be extremely different.

If the church and sovereign princes permit the negro trade; if the Christian, who curses in the name of God him who brings troubles and dissension into families, blesses the merchant who sails to the gold coast or to Senegal, to exchange the merchandize of which the Africans are fond for negroes; if, for the sake of this commerce, Europeans feel no remorse at keeping up an eternal war among those people, it is because, from the want of particular treaties and customs generally known by the law of nations, both the church and sovereign powers think that people are, with respect to each other, in the same situation as man in a state of nature before they entered into society, when they acknowledged no other laws but those of strength and cunning; when they had no convention among themselves, no property, and consequently there could be no robbery nor injustice. Even with respect to the particular treaties which nations enter into with each other, these never being guaranteed by a sufficient number of great nations, it appears that they can hardly ever cause them to be observed by force: and consequently, being like laws without power, they must frequently remain unexecuted.

When, by applying the general ideas of justice to nations,

my mind has reduced the question of this point, in order to discover why the people who break the treaties they have made
with others are less guilty than the private person who violates
the conventions made with society; and why, in conformity to
the public opinion, unjust conquests are less dishonourable to a
nation than a robbery is to a particular person ; it is sufficient
to recal to mind a list of all the treaties broken from time to
time by all nations. I then see that there is always a high
probability, that, without regard to these treaties, the governors
of every nation will take advantage of times of calamity to attack their neighbours, to conquer them, or at least to put it
out of their power to hurt them. Now, every nation being instructed by history may consider this probability sufficiently
great, to justify the belief that the infraction of a treaty, which
the prince finds it for his interest to violate, is a tacit clause of
all treaties, which are properly no more than truces; and that
consequently, in seizing a favourable opportunity of humbling
his neighbours, he only prevents them, since all nations, being
forced to expose themselves to the reproach of injustice, or of
bearing the yoke of servitude, are reduced to the alternative
of being slaves or sovereigns.

Besides, as it is almost impossible for any nation to preserve
itself, and as limiting the aggrandizement of an empire must,
as is proved by the history of the Romans, be considered as an
almost certain presage of its decay, it is evident that each nation may even believe itself the more authorized to make those
conquests that are called unjust, as not finding, for instance, in
the guarantee of two nations against a third, as much security
as an individual finds in his own nation against another individual; the treaty relating to it ought then to be much the less
sacred, as its execution is more uncertain.

Thus, when my mind has penetrated to this last idea, I discover the solution of the moral problem I had proposed to myself. I then perceive that the infraction of treaties, and that
kind of robbery which subsists between nations, must, as what
is past has proved, be a security for times to come, and still
continue till all states, or at least the greatest number of them,
have concluded general conventions; till the nations in con-

formity to the project of Henry IV. or the Abbé de saint Pierre, have reciprocally guaranteed their possessions; and engaged to take up arms against the people who shall attempt to subdue another; till chance shall have formed such a disproportion between the power of each state in particular, and that of all the others who are united, that these conventions may be maintained by force; and till the different nations have established among each other the same policy which a wise legislatur uses with respect to the citizens, when, by rewards affixed to good actions, and punishments to the bad, he lays the citizens under a necessity of being virtuous, by giving probity personal interest for its support.

It is then certain, that, in conformity to the public opinion, unjust conquests being not so contrary to the laws of equity, and consequently less criminal than robberies committed by private persons, they ought not to cast such dishonour on a nation as on a citizen.

This moral problem being resolved, if the progress made by my mind for that purpose be observed, it will be found that I at first recollected the ideas that were most familiar to me; then compared them with each other, and observed their agreement and disagreement in relation to the subject of my inquiry; that I at length rejected those ideas, in order to recollect others, and repeated this, till at last my memory presented the objects of comparison from which the truth I was in search of ought to flow.

Now, as the progress of the mind is always the same, what I have said on the discovery of one truth ought in general to be applied to all. I shall only remark on this subject, that, in order to make a discovery, we must necessarily have in our memories the objects from which truth is to be drawn.

If the reader recollects what I have said in the example I have just given, and in consequence of it would know whether all men well organized are really endued with an attention sufficient to raise their minds to the most lofty ideas, he may compare the operations of the mind in making a discovery, or when he simply follows the demonstration of a truth, and examine which of these operations supposes the most attention.

F F

In pursuing the demonstration of a proposition in geometry,
it is of no use to recal many objects to the mind; the master is
to lay before his pupil those proper to give the solution of the
problem he proposes to him.   But, whether a man discover a
truth or pursue a demonstration, he ought, in both cases, to
observe equally the relations that subsist between the objects
presented to him by his memory or his master.   Now, as he
cannot, without great hazard, present only to the mind the
ideas necessary to the discovery of truth, and consider none
but precisely the faces he ought to compare with each other,
it is evident that, in order to make a discovery, he ought to recollect a multitude of ideas foreign to the object of inquiry,
and to form a number of useless comparisons; comparisons
whose multitude may deter him.   He must then spend much
more time in discovering a truth than in pursuing a demonstration: but the discovery of this truth does not require, in any
one instance, a greater effort of attention than is supposed in
the pursuit of a demonstration.

To be assured of this, let us observe a student in geometry,
and we shall find, that he must apply so much the greater attention in considering the geometrical figures the master places
before him, as these objects being less familiar than those presented to him by his memory, his mind is at once employed by
a double care, in considering these figures, and in discovering
the relations that subsist between them: whence it follows
that the attention necessary to pursue the demonstration of a
proposition in geometry is sufficient for the discovery of truths
of a very different kind.   It is true, in this last case, the attention ought to be continued: but this continuance is properly
no more than the repetition of the same acts of attention.   Besides, if all men, as I said above, are capable of learning to
read, and of learning their mother tongue, they are all capable not only of the lively, but of the continued, attention requisite for the discovery of truth.

What continuity of attention must he use to know his letters,
to assemble them, form them into syllables, or to unite in his
memory objects of a different nature, that have only an arbitrary connection with each other, as the words Oak, Grandeur,

Love, which have no real connection with the things, idea, or sensation, they express? It is then certain, that if, by the continuance of attention, that is, by the frequent repetition of the same acts of attention, all men may successively engrave in their memory every word in a language, they are all endued with a force and continuity of attention necessary to raise those great ideas whose discovery places them in the rank of illustrious men.

But it may be asked, if all men are endued with the attention necessary to excel in one kind of study, when a contrary habit has not rendered them incapable of it, it is certain that this attention is more difficult to one man than to others: now to what other cause can this greater or less difficulty of attention be attributed, if it be not owing to a greater or less perfection of organization?

Before I make a direct reply to this objection, I shall observe, that attention is not foreign to the nature of man; that, in general, when we believe attention difficult to be supported, it is because we take the fatigue of weariness and impatience for the fatigue of application. In reality, if there be no man without desires, there is no man without attention. When it is reduced to a habit, it becomes a want: what renders it fatiguing, is the motive that determines us to it: if that be necessity, indigence, or fear, attention is then painful; but, if it be the hope of pleasure, attention itself then becomes a pleasure. Lay before a man two written copies equally difficult to read; the one a verbal process at law, and the other a letter from his mistress; and who can doubt that the attention would not be as painful in the first case as it would be agreeable in the second? From this observation, we may easily explain why attention is more painful to some than to others. It is not necessary for this purpose that there subsists between them any difference of organization: it is sufficient to shew, that here the pain of attention is always greater or less in proportion to the greater or less degree of the pleasure which each considers as the reward of his labour. Now, if the same objects are never of the same value in the opinion of different men, it is evident, that, in proposing to

different men the same objects as a reward, they have not an
equal reward in view ; and, being obliged to make the same
effort of attention, these efforts must consequently be more
painful to some than to others. We may then resolve the problem of a greater or less case of attention, without having recourse to the mystery of an unequal perfection in the organs
which produced it. But on admitting, in this respect, a difference in the organization of men ; in supposing, I say, they
have a warm desire of instruction, a desire of which all men
are susceptible ; there are none but will then find that they are
endued with a capacity of attention necessary to distinguish
themselves in an art. In fact, if the desire of happiness be
common to all men, and if it be their most lively sensation, it
is evident that every man will do whatever is in his power to
obtain it : now every man, as I have just proved, is capable of
a degree of attention sufficient to enable him to obtain the most
noble ideas. He will then make use of this capacity for attention, when, by the legislation of his country, his particular
taste, education, or happiness, shall become the prize to be
obtained by his attention. It will, I believe, be difficult to
resist this conclusion ; especially if, as I can prove, it is not
even necessary for a man to give all the attention of which he
is capable to be superior in one kind of study.

Not to leave any doubt with respect to this truth, let us consult experience, and examine the men of genius : they have
all experienced that it is not to the most painful efforts of attention that they owe the finest verses of their poems, the most
singular situations in their romances, and the most learned and
instructive of their philosophical works. They confess that
they owe them to the happy concourse of certain objects
which chance has placed before their eyes, or presented to
their memory ; and by comparing these, they have produced
those noble verses, those striking situations, and those grand
philosophical ideas ; ideas which the mind always conceives
with a greater promptitude and felicity, in proportion to their
being more true and general. Now, if in every work these
fine ideas, of whatsoever kind they may be, be in a manner
the strokes of genius, if the art employed about them be not a

work of time and patience, and what is called the labour of the brain, it is thence certain, that genius is less the price of attention than a gift of chance, which presents these happy ideas to all men, among whom those alone who are fond of glory are attentive to seize them. If chance be generally acknowledged to be the author of most discoveries in almost all the arts, and if in speculative sciences its power be less sensibly perceived, it is not perhaps less real; it no less presides at the opening of the finest-ideas. Thus they are not, as I have just said, the price of the most painful efforts of the attention; and it may be asserted, that the attention required in following the order of ideas, the manner of expressing them, and the art of passing from one subject to another*, is, beyond all contradiction, much more fatiguing; and that, in short, the most painful of all is the comparison of objects that are not familiar to us. For this reason the philosopher, capable of six or seven hours application to study, could not, without a very painful attention, spend six or seven hours either in examining witnesses or making a faithful and correct copy of a manuscript: hence it is evident, that the beginning of every science is always the most thorny. It is only owing to the habit we have acquired of considering certain objects, that we owe not only the facility with which we compare them, but also the just and rapid comparisons we draw from considering them with respect to each other. Thus, at the first glance of the eye, the painter perceives in a picture the faults with respect to the design and colouring: thus the shepherd, accustomed to consider his sheep, finds resemblances and differences between them, that makes him know them; and thus we are properly master only of the subject on which we have long meditated. It is in proportion to the greater or less degree of application with which we examine a subject, that our ideas of it are profound or superficial. It appears that works that have long employed our thoughts, and been long in composing, have greater strength; and that in those of sciences, as in mechanics, we gain in strength what is lost in time.

---

* Tantum series juncturaque pollet.

But, not to ramble from my subject, I shall repeat again, if the most painful attention be that which supposes the comparison of objects least familiar to us, and if that attention be required in the study of languages, every man being capable of learning his own language, all are consequently endued with a strength and power of attention sufficient to raise them to the rank of illustrious men.

There only remains, as a last proof of this truth, to recollect here, that error, as I have said, in my first essay, is always accidental, and not inherent in the particular nature of certain minds; and that all our false judgments are the effects of our passions, or of our ignorance: whence it follows, that all men are, by nature, endued with a mind equally just; and that, on its presenting to them the same objects, they would all form the same judgments. Now as the words a sound mind includes, in its most extensive signification, all minds, it follows, from what I said above, that all whom I call well organized, being born with a sound mind, they have all a natural power of acquiring the most lofty ideas*.

But it is replied, if this be the case, why do we see so few illustrious men? It is because study is attended with some trouble; and to conquer a disinclination to study, as I have already insinuated, a person ought to be animated by some passion.

In early youth, the fear of punishment is sufficient to force boys to study; but, in a more advanced age, when they do not meet with the same treatment, they must be induced to under-

---

* It must always be remembered, as I have said in my second discourse, that ideas, in their own nature, are neither lofty, great, nor little; that frequently the discovery of an idea called little does not suppose a less genius than the discovery of one that is lofty: that it is sometimes as necessary to seize with delicacy the ridicule of a character, as to perceive the mistakes of government; and that, if, by way of preference, the name of great and lofty be applied to discoveries of the last kind, it is from our meaning by the epithets lofty, great, and little, only such ideas as are more or less generally interesting.

go the fatigue of application, by the warmth of some passion, as, for instance, the love of glory. The force of attention is then proportioned to the force of the passion. Let us consider children : if they make a more equal progress in learning their own tongue than in a foreign language, it is because they are excited to it by more equal necessities ; that is, by eating and drinking, by the love of play, and by the desire of making known the objects of their love and aversion : now, wants nearly equal must produce effects that are also nearly equal. On the contrary, as the progress in a foreign language depends both on the method used by the master, the fear with which he inspires his scholars, and the interest parents take in the studies of their children, it is evident that their progress depending on such various causes, so combined and diversified, must, for this reason, be very unequal. Whence I conclude, that the great inequality of genius observable amongst men depends, perhaps, on their unequal desire of instruction. But this desire, it is said, is the effect of a passion : now, if we are obliged only to nature for the greater or less strength of our passions, it follows from thence that the mental abilities ought consequently to be considered as a gift of nature.

To this point, which is really delicate and decisive, the whole question is reduced. To resolve it, we must know both the passions and their effects, and enter into this subject in a very deep and circumstantial manner.

CHAP. V.

OF THE POWERS THAT ACT UPON THE SOUL.

EXPERIENCE alone can discover what these powers are. It informs us that laziness is natural to man; that attention gives him pain and fatigue*; that he gravitates incessantly towards

---

* The Hottentots will neither reason nor think. "Thought," say they, "is the scourge of life." How many Hottentots are there

repose as bodies towards a centre. He there remains strongly fixed, if he be not every moment repelled by two kinds of powers that counterbalance his laziness and inertia; on the one hand by strong passions, and on the other by hatred and lassitude.

Lassitude, or wearisomeness of inaction, is a more general and powerful spring than is imagined. Of all pains, this is doubtless the least; but nevertheless it is one. The desire of happiness makes us always consider the absence of pleasure as an evil. We would have the necessary intervals that separate the lively pleasures always connected with the gratification of our natural wants, filled up with some of those sensations that are always agreeable when they are not painful: we therefore constantly desire new impressions, in order to put us in mind every instant of our existence; because every one of these informations affords us pleasure. Thus the savage, as soon as he has satisfied his wants, runs to the banks of a river, where the rapid succession of the waves that drive each other forward make every moment new impressions upon him: for this reason, we prefer the sight of objects in motion to those at rest; and we proverbially say, that fire makes company; that is, it helps to deliver us from lassitude.

It is this necessity of being put in motion, and the kind of inquietude produced in the mind by the absence of any impression, that contains in part the principle of the inconstancy and improvement of the human mind, and which forcing it to

---

among us? These people are entirely devoted to indolence: to deliver themselves from all kinds of employment, they deprive themselves of every thing they can possibly do without.

The native inhabitants of the Caribbee Islands have the same aversion to thought and labour; they would sooner die with hunger than prepare their cassava bread, or make their pot boil. Their wives do every thing: they labour only one or two hours a day in cultivating the earth, and spend the rest of their time in their hammocks. If any person desires to buy their bed, they will sell it very cheap in the morning; for they will not give themselves the trouble of thinking whether they shall want it at night.

actuate all our senses must, after a revolution of an infinite number of ages, invent and carry to perfection the arts and sciences, and at length lead to the decay of taste*.

In fact, if the impressions made upon us are the more agreeable in proportion as they are more lively, and if the duration of the same impression blunts its vivacity, we must be desirous of those new impressions that produce in our minds the pleasure of surprise: artists ambitious of pleasing us, and exciting in us these kinds of impressions, ought therefore, after having in part exhausted the combinations of beauty, to substitute in its room the singular, because it makes a newer, and consequently a more lively, impression upon us. This, in polite nations, occasions the decay of taste.

To know still better the effect of lassitude upon us, and what the activity of this principle† is capable of producing,

---

* Perhaps, by comparing the slow progress of the human mind with the present state of perfection of the arts and sciences, we may form a judgment of the antiquity of the world. A new system of chronology might be made on this plan, that would be at least as ingenious as those that have hitherto appeared; but the execution would require great delicacy and sagacity of mind from him who undertook it.

† Lassitude, it is true, is not commonly very inventive; its spring is certainly too weak to enable us to execute grand enterprizes, and particularly to make us acquire great talents. It was not the languor of indolence that produced a Lycurgus, a Pelopidas, a Homer, an Archimedes, and a Milton; and we may assure ourselves that it is not the want of lassitude that makes us want great men. However, it sometimes produces great effects. It is sometimes capable of arming princes, and of drawing them to battle; and, when their first enterprizes are attended with success, it may make them conquerors. War may become an employment which habit renders necessary. Charles XII. the only hero who was ever insensible to the pleasures of love and of the table, was perhaps in part determined by this motive. But, if lassitude be capable of making a hero of this kind, it can never make a Cæsar or a Cromwell; it required a strong passion, to enable them to make the efforts of genius and skill necessary to clear the space that separated them from the throne.

let us observe mankind with an attentive eye; and we shall perceive, that the fear of lassitude prompts most of them to thought and action. In order to save themselves from it, at the hazard of too strong, and consequently disagreeable, impressions, men search with the greatest eagerness for every thing capable of putting them in motion: it is this desire that makes the common people run to see an execution, and the people of fashion a play; and it is the same motive in a gloomy devotion, and even in the austere exercises of penance, that frequently affords old women a remedy against the tiresomeness of inaction; for God, who by all possible means endeavours to bring sinners to himself, commonly uses with respect to them that of lassitude.

But especially at the age when the strong passions are enchained either by morals or the form of government, the wearisomeness of inaction plays its greatest part: it then becomes the universal mover.

At court and about the throne it is the fear of lassitude, joined to the smallest degree of ambition, that produces lazy courtiers of those who are but little ambitious. This makes them conceive little desires, form little intrigues, little cabals, little crimes, to obtain little places proportioned to the littleness of their passions: this makes a Sejanus, but never an Octavius; though it is, however, sufficient to raise them to those posts, where they indeed enjoy the privilege of being insolent, but search in vain to secure themselves from lassitude.

Such are, if I may be allowed the expression, both the active and inert forces which act on our souls; and, in obedience to these two opposite forces, we in general wish to be moved, without taking the trouble of moving ourselves. It is from this cause we desire to know every thing, without being at the pains of learning; and therefore, being more obsequious to opinion than to reason, which in every case would force us to undergo the fatigue of inquiry, men, on their entering into the world, accept indiscriminately all ideas presented to them, whether true or false *; and why, in fine, being impelled by the flux

_____

* Credulity is partly the effect of indolence. We have been habituated to believe a thing absurd; the falsity of such a belief is sus-

and reflux of prejudices, now towards wisdom, then towards folly, rational or irrational by mere accident, the slave of opi-

---

pected, but to be fully satisfied requires the fatigue of examination; thus we are not for undergoing; and thus choose rather to believe than examine. In such a disposition the most convincing proof of the falsity of an opinion will always appear insufficient. Every weak reasoning persuades; every ridiculous story is believed. I shall only produce one instance from Marini's account of Tonquin: " A religion," says this author, " was to be given to the Tonquinese, and that of the philosopher Rama, in the Tonquin language called Thic-ca, was made choice of. Its supposed origin, which they firmly believe, is as follows. One day the mother of the God Thic-ca had a vision of a white elephant, mysteriously formed in her mouth, and coming out of her left side. The dream, being ended, was realized, and she delivered of Thic-ca, who no sooner saw the light than he puts his mother to death; takes seven steps, marking the heaven with one finger and the earth with another; he boasts of being the only saint, in heaven or on earth. At seventeen years of age he marries three wives; at nineteen he forsakes his wives, and his son withdraws to a mountain, where he is instructed by two demons A-la-la and Ca-la-la. He afterwards comes among the people, by whom he is received, not as a teacher but as a pagod, or idol: he has four-score thousand disciples, among whom he selects five hundred, which number he afterwards reduces to one hundred, and these again to ten, who are called the ten great ones. This is what is told the Tonquinese, and is what they believe, though informed by a private tradition, that these ten great ones were his friends and confidants, and whom alone he did not deceive; for, after preaching his doctrine above forty-nine years, sensible of the approach of death, he called together all his disciples, and frankly addressed them in the following manner: " Hitherto I have deceived you; all that I told you is mere fiction: the only truth I have now to teach you is, that from nothing all came, and to it all shall return. Let me, however, advise you to keep my secret, and externally conform to my religion: there is no other way to keep the people in due subjection to you." Though this confession of Thic-ca on his death-bed be pretty generally known in Tonquin, yet the worship of that impostor still subsists, from a willingness of believing what they are accustomed to believe. Some scholastic subtleties, to which indolence gives the force of proof, have been sufficient for the disciples of Thic-ca through a cloud to aver this confession, and keep the Tonquinese in their belief.

nion is equally irrational in the eyes of the wise man, whether he maintains a truth, or advances an error. He is no better

---

The same laborious disciples have wrote five thousand volumes on the life of this Thic-ca. They maintain that he performed miracles; that immediately after his birth he assumed successively four-score thousand different forms; that his last metamorphosis was into a white elephant; and that hence is derived the extraordinary respect paid all over India to such animals. Of all august titles, that of king of the white elephant is most valued among Indian monarchs, and the king of Siam is stiled the king of the white elephant. The disciples of Thic-ca add, that there are six worlds; that on our dying in this we are born again in another; that the good man thus passes from one world to the other; and that, after this rotation, the wheel returns to its first position, and he is a second time born in this world: whence, at the seventh time, he departs in the plenitude of purity and perfection, and then having attained the utmost period of immutability finds himself exalted to the dignity of pagod, or idol. They hold a paradise and likewise a hell, from which, as in most false religions, the only way of escaping is to respect and be liberal to the Bonzes, and build monasteries. With regard to the devil, they relate, that he once had a dispute with the idol of Tonquin, which should be master of the earth. At last the devil agreed with the idol, that whatever it could cover with its robe should belong to him. On which the idol procured a robe made of such extent, that it covered the whole earth, and the baffled devil was obliged to retire into the sea, whence he sometimes returns; but flies immediately on the sight of the idol.

Whether these people had formerly any confused notion of our religion is not known; but one of the first articles of the creed of Thic-ca is, that there is an idol that saves mankind, and makes full satisfaction for their sins; and who, in order to have a more adequate knowledge and a more tender sense of the miseries of mankind, assumed the human nature.

Kolbe relates, that, among the Hottentots, there are many who maintain the same doctrine, and believe that their God has visibly appeared to their nation in the form of one of the most beautiful men among them; but the generality consider this tenet as a mere chimera, and pretend, that to metamorphose God into a man is to make him act a part very unbecoming his majesty. They pay him no worship; they say that God is good, and that our prayers are not regarded by him.

than the blind man who may accidentally tell the colour presented to him.

Thus the soul appears to be moved by the passions and a hatred of lassitude; by these it is rouzed from its natural tendency to rest, and surmounts the Vis inertiæ, to which it is always inclined to yield. But, however certain this proposition may appear, both in morality and natural philosophy, opinions are always to be established on facts; and in the following chapter I shall prove by instances, that it is the strong passions alone that prompt men to the execution of those heroic actions, and give birth to those grand ideas, which are the astonishment and admiration of all ages.

CHAP. VI.

OF THE POWER OF THE PASSIONS.

PASSIONS are in the moral what motion is in the natural world. If motion creates, destroys, preserves, animates the whole, that without it every thing is dead, so the passions animate the moral world. It is avarice which conducts ships over the deserts of the ocean; it is pride which fills up vallies, levels mountains, hews itself a passage through rocks, raises the pyramids of Memphis, digs the lake Mœris, and casts the Colossus of Rhodes. Love, it is said, formed the crayon for the first designer. In a country where revelation had never penetrated, it was love which, to sooth the grief of a widow, rendered disconsolate by the death of her young spouse, intimated to her the system of the immortality of the soul. It was the enthusiasm of gratitude which classed the benefactors of mankind among the Gods; which invented the false religions and superstitions, all of which, however, have not their source in such noble passions as love and gratitude.

It is therefore to strong passions that we owe the invention and wonders of arts; and consequently they are to be considered as the germ productive of genius, and the powerful spring that carries men to great actions. But, before we proceed, it may be proper to fix the idea I intend to convey by the word Strong-Passion. If men in general speak without understanding each other, it is owing to the obscurity of words; to this cause* may be attributed the prolongation of the miracle wrought at the tower of Babel.

By the word Strong-Passion, I mean a passion, the object of which is so necessary to our happiness, that without the possession of it life would be insupportable. This was Omar's idea of the passion, when he said, " Whoever thou art, that lovest liberty, desirest to be wealthy without riches, powerful without subjects, a subject without a master, dare to contemn death : kings will then tremble before thee, whilst thou alone shalt fear no person."

It is indeed only passions carried to this degree of force that can execute the greatest actions, defy dangers, pain, death, and heaven itself.

Dicearchus, the general of Philip, in presence of his whole army erects two altars, one to impiety, the other to injustice, sacrifices on them, and marches against the Cyclades.

Some days before the assassination of Cæsar, conjugal love, united with a noble pride, prevailed on Portia to make an incision in her thigh, to shew the wound to her husband ; and at

---

* For instance, if the word Red contain the several gradations from scarlet to carnation, let us suppose two men ; one has seen only scarlet, and the other carnation ; the first will very justly say, that red is a vivid colour; the other will be as positive, that it is a faint colour. For the like reason, two men may pronounce the word Will without understanding each other; for this word extends from the coldest to the most vehement degree of volition, which surmounts all obstacles. It is with the word Passion as with that of Understanding, its signification depends on the pronunciation. A man, who in a society of shallow persons is considered as weak, may be concluded simple : it is otherwise with him who is looked upon as a person of tolerable parts by geniuses of the first class; the choice of his company proves his superiority to common men. Here he is a middling orator, but would be the first in any other society.

the same time to say to him, " Brutus, you are meditating some great design which you conceal from me. I never before asked you an indiscreet question: I knew that our sex, however weak in itself, gathers strength by conversing with wise and virtuous men; and that I was daughter to Cato, and spouse to Brutus; but love rendered me so timerous, that I mistrusted my weakness. You see the essay I have made of my fortitude: judge from this trial of pain, whether I am worthy of your confidence."

It was the passion of honour and philosophic fanaticism alone that could induce Timicha, the Pythagorean, in the midst of torture, to bite off her tongue, that she might not expose herself to reveal the secrets of her sect.

Cato, when a child, going with his tutor to Sylla's palace, at seeing the bloody heads of the proscribed, asked with impatience the name of the monster who had caused so many Roman citizens to be murdered. He was answered, it was Sylla: " How," says he, " does Sylla murder thus, and is Sylla still alive?"—" Yes," it was replied, " the very name of Sylla disarms our citizens."—" O Rome," cried Cato, " deplorable is thy fate, since within the vast compass of thy walls not a man of virtue can be found, and the arm of a feeble child is the only one that will oppose itself against tyranny!" Then, turning toward his governor, "Give me," said he, " your sword; I will conceal it under my robe, approach Sylla, and kill him. Cato lives, and Rome is again free*."

In what climates has not this virtuous love of one's country performed heroic actions? In China, an emperor, being pursued by the victorious forces of a private patriot, in order to oblige this victor to disband his troops, had recourse to that superstitious respect which in that country a son pays to the

---

* It was the same Cato who, when retiring to Utica, being urged to consult the oracle of Jupiter Ammon, answered, " Oracles are for the fearful and the ignorant. The brave man is independent of the Gods, and knows when to live or die: he with composure offers himself to his fate, whether it be known or concealed." Cæsar, after having fallen into the hands of pirates, is still the same man, threatens them with death, and at landing makes good his words.

orders of his mother. He dispatched an officer, who, approaching her with his drawn poniard in his hand, told her peremptorily she must comply or perish. "Does thy master," answered she, with a disdainful smile, "flatter himself that I am ignorant of the tacit but sacred conventions between the people and their sovereigns, by which the people are to obey, and the kings to render them happy? He first broke the conventions. And thou, base tool of a tyrant, learn from a woman what in such cases is due to thy country." Then, snatching the poniard from the officer's hand, plunged it in her breast, saying, "Slave, if thou hast still any virtue, carry this bloody poniard to my son; bid him revenge the nation, and punish the tyrant. He has now nothing to fear, no cautions to observe for me: he is now at liberty to be virtuous.*"

---

* The passion of duty also animated Abdalla's mother, when her son, being forsaken by his friends, besieged in a castle, and urged to accept of an honourable capitulation offered him by the Syrians, consulted her how he should act, and she gave him this answer: "Son, when thou tookest up arms against the house of Ommiah, didst thou think it was espousing the cause of justice and virtue?" "Yes," answered he. "Oh! then," replied his mother, "what cause is there for deliberation? dost thou not know that cowards only are swayed by fear? wilt thou be the contempt of the Ommites? and shall it be said, that, when thou wert to determine between life and duty, thou didst prefer the former?"

It is the same passion for glory that, when the Roman army, perishing with cold for want of clothing, was on the point of dispersing, brought to the assistance of Septimus Severus the philosopher Antiochus, who, stripping himself before the army, leaped into a heap of snow, at which the troops cheerfully persevered in their duty.

Thrasea being one day counselled to make some submission to Nero, "How," said he, "shall I stoop so low to prolong my life a few days? No, death is a debt: I'll discharge it like a free man, and not pay it like a slave."

Vespasian, in a gust of passion threatening Helvidius with death, received this answer: "Did I ever tell you I was immortal? By putting me to death, you will act in character like a tyrant; I like a citizen, in receiving it without fear."

If the generous pride, the passion of patriotism and glory, determine citizens to such heroic actions, with what resolution and intrepidity do not the passions inspire those who aim at distinction in the arts and sciences, and whom Cicero calls the peaceable heroes? It is from a desire of glory, that the astronomer is seen, on the icy summits of the Cordeleras, placing his instruments in the midst of snows and frost; which conducts the botanist to the brinks of precipices in quest of plants; which anciently carried the juvenile lovers of the sciences into Egypt, Ethiopia, and even into the Indies, for visiting the most celebrated philosophers, and acquiring from their conversation the principles of their doctrine.

How strongly did this passion exert itself in Demosthenes, who, for perfecting his pronunciation, used every day to stand on the sea-shore, and with his mouth full of pebbles harangue the agitated waves! It was from the same desire of glory, that the young Pythagoreans submitted to a silence of three years, in order to habituate themselves to recollection and meditation; it induced Democritus* to shun the distractions of the world, and retire among the tombs, to meditate on those valuable truths, the discovery of which, as it is always very difficult, is also very little esteemed: in fine, it was this that prompted Heraclitus to cede to his younger brother the throne of Ephesus†, to which he had the right of primogeniture, that he might give himself up entirely to philosophy; which made the Athletic improve his strength, by denying himself the pleasures of love; it was also from a desire of popular applause that certain ancient priests renounced the same pleasures, and often, as Boindin pleasantly observes of them, without any other recompence for their continence than the perpetual temptation it occasions.

---

* Democritus was very rich, but he did not think this entitled him to neglect his mind, and to live in a flattered stupidity.

† Mison, son of the tyrant of Chenes, also renounced his right to his father's sceptre; and, being disengaged from all public duties, he used to retire among the solitary rocks, to indulge himself in profound reflections!

I have shewn that it is to the passions we owe most of the objects of our admiration; under their powerful influence we sustain dangers, pain, and death; and that they animate us to take the boldest resolutions.

I am now going to prove, that, in critical occasions, it is by their assistance only that great men are inspired to say, and act, and do, the best.

Let us here call to remembrance the memorable and celebrated speech of Hannibal to his soldiers on the day of the battle of Ticinus; and we shall own, that it could be inspired only by his hatred of the Romans and his passion for glory. " Fellow soldiers," said he, " heaven assures me of the victory. Let the Romans, not you, tremble. View this field of battle! It offers no retreat for cowards: we all perish, if any retire. What can be a more certain pledge of triumph? what plainer indidication of the protection of the Gods? They have placed us between victory and death!"

Can it be doubted that Sylla was not animated with these same passions, when Crassus asked an escort to go and raise new levies in the country of the Marsians, Sylla answered, " If you are afraid of the enemy, the escort I give you are your fathers, brothers, relations, and friends, who, massacred by the tyrants, cry for vengeance, and expect it from you."

When the Macedonians, wearied with the toils of war, desired Alexander to discharge them, it was pride and the love of glory that dictated to him this spirited answer: " Away, ingrates, lazy cowards! I'll subdue the world without you; Alexander will never want subjects and soldiers where there are men."

It is only from men of strong passions that such speeches can be expected. Genius itself, in such cases, can never supply the want of sentiment. We are ignorant of the language of passions we never felt.

Besides, it is not only in a single act, as eloquence in the passions; every kind are to be esteemed as the germ productive of superior understanding: it is they which, keeping a perpetual fermentation in our ideas, fertilize in us the same ideas which in frigid souls are barren, and would be no more than seed scattered on a rock.

It is the passsous which, having strongly fixed our attention on the object of our desire, causes us to view it under appearances unknown to other men, and which consequently prompt heroes to plan and execute those hardy enterprizes which, till success has proved the propriety of them, appear ridiculous, and indeed must appear so to the multitude.

"The cause," says Cardinal Richelieu, "why a timorous mind perceives an impossibility in the most simple projects, when to an elevated mind the most arduous seems easy, is, because, before the latter the mountains sink, and before the former mole-hills are metamorphosed into mountains.

It is, in effect, only a strong passion, which, being more perspicuous than good sense, can teach us to distinguish the extraordinary from the impossible, which men of sense are ever confounding; because, not being animated by strong passions, these sensible persons never rise above mediocrity, a proposition which I am now going to demonstrate, in order to prove the great superiority of the man of strong passions above any other, and that, in reality, great passions only can produce great men.

CHAP. VII.

OF THE SUPERIORITY OF THE MIND IN MEN OF STRONG PASSIONS ABOVE THE MEN OF SENSE.

If antecedently to success great geniuses of every kind are considered as romantic by the men of sense, it is because the latter, incapable of any thing great, cannot conceive the existence of the means great men employ in the execution of great things.

It is on this account, that great men must of consequence be derided till they excite admiration. When Parmenio, urged by Alexander to deliver his opinion on Darius's proposals of peace, said, " Were I Alexander, I would accept them," The

Macedonians doubtless, till victory justified that prince's apparent rashness, were better pleased with Parmenio's motion than with Alexander's answer: " And I also, were I Parmenio." One characterizes the man of sense, the other an extraordinary man. Now, the first class greatly exceeds in number that of the second. It is therefore evident, that, had not the son of Philip already gained the respect of the Macedonians by his signal exploits, and habituated them to extraordinary enterprises, his answer must have appeared absolutely ridiculous. None of them would have perceived the motive for it, either in the interior consciousness which this hero could have of the superiority of his courage and abilities, and the advantage both these qualities gave him over a luxurious effeminate people like the Persians; or, lastly, in the knowledge he had acquired, both of the temper of the Macedonians and his ascendency over their minds; and consequently of the facility of communicating to them, by his gestures, looks, and words, that intrepidity which animated himself. Yet these were the various motives which, enforced by an ardent thirst of glory, made him, with reason, conclude the victory much more certain than it appeared to Parmenio, and consequently inspired him with a bolder answer.

When Tamerlane fixed his engines before the ramparts of Smyrna, from which the forces of the Ottoman empire had lately been obliged to retire with great loss, he was aware of the difficulty of the enterprise; he well knew that he was attacking a place which the Christian powers might continually supply with provisions; but the passion for glory, which excited him to the enterprise, suggested to him the means of executing it. He fills up the large abyss of the waters, checks the seas, and baffles the European fleets by a dyke; displays his victorious standards on the breaches of Smyrna, and shews the astonished world that nothing is impossible to great men *.

---

* The same thing may be said of Gustavus, who, at the head of his army and artillery, availing himself of the time when the winter had consolidated the surface of the water, crossed the frozen seas for making a descent in Zeeland. He knew, as well as his officers, that his

When Lycurgus formed a plan for making Lacedemon a republic of heroes, he did not proceed by insensible alterations, according to the slow and therefore steady step of what is called wisdom. This great man, heated by a passion for virtue, perceived that by speeches, or supposed oracles, he could inspire his countrymen with the same sentiments that glowed in himself; and that, by seizing the first instant of ardour, he might change the constitution of the government, and bring about, in the manners of that people, a sudden revolution, which in the common methods of prudence would have required many years. He knew that passions are like volcanoes, whose sudden eruptions alter the channel of a river, which art could not have diverted but by digging another bed for it, and, consequently, not till after a long succession of time and prodigious expence. By this means he succeeded in a plan, perhaps the boldest ever undertaken, and which would have been too difficult for any sensible man, who, deriving that title only from his incapacity of being excited by strong passions, is also incapable of inspiring them.

Men of these passions, being intelligent judges in the various methods of kindling the fire of enthusiasm, have often had recourse to such, which sensible persons, for want of knowing this part of the human heart, have before the success always considered as puerile and ridiculous.

Such was the stratagem of Pericles, who, when marching towards a superior enemy, in order to make a hero of every soldier, conceals in a dark wood a man of an extraordinary stature, seated in a car, drawn by four white horses; he suddenly issues forth covered with a gorgeous mantle, on his legs glittering buskins, and his head adorned with radiant tresses: thus, he rapidly drives along the front of the army, calling out, " Pericles, the victory is thine! I promise it thee!"

Such was the method taken by Epaminondas for rouzing the

---

descent might be easily opposed; but he also knew that a wise temerity seldom fails of disconcerting the foresight of common men, that the boldness of the enterprises often secures their success, and that there are cases when the highest boldness is the highest prudence.

courage of the Thebans; he caused one night the arms hanging in a temple to be secretly removed, and persuaded the soldiers that the patron-gods of Thebes had made use of them in
order to come armed the next day, and join in battle with
them against their enemy.

Such, lastly, was the order given by Ziska on his death-bed,
when, still breathing the most furious hatred against the Catholics, who had persecuted him, he recommends to his partizans,
that, immediately after his death, they should flea him, and of
his skin make a drum, assuring them of the victory every time
they should beat this drum in their encounters with the Catholics; and this promise, seemingly so chimerical, was verified
by constant successes.

Thus it is seen, that the most decisive means, the best adapted for producing great effects, ever unknown to those who are
called men of sense, are discernible only by men of strong passions, who, in the circumstances of those heroes, would have
had the like sentiments.

Without the respect due to the reputation of the great Condé,
would it be thought, that a project of that prince, for recording
in every regiment the memorable actions and sayings of the
soldiers should prove the seed of emulation in the troops? Does
not the inexecution of this project convince us how little its
usefulness was perceived? How few, like the celebrated chevalier Folard, are sensible of the power of speeches on the sol-
diery? Does every body equally perceive all the beauty of that
saying of the Duke de Vendôme; when, seeing a body of his
troops flying, whilst the officers omitted nothing to rally them,
he throws himself among the fugitives, calling out to the officers, " Let the soldiers alone! This is not the place, but yon-
der," (pointing to a tree about a hundred paces off,) " whither
this corps is going to form again." Here the soldiers' courage
was perceivable; he thus revived in them the passions of shame
and honour, which they flattered themselves they still retained
in his eyes. By this resource alone they could have been
stopped, and thus they were again led on to action and to
victory.

Now can it be questioned such a speech had not its origin in the temper; and that, in general, all the ways made use of by great men for kindling in others the fire of enthusiasm have not been suggested to them by their passions? Where is the sensibleman who, for increasing the confidence and respect of the Macedonians, would have allowed Alexander to term himself the son of Jupiter Ammon? would have put Numa on feigning a private commerce with the nymph Egeria? would have advised Zamolxis, Zaleuxus, and Mneves, to pretend themselves inspired by Vesta, Minerva, or Mercury? Marius to have among his retinue a fortune-teller? Sertorius to consult his hind? and, lastly, who like the count de Dunois, would, for checking the progress of the English, have put the sword into the hands of a country girl?

Few extend their thoughts beyond the common mode of thinking; and still smaller is the number of those who dare* execute and speak what they think. If sensible men attempted to put such methods in practice, they would never be happy in the application, for want of a certain experimental acquaintance with the passions. They must follow beaten paths; if they forsake them, they bewilder themselves. Indolence is always the predominant quality in a man of sense: he has nothing of that activity of soul, by which a great man in power forms new springs for moving the world, or sows the seeds of future events. It is only to the man of passion, and him who thirsts after glory, that the book of futurity is open.

At the battle of Marathon, Themistocles was the only man of all the Greeks who foresaw the fight of Salamine, and who, by exercising the Athenians in naval affairs, prepared them for victory.

When Cato, the censor, a man whose sense exceeded his

---

* Yet by these alone is the human mind improved. When it is not a case of government, where the slightest faults may be productive of national evils, but only a scientifical point, the very errors of geniuses deserve the public applause and gratitude; for, in sciences, an infinite number of men must be mistaken, that others may no longer be mistaken. This line of Martial is applicable to them:

Si non errasset, fecerat ille minus.

sagacity, joined the senate determined to destroy Carthage, why did Scipio alone oppose the ruin of that city? Because he considered Carthage both as a rival worthy of Rome, and as a dyke for opposing the torrent of vices and corruptions then breaking into Italy. Employed in the politic study of history, habituated into meditation, and that laborious attention of which a passion for glory alone can render us capable, he attained a kind of divination. Accordingly, he predicted all the misfortunes that would fall on Rome, the very moment when the mistress of the world erected her throne on the ruins of all the monarchies of the universe; he in every country saw a Marius and a Sylla; and, when the Romans could perceive only triumphal palms, and hear the shouts of victory, he heard the proclamations of the sanguinary tables of proscription. That people were then like sailors, who, when the sea is smooth, and the zephyrs gently swell the sails and dimple the surface of the ocean, abandon themselves to levity and mirth, while the attentive pilot beholds, at the very extremity of the horizon, the storm which will soon throw the deep into a ferment.

If the Roman senate slighted Scipio's advice, it is because very few, by the knowledge of the past and present, see into futurity * ; it is because states, like the oak, the growth and decay of which is insensible to the ephemerical insects living under its shade, seem to them, as it were, in a state of immobility; and this apparent immobility they rather believe as being most flattering to their indolence, which thus thinks itself discharged from the solicitude of foresight and precaution.

It is in morality as in physics: the people think the ocean constantly chained within its bed, whereas the philosopher sees it successively discover and overflow vast tracts, and ships traversing those plains which were lately furrowed by the plough. The people behold with admiration the even summits of stupen-

---

* A slight present good frequently so inebriates a nation, that in its blindness it exclaims against the eminent genius who, in this slight present good, foresees many substantial evils. They imagine that, in branding him as a maleconcent, virtue punishes vice; whereas generally it is only folly laughing at judgement.

dous mountains; but the philosopher sees their aspiring tops gradually ruined by time tumbling down into the valleys, and filling them with their fragments. But to view the moral universe, like the natural, in a successive and perpetual destruction and reproduction, and thence to discern the remote causes of the overthrow of states, is the gift only of such as are inured to application. It is eagle-eyed passion which penetrates into the dark abyss of futurity: indifference is born blind and stupid. In a serene sky and pure air, the inhabitant of the town does not foresee the tempest: it is the attentive and interested eye of the husbandman that beholds, with terror, insensible exhalations rising from the surface of the earth, condensing in the air, and overspreading it with those clouds which will soon discharge themselves in dreadful lightnings and desolating hail, to the utter ruin of his promising crops.

If every passion be particularly examined, it will be found, that all are very sagacious in the pursuit of their objects; that they alone can some time perceive the cause of effects which the ignorant attribute to chance; consequently, that they alone can curtail, and perhaps one day totally destroy, the empire of this chance; of which each discovery necessarily contracts the limits.

If the ideas and actions arising from such passions as avarice and love are in general little valued, it is not that these ideas and actions do not often require great understanding and a multitude of combinations; but because both the one and the other are either indifferent or detrimental to the public, which, as I have proved in the preceding discourse, confers the appellations of virtuous or ingenious only on such actions and ideas as are useful to it. Now, of all passions, the love of glory is that alone which is never at a loss, that can always inspire such actions and ideas. It was this which inflamed an eastern monarch when he cried out, " Wretched are the sovereigns of slaves! Alas! the joys of just praise, which so delights the gods and heroes, are not made for them! Ye nations, added he, who have basely parted with the right of publicly blaming your masters, you have thereby lost the right of praising them: the panegyric of the slave is suspicious, and his unfortunate sovereign remains always in ignorance, whether he deserves esteem or contempt. How painful is this uncertainty to a noble soul!"

Such sentiments always suppose an ardent passion for glory. This passion is the soul of men of genius and talents in every kind; to this desire they owe the enthusiasm they have for their art, and which they sometimes carry so far, as to consider it as the only occupation worthy the mind of man; an opinion for which sensible persons call them madmen; but they are considered in another light by the knowing, who, in the cause of their madness, discern that of their abilities and success.

The conclusion of this chapter is, that the men of sense, those idols of the common people, are always very inferior to the men of passion; and that it is the strong passions which, rescuing us from sloth, can alone impart to us that continued attention productive of superior intellects. All that remains to confirm this truth is, to shew in the following chapter, that even they who are justly ranked among illustrious personages, when no longer supported by the ardour of passion, instantly sink into the class of the most ordinary men.

CHAP. VIII.

ON STUPIDITY, THE CONSEQUENCE OF THE CESSATION OF PASSIONS.

This proposition is a necessary consequence of the former. In effect, if a man, animated with the most violent desire of esteem, and as such capable of the strongest passion, finds himself able to satisfy this desire, he will soon cease to be animated with that passion, it being the nature of every desire to languish and die away, unless nourished by hope. Now, the same cause which extinguishes in him the passion for esteem will necessarily kill in him the germ of superior intellects.

Suppose persons no less ambitious of public esteem than the Turennes, the Condés, the Descartes, the Corneilles, the Richlieus, were made receivers of a tax, or the like; this station, depriving them of all hopes of glory, they would want even the common understanding necessary for such employments. Little adapted to the studies of edicts and tarifs, they would remain unqualified for a post odious to the public ; they would be filled with aversion and disgust for a science, in which he who has acquired the most profound and extensive knowledge, and who consequently retired to rest, in his own opinion, very learned and very respectable, may awake very ignorant and very use-less, should the government have thought fit to suppress or in-corporate these duties. Totally given up to the Vis inertiæ, such persons will soon become incapable of any kind of appli-cation.

This is the reason why, in the management of an inferior post, men born for great things are often found inferior to the most shallow understandings. Vespasian, who, on the throne, was the admiration of the Romans, would, whilst Prætor, have been the object of their contempt *. The eagle, which in its bold flight pierces the clouds, skims the surface of the earth with a less rapidity than the swallow. To destroy the ani-mating passion in a man is to deprive him at once of all his capacity; in this, Sampson's hair seems to be the emblem of passion; that being cut off, Sampson was reduced to a common man.

To confirm this truth by a second example, let us take a view of those eastern usurpers, who, endued with amazing boldness, necessarily blended great abilities; let us inquire, why most of them, when seated on the throne, shewed but little genius; why, very much inferior to the western usurpers, there is scarce one, as the form of the Asiatic governments sufficiently proves, who can be accounted a legislator: not that they always de-lighted in the calamities of their subjects, but because, having once obtained the crown, the object of their desire was ful-filled; because the pusillanimity, the subjection, and obe-dience, of a slavish people, ensuring them of the possession, the passion which had raised them to the empire ceased to ani-

---

* Caligula ordered Vespasian's robe to be dragged through the dirt for his neglecting to cause the streets to be cleaned.

mate them; that, being now without motives of a power to induce them to bear the fatigue of attention implied in the discovery and establishment of good laws, they are, as I have said
above, in the case of those men of sense, who, for want of a spirited desire, have never taken the pains necesary to free themselves from the delights of sloth. If, on the contrary, several
western usurpers have, when on the throne, displayed great
talents; if Augustus, Cromwell, and many others of a similar
genius, may be classed among legislators; it is because they had
to do with subjects of a more exalted turn of mind, and too
brave and generous patiently to bear the rein; the apprehen-
sion of losing the object of their desires still kept alive in them
the passion of ambition in all its former vivacity. Raised to
thrones on which sleep might have been fatal, they found it
absolutely necessary to conciliate their refractory subjects, to
enact laws useful in that juncture *, to impose on their people,
at least delude them with, the phantom of a transitory happiness, to make them amends for the real misfortunes attending a
usurpation.

Thus it is to the danger the latter were continually exposed
to on the throne, that they owed that superiority of talents
which raised them above most of the eastern usurpers! they
were in some respects like the man of genius, who, being the
but of criticism, and perpetually molested in the enjoyment of
a very precarious reputation, feels that it is not he alone who is

---

* This gained Cromwell the following just epitaph :
Ci git le destructeur d'un pouvoir légitime,
Jusqu'à son dernier jour favorisé des cieux,
Dont les vertus méritoient mieux
Que le sceptre acquis par un crime.
Par quel destin faut-il, par quelle étrange loi,
Qu'à tous ceux qui sont nés pour porter la couronne,
Ce soit l'usurpateur qui donne
L'exemple des vertus que doit avoir un roi !
The substance of which is :—Here lies the destroyer of regal power,
whom heaven constantly favoured, and whose virtues deserved some-
thing better than a sceptre acquired by guilt. Strange ! that from
usurpers the sons of majesty are taught the qualities becoming kings.

heated with the passion of vanity; and that if his renders him desirous of esteem, that of another will constantly withhold it, unless he take care, by useful and entertaining works and continual efforts of wit, to comfort them under the mortification of commending him. It is on the throne that this fear keeps the mind in a state of every kind of fecundity; this fear removed, the spring of the mind is broken.

Who doubts but that a natural philosopher often examines a physical problem, though sometimes of little importance to society, with infinitely more attention than a sultan bestows on the deliberation of a law, big with the happiness or calamity of thousands. If the latter bestows less time in weighing and digesting his ordinances and edicts, than a wit does in composing a sonnet or epigram, it is because thinking, which is always fatiguing, is as it were contrary to our nature*; and that a sultan, being above punishment and satire, was destitute of motives for overcoming sloth, the enjoyment of which is so agreeable to all mankind.

Thus we see the activity of the mind depends on the activity of the passions. It is therefore during the age of passion, that is from twenty-five to thirty-five and forty, that man is capable of the greatest efforts, both of virtue and genius. At this age, men born for great things have acquired a proper compass of learning, and their passions have yet scarce lost any thing of their force: but, beyond this term, our passions decline, and, as this is the period of mental acquisition, no new ideas are then acquired; and whatever superiority there may afterwards appear in their works, it is no more than the application and display of the ideas acquired in the time of the effervescence of the passions, but which hitherto had not been reduced to practice.

---

* Some philosophers have advanced this paradox, that slaves, under the hardest bodily labour, enjoyed perhaps in the tranquillity of their minds a compensation for all their sufferings; and that, by this tranquillity of mind, the condition of the slave was often in happiness equal to his master.

Farther, it is not only to age that the decay of the passions is to be attributed : we abate of our fondness for an object when the pleasure promised to ourselves from its possession does not equal the trouble of the acquisition. He who is fond of glory sacrifices his inclination to it no farther than he thinks the sacrifice will be repaid by the prize. On this account it was that so many heroes only could escape the snare of voluptuousness in the tumult of camps and the acclamations of victory : on this account it was, that, on a day of battle alone, the great Condé could master his choler, being then perfectly calm and sedate; it is on this account, if things called small may be compared with great, that Dupré, noted for a careless gait, never laid aside that aukward custom but on the stage, where he thought the admiration of the spectators sufficiently compensated for the trouble he took to please them. Habits and sloth are to be overcome only by a love of glory; and sometimes it is nothing but the greatest which will satisfy men, so that, if they cannot make themselves masters of almost the whole empire of esteem, most of them give themselves up to a scandalous sloth. Extreme pride and extreme ambition often produce in them the effect of indifference and moderation. In reality, it is a minute soul which desires a minute glory. If they who are so curious in dressing, figuring, and speaking, in assemblies, are generally incapable of great things, it is not only because by acquiring an infinity of minute talents and accomplishments they lose that time which they might employ in the discovery of exalted ideas, and the culture of eminent talents, but because the very pursuit of such a trivial glory implies a debility and narrowness in their desires. Accordingly, great men are seen for the most part utterly negligent of the minute cares and observances necessary to acquire a regard; these are ways they disdain. " In that young man," said Sylla, speaking of Cæsar, " who walks so immodestly along the streets, I see several Mariuses."

The reader, I hope, is now sufficiently convinced that the total absence of passion, if possible, would reduce us to the most absolute stupidity; and that the less we are animated by our passions, the nearer we approach that state*. Passions indeed are the celestial fire which vivifies the moral world ; it is to the passions that the arts and sciences owe their discoveries, and the soul its elevation. If they are also the sources of the vices and of most of the misfortunes of men, these misfortunes do not warrant moralists in condemning the passions, and exploding them under the appellations of madness and folly. Sublime virtue and discerning wisdom are two products of this folly, which should render it respectable in their eyes.

The general conclusion of what I have said on the passions is, that it is only their force that can counterbalance in us the force of indolence and inertia, pluck us from that indulgence and stupidity to which we are incessantly gravitating, and, lastly, endue us with that continuity of attention to which a superiority of talents is annexed.

But it will be said, has not nature, by thus kindling in some men a stronger disposition to mental passions than in others, given men unequal improvements? To this question, I answer, that, if to excel in one kind does not, as I have above shewn, require the utmost stretch of application, neither is it necessary for distinction in the same kind to be animated with the most fervent passion, but only with a degree sufficient for stimulating us to alertness and attention ; besides, it may be proper to observe, that, relatively to passions, there is not that difference between men as is imagined. To know whether nature in this respect has so unequally distributed its gifts, we must examine, whether all men are susceptible of passions; and, in order to this, we must go back to their origin.

---

* It is often from the want of passions that arises the obstinacy of persons of mean parts; their slender knowledge supposes that they never had any desire of instruction, or, at least, that this desire has been always very faint, very much below their fondness for sloth ; now he, who is not desirous of instruction, has never sufficient motives for altering his mind. To save himself the fatigue of imagination, he must always turn a deaf ear to the remonstrances of reason, and obstinacy in this case is the necessary effect of sloth.

CHAP. IX.

OF THE ORIGIN OF THE PASSIONS.

In order to arrive at this knowledge, we must distinguish the passions into two kinds : those immediately given us by nature, and those we owe to the establishment of society. And to know which of these passions has produced the other, let us transport ourselves in idea to the first ages of the world, and we shall there see that nature, by hunger, thirst, heat, and cold, informed man of his wants, and added a variety of pleasing and painful sensations ; the former to the gratifications of these wants, the latter to the incapacity of gratifying them : there we shall behold man capable of receiving the impressions of pleasure and pain, and born as it were with a love for the one, and hatred for the other. Such was man, when he came from the hand of nature.

In this state he had neither envy, pride, avarice, nor ambition ; sensible only of the pleasure and pain derived from nature, he was ignorant of all those artificial pains and pleasures we procure from the above passions. Such passions are then not immediately given by nature ; but their existence, which supposes that of society, also supposes that we have in us the latent seeds of those passions. If therefore we receive at our birth only wants, in those wants and in our first desires we must seek the origin of these artificial passions, which can be nothing more than the unfolding of the faculty of sensation.

Perhaps both in the moral and natural world, God originally implanted only one principle in all he created, and that what is, and what shall be, is only the unnecessary unfolding of this principle.

He said to matter, " I endow thee with power." Immediately the elements subject to the laws of motion, but wandering and confounded in the deserts of space, formed a thousand monstrous assemblages, and produced a thousand different chaoses, till they at last placed themselves in that equilibrium and natural order in which the universe is now supposed to be arranged.

He seems also to have said to man, " I endow thee with sensibility, the blind instrument of my will, that, being incapable of penetrating into the depth of my views, thou mayest accomplish all my designs. I place thee under the guardianship of pleasure and pain; both shall watch over thy thoughts and thy actions: they shall beget thy passions, excite thy friendship, thy tenderness, thine aversion, thy rage; they shall kindle thy desires, thy fears, thy hopes; they shall take off the veil of truth; they shall plunge thee in error, and, after having made thee conceive a thousand absurd and different systems of morality and government, shall one day discover to thee the simple principles, on the unfolding of which depends the order and happiness of the moral world."

Let us suppose that Heaven suddenly animates several men: their first employment will be to satisfy their wants, and soon after they will endeavour, by their cries, to express the impressions they receive from pleasure and pain. Those cries will constitute their first language, which, if we may judge from the poverty of the languages of the savages, must be very confined, and reducible to these first sounds. When mankind, by becoming more numerous, shall begin to spread over the surface of the earth, and, like the waves of the ocean, which cover its distant banks, and instantly retire into its capacious bed, many generations shall have appeared on the earth, and be swallowed up in the gulf wherein all things are forgotten; when families shall live nearer to each other; when the desire becomes common of possessing the same things, as the fruit of a certain tree, or the favours of a particular woman, it will excite quarrels and combats, and these beget anger and revenge; when, sated with blood, and weary of living in perpetual fear, mankind shall consent to lose a small part of that liberty they found so prejudicial in a state of nature, they will enter into conventions with each other, and these conventions will be their first laws; when they have formed laws, they will entrust some persons with the care of seeing them put in execution, and those will be the

first magistrates. These rude magistrates of a savage people
will inhabit the forests. After having in part destroyed the
animals, the people will no longer be able to live by hunting,
and the scarcity of provisions will teach them the art of
breeding and tending their flocks, which will supply their
wants; and the nations that subsisted by hunting will become
nations of shepherds. After a certain number of ages, when
these last will be extremely multiplied, so that the earth will
not in the same space yield nourishment for a greater number
of inhabitants without being cultivated by human labour,
the nations of shepherds will disappear, and give place to nations of husbandmen. The calls of hunger, in discovering
the art of agriculture, shall soon teach them that of measuring
and dividing the lands. This being done, every man's property must be secured to him, and thence will arise a number
of sciences and laws. Lands, from their different nature and
cultivation, bearing different fruits, men will purchase what
they want, by making exchanges with each other, and at
length perceive the advantage of a general exchange that
will represent all commodities; and, for this purpose, they
will make use of shells or metals. When societies are arrived
at this point of perfection, all equality between men will be
destroyed: they will be distinguished into superiors and inferiors; then the words good and evil, formed to express the
natural sensations of pleasure and pain we receive from external objects, will generally extend to every thing that can procure, increase, or diminish, either of these sensations; such
are riches and indigence: and then riches and honours, by the
advantages annexed to them, will become the general object
of the desires of mankind. Hence will arise, according to the
different forms of government, criminal or virtuous passions;
such as envy, avarice, pride, and ambition, patriotism, a
love of glory, magnanimity, and even love, which, being
given by nature only as a want, will be confounded with vanity, and become an artificial passion, that will, like the
others, arise from the unfolding of the natural sensibility.

However certain this conclusion may be, there are few men
who can clearly perceive the ideas from which it results.

Besides, by owning that our passions originally derive their source from natural sensibility, we may believe that, in the state in which polite nations are actually placed, these passions existed independently of the cause that has produced them. I propose then to follow the metamorphosis of the natural pleasures and pains into the artificial pleasures and pains; and to shew that, in the passions, such as avarice, ambition, pride, and friendship, which seem least to belong to the pleasures of sense, we always either seek natural pleasure or shun natural pain.

CHAP. X.

OF AVARICE.

GOLD and silver may be considered as objects agreeable to the eye; but, if we desired nothing more in their possession than the pleasures produced by the lustre and beauty of these metals, the avaricious man would rest satisfied with being allowed to contemplate freely heaps of gold and silver in the public treasury. But, as this view would be far from gratifying his passion, it necessarily follows, that the avaricious, of whatever class, either desire riches as the means of procuring pleasure, or as an exemption from the miseries with which poverty is attended.

This principle being established, I assert that man being, by nature, sensible of no other pleasures than those of the senses, these pleasures are consequently the only object of his desires. A fondness for luxury, magnificent equipages, expensive entertainments, and superb furniture, is then an artificial passion necessarily produced by the natural wants either of love or the pleasures of the table. Indeed, what real pleasure can this luxury and magnificence procure the avaricious voluptuary, if he do not consider them as the means of pleasing women, and obtaining their favours, if they are the objects of his fondness; or of imposing on men, and forcing them, by the uncertain hope of a reward, to remove from him every pain, and to assemble around him every pleasure?

With these avaricious voluptuaries, who certainly do not properly deserve to be called covetous, avarice is the immediate effect of the fear of pain and the love of pleasure. But it may be asked, how can this love of pleasure, or this fear of pain, be excited in the really avaricious, those wretched misers, who never part with their money to purchase pleasure? If they pass their lives in the want of common necessaries, and exaggerate to themselves and others the pleasures annexed to the possession of gold, it is merely to divert their attention from a misfortune which nobody can nor ought to pity.

However surprising the contradiction may be, that is found between their conduct and the motives from which they act, I shall endeavour to discover the cause, which, leaving them the incessant desire of pleasure, must always deprive them of its enjoyment.

In order to which, I shall observe, first, that this kind of avarice derives its source from an excessive and ridiculous fear of the possibility of indigence, and of the many evils with which it is accompanied. The avaricious are like those afflicted with a hypochondriac melancholy, who live in perpetual agonies, see themselves surrounded with dangers, and are afraid of being crushed by every one that approaches them.

This species of the avaricious we commonly find among those who were born in a state of indigence, and have themselves experienced the long train of evils with which it is attended. Their folly is therefore, in this respect, more pardonable than in men born in a state of affluence, among whom there are seldom found any of the avaricious, except the proud or voluptuous.

To explain how, among the former, the fear of wanting necessaries forces them to live in perpetual want, let us suppose any one of them, when sinking under the weight of poverty, forms a project for delivering himself from the painful burthen.— Hope immediately steps in to his assistance, and gives fresh vigour to his soul, which had been bowed down by indigence; revives his activity, and makes him search for protectors: she confines him to the anti-chambers of ministers, makes him cringe at the feet of the great, and devote himself to a very miserable life, till he has obtained a post that will raise him above want. But, when he is arrived at this desirable state, will pleasure be the only object of his pursuit? A man of this character, who is timid and distrustful, will have a lively remembrance of the evils he has experienced, and the same motives, that prompted the desire of delivering himself from them, will determine him to refuse the indulgence of every gratification, till he has acquired the habit of depriving himself of them. This man being once raised above want, if he be thirty-five or forty years of age, if the love of pleasure have its edge every moment blunted, and be less sensibly felt, what will he then do? He will become more difficult in his pleasures; if he be fond of women, he will have the most beautiful; and those favours are purchased at the dearest rate: he will therefore accumulate new riches, to gratify his new appetites. Now, if, in the time required for obtaining these acquisitions, distrust and timidity, which increase with age, and may be considered as the effects of the sensibility of our weakness, shew him that, in point of riches, he can never have enough; and if his insatiable thirst after them is found to be equally balanced by his love of pleasure; he will then be drawn by two different attractions. In order to obey both, this man, without renouncing pleasure, will prove to himself, that he ought, at least, to defer its enjoyment, till he has accumulated greater riches, when he may, without fear of futurity, employ himself entirely in the indulgence of present gratifications. If, in the new interval necessary to amass new wealth, age should suddenly render him insensible of pleasure, will he then change his manner of life? will he renounce habits, which the incapacity of acquiring new ones have rendered dear to him? No, he certainly will not! Satisfied in contemplating his riches, and with the possibility of the pleasures they are capable of procuring, he will endeavour to escape the pain of lassitude, by giving up himself entirely to his ordinary pursuits: he will become so much the more avaricious in his old age, as the habit of accumulating wealth is no longer counterbalanced by the desire of enjoying it, which will be strengthened by the mechanical fear of want, wherewith old age is always accompanied.

CHAP. XI.

OF AMBITION.

THE credit annexed to important posts, as well as to riches, preserves us from pain, procures us pleasures, and consequently is to be considered as the means of avoiding the one, and procuring the other. We may therefore apply to Ambition what I have said of Avarice.

Among the savage nations, whose chiefs or kings have no other privilege than that of being fed and clothed with what is caught by their warriors in hunting, the desire of being freed from these wants constitutes ambition.

Rome in its infancy appointed no other reward for great actions than as much land as one Roman could clear and till in a day; and this alone was sufficient to form heroes.

What I say of Rome, I say of all poor nations, among whom the ambitious desire only to be delivered from labour and fatigue. On the contrary, among opulent nations, where all who have any pretensions to great places have riches sufficient to procure not only the conveniences but the accommodations of life, ambition almost always flows from a love of pleasure.

But, it is said, that purple robes, coronets, and, in general, every mark of honour, can afford no natural satisfaction of pleasure; ambition then cannot be founded on a love of pleasure: but on the desire of esteem and respect, and is not therefore the effect of natural sensations.

If the desire of grandeur, I reply, were only kindled by the desire of glory and esteem, it would never excite ambition any where but in republics, such as Rome and Sparta, where dignities were commonly the insignia of the great virtues and the distinguished talents of which they were the reward. Among them, ambition might flatter pride, since it secured to a man the esteem of his fellow-citizens; and he, having always great enterprises to execute, might consider great posts as the means of rendering his glory conspicuous, and proving his superiority over others. Now the ambitious with equal ardour aspire to grandeur in ages where it is debased by the choice of the men who are raised to it, and consequently at the time when its possession is less flattering. Ambition is not then founded on the desire of esteem. In vain it is pretended, that, in this respect, the ambitious may deceive himself: the marks of respect, lavished upon him, inform him every moment that this honour is paid to his place, and not to him. He is sensible that the respect he enjoys is not personal; that it will vanish by the death or disgrace of the possessor; that the advanced age of the prince may be sufficient to destroy it; that then the persons, raised to the first employments, surround the sovereign like the golden clouds that attend the setting sun, whose splendor is obscured and disappears in proportion as that luminary sinks below the horizon. He has a thousand times heard, and has himself as often said, that honours are not purchased by merit; that promotion to great posts is no proof of merit in the eyes of the public; and that, on the contrary, it is generally considered as the price of intrigue and the meanness of importunity. If he doubt of it, let him consult history, and especially that of Byzantium, where he will see that a man may, at the same time, be invested with all the honours of an empire, and loaded with the contempt of nations. But, if it be supposed that the ambitious have a confused idea of the esteem they are desirous of obtaining, and that this is the only motive for their striving for important posts, it is easy to shew that this is not the true motive by which they are determined, and that in this particular they deceive themselves; since no one, as I shall prove, when I consider pride, can desire esteem for its own sake, but for the advantages it procures. The desire of greatness is not then produced by the desire of esteem.

To what then must we attribute the ardour with which persons seek for dignities? Why is the ambitious man like the young men of fortune, who love to shew themselves in public

in brilliant equipages, fond of appearing abroad, decorated
with marks of honour? It is because he considers these honours
as a proclamation that informs the people of his independence,
and of the power with which he is possessed of rendering, at
his pleasure, several of them happy or miserable; and that it
is for the interest of them all to merit his favour, which is
always proportioned to the pleasures they procure for him.

But, it will be asked, is not the ambitious fond of the respect
and homage of mankind? It is indeed their respect he desires;
but why does he desire it? In the homage paid to the great,
it is not the respectful gesture that pleases: if that gesture were
of itself agreeable, there is no rich man who would not procure
himself such happiness without going out of his house, and
striving after greatness. To please himself, he would hire
twelve porters, clothe them in magnificent habits, adorn them
with all the ribbons in Europe, and make them wait every
morning in his anti-chamber, to come daily to pay his vanity a
tribute of adulation and respect.

The indifference of the rich for this kind of pleasure, is a
proof that they are not fond of respect for its own sake, but as
it is an acknowledgment of the inferiority of other men, as a
pledge of their favourable dispositions, and of their eagerness to
avoid giving them pain, and to contribute to their pleasures.

The desire of greatness is then only founded on the love of
pleasure and the fear of pain. If this desire did not derive its
source from thence, what could be more easy than to undeceive
the ambitious? " O thou!" might a person say, " who art
scorched with envy, on contemplating the pomp and splendor
belonging to high posts, dare to exalt thyself to a more noble
pride, and their lustre shall cease to impose upon thee. Imagine for a moment that thou art as superior to other men as the
insects are inferior to them; then these courtiers will seem only
as bees that buz about their queen, and the sceptre itself will
appear no more than a glittering bauble."

Why do men never listen to such discourses? why will
they always pay respect to those who have little in their power,
and constantly prefer great places to great abilities? It is because greatness is a benefit which, like riches, is capable of

purchasing an infinite number of pleasures. Thus they are sought for with so much the more ardour, as they are capable of giving us a more extensive power over mankind, and consequently of procuring us a greater number of advantages. In proof of this truth, suppose the thrones of Ispahan and London were offered to our choice; there is hardly a man to be found who would not prefer the iron sceptre of Persia to that of England. Yet who can doubt, that, in the opinion of a good man, the latter would appear most desirable; and that, were he to make his choice, he would choose that where the king, being limited in his power, finds himself under a happy incapacity of injuring his subjects? If there be scarcely any of the ambitious, who would not rather choose to command the Persians, a nation of slaves, than the English, a free people, it is because an absolute authority over men renders them more attentive to please us, because they are informed by a secret instinct, that fear always pays more homage than love; because tyrants, atleast while living, have been generally more honoured than good kings; because gratitude has always raised less sumptuous temples to the beneficent gods, who bear the horn of plenty*, than fear has consecrated to the cruel and colossal dignities, who, borne on storms and tempests, and in lightnings, are painted with a thunderbolt in their hands; because, in short, being instructed by this knowledge, they are sensible that more is to be expected from the obedience of a slave than from the gratitude of a man who tastes the sweets of liberty.

The conclusion to be drawn from this chapter is, that the

---

* In the city of Bartam, the inhabitants offered their first fruits to the evil spirit, and nothing to the great Deity, who, they say, is good, and stands is no need of these offerings. Vincent le Blanc.

The inhabitants of Madagascar believe there is a good and an evil spirit. Before they eat, they make an offering to God, and another to the demon. They begin with the latter, and, throwing a piece on the right side, say, " That is for thee, my lord devil." They afterwards throw a piece on the left side, saying, " That is for thee, my Lord God." They make no prayers to him. Collect. of edifying Letters.

desire of greatness is always produced by the fear of pain or the love of sensual pleasure, to which all the other pleasures must necessarily be reduced Those derived from power and respect do not properly deserve the name, they having obtained it only because hope, and the means of procuring pleasures, are pleasing sensations; but these sensations only derive their existence from natural pleasure*.

I am very sensible that in the schemes, the enterprises, the crimes, the virtues, and the dazzling pomp of ambition, it is difficult to perceive the operations of natural sensibility. How in haughty ambition, who, with her arm smoking with slaughter, sits in the midst of a field of battle, on a heap of carcases, and in token of victory claps her wings dropping with blood; how, I say, in this figure of ambition, shall we discover the daughter of pleasure? how shall we imagine, that by the dangers, the labours, and the fatigues, of war, men are only in the pursuit of pleasure? Yet it is she alone, I maintain, who, under the name of libertinism, recruits the armies of almost all nations. People love pleasure, and consequently the means of procuring it: they desire riches and honours, and, inspired also by indolence, would make their fortune in a day. Now war, which promises the soldiers the plunder of cities and the officers honours, at the same time flatters their indolence and impatience. Men therefore more freely endure the fatigues of war†

---

* To prove that ambition is not produced by the natural pleasures, some may perhaps say, that this passion arises from a vague desire of happiness. But I shall ask, what is the vague desire of happiness? It is a desire that has no determinate object. I would know, if the man, who, without loving any particular woman, loves the sex in general, is not animated by a desire of natural pleasure? Whenever we give ourselves the trouble of decompounding the vague sensation of love or happiness, we always find the natural pleasure at the bottom of the crucible. It is the same with the ambitious as with the avaricious, who would not be covetous of money, if it could not be given in exchange for pleasure, or be made the means of escaping pain. Nobody desires money in a city like Sparta, where money had no currency.

† "Repose," says Tacitus, "is to the Germans a state of violence

than the labours of agriculture, which affords them only a distant prospect of wealth. Thus the ancient Germans, the Celtes, the Tartars, the inhabitants on the coast of Africa, and the Arabs, were always more fond of robbery and piracy than of the cultivation of the earth.

It is with war as with high play, which is preferred to playing for small sums, even at the risque of ruin; because playing deep flatters us with the hope of immediately obtaining great riches.

To take every thing that looks like a paradox from the principles I have just established, I shall, in the title of the next chapter, expose the only objection I have not yet answered.

CHAP. XII.

IF MAN IN THE PURSUIT OF GREATNESS SEEKS ONLY THE MEANS OF AVOIDING PAIN AND ENJOYING NATURAL PLEASURE, WHY DOES PLEASURE SO OFTEN ESCAPE FROM THE AMBITIOUS?

WE may divide ambitious men into two kinds. Unhappily for society, there are some men who are enemies to the felicity of others, and desire high posts, not to enjoy the advantages they procure, but to delight in the miseries of the unfortunate, to torment mankind, and to sport with their distresses. This species of ambitious men are of a character not unlike that of the false devotees, who are generally esteemed wicked; not because the law they profess is not a law of love and charity, but because the men who are commonly led to embrace an austere devotion* are dissatisfied with this lower world, and

---

they incessantly sigh after wars, in which they soon distinguish themselves; they are more fond of fighting than of labour."

* Experience proves that, in general, the persons of a character most inclined to deny themselves certain pleasures, and to embrace the austere maxims and practices of a particular kind of devotion, are commonly of a very unhappy disposition. This is the only way

can hope for happiness only in another, and being gloomy, timid, and dissatisfied, they endeavour by the view of the misfortunes of others to divert their attention from their own. The ambitious of this cast are but few in number; they have no greatness and nobleness of soul; they are ranked among tyrants, and by the nature of their ambition are deprived of all pleasures.

The other class of the ambitious comprehends almost the whole number, and amongst these I include all who, in the possession of great places, seek only for the advantages annexed to them. Of these there are some, who, from their birth or situation, are at first raised to important posts, whence they may sometimes unite pleasure and ambition: they are born as it were in the middle* of the course they have to run. This is not the case of the man in moderate circumstances, who, like Cromwell, would rise to the highest posts. In entering the path of ambition, in which the first steps are commonly the most difficult, he has a thousand intrigues to invent, and a thousand friends to manage; he has at one and the same time the care of forming grand projects, and the particulars in relation to their execution. Now to discover how such men, who are warmly engaged in the pursuit of every pleasure, and ani-

---

of explaining, how so many sectaries have been able to unite the holy and mild principles of religion to so much wickedness and want of toleration,—a want of toleration proved by such a number of massacres. If youth, when no obstacle is opposed to the passions, is commonly more humane and generous than old age, it is because the mind is not yet hardened by misfortunes and infirmities. The man of a generous disposition is gay and obliging, and he alone says, " Let all the world partake of my joys." But the man of a gloomy temper is wicked. Cæsar said, speaking of Cassius, " I dread these men with pale meagre countenances; it is not so with the Antonies, who are wholly taken up with pleasure: their hands gather flowers, and are never employed in sharpening poniards." This is a fine observation of Cæsar, and is more generally true than is imagined.

* Ambition in them, is, if I may so express myself, rather an appendage of their rank than a strong passion, stimulated by obstacles, and triumphing over all opposition.

mated alone by this motive, are so often deprived of it, let us suppose, that, greedy of these pleasures, and struck with the eagerness with which people endeavour to anticipate the desires of the great, such a man endeavours to raise himself to the first posts. If he be born in those countries where the people have the disposal of favours, where the public esteem can only be obtained by services done to his country, and where merit is consequently necessary; or, if he be born under an absolute despotic government, as that of the Mogul, where honours are purchased by intrigue; or wherever else he received his birth; he can afford little time for pleasure. To prove it, I will take the pleasure of love for an instance, not only as the most lively of all the passions, but also as the most universal spring of civilized society; for it is proper to observe by the way, that there is in every nation a natural want that may be considered as the universal soul of that nation. Among the savages in the North, who are often exposed to the most dreadful famine, and are always employed either in hunting or fishing, all their ideas flow from hunger and not love: this want is in them the seed of all their thoughts. Thus all the combinations formed by their minds turn on the stratagems used in hunting and fishing, and on the means of supplying the calls of hunger. On the contrary, the love of women is, among civilized nations, the main spring by which they are moved*. In these coun-

---

* Not that these are the only motives that may kindle the fire of ambition. In countries where the inhabitants are poor, as I have observed above, the power of supplying their wants is the object to which the ambitious aspire. In despotic states, the fear of the punishment to which a person may suddenly be put, by the caprice of a tyrant, may also form ambitious men; but in civilized nations it is a vague desire of happiness—a desire that is constantly derived, as I have already shewn, from the pleasures of sense, that most commonly inspires a love of greatness. Now, from among these pleasures, I was doubtless in the right to choose that of women, as the most lively and powerful. As a proof that we are animated by pleasures of this kind, it appears that we are only capable of the acquisition of the great abilities and desperate resolutions, necessary to ascend to high

tries love invents and produces every thing: magnificence,
and the arts of luxury, necessarily flow from the love of women,
and a desire to please them; and even our inclination to impose one on another, by the splendor of wealth and greatness,
is only a new method of seducing them. Let us then suppose,
that a man, born without a fortune, but fond of the pleasures
of love, has observed that the women comply the more easily
with the desires of a lover, in proportion as the elevation of his
rank will reflect the greater honour on her; and that, being thus
filled with ambition by his passion for women, he aspires to the
post of general, or to that of prime minister; in order to obtain
those places, he must apply his whole care in acquiring abilities,
or in forming intrigues. Now the kind of life most proper to
enable him to become a man of deep art, or a person of merit,
is entirely opposite to a life of gallantry; women being pleased
with assiduities that are incompatible with the life of an ambitious man. It is then certain that in youth, and till he obtain
those great places that will induce the women to exchange
their favours for the honour and credit of his embraces, he must
deprive himself of the enjoyment of his favourite gratification,
and sacrifice almost for ever present pleasures to the hope of
enjoying future delights. I say almost for ever, because the
road of ambition is commonly very long in running. Not to
mention those, whose ambition is increased as soon as satisfied,
and whose desires are no sooner accomplished than new ones
succeed; who from being ministers would be kings; who
from being kings would aspire, like Alexander, to universal
monarchy, and would ascend a throne where the respect of the
whole world would assure them, that the whole world was em-

---

posts, in the time of youth, that is, at an age when the natural wants
are more warmly felt. But old men ascend with pleasure to great
employments: they do so, they accept of them, they desire them;
but this desire does not deserve the name of a passion, since they are
no longer capable of those hardy enterprises and extraordinary efforts
of mind that spring from the passions. The old man may proceed
by habit along the course in which he set out in his youth, but he can
never begin a new one.

ployed in contributing to their happiness: without mentioning,
I say, these extraordinary men, and supposing even moderation
in ambition, it is evident that a man, who becomes ambitious
from the love of women, will not, in common, obtain the highest
posts till he arrive at the age when his desires will be extinguished.

But, supposing that his desires are still luke-warm, scarcely
has he obtained his wishes, when he finds himself placed on a steep
and slippery rock; he sees himself on every side the but of the
envious, who stand about him with their bows bent, ready to
pierce him with their arrows. He then discovers, with horror,
the tremendous abyss that opens for him; he perceives that by
his fall, as a sad appendage of greatness, he will be miserable
without being pitied; exposed to insults from those whom he
had affronted by his pride; he will be the object of the contempt of his rivals,—a contempt more painful than any outrage
they could offer him; that, being the derision of his inferiors,
they will then free themselves from that tribute of respect,
which, in the enjoyment, may some time appear troublesome;
but its loss is insupportable, when habit has rendered it a want.
He sees then, that, deprived of the only pleasure he had ever
tasted, and reduced to a state of debasement, he will no longer
enjoy the contemplation of his grandeur, like the avaricious
man in contemplating his wealth, with the possibility of obtaining all the enjoyments they are capable of affording him.

This ambitious man is then by the fear of pain, and the lassitude of indolence, kept in the course he entered from a love
of pleasure: the desire of preserving succeeds the desire of
acquiring. Now the care necessary to maintain his dignities
being nearly the same as those by which he acquired them,
it is evident that he must spend his youth and riper age in the
pursuit and preservation of those places, that were only desired
as the means of obtaining the pleasures that always fly from
him. Thus, being advanced to an age at which he is incapable
of a new kind of life, he gives himself up entirely to his old
employments, and must do so; because a mind, continually
agitated by fear and lively hopes, and incessantly actuated by
strong passions, will always prefer the torments of ambition to

the insipid calm of tranquil life. Like the vessels which the waves still carry towards the south, when the north wind has ceased to blow, men follow in old age the same direction that was given them by their passions in their youth.

I have now shewn how the ambitious man, called to greatness by a passion for women, enters into a rugged path. If he, by chance, meet with some pleasures, these are always mixed with bitterness; he tastes them with delight only, because they are very rare, and strewed here and there, like the trees scattered far from each other in the deserts of Lybia, whose scorched leaves can afford no agreeable shelter, except to the burnt African who reposes under them.

The contradiction we perceive between the conduct of an ambitious man, and the motives from which he acts, is then only so in appearance; ambition, therefore, is kindled by a love of pleasure and a fear of pain. But it may be said, that though avarice and ambition are the effects of a natural sensibility, pride, at least, cannot be derived from the same source.

CHAP. XIII.

OF PRIDE.

PRIDE is only a true or false opinion of our own excellence,—an opinion which, depending on the advantageous comparison we make between ourselves and others, must consequently suppose the existence of men, and even the establishment of society.

The sensation of pride is not then innate, like those of pleasure and pain: pride is therefore an artificial passion, that supposes the knowledge of beauty and excellence. Now excellence and beauty are only what the greatest number of mankind have always considered as such. The idea of esteem then preceded that of being worthy of esteem; but these ideas were soon confounded together. Thus the man, who, animated by the noble and pompous desire of pleasing himself, and satisfied with his own esteem, believes that he looks with indifference on the general opinion, is, in this particular, the dupe of his own pride, and mistakes the desire of being esteemed for the desire of being worthy of esteem.

In reality, pride can never be any thing more than a secret and disguised desire of the public esteem. Why will the same man, who, in the forests of America, derives his vanity from the strength and agility of his body, be less proud of these advantages in France, where their want is compensated by more essential qualifications? It is because strength and agility of body neither can nor ought to be so much esteemed by a Frenchman as by a savage.

To prove that pride is only a disguised love of esteem, let us suppose a man solely possessed by the desire of raising in his mind an assurance of his own excellence and superiority. Upon this supposition, that superiority, which is the most personal and the most independent of chance, will doubtless appear the most flattering; and, therefore, if he be to choose either literary or military glory, he would give the preference to the former. Would he contradict Cæsar himself? would he not confess with that hero, that the laurel of victory is, by the sensible part of the public, always divided between the general, the soldier, and chance; and that, on the contrary, the laurels of the Muses belong without participation to those whom they inspire? would he not confess that chance might often place ignorance and cowardice on the triumphant car, and that it has never crowned the brow of a stupid author?

In consulting only his pride, that is, the desire of entertaining a high opinion of his own excellence, it is certain, that literary glory would appear the most desirable. The preference we give a great general above a profound philosopher, would not, in this respect, alter his opinion : he would perceive, that, if the public have a higher esteem for the general than for the philosopher, it is because the talents of the first have a more speedy influence on the public happiness, and that the maxims of a wise man must appear of immediate use only to a small number of those who are desirous of instruction.

Yet, if there be nobody in France who would not prefer the glory of arms to that of literature, I conclude from thence, that it is only to the desire of being esteemed that they owe the desire of being worthy of esteem, and that pride is nothing more than the love of esteem.

In order to prove that this passion of pride or esteem is produced by the senses, it is proper now to inquire if any one desires esteem for its own sake, and if this fondness for esteem is not the effect of the fear of pain and the love of pleasure.

To what other cause, in fact, can be attributed the solicitude with which people endeavour to obtain the esteem of the public? Is it owing to an inward distrust of our merit, and consequently to pride, that, being desirous of esteeming ourselves, and not being able to do it alone, we want the public suffrage to prop the high opinion we have of ourselves, in order to enjoy the delicious thoughts of our own excellence?

But if we owe the love of esteem only to this motive, then the most extensive esteem, that is, such as should be granted by the greatest number of men, would, without doubt, appear the most flattering and desirable, as the most proper to silence in our minds an importunate distrust, and to make us rest satisfied with our own merit. Now, supposing that the planets were inhabited by beings like ourselves, and that one of the inhabitants of those worlds came every moment to inform us of what passed there, and that a man had the choice either of having the esteem of his own country, or that of all those celestial worlds; upon this supposition, is it not evident, that he would desire the most extensive esteem, that is, that of all the planetary inhabitants, and that they should give him the preference to all his fellow-citizens? There is, however, nobody, who, in this case, would not determine in favour of the national esteem. We then do not owe this love of esteem to our desire of being firmly assured of our own merit, but to the advantages this esteem procures for us.

In order to be convinced of this, let any man put the following question to himself, Whence comes the solicitude with which those, who declare themselves the most anxiously fond of the public esteem, seek for high posts in those periods of time, when, crossed by intrigues and cabals, they can be of no service to their country; and when, consequently, they will be exposed to the derision of the public, who, always equitable in their judgments, despise the man who is so indifferent with respect to esteem, as to accept of a post, the duties of which he cannot worthily discharge? Let him also ask himself, why a man is more delighted at having the esteem of a prince than that of a private person of no consequence? and it will be found that in every case our fondness for esteem is always in proportion to the advantages that may accrue from it.

If we prefer the esteem of the ignorant multitude to that of a few select persons, it is because we see a greater number of men subject to that kind of empire which esteem rules over minds; and because a greater number of admirers more frequently lay before us an agreeable image of the pleasures they may procure for us.

For this reason, we are quite indifferent with respect to the admiration of a people with whom we have no connection; there are few Frenchmen who would be much affected by the esteem felt for them by the inhabitants of Great Thibet. If there are men who would possess universal esteem, and be anxious for possessing that of the Terra Australis, this desire is not the effect of a greater love of esteem; but only flows from the habit they have acquired of uniting the idea of a greater happiness to the idea of a greater esteem *.

The last and the strongest proof of the truth of what is here advanced is, the disgust people have for esteem †, and the scarcity there is of great men, in the ages when no rewards are adjudged to merit. It appears as if a man, capable of exerting great talents or great virtues, enters into a tacit contract with his country, by which he promises to render himself illustrious by his abilities, and by actions that shall be of use to his fellow-

---

* Men are habituated by the principles of a good education to confound the idea of happiness with that of esteem. But under the name of esteem they really desire only the advantages it procures.

† Little is done to merit esteem in countries, where it produces no fruit: but, whenever it procures great advantages, people run to it, like Leonidas, to defend with three hundred men the pass of Thermopylæ.

citizens, provided they will have the gratitude to ease his pains
and assemble about him every pleasure.

To the negligence and punctuality of the public in fulfilling
these tacit engagements is owing, in all ages and countries, the
multitude or the scarcity of great men.

We do not then love esteem for its own sake, but only for
the advantages it procures. In vain would people arm themselves against this conclusion, with the example of Curtius: a
fact, that stands almost alone in history, can prove nothing
against principles so abundantly supported by experience,
especially when that very fact may be attributed to other principles, and naturally explained by other causes.

In order to form a Curtius, it is sufficient that a man, weary
of life, finds himself under that unhappy disorder of body that
renders so many of the English suicides; or that in a very superstitious age, like that in which Curtius lived, a man should
arise, who, having more superstition and credulity than the
rest, should fancy, that by sacrificing himself, he should obtain
a place among the gods. Upon either of these suppositions, he
might devote himself to death, either to put an end to his miseries, or to enter into the possession of celestial pleasures.

The conclusion of this chapter is, that people desire to be
worthy of esteem only to enjoy esteem, and that they desire
esteem only to enjoy the pleasures annexed to it: a fondness for
esteem is then a disguised love of pleasure. Now, if there be
only two sorts of pleasures, the one the pleasures of sense, and
the other the means of acquiring them, (for these means are
ranked in the class of pleasures, because the hope of obtaining
them is the beginning of pleasure, but of a pleasure that has no
real existence till this hope is realized,) natural sensuality is
then the seed that produces pride, and all the other passions,
among which I include friendship; which, being in appearance more independent of the pleasures of sense, deserves to be
examined, in order to confirm, by this last example, all that has
been here said on the origin of the passions.

CHAP. XIV.

OF FRIENDSHIP.

LOVE implies want, and there is no friendship without it; for this would be an effect without a cause. All men have not the same wants, and therefore the friendship that subsists between them is founded on different motives: some want pleasure or money, others credit; those conversation, and these a confident, to whom they may disburthen their hearts. There are consequently friends of money *, of intrigue, of the mind,

---

* Persons have hitherto taken intolerable pains to repeat after each other, that those ought not to be reckoned in the list of friends, whose interested views makes them love us only for our money. This kind of friendship is certainly not the most flattering; but it is nevertheless a real friendship. Men, for instance, love in a comptroller-general the power he has of obliging them; and in most of them the love of the person is incorporated with the love of the money. Why is the name of friendship refused to this sensation? Men do not love us for ourselves, but always on some other account, and the above-mentioned is as good as any other. A man is in love with a woman; can it be said that he does not love her, because he only admires the beauties of her eyes or complexion? But, it is said, the rich man, when reduced to poverty, is no longer beloved. This is not denied; but when the small-pox robs a woman of her beauty, all addresses to her commonly cease; though this is no proof that she was not beloved while she was beautiful. Suppose a friend, in whom we had the greatest confidence, and for whose mind, disposition, and character, we had the highest esteem, had suddenly become blind, deaf, and dumb; we should regret in him the loss of a friend; we should still respect his memory; but, in fact, we should no longer love him; because he would have no resemblance of the man we had loved. If a comptroller-general falls into disgrace, we no longer love him, for this reason, because he is the friend who is suddenly become blind, deaf, and dumb. It is nevertheless true, that the man anxious for money has great tenderness for him who can procure it for him. Whoever has this want of money, is born the friend of the post of comptroller-general, and of him who possesses it. His love is inscribed

and of misfortune. Nothing can be of more use than to consider friendship under this point of view, and to form clear ideas of it.

In friendship, as in love, people form the most romantic ideas: they always search for the hero, and every instant think they have found him: they hang upon the first that offers; they love him, while they know little of him, and are desirous of knowing him better; but no sooner is their curiosity satisfied than they are disgusted. They have not found the hero of romance. Thus we become susceptible of some regard, but are incapable of friendship. It is therefore for the interest of friendship itself that we should have clear ideas of it.

I confess, that, in considering it as a reciprocal want, it cannot but be acknowledged, that it is very difficult for the same wants, and consequently for the same friendship *, to subsist between two men for a long course of time; and, therefore, nothing is more uncommon than friendship of long standing †.

---

in the inventory of the moveables and utensils belonging to his office. It is then our vanity that makes us refuse giving the name to so selfish and necessary a passion. Upon which, I shall observe, that the most solid and durable friendships are commonly those of virtuous men, however villains themselves are susceptible of it. If, as we are forced to confess, friendship is only the sensation by which two men are united, we cannot deny, but that friendship subsists between the wicked, without contradicting the most authentic facts. Can we, for instance, doubt that two conspirators may be united by the warmest friendship? that Jaffier did not love James Piero? that Octavius, who was certainly not a virtuous man, did not love Mecænas, who was at best but a weak man? The power of friendship is not in proportion to the honesty of two friends, but to the force of the interest by which they are united.

* The circumstances in which two friends ought to be found, being once given, and their characters known; if they are ever to quarrel, there is no doubt but that a man of penetration, by foreseeing the time when these two men would cease to be reciprocally of use to each other, might calculate the moment when their rupture would happen, as an astronomer calculates the time of an eclipse.

† We ought not to confound with friendship the chains of habit, the respectful esteem felt for an acknowledged friend, or that happy

Friendship is much more durable than love; and yet has, however, its birth, its increase, and decay; but those who have not felt its power, never pass from the warmest friendship to the severest hatred, nor are they ever exposed to the pain of detesting him they have loved. Does a friend disappoint our expectations? we are not enraged against him: we give a sigh to human nature, and with tears exclaim, My friend has no longer need of me!

It is difficult enough to form clear ideas of friendship. With respect to this passion, all about us contribute to deceive us. There are some, who, to render themselves more worthy of esteem in their own eyes, exaggerate to themselves their affection for their friends; make romantic descriptions of friendship, and persuade themselves that they are real; till a proper occasion, by undeceiving both them and their friends, convinces them that they did not love them so much as they thought they did.

These frequently pretend, that they are desirous of loving, and of being warmly beloved. But we are never so violently affected with the virtues of a man as when we first see him; for, as custom renders us insensible to personal beauties, a good understanding, and even the qualities of the soul, we are never so strongly agitated as by the pleasure of surprise: a man of wit said pleasantly enough on this occasion, that those, who would be beloved * with such warmth, ought in friendship, as well as in love, to have many new passions, but none of them lasting; because, added he, the beginnings in both have always the most lively and tender moments.

---

point of honour, so useful to society, that makes us keep an acquaintance with those whom we call our friends. We perform the same services for them, that we did when they filled us with the warmest sensations; though in reality we do not want their company, and do not love them.

* Friendship is not, as some people pretend, a perpetual tender sensation, because mankind are never constant in any thing. Between the most cordial friends there happen moments of coolness: friendship is then a continual succession of warmth and coolness; the latter are very rare.

But for one who imposes on himself, there are ten hypocrites in friendship, who pretend to have the sensations they do not feel, make many dupes, but are never dupes themselves.— They paint friendship in lively but false colours; being only attentive to their own interest, they endeavour to make others model themselves in their favour after the portrait they draw of that passion *.

Man being exposed to so many errors, it is very difficult to obtain adequate ideas of friendship. But what evil, say they, is there in exaggerating a little the force of this sensation? The evil of habituating men to expect from their friends perfections not to be found in human nature.

An infinite number of sensible men, seduced by such pictures, have long pursued a vain chimera; but, being at length enlightened by experience, are become disgusted with friendship, for whose connections they had been well adapted, had they not formed ideas of it that were too romantic.

Friendship supposes a want; and the more this want is felt, the more lively will be the friendship: the want is then the measure of the sensation. A man and woman, escaping shipwreck, save themselves on a desert island; where, having no hope of ever seeing their native country, they are forced to lend their mutual assistance, to defend themselves from the wild beasts, to enjoy life, and to escape despair: no friendship

---

* It may, perhaps, require courage, and a capacity for friendship, to enable a person to give a clear idea of it; for we are at least certain of raising against us the hypocrites in friendship: there are some of these, who, like bragging cowards, are always boasting of their exploits. Let those who pretend to be susceptible of friendship, read the Toxaris of Lucian, and ask themselves if they are capable of the actions which friendship made the Scythians and Greeks perform? If they examine themselves with sincerity, they will confess, that, in this age, we have not even the idea of this kind of friendship. Thus, among the Scythians and Greeks, friendship was placed in the rank of the virtues. A Scythian could not have above two friends; but he was to stop at nothing in serving them. They were in part animated by the love of esteem, under the name of friendship; for friendship alone would never have been so courageous.

can be more warm than that between this man and woman, who would have perhaps hated each other, had they remained at Paris. If one of them happen to perish, the other has really lost the half of himself; no grief can equal his: he must have dwelt alone in a desert island, who can be sensible of all its violence?

As the force of friendship is always proportioned to our wants, there are forms of government, manners, circumstances, and, in short, ages, more favourable to friendship than others.

In the ages of chivalry, when they chose a companion in arms, and two knights shared in the glory and danger, and when the cowardice of one might cost the life and honour of the other, they became, from interest, more careful in the choice of their friends, and consequently more closely united to them.

When the fashion of duels supplied the place of chivalry, the men, who with their friends daily exposed themselves to the danger of death, became more dear to each other. Friendship then was held in great veneration, and reckoned among the virtues: it supposed in the knights and duellists great loyalty and valour; virtues that were honoured, and ought to be so, as these virtues were almost always in action*.

It is proper sometimes to recollect, that the same virtues are, at different times, more or less valued, according to their unequal use in different ages.

Who doubts that in revolutions and times of distress, and in a form of government that seems to favour factions, friendship is stronger and more courageous than when every thing is in a state of tranquillity? History furnishes us with a thousand examples of heroism of this kind. Friendship then supposes a man possessed of courage, discretion, firmness, knowledge, and prudence: qualities that being absolutely necessary in troublesome times, and rarely to be found in the same man, ought to render him extremely dear to his friend.

---

* BRAVE was then synonymous to HONEST; and, from the remains of ancient custom, we still say a BRAVE'MAN, when we mean one who is loyal and honest.

Our manners do not require the same perfections * in our friends, because these perfections are of no use to us: we have no important secrets to trust, nor battles to fight, and consequently have no occasion either for prudence, knowledge, discretion, or courage, in a friend.

In the actual form of our government, the individuals are not united by any common interest. In order to make our fortunes, we have less need of friends than of an infinite number of protectors. Luxury, and what is called the spirit of society, have secured a great number of men from the want of friendship. No motive, no interest, is now sufficient to make us overlook the seeming or real faults of our friends.— There is therefore no friendship†; we do not affix to the word friend even the same ideas as formerly; we may in this age cry out with Aristotle ‡, " O my friends! no longer is there a friend to be found."

Now, if there are ages, manners, and forms of government, wherein there is more or less need of a friend, and if the

---

* In the present age, friendship requires scarcely any qualifications. An infinite number of men give themselves out for true friends, in order to appear of some consequence. Others become hackney solicitors in other people's affairs, in order to escape the pain of having nothing to do: others perform services, but make the persons they have obliged pay dear for them, by the loss of their liberty ; and some few others, in short, believe themselves worthy of friendship, because they are the sure guardians of a secret, and have the virtues of a strong box.

† Thus, says the proverb, we should say we have many friends, and think we have but few.

‡ Every body repeats after Aristotle, that there is no such thing as a friend to be found, and yet each maintains that he is a good friend. Two such contradictory propositions can only arise from the great number of hypocrites in point of friendship, and there being many men who do not know themselves.

These last, as I have already said, will oppose some of the propositions in this chapter. I shall have their clamours against me ; but, unhappily for them, I have experience on my side.

warmth of friendship is proportioned to the greatness of this want, there are also situations in which the heart becomes more easily opened to the admission of friendship; and these are commonly those where we have more frequent need of the assistance of others.

The unfortunate are, in general, the most tender friends: united by their reciprocal distresses, they enjoy, while condoling the misfortunes of a friend, the pleasure of being affected with their own.

What I have said on circumstances, I also say of characters: there are some who cannot live without a friend. The first are those of a weak and timid disposition, who, in their whole conduct, never conclude on any thing without the advice and assistance of others: the second are, the persons of a gloomy, severe, and tyrannical, temper, who are the warm friends of those over whom they vent their spleen; these are like one of the wives of Socrates, who, at the news of the death of that great man, became more inconsolable than the second, who, being of a mild and amiable disposition, lost in Socrates only a husband, while the other lost in him the martyr of her capricious temper, and the only man who could bear with it.

There are, in short, men free from all ambition or strong passions, and whose sole delight is in the conversation of men of sense and learning. In the present system of manners, the men of this cast, if they are virtuous, are the most tender and faithful of their friends. Their souls, always open to friendship, know all its charms; and having, upon my supposition, no passion that can counterbalance this sensation, it becomes their only want: thus they are sensible of a very rational and courageous friendship, without however having so much as that of the Greeks and Romans.

From a contrary reason, people are, in general, the less susceptible of friendship, in proportion as they are more independent of other men. Thus the rich and powerful are commonly but little sensible of friendship; and generally pass for men without feeling. In fact, whether men are naturally cruel whenever they can be so with impunity, whether the rich and powerful consider the miseries of others as a reproach to their own happiness; or, in short, whether they desire to be delivered from the importunate requests of the unhappy, it is certain, that they almost constantly treat the miserable with inhumanity *. The sight of the unfortunate has on most men the effect of Medusa's head: at his aspect, hearts are turned to stone.

There are, besides, some persons quite indifferent with respect to friendship; and others who enjoy a self-sufficiency †. Accustomed to seek for, and to find, happiness in themselves, and being become too knowing to be made dupes, they cannot preserve a happy ignorance of the wickedness of mankind; a precious ignorance, which in early youth locks so closely the bonds of friendship; thus they are but little sensible of the charms of this sensation; not that they are now incapable of feeling it. These are often, as a very sensible lady said, rather disabused than insensible.

---

* The least fault a man in distress commits is a sufficient pretence for the rich to refuse him all assistance; they would have the unhappy entirely perfect.

† There are few men of this class; the power of finding a sufficiency in ourselves, which is made an attribute of the Deity, and we are forced to revere in him, is always placed in the rank of the vices, when it is found in man. Thus we blame under one appellation, what we admire under another. How many times have people, under the name of insensibility, reproached M. de Fontenelle for the power of being self-sufficient; that is, of being one of the wisest and happiest of all mankind.

As the princes of Madagascar make war on their neighbours, whose flocks are more numerous than theirs, they always repeat these words, " Those are our enemies who are richer and more happy than we;" so we may assure ourselves, that, after their example, most men declare war against the wise. They hate in him a moderation of temper, which, reducing his desires to his possessions, makes him a reproach to their conduct, and renders the wise too independent of them. They regard this independence as the seed of all the vices, because they perceive that the source of humanity would be dried up, as soon as a period was put to their reciprocal wants.

These wise men ought, however, to be very dear to society. If

It follows, from what I have said, that the power of friendship is always proportioned to men's want of each other * ; and
that this want is varied according to the difference of ages,
manners, forms of government, circumstances, and characters.
But if friendship, it be objected, be a want, it is at least no
natural want. What is a friend? Is it not a relation of choice?
We desire a friend to live, in a manner, in him, to pour out

---

extraordinary wisdom sometimes renders them indifferent with respect
to the friendship of particular persons, it also makes them, as we find
from the example of the Abbé de Saint Pierre and Fontenelle, pour
out on human nature in general all those tender sensations which the
most lively passions force us to lavish on a single individual. Far
different from those men who are not good, because they have been
imposed upon, and whose goodness decreases in proportion as they
obtain more knowledge, the wise man alone may be constantly good,
because he alone knows mankind. Their wickedness does not fill him
with indignation : he, like Democritus, sees in them none but fools or
children, against whom it would be ridiculous to be offended, and who
are more worthy of pity than of anger. He considers them with the
eye of a mechanic, who examines the working of a machine, and,
without insulting humanity, complains that nature has united the preservation of one being to the destruction of another; that to afford
nourishment, he orders the hawk to seize in his talons the dove; made
it necessary for the insect to be devoured; and rendered every being
an assassin.

If the laws alone are dispassionate judges, the wise man, in this
respect, resembles the laws. His indifference is always just and impartial; this ought always to be considered as one of the greatest virtues of a placeman, whose too great want of friends always lays him
under the necessity of being guilty of some act of injustice.

In fine, the wise man alone may be generous, because he is independent. Those, united by reciprocal bonds of utility, cannot be
liberal to each other. Friendship can only make exchanges, and nothing but independence can offer gifts.

* If we loved a friend only for himself, we should never consider
any thing but his happiness; we should not reproach him for being
so long without seeing or writing to us: we should say that he had
probably spent his time more agreeably, and should rejoice in his
happiness.

our soul into his, and to enjoy a conversation which confidence always renders delightful. This passion is then founded neither on the fear of pain nor the love of sensual pleasure. But, I reply, in what does the charm of the conversation of a friend consist? It is in the charm of speaking of ourselves. Has fortune placed us in a comfortable situation? We converse with a friend, on the means of increasing our wealth; our honour, our credit, and our reputation. Are we in low circumstances? We seek with the same friend the means of delivering ourselves from indigence; and his conversation saves us, at least, the weariness we should feel, while under misfortunes, from the pain of engaging in indifferent conversations. It is always of these pains, or of these pleasures, that a person talks to his friend. Now, if there be no true pleasures or pains, as I have already proved, but physical pain and pleasure; if the means of procuring them arise from the pleasure of hope, which supposes the existence of the first, and are only a consequence of them; it follows, that friendship, as well as avarice, pride, ambition, and the other passions, is the immediate effect of physical sensibility.

As the last proof of this truth, I am going to shew that, with the assistance of these pleasures and pains, we may excite in our minds all kinds of passions; and that therefore the pleasures and pains of sense are the prolific seed of all sentiment.

CHAP. XV.

THAT THE FEAR OF NATURAL PAIN, OR THE DESIRE OF NATURAL PLEASURE, MAY EXCITE ALL THE PASSIONS.

If we open history, we shall find, that in all the countries where certain virtues were encouraged by the hope of sensual pleasures, these virtues were more common, and cast a greater lustre,

Why were the Cretans, the Bœotians, and, in general, all the people most addicted to love, most distinguished by their bravery? It is because the women granted their favours only to the brave; because the pleasures of love, as Plutarch and Plato observe, are most proper to exalt the minds of the people, and the most worthy of rewarding heroes and virtuous men.

It was probably from this motive that the Roman senate, the vile flatterers of Cæsar, resolved, as some historians relate, to grant him, by an express law, the right of enjoying all the Roman ladies. This is also the reason which, according to the Grecian manners, made Plato say, that, after a battle, the most beautiful ought to be the reward of the most valiant; a project of which Epaminondas himself had some idea, since, at the battle of Leuctra, he placed the lover by the side of his mistress; a method which he always considered as most proper to secure military success. How greatly indeed are we influenced by the pleasures of sense! They rendered the sacred battalion of the Thebans invincible; they inspired ancient nations with the greatest courage, when the conquerors divided between them the riches and the women of the conquered; they, in short, formed the character of those virtuous Samnites, among whom the greatest beauty was the reward of the greatest virtue.

To confirm this truth by a more circumstantial example, let us examine by what means the famous Lycurgus diffused into the hearts of his fellow-citizens the enthusiasm, and, if I may use the term, the fever, of virtue; and we shall see that if no people surpassed the Lacedæmonians in courage, it was because no people honoured virtue more, and gave greater rewards to valour. Let us call to mind those solemn festivals, where, according to the laws of Lycurgus, the young and beautiful Lacedæmonian women advanced half naked, and danced in the assembly of the people. There, in the presence of the nation, they insulted, by strokes of satire, those who had in battle discovered any symptoms of cowardice, and celebrated in their songs the young warriors who had distinguished themselves by some great exploits. Now, who

can doubt that the coward, made a but before the whole nation, at which these young girls shot their bitterest raillery,
must be tormented with shame and confusion, and filled with
the most severe repentance? What a triumph, on the contrary, was here for the young heroes, who received the palm
of glory from the hand of beauty; who read esteem in the
countenances of the old men, and love in the eyes of the fair,
with the assurance of those favours, the very hope of which
is a pleasure! Can we doubt that the young warrior was then
intoxicated with virtue? Thus the Spartans, eager for the
fight, rushed with fury into the midst of the enemies' battalions, and, on every side surrounded with death, sought for
nothing but glory. Every thing in this legislation concurred
to metamorphose men into heroes. But to establish it, Lycurgus must have been convinced, that pleasure is the only
and universal principle of action, and been sensible that women, who every where else seem, like the flowers of a fine
garden, to be only made for the ornament of the earth, and
to please the eye, might be applied to a nobler use; that the
fair, sunk and degraded among almost all the people of the
world, might enter into a partnership of glory with the men,
divide with them the laurels they made them gather, and at
length become one of the most powerful springs of the legislation.

Indeed, if the pleasure of love be to man the most lively of
his pleasures, what fruitful seeds of courage are included in it,
and what ardour for brave actions may be inspired by the desire of women* ?

Whoever will examine himself in this particular, will be
sensible that, if the Spartans had been more numerous, that if
more infamy could have been heaped on the coward, that if
it had been possible to have paid still more respect and homage to valour, Sparta would have carried still farther the enthusiasm of virtue.

---

* To what dreadful dangers did it expose David himself, when, to
obtain Michal, he laid himself under an obligation to cut off and
bring to Saul the foreskins of two hundred Philistines?

Let us suppose as a proof of this, that penetrating, if I may thus express myself, more deeply into the views of nature, she had adorned beautiful women with so many charms, and affixed the highest degree of pleasure to their enjoyment, to render them the reward of the most exalted courage. Let us suppose also, that, after the example of those virgins, consecrated to Iris or to Vesta, the most beautiful of the Spartan ladies had been consecrated to merit; that, being presented naked in the assemblies of the people, they had been carried off by the warriors, as prizes obtained by their courage; and that these young heroes had experienced at the same instant the double intoxication of love and glory: however fantastical and distant from our manners this may appear, it is certain that it would have rendered the Spartans still more brave and valiant, since the force of virtue is always proportioned to the pleasure allotted for its reward.

I shall observe on this subject, that, chimerical as this custom is in appearance, it is still in use in the kingdom of Bisnagar, of which Narsinga is the capital. To raise the courage of the warriors, the king of that country, according to the accounts of travellers, purchases, entertains, and dresses in the most magnificent manner, beautiful women, solely appropriated to the pleasures of the warriors who have distinguished themselves by some glorious exploits. By this means he inspires his subjects with the greatest courage, and draws to his court all the warriors of the neighbouring nations, who, flattered by the hope of enjoying these beautiful women, abandon their country, and settle at Marsinga, where they feed only on the flesh of lions and tigers, and drink nothing but the blood of those animals*.

---

* The women among the Gelons were obliged by the laws to do all the works that required strength, as building of houses, and cultivating the earth: but, to reward them for their pains, the same law granted them the privilege of lying with every warrior they liked. The women were much attached to this law. See Bardezanes, quoted by Eusebius in his Evangelical Preparation.

o o

It follows, from the above-mentioned examples, that the pains and pleasures of the senses are capable of inspiring all the passions, sensations, and virtues. Therefore, without having recourse to distant ages and countries, I shall cite, as the last proof of this truth, those ages of chivalry when the women taught their pupil knights both the art and the catechism of love.

In these times, as Machieval remarks, and so early as when the French made their descent into Italy, they appeared so brave and so sensible to the posterity of the Romans, that they were animated by the greatest courage ; because, as that historian adds, the women granted their favours only to the most valiant. In order to judge of the merit and tenderness of a lover, they required proofs that he had taken prisoners in wars, scaled the walls of a city, or taken a post from an enemy. They chose rather to have a lover perish than to fly. A knight was then obliged to fight, in order to maintain the beauty of his lady, and the excess of his tenderness. The exploits of the knights were the perpetual subjects of conversation and romances, that always recommended gallantry. The poets direct the knight in the midst of the dangers of the battle, to have the picture of his lady present in his mind ; and in tournaments, before the charge was sounded, he was to lift up his eyes to his mistress, as the following ballad proves:

> " Servants d'amour, regardez doucement,
> " Aux eschaffauds, anges de paradis ;
> " Lors jousterez fort & joyeusement,
> " Et vous serez honorez & cheris."

Which may be thus translated :

> " Ye gallant knights, before ye toss the lance,
> " Or to the deeds of chivalry advance,

The inhabitants of Florida have a very strong and agreeable drink, which they never present to any, except the warriors, who have distinguished themselves by their bravery. Collection of edifying Letters.

" Behold that radiant circle of the fair,
" To those bright forms direct your votive pray'r ;
" Implore the aid of their angelic eyes,
" Nor fear to die, when beauty is the prize."

Thus every thing dictated love; and by what more powerful motive can the mind be affected ? Is not the step, the look, the least gesture, of beauty sufficient to charm and intoxicate themselves ? Is it not in the power of women to give souls and bodies, at their pleasure, to the fool and the feeble ? And did not the Phœnicians, under the names of Venus, or Astarte, raise altars to beauty?

These altars could only be pulled down by our religion : for what object can there be, to him who is not enlightened by the eye of faith, more worthy of our adoration than that to which Heaven has granted the precious trust of the most lively of our pleasures ?—pleasures, whose enjoyment alone may enable us to support the painful burthen of life, and comfort us under the misfortunes that attend our existence.

The general conclusion of what I have said on the origin of our passions is, that sensual pain and pleasure give thought and action to man, and are the only counterpoise that moves the moral world.

The passions are then in us the immediate effect of physical sensibility : now, all men are susceptible and sensible of passions; all consequently carry within them the prolific seeds of the mental faculties. But, it may be said, that, though all men have sensibility, they have it not in the same degree ; thus, for instance, we see whole nations indifferent with respect to a love of glory and virtue : now, if men are not susceptible of such strong passions; if all are not capable of the same continuance of attention, that must be considered as the cause of the great inequality of their intellectual faculties; hence it follows, that nature has not given to all men the same mental powers.

In answer to this objection, it is not necessary to inquire whether all men are endued with equal sensibility; this question, which would be more difficult to resolve than is imagined, would be foreign to my subject. What I propose is to inquire whether all men are not at least susceptible of passions strong enough to furnish them with that continued attention necessary to give a superiority of mind.

For this purpose, I shall first refute the argument drawn from the insensibility of certain nations to the passion and glory of virtue; an argument from which some have endeavoured to prove that all men are not susceptible of passions. I say then, that the insensibility of these nations ought not to be attributed to nature, but to accidental causes, such as the different forms of governments.

CHAP. XVI.

TO WHAT CAUSE WE OUGHT TO ATTRIBUTE THE INDIFFERENCE OF CERTAIN NATIONS WITH REGARD TO VIRTUE.

To determine whether the indifference of certain nations with respect to virtue depends on nature or the particular form of governments, we must first know man; penetrate even into the abyss of the human heart; and recollect, that, being born sensible of pleasure and pain, he owes, to this physical sensibility, his passions; and that to his passions he owes all his virtues and vices.

These principles being laid down, in order to resolve the question above proposed, we must at length examine whether the same passions, on being moulded by different forms of government, do not produce in human beings the opposite vices and virtues.

Suppose a man be so in love with glory as to sacrifice to it all his other passions: if, by the form of government, glory be constantly the reward of virtuous actions, it is evident this man will be always under a necessity of being virtuous; and that to form a Leonidas and an Horatius Cocles, there needs no more than to place him in a country and in circumstances like theirs.

But, it is objected, that there are few men who raise the passion to this height. To which I reply that none but the man who enters deeply into this passion can penetrate into the sanctuary of virtue. This is not the case with respect to the men incapable of lively passions, and who are called honest men : if the latter are kept in the path of virtue at a distance from this sanctuary, it proceeds from their being constantly held there by the fetters of indolence, which they have not the strength to break.

The virtue of the former is alone rational and active; but it does not increase, or at least arrive at a certain height, except in warlike republics ; because in no other form of government the public esteem can raise them above other men, and procure them greater respect ; this esteem is therefore the most pleasing, the most desirable, and the most proper, to produce great effects.

The virtue of the latter being grafted on indolence, and produced, in a manner, by the absence of strong passions, is only a passive virtue, which, being attended with little knowledge, may be dangerous in the first and most important posts, though otherwise it is a sure guide. It is common to all who are called honest men, who are more esteemed for the evils they do not commit than for the good they perform.

With respect to the men of strong passions, whom I have just mentioned, it is evident that the same desire of glory which, in the early ages of the Roman republic, produced such men as Curtius and Decius, must have formed a Marius and an Octavius in those periods of trouble and revolutions, when glory, as in the latter times of the republic, was only connected with tyranny and power. What I have said of the passion for glory, I apply to the love of esteem, which is only a diminutive of the love of glory, and the object that attracts the desires of those who cannot arise to fame.

This desire of esteem must in like manner produce, in different ages, opposite virtues and vices. When interest is a surer path to preferment than merit, this desire makes men of intrigue and flatterers; when money is more honoured than virtue, it produces avaricious men, who seek for riches with as much eagerness as the first Romans fled from them, when they were ashamed to have them in their possession; whence I conclude, that, from the influence of different manners and governments, the same desire must necessarily produce a Cincinnatus, a Papyrius, a Crassus, and a Sejanus.

I shall observe, by the way, on this subject, the difference there is between the ambitious of glory and the ambitious of high posts or of riches. The first can never be otherwise than great criminals, because great crimes, from the superiority of the talents necessary to the commission of them, and the extraordinary advantages united with the success, can alone impose so far on the imagination of mankind, as to extort their admiration,—an admiration founded on the inward and secret desire of resembling these illustrious criminals. Every man in love with glory is then incapable of all little crimes. If this passion made a Cromwell, it never made a Cartouche. From whence I conclude, that Sylla and Cæsar, in any other situations than those uncommon and extraordinary ones in which they found themselves, would, by the nature even of their passions, have remained faithful to virtue; while the cunning and avaricious, influenced by the baseness and obscurity of their vices, have daily opportunities of committing new ones.

Having shewn how the same passion, which impels us to the love and practice of virtue, may in different ages and governments produce the opposite vices, let us now endeavour to penetrate more deeply into the human heart; and discover why, in any government whatsoever, man, variable in his conduct, is determined by his passions sometimes to good, and at others to bad, actions: and why his heart is an amphitheatre, always open to the contests between virtue and vice.

In order to resolve this moral problem, it is necessary to search into the cause of the successive disquietude and sleep of conscience, into the source of those confused and various emotions of soul, and of those inward struggles which the tragic poet presents with such success on the stage, only because the spectators have all had the same inward feelings;

and we must ask ourselves, what are these two selfs, which
Paschal* and some Indian philosophers have acknowledged in
their own breasts?

To discover the universal cause of all these effects, it is sufficient to observe that men are not moved by one single species
of sensations; that none of them are completely animated by
those solitary passions that fill the whole capacity of the soul;
that, drawn by turns by different passions, some of which are
conformable and others contrary to the general interest, every
man is subject to two different attractions, one of which leads
him to virtue, and the other to vice. I say every man; for
the probity of none was ever more universally acknowledged
than that of Cato and Brutus, because no man can flatter himself with being more virtuous than these two Romans: the
former, however, surprised by a desire of avarice, committed
some instances of extortions in his government; and the latter,
moved by the entreaties of his daughter, obtained of the
senate, in favour of Bibulus, his son-in-law, a grant he had
refused to Cicero, his friend, on account of its being contrary to the interest of the republic. This is the cause of the
mixture of vice and virtue perceivable in all hearts, and the
reason why there is neither pure virtue nor unmixed vice upon
earth.

Now, in order to know what it is that denominates a man
virtuous or vicious, it must be observed, that, among the
passions by which every man is animated, there is necessarily
one that principally presides over his conduct, and has a greater
influence over his mind than all the others.

In proportion then as the latter commands more or less imperiously, and is, in its own nature, or from particular circum-

---

* In the school of Vedantam, the Brachmans of that sect teach
that there are two principles, the one positive, which is the ME; the
other negative, to which they give the name of Maya, or OF ME,
that is error. Wisdom consists in delivering ourselves from Maya,
and in persuading ourselves, by a constant application, that the ME
is the only eternal infinite being : the key of the deliverance is in
these words, the ME is the Supreme Being.

stances useful or prejudicial to the state, the man is more frequently determined either to good or to evil, and receives the name of virtuous or vicious.

I shall only add, that the strength of his virtues or vices will be always proportioned to the vivacity of his passions, and their strength to the degree of pleasure he receives from indulging them. For this reason in early youth, which is most sensible of pleasure and of the strength of the passions, we are generally capable of greater actions.

The most exalted virtue, as well as the most shameful vice, is the effect of the greater or less intenseness of the pleasure it affords us.

Thus we can form no exact idea of the degree of our virtue, till we have discovered, by a scrupulous examination, the number and degrees of those pains which a passion, as for instance, the love of justice or of glory, may enable us to support. The person to whom esteem is every thing, and life nothing, will, like Socrates, submit rather to suffer death, than meanly to beg for life. He who is become the soul of a republican state, in which pride and glory render him passionately desirous of the public welfare, will, like Cato, prefer death to the mortification of seeing himself and his country submit to the yoke of arbitrary power. But such actions are the effect of the greatest love of glory. This is the highest pitch to which the strongest passions can attain, and here nature has fixed the bounds of human virtue.

In vain would we deceive ourselves; we necessarily become the enemies of men, when we can no otherwise be happy than by their misfortunes*. It is the pleasing conformity we find between our own interest and that of the public, a conformity generally produced by the desire of esteem, that gives us those tender sentiments that are rewarded by their affection. He who to be virtuous must always conquer his inclinations, must necessarily be a wicked man. The meritorious virtues are

---

* *Secundum id quod amplius nos delectat operemur necesse est*, says St. Augustin.

never certain and infallible virtues*. It is impossible in practice for a man to deliver himself up, in a manner, daily to a war with the passions, without losing many battles.

Being always forced to yield to the most powerful interest some of that love for esteem, we never sacrifice any great pleasure to it, but those it procures. If, on certain occasions, sacred personages have sometimes exposed themselves to the contempt of the public, it is because they would not sacrifice their salvation to their glory; and if some women resist the solicitations of a prince, it is because they believe, that his conquest would not recompence them for the loss of their esteem: thus, there are few insensible to the love of a king, who is young and charming; and none who resist such beneficent, amiable, and powerful, beings as we paint the sylphs and genii, who, by a thousand allurements, can at once intoxicate all the senses of a mortal.

This truth, founded on self-love, is not only known, but even acknowledged, by the legislators.

Convinced that self-love is, in general, the strongest passion of mankind, the legislators have never pronounced it criminal, for a man to kill another in his own defence, nor blamed a citizen for not devoting himself to death, like Decius, for the preservation of his country.

The virtuous man is not then he who sacrifices his pleasures, habits, and strongest passions, to the public welfare, since it is impossible that such a man should exist†; but he whose strongest passion is so conformable to the general interest, that he is almost constantly necessitated to be virtuous. For this reason, he approaches nearer to perfection, and has a

---

* In the haram it is not to the meritorious virtues, but to impotency, that the Grand Seignior entrusts his women.

† If some men have seemed to sacrifice their interest to the public welfare, it is because, in a good form of government, the idea of virtue is so united to that of happiness, and the idea of vice to that of contempt, that they are hurried away by a lively sensation, the origin of which is not always to be discovered; and from this motive perform actions that are often contrary to their interest.

greater claim to the name of being a virtuous man, who requires stronger motives of pleasure, and a more powerful interest, in order to determine him to do a bad action, than are necessary to his performing a good one, and consequently supposes that he has a greater passion for virtue than for vice.

Cæsar was, without doubt, not the most virtuous among the Romans; yet, if he would not renounce the title of a good citizen without taking that of the master of the world, we have not, perhaps, a right to banish him from the class of honest men. In fact, among the virtuous, who really deserve that title, how few are there, who, if placed in the same circumstances as Cæsar was, would refuse the sceptre of the world, especially if, like Cæsar, they thought they had those superior talents that secure the success of great enterprises? Less abilities would perhaps render them better citizens; and a moderate degree of virtue, supported by a greater anxiety for the success, would be sufficient to deter them from engaging in so bold a project. Indeed, sometimes a want of talents preserves us from vice; and frequently to the same defect we owe all our virtues.

We are on the contrary less virtuous, as less powerful motives lead us to the commission of a crime. Such, for instance, is that of some of the emperors of Morocco, who, solely from the motive of making a parade of their dexterity, would, with one blow of a sabre, in mounting a horse, cut off the head of the groom who held the stirrup.

This is what distinguishes the virtuous from the vicious man, in a manner the most clear, precise, and conformable, to experience; on this plan the public might make an exact thermometer, which would shew the various degrees of virtue and vice in each citizen, if, by penetrating to the bottom of the heart, we could discover there the value that each sets on his virtue. But the impossibility of arriving at this knowledge forces us to judge of men only by their actions,—a judgment extremely faulty in every particular, but on the whole sufficiently conformable to the general interest, and almost as useful as if it were just.

After having inquired into the influence of the passions, and explained the cause of that mixture of virtue and vice observable in all men; having stated the limits of virtue, and at length fixed the idea that belongs to the word virtuous; we are now at liberty to judge, if we ought to attribute the indifference of certain nations for virtue to nature, or to a particular legislation.

If pleasure be the only object of man's pursuit, we need only imitate nature, in order to inspire a love of virtue. Pleasure informs us of what she would have done, and pain what she forbids, and man will readily obey her mandates. Why may not the legislature, armed with the same power, produce the same effects? Were men without passions, there would be no means of producing a reformation; but the love of pleasure, against which men, possessed of a probity more venerable than enlightened, have constantly exclaimed, is a bridle by which the passions of the individuals might always be directed to the public good. The hatred most men have for virtue is not then the effect of the corruption* of their nature, but of the imperfection of the legislation. It is the legislation, if I may venture to say so, that excites us to vice, by mingling it with pleasure; the great art of the legislator is that of separating them, and making no proportion between the advantage the villain can receive from his crime, and the pain to which he exposes himself. If among the rich men, who are often less virtuous than the indigent, we see few robbers and assassins, it is because the profit obtained by robbery is never to a rich man proportionable to the hazard of a capital punishment: but this is not the case with respect to the indigent; for the disproportion falling infinitely short of being so great with respect to him, virtue and vice are in a manner placed in an equilibrium. Not

---

* If robbers are as faithful to the agreements made between themselves as honest men, it is because the common danger, by which they are united, necessitates them to it. From the same motive people discharge their debts contracted at play, and with such assurance become bankrupts to their creditors. Now, if interest make villains do what virtue makes honest men perform, who can doubt that, by dexterously managing the principle of interest, a judicious legislator might lay all men under a necessity of being virtuous.

that I would here pretend to insinuate, that men ought to be driven as with a rod of iron.   In an excellent legislation, and among a virtuous people, contempt, which deprives man of all consolation, and leaves him desolate in the midst of his native country, is a motive sufficient to form virtuous minds.   Every other kind of punishment renders men timid, inactive, and stupid.   The kind of virtue produced by the fear of punishment resembles its origin; this virtue is pusillanimous, and without knowledge; or rather fear, which only smothers vice, but produces no virtues.   True virtue is founded on the love of esteem and glory, and the fear of contempt, which is more terrible than death itself.   I cannot cite here a more apposite example, than the answer which the English Spectator puts into the mouth of a soldier fond of duelling, who thus addresses Pharamond, who reproached him for having disobeyed his orders.   " How could I obey such orders ?" said the soldier: " Thou punishest indeed with death those who violate them, but with infamy those who obey them! Know, then, that I fear death less than infamy !"

I might conclude from what I have said, that the love or indifference of certain nations for virtue does not arise from nature, but from the different constitutions of states: but, however just this conclusion might be, it would not be sufficiently proved, if I did not endeavour to throw more light on this subject, by searching more particularly into such governments as are either free or despotic, for the causes of this love or indifference for virtue.   I shall first inquire into the nature of a despotic government; and, in order to obtain a more accurate knowledge of this subject, I shall examine what motive it is that can excite in man such an unbridled lust of arbitrary power as is felt in the East.

I choose the East for an example, because an indifference with respect to virtue is no where constantly felt but in governments of that kind.   In vain do some jealous neighbouring nations accuse us with already bending under the yoke of eastern despotic power: I say that our religion does not permit princes to usurp such a power; that our constitution is monarchical, and not despotic; that the individuals may consequently be stripped of their property by law, but not by arbitrary authority; and that our princes claim the title of monarchs, and not that of uncontroulale sovereigns; that they acknowledge themselves bound by the fundamental laws of the kingdom, and declare themselves the fathers, and not the tyrants, of their subjects. Besides, a despotic power could not be established in France, without the whole country being soon subdued. This kingdom is not like Turkey and Persia; those empires are defended by vast deserts, and their immense extent, supplying the depopulation occasioned by despotic power, always furnishes fresh armies for the sultan. In a country like ours, surrounded by wise and powerful nations, the minds of the people could not be sunk with impunity; and France, depopulated by tyranny, would soon fall a prey to these nations. The prince, in loading the hands of his subjects with irons, would only bow them to the yoke of slavery, to render himself subject to the yoke of the neighbouring princes. It is then impossible for him to form such a project.

CHAP. XVII.

OF THE UNIVERSAL DESIRE OF BEING DESPOTIC, THE MEANS EMPLOYED TO ARRIVE AT THIS POWER, AND THE DANGER TO WHICH IT EXPOSES KINGS.

This desire derives its source from the love of pleasure, and consequently from the nature of man himself. Every one would be as happy as possible;—every one would be invested with the power of forcing men to contribute to their happiness to the utmost of their power; and for this reason every one desires to command.

All people are either governed according to laws and established conventions, or by an arbitrary will. In the first case, the power over them is less arbitrary, and they are not under so great a necessity of pleasing the prince; besides, he that would govern a people according to their laws must know them, reflect upon them, and endure the fatigue of studying them,—

from which indolence always seeks to be delivered. In order to gratify this indolence, he aspires to an absolute power, which, exempting him from all care, study, and the fatigue of attention, makes his fellow-creatures the abject slaves of his will.

According to Aristotle, a despotic government is that in which all men are slaves, and only one free.

This is the motive that induces every man to desire to be despotic. In order to be so, he must demolish the power both of the great and of the common people, and consequently divide the interest of the citizens. In a long succession of ages, opportunities will offer, and almost all sovereigns, being animated by a view of their interest more lively than rational, embrace them with avidity.

On this anarchy of interests is established the despotic power of the East, resembling the picture given by Milton of the empire of Chaos, which, says he, extends its royal pavilion over a barren and wasteful abyss, where Confusion, involved in herself, maintains the anarchy and discord of the elements, and governs each atom with a sceptre of iron.

A division being once sown between the citizens, it is necessary to debase and degrade their minds, by brandishing the sword of tyranny, and making it dazzle in their eyes; to place the virtues in the rank of crimes, and to punish them as such. To what cruelties of this kind have not only the despotic power of the East, but even that of the Roman emperors, been carried? "Under the reign of Domitian," says Tacitus, "the virtues were decrees of death. Rome swarmed with informers; the slave was a spy on his master, the freedman on his patron, the friend on his friend." In those calamitous ages, the virtuous man did not advise the commission of crimes, but he was obliged to wink at them. Had he shewn more courage and firmness on such occasions, it would have been treated as a crime against the state. Among the degenerate Romans, weakness was the heroism. In that reign were punished Senecio and Rusticus, the panegyrists of the virtues of Thrasea and Helvidius; those illustrious orators were treated as criminals of state, and their works burnt by public authority. Celebrated writers, such as Pliny, were reduced to compose grammatical books, because every work, on a more elevated subject, might have given umbrage to the tyrant, and have been dangerous to the author. The learned, who had been invited to Rome by an Augustus, a Vespasian, an Antoninus, and a Trajan, were banished by a Nero, a Caligula, a Domitian, and a Caracalla : the philosophers were driven away, and the sciences proscribed. " These tyrants," says Tacitus, " endeavoured to obliterate whatever had the marks of genius and virtue."

By thus keeping the mind in the perpetual tremors of fear, tyranny debases it to her purposes. It is she who in the East has invented those cruel tortures and punishments practised there * ;—punishments sometimes necessary in those detestable countries, because the people are invited to commit crimes, not only by their misery, but also by the example of the sultan, who teaches them to despise justice.

These are both the motives on which the love of despotic authority is founded, and the means employed to arrive at it. Thus, foolishly in love with arbitrary power, kings inconsiderately throw themselves into a road interrupted by a thousand precipices, down which a thousand tyrants have fallen. Let us here venture, for the good of human nature, and that of sovereigns, to lend them some light, and to shew them the dangers to which, under such a government, they and their people are exposed. Let them from henceforward keep far from them every perfidious counsel, that inspires them with the desire of arbitrary power; and let them at length know, that the strongest and most masterly treatise against tyranny would be a treatise on the happiness and preservation of kings.

But, it is said, who can conceal this truth from them? why do not they compare the small number of princes banished from England with the prodigious number of Greek and Turkish emperors murdered on the throne of Constantinople? If the sultans, I reply, are not deterred by these terrible examples, it is

---

* The punishments, in use almost all over the East, fill the human mind with horror, because the tyrant who orders them is himself above the laws. This is not the case in republics, where the laws are always mild, because those who establish submit to them.

from their not having this picture habitually present to their minds: it is from their being continually prompted to despotism, by the wretches who would share with them the arbitrary power; and because most of the eastern princes, being governed by the will of a vizier, yield, through weakness, to his desires, and are not sufficiently informed of their injustice by the noble resistance of their subjects.

The entrance into despotism is easy. The people seldom foresee the evils a confirmed tyranny prepares for them; and, if they at last perceive it, it is not till they sink under the yoke, are changed on all sides; and, being unable to defend themselves, only wait trembling for the punishment to which they must be condemned.

Emboldened by the weakness of the people, the princes become despotic tyrants. They do not know, that they themselves suspend over their heads the sword that is to give them the mortal blow; that, to abrogate all law, and reduce every thing to arbitrary power, they must perpetually have recourse to force, and often employ the soldier's sword. Now, the habitual custom of making use of such methods, either provokes the citizens to revolt, and invites them to revenge, or insensibly accustoms them to know no other justice than force.

Though a long time be required to spread such an idea among the people, it forces its way at last, and reaches even to the soldiers, who, at length, perceiving that no collective body in the state is capable of resisting them, and that the prince, odious to his subjects, owes all his power to them, their souls are open to the most audacious projects, and they long to better their condition. If then a bold and courageous man flatters them with the hope of plundering some great cities, such a man, as all history proves, is sufficient to cause a revolution;— a revolution that is always speedily followed by a second; since, in despotic states, as the illustrious president de Montesquieu observes, the tyrants are often assassinated, without destroying the tyranny. When once the soldiers know their strength, it is impossible to keep them within just bounds. I could cite on this occasion all the Roman emperors proscribed by the Pretorian bands, for resolving to free the country from the tyranny of the soldiers, and to re-establish the ancient discipline of the army.

The despotic tyrant then, in order to command slaves, is forced in his turn to obey his ever turbulent and imperious troops. But the case is very different, when the prince has created in the state a powerful body of magistrates, by whom the people, being judged, obtain ideas of justice and equity; the soldiers, being always taken out of the body of the citizens, preserve in their new state some idea of justice; besides, they are sensible that the entire body of the citizens, called together by the prince and the magistrates, under the standard of the laws, would oppose any bold attempt, and let the valour of the army be ever so great, it must at length be overpowered by numbers. Hence, the soldiers are kept within the bounds of duty by sentiments of justice and fear.

A powerful body of magistrates is then necessary to the safety of kings: it is a buckler, behind which both the prince and people are sheltered, the one from the madness of sedition, and the other from the cruelties of tyranny.

The Khalif Aaron Al-Raschid reflecting on this subject, in order to preserve himself from the dangers which on all sides surround despotic princes, one day asked his brother, the celebrated Beloulh, what advice he could give him on the manner of reigning well? "Make thy will," said he, "conformable to the laws, and not the laws to thy will. Reflect, that men without merit are always craving, and that great men are so modest that they seldom ask; refuse then the requests of the one, and prevent those of the other. Load not thy people with taxes too burthensome; and recollect on this subject, the advice which king Nouchirvon the Just gave to his son Ormous: "My son," said he, "nobody will be happy in thine empire, if thou thinkest only of pleasure. When thou art reclined on thy pillow, and ready to taste the sweets of sleep, remember those whom oppression keeps awake; when a splendid repast shall be served up before thee, think on those who languish in misery; when thou ramblest through the delightful groves of thine haram, remember that there are those who are unfortunate, and whom tyranny keeps in irons.—I shall only

add one word more," said Beloulh ; " receive into thy favour
men eminent in the sciences, and conduct thyself by their advice, in order that monarchy may be obedient to the written
law, and not the law to monarchy *."

Themistius†, being commissioned by the senate to harangue
Jovianus on his advancement to the throne, made nearly the
same discourse to that emperor : " Remember," said he, " that,
though the army has raised thee to the empire, thou must learn
from the philosophers the art of governing ; the first has given
thee the purple of the Cæsars ; but the latter will teach thee
how to wear it worthily."

Even among the ancient Persians, the most abject and dastardly of all people, the philosophers, who inaugurated the
princes, were allowed to repeat these words to them at their
coronation§ : " Know, O king, that thine authority shall cease
to be lawful on the very day that thou ceasest to render the
Persians happy." A truth of which Trajan appears to be fully
sensible, when, being raised to the throne, and presenting the
sword, as usual, to the præfectus pretorio, he said, " Receive
from me this sword, and make use of it under my reign,
either to defend in me a just prince, or to punish in me a
tyrant."

Whoever, under pretence of supporting the authority of his
sovereign, would stretch it to an arbitrary power, is at the
same time a bad father, a bad citizen, and a bad subject : a
bad father and a bad citizen, because he would load his posterity and his country with the chains of slavery ; and a bad
subject, because, by changing a lawful for an arbitrary authority, he is summoning up ambition and despair against the
king. I call to witness the thrones of the East, so often stained
with the blood of their sovereigns‡. If the sultans well un-

* See Chardin, vol. v.
† Critical History of Philosophy, by M. Deslandes.
§ Ibid.
‡ Notwithstanding the attachment of the Chinese to their sovereigns,
which has often led several thousands of them to sacrifice themselves

derstood their own interest, it would never permit them either to wish for such a power, or in this respect to yield to the desires of their viziers. Kings ought to be deaf to such advice, and to recollect that their highest interest requires, if I may so express myself, that they should set a proper value on their kingdom, in order that it may be enjoyed by them and their posterity. This true interest can only be understood by intelligent princes : in others, the contemptible glory they propose to themselves, by commanding absolutely, and the love of indolence, which conceals from them the dangers with which they are surrounded, will always prevent their engaging in more noble pursuits; hence all governments perpetually tend towards despotic power.

CHAP. XVIII.

THE PRINCIPAL EFFECTS OF DESPOTIC POWER.

I SHALL first distinguish despotic power into two kinds; one, suddenly established by force of arms in a virtuous nation, that bears it patiently. This nation is like an oak bent down by main force, whose elasticity soon breaks the ropes which hold it down. Greece furnishes a multitude of instances of this kind.

The other is founded by time, luxury, and effeminacy. The nation among whom it is established is like an oak, which, being bent down by little and little, insensibly loses the elasticity necessary to make it rise and recover its first state. Of this last kind of despotic power I shall treat in this chapter.

In nations subject to this kind of government, the men in high posts can have no clear idea of justice; they are in this respect plunged into the most profound ignorance. Indeed,

---

on the tomb of their monarchs, yet how many revolutions has the ambition of arbitrary power excited in that empire? See the History of the Huns, by M. de Guignet, in the article of China.

what idea can a vizier form of justice? He does not even know, that there is such a thing as the public welfare; yet destitute of this knowledge he must wander here and there without a guide. The ideas of just and unjust, received in early youth, insensibly become obscured, and at length entirely disappear.

But who, it is objected, can conceal this knowledge from the viziers? How can they acquire it, I reply, in these despotic countries, where the citizens have no share in the management of public affairs; where the person, who fixes his attention on the misfortunes of his country, meets with the eye of resentment; where the mistaken interest of the sultan is opposed to the interests of his subjects; and where, to serve the prince, is to betray the nation? In order to be just and virtuous, it is necessary that they should know what are the duties of a prince and his subjects, and study the reciprocal engagements that bind together all the members of society. Justice is no more than a consummate knowledge of these engagements. To rise to this knowledge, they must think; but what man among a people subject to arbitrary power dares to think? Indolence, inutility, inaction, and even the danger of thinking, soon draw after them an incapacity of thought; for they think but little in countries where they keep their thoughts concealed. It would be an idle surmise to say, that they are silent from prudence; but this does not prevent their thinking. It is certain, that they are void of thought, and that great and noble ideas are never formed in the heads of those subject to arbitrary power.

In those countries people are never animated by that opinion of their own importance, and that giddiness which foretells the destruction of empires. Every one keeping his eyes fixed on his private interest, never places them on that of the public.— The people then can have no idea either of the public welfare or the duty of citizens; and the viziers, being taken from the body of the nation, must, on entering their office, be void of every principle that can teach them a wise administration, or a proper distribution of justice; the people then must seek for great places, not with a view of doing good, but to make their court to the sovereign, in order to obtain a share of his power.

But, even supposing them animated with the desire of doing good, their ignorance prevents their being able to accomplish it; and the attention of the viziers being necessarily engrossed by the intrigues of the seraglio, they have not leisure for reflection.

Besides, to obtain knowledge, they must expose themselves to the fatigue of study and meditation; and what motive can engage them to take this trouble? They are not stimulated to it even by the fear of censure *.

If we may be allowed to compare small things with great, let us take a survey of the republic of letters. If the critics were banished from thence, is it not obvious, that authors being freed from the salutary fear of censure, which now compels them to take pains in improving their talents, they would then present the public with only rude and imperfect pieces? This is exactly the case of viziers; this is the reason of their inattention to the administration of affairs, and the cause of their never condescending to consult men of learning †.

What I have said of the viziers, may be applied to the sultans. Princes do not escape the general ignorance of their own nation: their eyes are, even in this respect, covered with a thicker darkness than those of their subjects. Almost all, who are intrusted with their education, or who surround them, being eagerly desirous of governing under their name, have an interest in rendering them stupid ‡. Thus, the prince destined

---

* For this reason the English esteem the liberty of the press one of the most valuable of their privileges.

† The president de Montesquieu's authority has been quoted in the parliament of England, because the English are a free people: and in relation to laws and the administration of affairs, Peter the Great consulted the famous Leibnitz, because one great man is not ashamed to consult another; and because Russia, by its commerce with the other European nations, may obtain more knowledge than other eastern nations.

to reign, being shut up in the seraglio till the death of his father, passes from the haram to the throne, without any clear idea of the knowledge of government, and before he has even been once present at a divan.

Wherefore then, after the example of Philip of Macedon, whose superior courage and understanding did not inspire him with a blind self-confidence, and who paid his pages for repeating to him every day, " Remember, Philip, that thou art a man," why should not viziers sometimes allow critics to put them in mind of being men * ? Wherefore, I say, cannot they without a crime, doubt of the justice of their decisions, and repeat after Grotius, " That every decree, or every law, which people are forbid to examine, and to censure, can never fail of being unjust ?"

It is because these viziers are but men. Are there many among the authors who would have the generosity to spare the critics, had they the power to punish them ? It is at least only the men of a superior genius and of an elevated character, who, sacrificing their resentment to the public advantage, would preserve in the republic of letters the critics, so necessary to the progress of the arts and sciences. How then can such generosity be required from a vizier ?

" There are," says Balzac, " but few ministers so generous as to prefer being praised for their clemency, which lasts as long as the families of those they have preserved, to the plea-

___

even among ourselves, Louis XIII. in one of his letters, complains of the Marshal d'Ancre. " He opposes," says he, " my walking in the streets of Paris, and allows me no pleasures but those of hunting, and taking a few turns in the Thuilleries : he has forbid the officers of my houshold, as well as all my subjects, to converse with me on serious affairs, and to speak to me in private." It seems as if, in every country, pains are taken to render the princes but little worthy of the throne, where they are called to it by their birth.

* There is not a person like the Duke of Burgundy to be found in the East. That prince read all the libels made against him and Louis XIV. He was desirous of being informed, and was sensible that hatred and humour can alone, sometimes, dare to present the truth to kings.

sure of revenge, though the latter passes away as swiftly as the fall of the axe that separates the head from the body." Few viziers deserve the praises given n Sethos to queen Nephta, when the priest, pronouncing her panegyric, says, " she pardoned like the Gods, with the full power of punishing."

Those in power will be always unjust and vindictive. M. de Vendome said, pleasantly enough on this subject, that in the march of armies he had often inquired into the quarrels between the mules and the muleteers; but, to the disgrace of human nature, reason was almost always on the side of the mules.

M. de Vernay, who was so well skilled in natural history, that by the bare inspection of the tooth of an animal he knew whether it was carnivorous or fed on grass, often said, " Let me only see the tooth of an unknown animal, and by that I shall judge of its manners." After his example, a moral philosopher may say, " Shew me the degree of power wherewith a man is invested, and by that I shall form a judgment of his justice." In vain should we attempt to disarm the cruelty of the viziers, by repeating after Tacitus, that the punishment of critics is only the trumpet that informs posterity of the disgrace and vices of their executioners. In despotic states, people care, and indeed cannot avoid caring, but little for glory and posterity, since they do not love, as I have already observed, esteem for its own sake, but for the advantages it procures; since nohing is granted to merit, and there is nothing which they dare refuse to power.

The viziers having then no interest in improving their minds, and consequently in supporting censure, they must generally remain ignorant *. The Lord Bolingbroke says on this subject,

---

* As all the citizens are very ignorant of what constitutes the public welfare, most of the projectors in those countries are either cheats, who have no particular use in view, or people of mean abilities, who cannot seize, at a single glance, the long chain by which the several parts of a state are connected together, and consequently they always propose schemes that are inconsistent with the general system of government: for this reason, they seldom dare to expose them in their works to public view.

" When young, I at first considered those who governed the
nations as superior intelligences; but," he adds, " experience
soon undeceived me. I examined those who were at the
helm of affairs in England, and soon found that the Great were
like those gods of Phœnicia, on whose shoulders were fixed
the head of a bull, as a mark of supreme power; and that, in
general, men were governed by the greatest blockheads among
them." This truth, which Bolingbroke applied, perhaps from
humour, to England, is, doubtless, not to be disputed in almost
all the empires of the east.

CHAP. XIX.

THE ABJECT AND SUBMISSIVE SUBJECTION, IN WHICH THE PEOPLE ARE KEPT, OCCASIONS THE IGNORANCE OF THE VIZIERS, AND IS THE SECOND EFFECT OF DESPOTIC POWER.

THOUGH the viziers, it is objected, may not find it for their
interest to improve their minds, yet it is most certainly for the
interest of the public, that they should not be ignorant, since
every nation desires to be well governed: what then is the
reason, that no citizen in those countries has the virtue to reproach the viziers for their ignorance and injustice, and to force
them by the fear of contempt to become good citizens? It is
because the property of despotic power is to debase and degrade the mind.

In states where the law alone dispenses punishments and rewards, and where obedience is paid to none but the laws,
the virtuous, dwelling in safety, contract a boldness and firmness of soul, that cannot subsist in a country which is the seat
of despotic power, where property, life, and liberty, depend
on the caprice* and arbitrary will of one man. In these countries it would be as imprudent to be virtuous, as it would have

---

* We can find no instance in Turkey like that which happened in
Scotland, of the laws punishing the sovereign for an act of injustice
committed against a subject. At Malcolm's accession to the throne

been to be viscious in Crete and Lacedemon. There no man rises up against injustice, and, rather than applaud it, cries with the philosopher Philoxenes, "Let me be carried back to the quarries."

In these governments, how difficult would it be to be virtuous? To what dangers would a person of probity be exposed? Suppose a man in love with virtue; would we have such a man perceive, that the injustice or incapacity of the viziers or satraps was the cause of the miseries of the public, and yet be silent? this would be a contradiction. Besides, a mute probity would here be of no use. The more virtuous this man was, the more eager would he be to point out him on whom the national contempt ought to fall: and I even maintain, that he ought to do it. Now, from the injustice and weakness of a vizier invested, as I have said above, with the power necessary to condemn merit to the greatest torments, this man would be so much the sooner delivered to the mutes, in proportion to his being more the friend of virtue than of his country.

As Nero, when on the stage, extorted the applauses of the spectators, more barbarous than himself; so the viziers require the praises of even those they use ill, and overload with taxes. They are like Tiberius, under whose reign the sighs and cries of the unhappy wretches under oppression were construed to proceed from a factious spirit, because every thing is criminal, says Suetonius, under a prince who is constantly stung with his own guilt.

There is not a vizier, who would not reduce mankind to the condition of those ancient Persians, who, being cruelly whipped by the order of their prince, were obliged to appear before him: "We come," said they, "to thank thee for having condescended to remember us."

---

of Scotland, a nobleman presented to him the patent of his privileges, entreating his majesty to confirm them: but the king took the patent, and tore it in pieces. The nobleman complained of this to the parliament, who decreed, that the king should sit on his throne, and in the presence of the whole court stitch the nobleman's patent together with a needle and thread.

The noble boldness of a citizen, so virtuous as to reproach the viziers for their ignorance and injustice, would be soon followed by his punishment*, to which nobody would expose themselves. Nobody, you will say, but the brave man, the hero. He might do it, I reply, when supported by the hope of esteem and glory ; but, if he is deprived of this hope, his courage abandons him. Among a slavish people, the name of factious is given to a generous citizen ; and there will be found those who approve his punishment. There is no crime on which praise is not lavished, in a state where an abject meanness is become the mode. " If the plague," says Gordon, " had garters, pensions, and ribbons, to bestow, there are churchmen vile enough, and civilians base enough, to maintain, that the plague reigns by divine right; and that to withdraw ourselves from its malignant influences is a sin against God." It is then more prudent in these countries to be the accomplice than the accuser of knaves; for virtue and talents are always the but of tyranny.

On the conquest of India by Thamas Kouli Khan, the only man worthy of esteem, whom that prince found in the Mogul's empire, was one named Mahmouth, and this Mahmouth was banished.

In countries subject to a despotic government, the love of the esteem and acclamations of the people is so criminal, that the prince always punishes those who obtain them. Agricola, after having triumphed over the Britons, in order to escape the applauses of the people, as well as the fury of Domitian,

---

* When a vizier commits a fault during his administration, if the public suffer by it, the people complain, and the vizier's pride is offended : but, so far is he from changing his measures, and trying by a better conduct to calm their too just complaints, that he solely employs himself in methods of imposing silence on the citizens. These methods of force exasperate them, and they redouble their cries : the vizier has then only two parts to take, either to expose the state to revolutions, or to carry despotic power to that excess which always threatens the ruin of empires. This last choice is most commonly preferred by the viziers.

passed the streets of Rome in the night, in his way to the emperor's palace : the prince embraced him coldly : Agricola retired ; and the conqueror of Briton, says Tacitus, was instantly lost in the crowd of other slaves.

In those unhappy times, one might have cried out at Rome, with Brutus, " O virtue, thou art but an empty name!" How can we expect to find it amongst a people who live in perpetual agonies, and whose minds, being broke with fear, have lost all their force and vigour? Among such people, we only meet with powerful insolence, and abject dastardly slaves. What picture can be more humbling to human nature than the audience of a vizier, when, with a grave and stupid air of importance, he advances into the midst of a crowd of clients, who, grave, mute, and immoveable, with their eyes fixed and cast down, wait trembling for the favour of a look*, nearly in the attitude of those bramins, who, with their eyes fixed on the end of their noses, wait for the blue and divine flame with which Heaven is to bestow its illuminations, and whose appearance, according to them, is to raise them to the dignity of a pagod!

When we see merit thus humbled before an ignorant vizier, or even a despicable eunuch, we cannot help calling to mind the ridiculous veneration in which cranes are held at Japan, where the name of that bird is never uttered without its being preceded by O-thurisama, or, my lord.

---

* The vizier himself never enters the divan, when the sultan is there, without trembling.

CHAP. XX.

THE CONTEMPT OF VIRTUE, AND THE FALSE ESTEEM PEOPLE AFFECT TO HAVE FOR IT, THE THIRD EFFECT OF DESPOTIC POWER.

SINCE, as I have already proved in the preceding chapters, the ignorance of the viziers is a necessary consequence of despotic forms of government; the ridicule, which in those countries is cast on virtue, seems equally to proceed from the same effect.

Is it to be doubted, that, in the sumptuous repasts of the ancient Persians, and in their elegant evening entertainments, they ridiculed the frugality and coarse food of the Spartans? and that the courtiers, accustomed to cringe in the anti-chamber of the eunuchs, in order to obtain the disgraceful honour of being their sport, did not give the name of ferocity to the noble pride which forbade the Greeks prostrating themselves before the great king.

A slavish people cannot avoid treating with ridicule bravery, magnanimity, disinterestedness, a contempt of life, and all the virtues founded on patriotism and liberty. In Persia, they must then have treated as a fool, and the enemy of a prince, every virtuous subject, who, struck with the heroism of the Greeks, exhorted his fellow-citizens to assemble, and, by a speedy reformation of the government, prevent the approaching ruin of an empire, where virtue was despised*. The Persians, to escape the mortification of thinking themselves mean, were under the necessity of considering the Greeks as ridiculous. We can never be struck by any sentiments that do

---

* At the very moment when three hundred Spartans defended the pass of Thermopylæ, some Arcadian deserters were giving Xerxes an account of the Olympic games, when a Persian lord cried out— " What men are we going to fight! Insensible of interest, they are only greedy of glory !"

not affect us in a lively manner. A brave citizen, who is had in veneration wherever the rank of a citizen subsists, must ever pass for a fool in all despotic governments.

Among us Europeans, who approach nearer to the heroism of the Greeks than to the servility of the eastern empires, how many great actions would be deemed foolish, were they not consecrated by the admiration of all ages! To this admiration is to be ascribed our not mentioning as ridiculous the order sent by the people of Sparta to King Agis, before the battle of Mantinea: "Take no advantage of superiority of numbers; send back a part of the troops, and fight the enemy with equal force." In like manner we should treat as ridiculous the answer made by Callicratidas, general of the Lacedemonian fleet, before the battle of Argineuses. Hermon advising him not to engage the Athenian fleet with unequal force, "O Hermon," he replied, "the gods forbid that I should follow an advice that would be attended with such fatal consequences to my country. Sparta shall not be dishonoured by her general. Here both I and my army must either conquer or perish. Is it for Callicratidas to teach the art of making a retreat to men who, to this day, have never inquired what were the numbers of the enemy, but only where they were encamped?" So bold and noble an answer would to most men appear foolish. What men have such an elevation of soul, such a profound knowledge of politics, as to perceive, like Callicratidas, the importance of cherishing in the Spartans that obstinate bravery that rendered them invincible? This hero knew that to be incessantly employed in cherishing their sentiments of courage and glory, too much prudence might blunt their edge; and that a nation can have none of the virtues, without having the scruples that attend them.

Half politicians, for want of comprehending a sufficient extent of time, are always struck in too lively a manner with a present danger. Accustomed to consider every action independently of the chain by which they are all united, when they think of correcting the success of any virtue that prevails among a people, they too often only take from them the palladium to which is fixed their success and glory.

It is then to this ancient admiration that we owe our still continuing to admire these actions: this admiration is then only hypocritical, or the effect of prejudice. A felt admiration would necessarily lead us to imitation.

Now, what man is there, among those who pretend to be passionately fond of glory, who would blush at a victory, that was not entirely owing to his bravery and military skill? Are there many Antiochus Soters? That prince, sensible that he owed the defeat of the Galates only to the terror and confusion into which they were thrown by the unexpected sight of the elephants, shed tears on his triumphal palms, and on the field of battle caused trophies to be raised to his elephants.

They boast of the generosity of Gelon. After the defeat of the innumerable army of the Carthaginians, when the conquered expected the hardest conditions, that prince only required of the humbled Carthaginians the abolition of the barbarous sacrifices of their own children, whom they offered to Saturn. That conqueror would reap no other advantage from his victory than the conclusion of the only treaty that perhaps was ever made in favour of human nature. Among so many admirers, why has Gelon no imitator? A thousand heroes have by turns subdued Asia: however, there is not one who, sensible of the miseries suffered by the human race, has improved his victory, by freeing the Orientals from that weight of wretchedness and degradation into which they have been sunk by despotic power. None of them have destroyed those houses of grief and lamentation where jealousy without remorse mutilates the unhappy persons destined to guard their pleasure, and condemned to the punishment of having desires always reviving and always impotent. People have then no esteem for Gelon's action, but what is hypocritical, or the effect of prejudice.

We honour valour, but it is less than it was honoured at Sparta: therefore we do not experience, at the view of a fortified town, the sensations of contempt felt by the Spartans. Some of them, passing under the walls of Corinth, asked— " By what women is this city inhabited?"—" These are," they were told, " the Corinthians."—" Do not these mean-spirited and cowardly men know," they resumed, " that the only ramparts impenetrable to the enemy are citizens determined to die?" Such courage and elevation of soul are only to be found in warlike republics. With whatever love we are animated for our country, we do not see the mother, after the loss of a son killed in battle, reproach her other sons who have survived the defeat. We do not take example from those virtuous Spartans: after the battle of Leuctra, ashamed of having borne in their wombs men capable of flying, those, whose children had escaped the slaughter, retired to the innermost parts of their houses, in mourning and silence; while, on the contrary, the mothers, whose sons died fighting, filled with joy, and, with their heads crowned with flowers, went to the temple to return thanks to the gods.

However brave our soldiers may be, we do not see a body of twelve hundred men sustain, like the Swiss at the battle of St. James l'Hospital*, the efforts of an army of sixty thousand men, who paid for their victory by the loss of eight thousand soldiers. We no longer see governments treat as cowards; and condemn as such, ten soldiers, who, escaping from the slaughter of that battle, brought home the news of so glorious a defeat.

If in Europe itself we have only a barren admiration of such actions and such virtues, what contempt must the people of the East feel for the same virtues? Who can make these think of

---

* M. Duclos, in the History of Louis XI. says, that the Swiss, to the number of three thousand, sustained the shock of the Dauphin's army, composed of fourteen thousand French and eight thousand English. The battle was fought near Bottelin, and the Swiss were almost all slain.

At the battle of Morgarten, thirteen hundred Swiss routed the Archduke Leopold's army, composed of twenty thousand men. Near the Wesen, in the canton of Glaris, three hundred and fifty Swiss defeated eight thousand Austrians: every year they celebrate the memory of this defeat on the field of battle, when an orator makes a panegyric on this action, and reads the list of the three hundred and fifty names.

them with respect? Those countries are peopled with abject
vicious minds; and when the virtuous men in a country are
not sufficiently numerous to give the bent to a nation, it necessarily receives it from those who are corrupt. These last,
always interested in ridiculing the sensations they do not feel,
render the virtuous silent. Unhappily there are but few who
do not yield to the clamours of those by whom they are surrounded, who are courageous enough to brave the contempt of
their country, and have the judgment to think that the esteem
of a nation, placed on a certain degree of degradation, is less
flattering than dishonourable.

Did the little value set on Hannibal, at the court of Antiochus, dishonour that great man? did the cowardice, with
which Prusias would have sold him to the Romans, stain the
glory of that illustrious Carthaginian? In the eyes of posterity, it has only dishonoured the king, the council, and the
people, who deliberated upon it.

The result of what I have said is, that people have really
in despotic empires only a contempt for virtue, and that nothing but the name is honoured. If every day we invoke this
virtue, and require it of the citizens, it is only, in this case,
with virtue as with truth, it is demanded on condition we are
so prudent as to conceal it.

———

CHAP. XXI.

OF THE DESTRUCTION OF EMPIRES SUBJECT TO AR-
BITRARY POWER: THE FOURTH EFFECT OF TY-
RANNY.

THE indifference of the eastern nations with respect to
virtue, their ignorance, and abject state of mind, necessarily
follow from the form of their government, and must at the
same time render citizens dishonest to each other, and void of
courage with respect to an enemy.

From this source we may trace the astonishing rapidity with
which the Greeks and Romans subdued Asia. How could

slaves, educated and nurtured in the anti-chamber of a master, stifle, at the sight of the Roman swords, the habitual sensations of fear they had contracted from arbitrary power? How could men, so debased, without elevation of mind, accustomed to trample on the weak, and to cringe before the powerful, avoid yielding to the magnanimity, the policy, the valour, of the Romans, and shew themselves equally dastardly in counsel and in the field of battle?

If the Egyptians, as Plutarch says, were successively the slaves of all nations, it was owing to their being subject to the most severe despotic power : thus they almost constantly gave proofs of cowardice. When King Cleomenes, being driven from Sparta, took refuge in Egypt, he was imprisoned by the intrigues of a minister, named Sobisius ; but having killed his guard, and broken his fetters, the prince presented himself in the streets of Alexandria ; but in vain did he exhort the citizens to revenge him, to punish the injustice of his treatment, and shake off the yoke of tyranny : every where, says Plutarch, he found only immoveable admirers. These base and cowardly people had only that species of courage which made them admire great actions, but not that which would excite them to imitate them.

How can a slavish people resist a free and powerful nation ? In order to make use of arbitrary power with impunity, the tyrant is forced to enervate the minds and the courage of his subjects. What renders him formidable at home, renders him weak abroad : with liberty, he banishes from his empire, all the virtues. " They cannot," says Aristotle, " inhabit base and servile minds."—" We must," says the illustrious president de Montesquieu, whom we have already quoted, " begin by being bad citizens, in order to become good slaves." They could only oppose against the attacks of a people like the Romans, councils and generals absolutely unacquainted with political and military knowledge, taken from that very nation, whose courage was softened, and whose minds were debilitated ; it then necessarily followed that they must have been overcome.

But, it is said, the virtuous have however shone with the greatest lustre in despotic states. This is true, when it has happened that the throne has been successively possessed by several great men. Virtue benumbed by the presence of ty-ranny, revives at the appearance of a virtuous prince: his presence may be compared to that of the sun; when his light pierces and disperses the black clouds that cover the earth, all nature revives, every thing glows with new life; the plains are peopled with laborious husbandmen, the groves resound with aerial concerts, and the winged inhabitants of the skies fly to the tops of the oaks, to welcome the returning sun. " O happy times," cries Tacitus, under the reign of Trajan, " when people obey only the laws, when every one may think freely, and freely tell his thoughts, when every heart flies to the prince, and the sight of him is a benefit!"

The lustre thrown upon such nations is always but of short duration. If sometimes they attain to the highest pitch of power and glory, and become illustrious by success of all kinds, this success being united, as I have already said, with the wisdom of the kings who governed, and not with the form of government, has always been as fleeting as brilliant: the strength of such states, however it may impose upon us, is but an illusion; it is the Colossus of Nebuchadnezzar, whose feet were of potter's clay. These empires resemble the lofty pine, whose top reaches to the heavens; the beasts of the field, and the birds of the air, seek for shelter under its branches; but, being fixed to the earth by too weak a root, is overthrown by the first storm. Such states have but a momentary existence, if they are not surrounded by nations, who have little dispo-sitions for great enterprizes, and are subject to arbitrary power. The respective strength of such nations consists then in an equilibrium of weakness. If a despotic empire has re-ceived a shock, and the throne cannot be secured without a manly and courageous resolution, that empire is destroyed.

The people who groan beneath the yoke of arbitrary power have then only a momentary success, a mere flash of glory, and must, sooner or later, submit to a free and enterprising nation. But supposing that particular circumstances and situations save them from this danger; the bad administration of these kingdoms is sufficient to destroy, to depopulate, and to turn them into desarts; the lethargic languor that successively seizes all the members, produces this effect. The property of despotic power is to stifle the passions : now when minds have, by the want of passions, lost their activity ; when the citizens are in a manner rendered stupid by the opium of luxury, indolence, and softness, the state then falls into a consumption : the apparent calm it enjoys, is, in the eyes of men of understanding, a languid state that is the forerunner of its dissolution. The passions are necessary in a nation, and are its life and soul; the people who have the strongest, are in the end triumphant.

The moderate effervescence of the passions is salutary to an empire; which in this respect resemble the sea, whose stagnate waters, on becoming corrupt, would exhale vapours that would prove fatal to the universe, if they were not purified by the rising of tempests.

But, if the grandeur of nations subject to arbitrary power is only momentaneous, it is not so in governments where the power, as in Rome and Greece, is divided between the people, the nobility, or the kings. In those states, private interest, closely connected with that of the public, changes men into citizens. It is in such states only that the people, whose success depends on the constitution of the government, may hope that it will be of long duration. The necessity in which the citizens here find themselves, of being employed about important objects, and the liberty of thinking and speaking whatever they please, give greater strength and elevation of mind ; the boldness of their thoughts have an influence on their hearts, and make them conceive more extensive, more courageous projects, and execute them with greater intrepidity. I shall even add, that if private interest is not intirely separated from that of the public, if the manners of a people, like those of the Romans, are not as corrupt as they were in the time of Marius and Sylla; the spirit of faction, which obliges the citizens to watch, and be a mutual restraint on each other, is the preserving genius of these empires. They are maintained only by a

counterbalance of opposite interests. Never are the foundations of these states more secure, than at the time when these
exterior ferments appear ready to overthrow them. Thus, the
bottom of the sea is calm and tranquil, even when the north
winds, let loose on its surface, seems to turn it up from its
abyss.

After having discovered in the despotic power of the eastern
nations, the cause of the ignorance of the viziers, the indifference of the people with respect to virtue, and the overthrow of
empires subject to that form of governments, I shall now proceed to shew the opposite effects produced from other political
constitutions.

CHAP. XXII.

OF THE LOVE OF CERTAIN NATIONS FOR GLORY AND VIRTUE.

THIS chapter is so necessary a consequence of the preceding,
that I should think myself excused from all farther examination
of this subject, were I not convinced, that an explanation of the
means proper to necessitate men to virtue, would be agreeable
to the public, and that such disquisitions are instructive even to
those who are most virtuous. I therefore enter into this subject. I cast my eyes over the republics more fruitful in virtuous men: I stop them at Greece and Rome, and see a multitude of heroes arise. Their great actions, preserved with care
in history, seem collected there, to spread the odour of virtue
into the most corrupt and distant ages: it is with these actions
as with the vases of incense, which, placed on the altars of the
Gods, are sufficient to diffuse their perfume over the vast extent
of their temples.

Whoever considers the virtuous actions history has trans-
mitted of these people, and would discover the cause, they will
find that it proceeded from the address with which the legislators of those nations united private and public interest*.

---

* In this union consists the true spirit of the laws.

I take the action of Regulus for a proof of this truth. Supposing in this general, no sentiment of heroism, not even those with which he must have been inspired by a Roman education; I maintain, that, in the age when that consul lived, the legislation was, in certain respects, brought to such a degree of perfection, that had Regulus consulted merely his own personal interest, he could not avoid the generous action he performed. For whoever calls to mind the discipline of the Romans, and that flight, and even the loss of their buckler in battle was punished with the bastinado, under which the guilty commonly expired, must be convinced that a consul conquered, made prisoner, and deputed by the Carthaginians to treat about the exchange of prisoners, could not appear before the Romans, without the fear of that contempt, which is always so humbling to republicans, and so insupportable to an elevated mind. Hence the only part Regulus had to take, was to efface, by some heroic action, the shame of his defeat. He therefore opposed the treaty of exchange, which the senate was ready to sign. He doubtless exposed his life by this advice: but the danger was not imminent; it was very probable, that, astonished by his courage, the senate would be only the more eager for concluding a treaty, that would restore to them so virtuous a citizen. Besides, supposing the senate was brought over by his advice, it was very probable, that the Carthaginians, from the fear of reprisals, or an admiration of his virtue, would not make him suffer the punishment, with which they had threatened him. Regulus did not then expose himself to any danger, to which, I will not say an hero, but even a sensible and prudent man, would have presented himself, to avoid the contempt, and obtain the admiration, of the Romans.

There is then an art of necessitating men to perform heroic actions; not that I would pretend to insinuate here, that Regulus did nothing more than obey this necessity, nor do I mean to stain his glory; the action performed by Regulus was, doubtless, the effect of an impetuous enthusiasm, which led to virtue; but such an enthusiasm could no where be kindled but at Rome.

The virtues and vices of a nation are always necessary effects of its legislation; and it was doubtless the knowledge of this

truth, that made way for that excellent law in China ; to fertilize the seeds of virtue, the mandarins participate in the glory
or shame of the virtuous or infamous actions committed in their
governments*; and, in consequence of them, those mandarins
are raised to superior, or degraded to inferior posts.

How can it be doubted, that virtue is not among all nations
the effect of the greater or less degree of wisdom in the administration ?   If the Greeks and Romans were so long animated
by these manly and courageous virtues, which Balzac calls
" the excursions of the soul beyond the common duties," it is
because the virtues of this king are almost constantly peculiar
to the nations, where each citizen has a part in the sovereignty.

It is only in these countries that we find a Fabricius. Being
pressed by Pyrrhus to follow him to Epirus: " Pyrrhus," said
he, " thou art doubtless an illustrious prince, and a great warrior; but thy people groan in misery. What rashness would
it be to take me into Epirus ? Canst thou doubt that thy people, soon ranged under my law, would not prefer exemption
from tribute, to being overloaded with taxes, and security to
the uncertainty of their possessions ? To-day thy favourite, to-
morrow I should be thy master."   Such a discourse could only
be pronounced by a Roman. In republics we perceive, with
astonishment, how far the heighth of courage, and the heroism
of nations may be carried †. I shall mention Themistocles for

---

* This is not the case in the other empires of the East, where the
governors are only employed in levying taxes, and opposing seditions.
Besides, they are not required to trouble themselves about the happiness of the people in their provinces; their power in this respect is
even very limited.

† We see from cardinal Mazarine's letters, that he was sensible of
the advantages of this form of government. He was afraid that England, by forming a republic, would become too formidable to its neighbours. In a letter to M. le Tellier, he says, " Don Louis and I know
very well, that Charles II. is out of the kingdoms that belong to him ;
but among all the reasons that may engage the kings our masters, to
think of his restoration, one of the strongest is, hindering England
from forming a powerful republic, which, in the end, would give all its
neighbours cause to look about them."

an example of this kind : a few days before the battle of Salamis, that warrior, insulted in full council by the Spartan general, made no other reply to his menaces than these words,
" Strike, but hear." To this example I shall add that of Ti-
moleon : he was accused of a misdemeanor, and the people
were ready to cut his accusers in pieces; but he stopped their
fury by saying, " O Syracusans, what are you going to do ?
Think that every citizen has a right to accuse me : take care,
lest by giving way to your gratitude, ye do not injure that very
liberty, which it is my glory to have restored to you."

If the Greek and Roman history is full of these heroic strokes,
and if we in vain search the whole history of despotic power to
find the like ; it is only because, in these governments, private
interest is never united to that of the public ; because, in these
countries, among a thousand qualities, they do honour only to
baseness, and reward none but those of moderate abilities* ;
and because, to these men of moderate abilities, the administration of public affairs is almost always intrusted ; while men
of genius are excluded. They are of opinion, that these being
restless and too active, they would disturb the repose of the
state ; a repose that may be compared to the momentary still-
ness of nature preceding a tempest. The tranquillity of a state
does not always prove the happiness of the subject. In arbitrary governments, the men are like those horses, whose noses
being wrung, suffer, without flinching, the most cruel operations, while the courser at liberty prances at the first touch.
In these countries, a lethargy is taken for tranquillity. The
love of glory, unknown to these nations, can only be preserved
in a body politic, by the mild fermentation that renders it
sound and robust, and calls forth every virtue and every talent.
The ages most favourable to literature have, for this reason,
always been most fruitful in great generals and great politicians : the same sun gives life to the cedar and the plane-
tree.

---

* In these countries genius and abilities are only honoured in great
princes, and great ministers.

Moreover, this passion for glory, which was deified by the Pagans, has received the homage of all republics, but principally of those that are poor and warlike.

CHAP. XXIII.

THAT POOR NATIONS HAVE BEEN ALWAYS MORE GREEDY OF GLORY, AND MORE FRUITFUL IN VIRTUOUS MEN, THAN-OPULENT NATIONS.

THE heroes in commercial republics seem to appear only to destroy tyranny, and then to vanish. It was in the infancy of the liberty of the Dutch, that Balzac, speaking of that nation, said, " that they deserved to have God for their king, since they could not bear to have a king for their god." The soil proper for the production of great men in republics, is then soon exhausted. The glory of Carthage disappeared with Hannibal. The spirit of commerce there, necessarily destroyed that of valour. " Rich nations," says Balzac, " are governed by the force of lucrative reasons, and not according to moral institutions, which propose motives to great and honest enterprizes."

A virtuous courage is only preserved among poor nations. The Scythians were, perhaps, the only people who sung hymns in honour of the gods, without asking any favours, from their being persuaded that the courageous could want for nothing. Subject to commanders, whose power was sufficiently extensive, they were independent, because they ceased to obey their chiefs, when they ceased to obey the laws. There are no rich nations who resemble the Scythians, in having no other want but that of glory. Wherever commerce flourishes, riches are preferred to glory, because riches afford an exchange for all pleasures, and it is more easy to acquire them.

What a sterility of virtues and talents must this preference occasion. The decrees of glory never proceeding, but from public gratitude, its acquisition is always the reward of services rendered to our country; and the desire of obtaining it, constantly supposes the desire of performing services, that may be of use to the nation.

This is not the case with the desire of riches. They may, sometimes, be the reward of stock-jobbers, of meanness, of spies, and very often of crimes; they seldom fall to the share of those who have the greatest abilities, or of those who are most distinguished by their virtues. The love of riches does not necessarily lead to the love of virtue. Commercial nations ought therefore to be more fruitful in good merchants than in good citizens, and in great bankers than in heroes.

It is not then in the land of luxury and of riches, but in that of poverty, that the sublime virtues grow and flourish *; nothing is so uncommon as to meet great minds in opulent empires †; the citizens there contract too many wants. Whoever has multiplied them, has given tyranny hostages for his baseness and cowardice. Virtue, with which few are satisfied, can alone secure the people from corruption. It was this kind of virtue that dictated the answer of an English lord, distinguished by his merit, to a minister. The court, finding it for the interest to bring him over to their party, Mr. Walpole waited upon him: " I come from the king," said he, " to assure you of his protection; to let you know, that he is sorry for his not yet having done any thing for you; and to offer you a post more suitable to your merit." " Sir," replied the nobleman, " before I answer your proposal, permit me to have my supper served up." Immediately was brought in the remains of a leg of mutton, on which he had dined; then, turning to Mr. Walpole, " Sir," said he, " do you think that a man, who can be contented with such fare, can be easily gained over? Tell his

---

* To which I add happiness. What it is impossible to say of individuals may be said of nations—that the most virtuous are always the most happy, though they are not the most rich and commercial.

† " Among all the nations of Germany, the Sucones," says Tacitus, " after the example of the Romans, set a value on riches, and like them have submitted to despotic power."

majesty what you have seen; this is the only answer I have to make *".

Such a discourse could only proceed from a person who knew how to contract the circle of his wants: but how few persons, in a rich country, can resist the perpetual temptation of superfluities! What virtuous men does poverty give to a nation, whom luxury would have corrupted! " O philosophers," Socrates often said, " you who represent the Gods on earth, learn, like them, to be self-sufficient, and to be contented with little; especially, go not cringing to solicit princes and kings." " Nothing can be more firm and virtuous," says Cicero, " than the first ages of Greece; they were terrified at no danger, they were discouraged at no obstacles, and no respect restrained them, or made them sacrifice the truth to the absolute will of princes." But these philosophers were born in poor countries; therefore their successors did always preserve the same virtues. Those of Alexandria were reproached with having too much complaisance for the princes their benefactors, and with purchasing, by their meanness, the tranquil leisure those princes suffered them to enjoy. On this subject, Plutarch cries out, " What sight can be more degrading to human nature, than to see sages prostitute their praises to men in place! Must the courts of kings be so often the rocks on which wisdom and virtue split! Ought not the great to be sensible, that all who entertain them, with things of only a frivolous nature, deceive them †? The true manner of serv-

---

* This story I find related of a member of parliament, in the reign of Charles II. in the General Dictionary.

† There was doubtless a time when men, distinguished by their wisdom, had a right to speak only to princes, in order to tell them what was truly useful. Hence, the philosophers of India left their retreat but once in a year: this was to repair to the king's palace, where each of them uttered, with a loud voice, his political reflections on the administration, and the changes and regulations they would have made in the laws. Those, whose reflections were for three times successively judged false or trivial, lost their right of speaking. Crit· Hist. of Philosophy, tom. II.

ing them is to reprove them for their vices and bad conduct, and to let them know, that it ill becomes them to spend their days in diversion. This is the only language proper to a virtuous man; lying and flattery should never dwell upon his lip."

This exclamation of Plutarch is very fine; but it is a greater proof of his love of truth than of his knowledge of human nature. It is the same with respect to Pythagoras: "I refuse," says he, "the name of philosophers to those who give into the corruption of courts; those alone are worthy of the name, who are ready to sacrifice before kings their life, their riches, their dignities, their families, and even their reputation. By this love of truth," he adds, "we participate with the divinity, and become united to him in the most noble and intimate manner."

Such men do not indifferently arise in all kinds of governments: they are produced, either by a philosophical enthusiasm that is speedily extinguished, by a singular education, or by an excellent legislation. The philosophers mentioned by Plutarch and Pythagoras have almost constantly been born in poor nations, passionately fond of glory.

Not that I regard indigence as the source of virtues: it is to the greater or less wisdom in the administration of honours and rewards that we must attribute the production of great men among all nations. But what can scarcely be imagined is, that virtue and abilities are no where to be recompenced in so flattering a manner as in poor and warlike republics.

CHAP. XXIV.

PROOF OF THIS TRUTH.

To take from this proposition the air of a paradox, it is sufficient to observe, that the two most general objects of the desires of mankind are wealth and honours. But of these two objects, men are most desirous of honours; they are dispensed in a manner flattering to self-love.

The desire therefore of obtaining them renders men capable of the greatest efforts, and it is then that they perform prodigies. Now these honours are no where distributed with more justice than among the people, who, having no other money to pay for the services rendered to their country, have consequently the greatest interest in supporting their value : thus, the poor republics of Greece and Rome have produced more great men than all the vast and rich empires of the East.

Among the nations opulent and subject to despotic power, people place, and ought to place, more value on money than on honours. As honours received their value from the manner in which they are administered, and as in the East the sultans are dispensers of them, it appears, that they must bring them into discredit by the ill choice they make of those whom they adorn with them. Thus, in those countries, honours are properly mere titles only : they cannot flatter pride in a very lively manner, because they are seldom united with glory, which is not in the power of princes, but in that of the people only, to bestow ; since glory is nothing more than the acclamation of public gratitude. Now, when honours are debased, the desire of obtaining them grows cool, and this desire no longer enables men to perform great things ; they become in a state a spring without force, and therefore placemen justly neglect to make use of them.

There is a district in America, where, when an Indian has gained a victory, or managed a negotiation with dexterity, they say to him in an assembly of the nation, " Thou art a man." This eulogium is a more powerful incentive to great actions than all the dignities proposed by despotic states to those who render themselves illustrious by their talents.

In order to be fully sensible of the contempt which must be sometimes thrown on honours, from the ridiculous manner in which they are bestowed, let us remember the abuse that was made of them in the reign of Claudius : " Under that emperor," says Pliny, " a citizen killed a raven, remarkable for his dexterity : this citizen was put to death, and a magnificent funeral was made for the bird ; a musician, playing on a flute, preceded the bed of state, on which the raven lay, which was supported by two slaves, and in the procession followed an infinite number of people of both sexes and of all ages. Upon this subject, Pliny cries out, " What would our ancestors say, if in Rome itself, where our first kings were interred without pomp, where they did not revenge the death of the destroyer of Carthage and Numantia, they had assisted at the obsequies of a raven !"

But, you will say, in countries subject to arbitrary power, honours are however sometimes the reward of merit. They doubtless are so : but they are oftener the reward of vice and meanness. Honours are in these governments like the scattered trees in a desert, whose fruits are sometimes carried off by the birds of heaven, but become too often the prey of the serpent, which from the foot of the tree ascends even to its top.

Honours being once degraded, services performed for the state can only be paid for with money. Now every nation, who discharges its obligations only with specie, soon becomes overcharged with expences, and in a little time insolvent; there is then no reward for virtue and abilities.

In vain, is it said, that, instructed by want, princes in this extremity ought to have recourse to the payment of their obligations with honours : for as in poor republics, where favours are distributed by the body of the nation, it is easy to raise the value of honours, nothing can be more difficult than to render them valuable in despotic countries.

What probity would that administration shew, that should endeavour to reward with honours! What strength of mind would it require to resist the intrigues of courtiers! What discernment to grant these honours only to persons of great talents and distinguished virtues, and constantly to refuse them to those of mean abilities, who would discredit them! What justness of thought would it demand, to seize the precise moment, when these honours, by becoming too common, would no longer excite the citizens to make the same efforts, and when they ought consequently to create new ones!

It is not the same with honours as with riches. If the public interest forbids the melting down the gold and silver specie, it on the contrary requires, that honours should not be bestowed

as a reward, when they have lost the value which they only receive from the opinion of the people.

I shall observe on this subject, that we cannot, without astonishment, consider the conduct of most nations, who employ
so many men in the management of their revenues, and appoint
none to watch over the distribution of honours. Yet what can
be of greater use, than a severe scrutiny into the merit of those
whom they raise to dignities? Why has not each nation a
court, in which, by a profound and strict examination, they
may ascertain the reality of those talents that are to be rewarded? What a value would such an examination give to
honours! What a desire to merit them! What a happy
change would this desire produce, not only in private education, but by little and little, in that of the public! A change,
on which, perhaps, depends all the difference observable between nations.

Among the base and cowardly courtiers of Antiochus, how
many would there have been had they been educated from
their infancy at Rome, who would, like Popilius, have drawn
a circle about that king, beyond which he could not pass
without rendering himself a slave, or the enemy of the Romans!

Having proved that great rewards produce great virtues, and
that the wise distribution of honours is the strongest band which
legislators can use to unite the private and general interest, and
to form good citizens; I think I have a right to conclude from
thence, that the love or indifference of certain nations for virtue is an effect of the different forms of their governments.
Now, what I have said of the love of virtue, which I take for
an example, may be applied to any other of the passions. We
ought not then to attribute to nature that unequal degree of
passions, of which different nations appear susceptible.

As the last proof of this truth, I am going to shew, that the
strength of our passions is always proportioned to the force
of the means employed to excite them.

CHAP. XXV.

OF THE EXACT RELATION BETWEEN THE STRENGTH OF THE PASSIONS AND THE GREATNESS OF THE REWARDS PROPOSED TO MANKIND.

In order to be sensible of this connection, it is necessary to have recourse to history. I open that of Mexico: I see heaps of gold affording the avarice of the Spaniards greater riches than they could have procured by the plunder of all Europe.— Animated by the desire of possessing them, these very Spaniards quit their substance and their families, and, under the conduct of Cortez, undertake the conquest of the new world; combat at once the climate, want, numbers, and valour; and, by a courage as obstinate as impetuous, triumph over them all.

More heated still by the lust of gold, and more greedy of riches, as they were more indigent, I see the Buccaneers pass from the northern to the southern seas, attack impenetrable intrenchments, defeat, with a handful of men, numerous bodies of disciplined soldiers; and often, having ravaged the coasts of the Pacific Ocean, open to themselves a new passage into the northern seas, by surmounting, with incredible fatigue, continual combats, and a courage that was proof against every thing, all the obstacles which men and nature threw in their way.

If I cast my eyes on the history of the north, the first people, who present themselves to my view, are the disciples of Odin. They are animated with the prospect of a reward, which, though imaginary, is the greatest of all, when realized by credulity. Thus, while they are actuated by a lively hope, they shew a courage, which, being proportioned to a celestial recompence, is even superior to that of the Buccaneers. " Our warriors, greedy of death," says one of their poets, " seek for it with fury; being struck in battle by a mortal blow, they fall, and laughing die." This truth is confirmed by one of their kings, named Lodbrog, when, crying out in the field of battle, " With what unknown joy am I seized! I die: I hear the voice of Odin call me; already the gates of his palace are opened; I see, coming from thence, beautiful virgins half naked;

they wear a blue scarf, which augments the whiteness of their bosoms; they advance towards me, and offer me the most delicious beer, in the bleeding skulls of my enemies."

If from the north I pass to the south, I see Mahomet, the creator of a new religion like that of Odin, call himself the envoy of heaven, proclaim to the Saracens, that the Most High had delivered to them the earth, that he would make terror and desolation march before them; but that they must merit the empire by their valour. To excite their courage, he teaches, that the eternal has thrown a bridge over the abyss of hell, narrower than the edge of a scimetar; and that, after the resurrection, the brave will skip over it with a light foot, in order to arrive at the celestial abodes; while the coward, falling from this bridge, will be precipitated into the jaws of the horrible serpent that inhabits the dark cavern of the house of smoke.

To confirm the mission of the prophet, his disciples add, that, mounted on Al-borak, he passed through the seven heavens, saw the angel of death, and the white cock, which, with his feet fixed on the first heaven, concealed his head in the seventh: that Mahomet cut the moon in two; made fountains issue from his fingers; gave speech to the brutes; caused himself to be followed by the forests, and saluted by the mountains*; and that, beloved of God, he brought the law, dictated to him by the Almighty.

---

* Many other miracles are related of Mahomet. A restive camel, having perceived him at a distance, came to him, they say, and fell on his knees before the prophet, who, stroking him, ordered him to amend. It is said, that at another time the same prophet fed thirty thousand men with a sheep's liver. Father Maracio does not dispute the fact, but pretends, that this was the work of the devil. With respect to the prodigies that are still more astonishing, such as cutting the moon in two, making the mountains dance, and a roasted shoulder of mutton speak, the Mussulmans assert, the performance of such amazing prodigies, so much above all human strength and cunning, was absolutely necessary to convince stubborn minds, which are always very difficult to be persuaded of the truth of miracles.

Struck by these recitals, the Saracens listened to the discourse of Mahomet with the more credulity, as he gave them the most voluptuous descriptions of the celestial abodes designed for the brave. Interested by the pleasures of sense to be enjoyed in Paradise, I see them glowing with the warmest zeal, and, sighing incessantly after the houris, rush with fury upon their enemies. "Warriors!" cried in battle one of their generals, named Ikrimach, "I see those beautiful virgins with black eyes: they are fourscore in number. If one of them should make her appearance on earth, all its sovereigns would quit their thrones to follow her. But what do I see!—one of them advances; she has gold buskins on her legs; in one hand she holds a handkerchief of green silk, and in the other a topaz cup: she beckons me with her head, saying, 'Come hither, my well-beloved.' Stay for me, divine houris: I rush among the battalions of the Infidels; I give, I receive, death; and fly to thee!"

While the credulous Saracens thus distinctly saw the houris, their love of conquests, being proportionable to the greatness of the rewards they expected, animated them with a courage superior to that inspired by the love of our country: it therefore produced the greatest effects; for, we see, that, in less than one century, they subdued more nations than the Romans had conquered in six hundred years.

Thus the Greeks, who were superior to the Arabs in number, discipline, arms, and warlike machines, fled before them like doves at the sight of the hawk*. All the nations leagued together could only have opposed an ineffectual barrier against them.

The Persians, according to Chardin, believe that Fatima, Mahomet's wife, was in her life-time carried up to heaven. They celebrate her assumption.

* The Emperor Heraclius, astonished at the numerous victories obtained over his armies, assembled a council composed rather of divines than statesmen: the evils to which the nation was exposed were laid before them, and they inquired into the cause; upon which they concluded, according to the custom of those times, that the Almighty

In order to resist them, it would have been necessary to arm
the Christians with the same spirit as that with which the law
of Mahomet animated the Musselmans; to promise heaven and
the palm of martyrdom, as St. Bernard did in the time of the
Crusades, to every warrior who died fighting the Infidels,—a
proposal the Emperor Nicephorus made to the bishops who
were assembled. But they, wanting the judgment of St. Bernard, unanimously rejected it*. They did not perceive, that
this refusal would discourage the Greeks, promote the extinction of Christianity, and the progress of the Saracens, to which
they could oppose no other defence than a zeal equal to their
fanaticism. These bishops, therefore, continued to attribute
the calamities that laid waste the empire to the crimes of the
nation, though a judicious eye might have discovered the cause
in the blindness of these very prelates, who, in such conjunctures, might be considered as the scourges heaven made
use of to afflict the empire.

The astonishing success of the Saracens depended so much
on the strength of their passions, and the strength of their pas-

---

was offended at the crimes of the nation; and that the only way
of putting a stop to so many misfortunes was by prayer, fasting,
and tears.

This resolution being taken, the emperor considered none of the resources that still remained after so many disasters,—resources that
would, at first, have presented themselves to his mind, if he had
known that courage only sprang from the passions; that, ever since
the destruction of the republic, the Romans being no longer animated
by the love of their country, their sending men without passions
to fight such fanatics was opposing fearful sheep against ravenous
wolves.

* They alledged, in favour of their opinion, the ancient discipline
of the eastern church, the thirteenth canon, and the letter of St. Bazil
the Great to Amphilochus. This letter declares, that " every soldier that killed an enemy in battle could not receive the communion
for three years after." Whence it may be concluded, that, though it
is of the greatest advantage to be governed by a man of sense and
discernment, nothing can sometimes be more dangerous than being
governed by a saint.

sions on the means made use of to excite them, that these very
Arabs, these warriors so formidable, before whom the earth
trembled and the armies of the Greeks fled, and were dispersed
like the dust before the wind, trembled themselves at the
sight of a sect of Mussulmans named Saffrians*. Inflamed, like
all reformers, with the fiercest pride and a firm belief, these
sectaries saw more distinctly the celestial pleasures which hope
presented to the other Mussulmans at a confused distance.
Thus, these furious Saffrians resolved to purge the earth of
its errors, enlighten or exterminate the nations, which at their
appearance, they said, ought to be struck with light or terror,
and quit their prejudice as speedily as an arrow is shot from
a bow.

What I have said of the Arabs and Saffrians may be applied
to all the nations influenced by the motives of religion; it is
here the unequal degree of credulity, which among different
nations produces the equilibrium of their passions and courage.

In regard to passions of another kind, it is still the unequal
degree of their strength, always occasioned by the diversity
of their governments, and the situations·of the people, which
in the same emergencies determines them to act in so different
a manner.

When Themistocles went armed, to raise considerable subsidies on the rich allies of the republic, " Those allies," says
Plutarch, " made haste to furnish him, because a fear, proportioned to the riches he might take from them, rendered
them submissive to the will of the Athenians. But when
the same Themistocles addressed himself to indigent peo-

---

* These Saffrians were so formidable, that Adi, a captain of great
reputation, having received orders to attack with six hundred men
a hundred and twenty of those fanatics, who were assembled in the
government of a man named Ben Mervan, that captain represented,
' that each of these sectaries, longing for death, might attack with advantage twenty Arabs; and that therefore the inequality of courage
not being, on this occasion, compensated by the inequality of numbers, he would not hazard a battle, which the determined valour of
these fanatics rendered so unequal.'

ple, and, disembarking at Andos, made the same demand to
those islanders, declaring that he came attended by two powerful deities, " Necessity and Force, which," said he, " always
bring persuasion in their trains." " Themistocles," they replied, " we should, like the other allies, submit to thine orders,
if we were not also protected by two deities as powerful thine,
Indigence and Despair, which spurn at Force."

The vivacity of the passions depends, therefore, on the
means employed by the legislator in kindling them, or in the
situations in which fortune has placed us*. The more lively
our passions are, the greater are the effects produced by them.
Thus success, as all history proves, constantly attends the people who are animated by strong passions,—a truth too little
known, the ignorance of which has opposed the progress that
otherwise might have been made in the art of inspiring the passions: this art is at present unknown even to those politicians
of reputation who calculate pretty justly the interest and
strength of a state, but have never perceived the singular resources which, in critical conjunctures, might have been drawn
from the passions, when people have the art of exciting them.

---

* Insignificant means always produce insignificant passions and
insignificant effects: grand motives are required to excite us to perform bold enterprizes. It is weakness, rather than folly, which in
most governments perpetuates the abuse. We are not so inferior as
we appear to be to posterity. Is there a man, for instance, who does
not perceive the absurdity of the law, which prohibits citizens disposing
of their effects before they are twenty-five years of age, and yet, at
sixteen, allows them to dispose of their liberty, by becoming monks?
Every one knows the remedy of this evil, and perceives at the same
time the difficulty of applying it. What obstacles does the interest of
some societies raise against the public interest in this respect! What
long and painful efforts of courage and judgment, and what constancy,
does the execution of such a project suppose! Perhaps it would be
necessary, in order to make the attempt, that placemen should be
prompted by the hope of the greatest glory, and flatter themselves
that public gratitude would every where erect statues to their memory.
We ought always to recollect, that in morality, as well as in natural
philosophy and mechanics, the effects are always proportioned to the
causes.

The principles of this art, though as certain as those of geometry, appear in fact to have been hitherto perceived only by great men with respect to war and politics. Upon which I shall observe, that, if the virtues, the courage, and consequently the passions, with which soldiers are animated, contribute no less to obtain a victory than the order in which they are ranged, a treatise on the art of inspiring them would be of no less use to generals than the excellent treatise of the illustrious chevalier Folard on Tactics*.

It was the passions, united to the love of liberty and the hatred of slavery, more than the skill of the engineers, that occasioned the celebrated and obstinate defence of Abydos, Saguntum, Carthage, Numantia, and Rhodes.

In the art of exciting the passions, Alexander excelled almost all other great generals: to this art he owed those instances of success, so often attributed, by those who are called men of sense, to chance or a foolish rashness, because they do not perceive the almost-invisible springs by which that hero performed so many prodigies.

The conclusion of this chapter is, that the strength of the passions is always proportioned to the strength of the means made use of to inspire them. Now I ought to examine, if these very passions may in all men, well organized, be carried to such a height as to endue them with that continued attention to which superiority of genius is attached.

CHAP. XXVI.

OF WHAT DEGREE OF PASSION MEN ARE SUSCEPTIBLE.

If, in order to determine this degree, I transport myself over the mountains of Abyssinia, I there see men, at the order of their

---

* Discipline is, in a manner, nothing else but the art of inspiring soldiers with a greater fear of their officers than of the enemy. This fear has often the effect of courage: but it cannot prevail against the fierce and obstinate valour of people animated by fanaticism, or a warm love of their country.

khalifs, become impatient of death, and precipitate themselves
on the points of poniards and rocks, and others into the abyss of
the sea: no other reward is, however, proposed to them, besides
the celestial pleasures promised to all Mussulmans; but their
possession appears more certain; consequently the desire of
enjoying them makes more lively impressions on their minds,
and their efforts to merit them are proportionally greater.

In no other place, besides Ayssinia, is so much care and art
employed to confirm the belief of these blind and zealous executioners of the will of their prince. The victims destined
to this employment can no where receive an education so proper to form fanatics. Transported from the most tender age
into a distant, wild, and lonesome, part of the seraglio, where
reason is made to wander in the darkness of the Mussulmans'
faith, they are informed of the mission and the laws of Mahomet, the prodigies performed by that prophet, and the absolute resignation due to the orders of the khalifs: there, by giving them the most voluptuous descriptions of paradise, they
fill them with the most ardent desire for celestial pleasures.
Scarcely have they arrived at that age, when, they become sensible of pleasure, when, by impetuous desire, nature indicates their
impatience and power of enjoying the most lively gratifications,
than, in order to fortify the belief of a young man, and to en-
flame him with the most violent fanaticism, the priest, after having mixed an intoxicating liquor in his drink, transports him,
during his sleep, from his gloomy abode to a delightful grove
appointed for that use.

There, reclined on a bed of flowers, surrounded with spout-
ing fountains, he reposes till Aurora, by giving form and colour
to the universe, awakes all the productive powers of nature,
and makes love circulate in the veins of youth. Struck with
the novelty of the objects that surround him, the young man
looks about, and fixes his eyes on several fine women, whom
his credulous imagination transforms into houris. These, being accomplices in the cheat formed by the priest, are instructed in the art of seducing; he sees them advancing
towards him, dancing; they enjoy his surprise; by a thousand
sportive motions they excite in him unknown desires, oppose

the slight gauze of a pretended modesty to the impatient wishes with which they inflame him: they, at length, yield to love; then, changing those sportive actions to caresses, plunge him in delight. This intoxication is succeeded by a voluptuous repose, which is soon interrupted by fresh pleasures; till the young man's desires being gratified, he is conducted by these women to a delicious banquet, where he is again intoxicated with liquor, and carried, during his sleep, to his first abode. There he no sooner awakes, than he seeks for the objects with which he had been enchanted; but, like a deceitful vision, they are vanished from his sight; he still calls the houris: he finds none near him but the Imans: he relates to them his dream, which is no sooner ended, than, placing their foreheads, on the earth, the Imans say, "O vessel of election! O my son! doubtless our holy prophet has taken thee up into paradise, to give thee a foretaste of the pleasures reserved for the faithful, in order to strengthen thy faith and courage. Merit, therefore, so particular a favour, by being absolutely devoted to the orders of the khalifs."

By a similar education the dervises animated the followers of Ismael with the firmest belief: thus they made them entertain a hatred of life and a love of death, which they considered as the gate that afforded an entrance to celestial pleasures, and inspired them with that determined courage which for some time astonished the universe.

I say for some time, because this kind of courage soon disappears with the cause that produced it. Of all the passions, that of fanaticism founded on the desire of pleasure is, doubtless, the strongest, and always the least durable, because fanaticism being only founded on prejudice and deceit, reason must insensibly sap its foundation. Thus the Arabs, the Abyssinians, and in general all the Mahometan nations, within the space of one century, lost all that superiority of courage which had distinguished them from all other people; and, in this particular, they were much inferior to the Romans.

The bravery of these last, excited by a spirit of patriotism, and founded on real and temporal rewards, would always have been the same, if luxury had not passed into Rome with the spoils of Asia; if the desire of riches had not broke the chain that united personal and general interest, and had not at once corrupted the manners and form of government among that people.

I cannot help observing with respect to these two kinds of courage, the one founded on religious fanaticism, and the other on the love of our country, that the latter is the only one with which a wise legislator ought to inspire his fellow-citizens. A fanatic courage is soon weakened and extinguished. Besides, this courage deriving its source from the blindness of superstition, a nation has no sooner lost its fanaticism than nothing remains but its stupidity; and it then becomes the contempt of all nations, to which it is in every respect really inferior.

It is to the Mussulman's stupidity that the Christians owe so many advantages obtained over the Turks, who, by their numbers alone, says the chevalier Folard, would be too formidable, if they made some slight changes in the order of battle, their discipline, and arms; if they quitted the sabre for the bayonet, and could lay aside the ignorance in which they will ever be kept by superstition; for their religion, he adds, is only fit to eternize the stupidity of that nation.

I have shewn, that the passions are capable of making us perform prodigies,—a truth proved both by the desperate courage of the followers of Ismael; by the meditations of the Gymnosophists, whose probation is not finished till after a retreat of thirty-seven years spent in silence and study; by the barbarous and continued macerations of the Fakers; by the revengeful fury of the Japanese*; by the duels of the Europeans; and, in short, by the firmness of the Roman gladiators, who, on receiving a mortal blow, fell and died with the same courage with which they had fought.

All men, as I propose to prove, are then, in general, susceptible of a degree of passion more than sufficient to make them triumph over their laziness, and to endue them with that con-

---

* One of these rips open his belly in the presence of the person who has offended him; upon which the latter is, under pain of infamy, obliged to follow his example, and rip up his.

tinuance of attention to which superiority of knowledge is attached.

The great inequality of mind observable in mankind, therefore, only depends on the different education they receive, and
the unknown and varied chain of circumstances in which they
are placed.

In fact, if all the operations of the mind are reducible to perceiving, remembering, and observing, the relations that subsist
between different objects, and their connection with us, it is
evident that all men being endued, as I have already shewn,
with sense, extent of memory, and, in short, with the capacity
of attention necessary to render them capable of the highest
ideas; among men who are well organized*, there are consequently none who may not render themselves illustrious by
great talents.

I shall add, as a second demonstration of this truth, that all
the false judgments, as I have proved in my first discourse, are
the effect either of ignorance or of the passions: of ignorance,
when we have not in our memory the subjects of comparison
from whence the truths we are in search of ought to result: of
the passions, when they are so modified that we have an interest in seeing objects different from what they really are. Now
these causes, which are the only general ones that produce our
errors, are entirely accidental.

Ignorance, in the first place, is not necessary; it is not produced by any defect in the organization, since there is no man,
as I have shewn in the beginning of this discourse, who is not
endued with a memory capable of containing infinitely more objects than are required for the discovery of the most important
truths. In regard to the passions, the natural wants being the
only passions immediately given by nature, and the wants being
never deceitful, it is evident that the want of just thinking is
never produced by a defect in the organization; and that we
have all the power of forming the same judgments on the same
things. Now to have the same view of them is to have equal

---

* That is, those in whose organization we perceive no defect, which
is the case with most men.

abilities of mind.   It is then certain, that the inequality of abilities, observable in the men whom I call well organized, does no
ways depend on the greater or less degree of the excellence of
their organization *, but on the different education they have
received, on the various circumstances in which they have been
placed, and, in short, on the little aptitude they have for
thought, from the hatred they have contracted in early youth
for application, of which they become absolutely incapable in a
more advanced age.

How probable soever this opinion may be, as its novelty may
still produce surprise, since we with difficulty lay aside ancient
prejudices, and, in short, as the truth of a system is proved by
the explication of the phænomena that depend upon it ; I am
going, in consequence of my principles, to shew, in the following chapter, why so few persons of genius are to be found
among mankind, when all are formed to be of this class.

CHAP. XXVII.

OF THE AGREEMENT OF FACTS WITH THE PRINCIPLES
ABOVE ESTABLISHED.

EXPERIENCE seems to contradict my doctrines, and this apparent contradiction may render my opinions suspected.   " If all
men," say they, " have equal capacities, why in a kingdom,

---

* I observe on this subject, that the title of a man of genius, as I
have shewn in the second discourse, is not granted on account of the
number or delicacy, but the happy choice, of the ideas presented to the
public ; and if chance, as experience proves, determines us to engage
in more or less interesting studies, and almost constantly makes us
choose the subjects of which we treat ; those who consider genius as a
gift of nature are, upon this supposition, obliged to confess that genius is rather the effect of chance than the excellence of the organization ; and that it cannot be considered as the mere gift of nature,
unless the word *nature* be extended to the eternal and universal chain
which binds together all the events that happen in the world, and in
which the idea even of chance is comprehended.

composed of fifteen or eighteen millions of people, do we see so few of such men as Turenne, Rony, Colbert, Descartes, Corneille, Moliere, Quinault, le Brun, and, in short, of those men who are mentioned as an honour to their age and country?

To resolve this question, let us examine the vast concourse of circumstances absolutely necessary to form illustrious men of what kind soever, and we shall acknowledge, that men are so rarely placed in that happy concourse of circumstances, that geniuses of the first order must be in fact as scarce as they are found to be.

Supposing in France sixteen millions of persons endued with the most happy disposition of mind, supposing an ardent desire in the government of calling forth these dispositions, yet, as experience shews, books, men, and the assistance proper to unfold these dispositions, are only to be found in an opulent city, it is, consequently, among the eight hundred thousand persons who live, or have long lived at Paris*, that we ought to find men superior in the different arts and sciences. Now, if from these eight hundred thousand persons we first deduct half, that is, the women, whose education and manner of life oppose the progress they might make in the arts and sciences; if we exclude also children, old men, artizans, manufacturers, monks, domestics, soldiers, the merchants, and, in general, all those who by their stations, dignities, and riches, are subject to employments, or given up to pleasure, which take up a part of their time; if we consider, in short, the small number of those, who are placed in their youth in that station where they feel no other pain than that of not being able to comfort all the miserable, and who can, without inquietude, give themselves up entirely to study and reflection; it is certain, that this number

---

* If we run over the list of great men, we shall see that Moliere, Quinault, Corneille, Condé, Pascal, Fontenelle, Mallebranche, &c. have been under a necessity of improving their minds by the assistances· to be obtained in the capital; that country talents are always condemned to obscurity; and that the muses, so fond of woods, meadows, and fountains, would be no better than country lasses, if they did not from time to time breathe the air of great cities.

cannot exceed that of six thousand; that of these six thousand, there are not six hundred animated with the desire of instruction; that of these six hundred, there are not half of them animated with this desire, with the degree of warmth proper to fertilize grand ideas; that we cannot reckon a hundred who add to the desire of instruction the constancy and patience necessary to carry their abilities to perfection, and who thus unite two qualities, which vanity, too impatient of producing itself to view, ever hinders being united; in these there are not, perhaps, fifty who in their early youth have always applied to the same kind of study, who have always been insensible to love and ambition, and who have not in too varied studies, in pleasures, or intrigue, lost the moments, the loss of which is always irreparable to whoever would render himself superior in any science or art whatsoever. Now of these fifty, who, divided by several kinds of study, will produce only one or two of each kind, if I deduct those who have not read the works, lived with the men most proper to enlighten them; and from this number, thus reduced, I still retrench all those whose progress has been stopped by death, the reverses of fortune, or other accidents; I say, that under the actual form of our government, the multitude of circumstances, the concourse of which is absolutely necessary to form great men, opposes their multiplication, and the men of genius must be as uncommon as they really are.

We ought then only to search into morals for the true cause of the inequality observable in various minds: to account, therefore, for the scarcity or multiplicity of great men in certain ages or countries, we have no reason to have recourse to the influence of the air and the different climates, which, so constantly repeated, have been always contradicted both by history and experience.

If the different temperature of climates had such an influence on the mind and its capacities, how comes it that the Romans*, so magnanimous, so brave, under a republican government, are

---

* Though some people acknowledge that the Romans, at present, do not resemble the ancient Romans, yet they pretend that they have this in common, their being the masters of the world. " As ancient

now so dastardly and effeminate? How comes it that the Greeks and Romans, who were formerly so worthy of esteem for their wit and virtue, and were the admiration of the earth, are now dwindled into contempt? How comes it that those Asiatics, so brave under the name of Eleamites, were so cowardly and base in the time of Alexander, under that of Persians; and yet under the name of Parthians became the terror of Rome, and that in an age when the Romans had lost none of their courage and discipline? How comes it that the Spartans, the most brave and virtuous of the Greeks, while they were religious observers of the laws of Lycurgus, lost their reputation for both, when, after the Peloponnesian war, they suffered gold and luxury to be introduced among them? How comes it that the ancient Cattæ, so formidable to the Gauls, are now void of the same courage? How comes it that the Jews, so often defeated by their enemies, shewed under the conduct of the Maccabees a courage worthy of the most warlike nation? How comes it that the arts and sciences have been by turns cultivated and neglected by different nations, and have successively run through almost all climates?

In one of Lucian's dialogues, that philosopher says, " It was not in Greece that I made my first abode. I began by directing my steps towards the Indus; and the Indian, to hear me, humbly descended from his elephant. From the Indies, I turned towards Ethiopia; I transported myself into Egypt; from Egypt, I went to Babylon; I stopped in Scythia; I returned by Thrace. I conversed with Orpheus, and Orpheus brought be into Greece."

Why did philosophy pass from Greece into Hesperia, from Hesperia to Constantinople and Arabia? and why, repassing Arabia into Italy, has it found an asylum in France, England, and even in the north of Europe? Why do we no longer find a Phocion at Athens, a Pelopidas at Thebes, and a Decius at Rome? The temperature of these climates is not changed: to

---

Rome," say they, " conquered it by her virtues and her valour, so modern Rome has reconquered it by her plots and political artifices; and Pope Gregory VII. is the Cæsar of this second Rome."

what then ought we to attribute the transmigration of arts, sciences, courage, and virtue, if it is not to be ascribed to moral causes?

To these causes we owe the explanation of an infinite number of political phænomena, which people in vain endeavour to explain by physical causes. Such are the conquests of the people of the north, the slavery and allegorical genius of the orientals, and the superiority of certain nations in certain sciences ;—a superiority which they will cease, I think, to attribute to the different temperature of the climate, when I have rapidly pointed out the cause of these principal effects.

CHAP. XXVIII.

OF THE CONQUESTS OF THE NORTHERN NATIONS.

THE physical cause of the conquests, made by the inhabitants of the northern part of Europe, is said to be derived from that superiority of courage or strength which nature has given to the northern nations preferably to those of the south. This opinion, so proper to flatter the pride of the nations of Europe, most of which derive their origin from those people, has met with no opposition. However, in order to assure ourselves of the truth of so flattering an opinion, let us examine, whether the inhabitants of the north are really possessed of greater bravery than those of the south. For this purpose, let us first inquire what courage is, and ascend up to the principles that may throw a light upon one of the most important questions in morality and politics.

Courage in animals is only the effect of their wants, and, these being gratified, they become cowards: the famished lion attacks a man; the lion, whose stomach is filled, flies from him. The hunger of animals being once appeased, the self-love of every being, so necessary to its preservation, makes it fly from all danger. Courage in animals is, therefore, an effect of their want. We give the epithet of timid to the animals who feed on grass, only because they are not forced to fight for food, and have no motive to brave dangers: if they have a want, they become courageous; the stag in rutting time is as furious as a beast of prey.

Let us apply to man, what I have said of animals. Death is always preceded by pain, and life always accompanied with some pleasure. We are then attached to life by the fear of pain, and the love of pleasure: the happier life is, the more are we afraid to lose it; and from thence proceeds the horror felt by those who live in plenty at the approach of death. On the contrary, the less happiness there is in life, the less do people regret to leave it: hence proceeds the insensibility with which the peasant waits for his dissolution.

Now, if the love of our being is founded on the fear of pain and the love of pleasure, the desire of being happy is more powerful than the desire of life. To obtain the object in the possession of which we place our happiness, every one is capable of exposing himself to dangers, either of a greater or a less nature, but always proportioned to the greater or less warmth of desire the person feels for possessing that object*. To be absolutely without courage, it is necessary to be absolutely without desire.

The objects of the desires of mankind are various; they are animated with different passions, as avarice, ambition, the love of their country, that of women, &c. Consequently, the man capable of the boldest resolution, to gratify one particular passion, will be without courage when another passion is concerned. We have a thousand times seen the buccaneer animated by a valour more than human, when stimulated by the hope of booty, yet find himself without the courage to revenge an affront. Cæsar, whom no danger could terrify in his march to glory, mounted with trembling into his car, and never sat down in it till he had superstitiously repeated three times a certain verse, which he imagined had the power to keep him from being thrown from it†. The fearful man, whom every danger affrights, may be

---

* The most courageous nation is, consequently, that where valour is best rewarded, and cowardice most punished.

† See the Critical History of Philosophy.

animated with the most desperate courage in the defence of
his wife, his mistress, or his children. In this manner we may
explain a part of the phænomena of courage, and the reason
why the same man is brave or timorous according to the various
circumstances in which he is placed.

After having proved that courage is the effect of our wants,
a force communicated to us by our passions, and that it is
exerted on obstacles which chance, or the interest of others,
opposes to our happiness, it is proper now to prevent all objections, and, to throw a greater light on a subject of such importance, to distinguish two kinds of courage.

The one, which I call true courage, consists in seeing danger
as it is, and facing it. The other has, in a manner, nothing but
effects : this kind of courage, common to almost all men, makes
them brave dangers, because they are ignorant of them ; for
the passions, by fixing all their attention on the object of their
desires, conceals from them, at least, a part of the danger to
which they expose themselves.

To have an exact measure of the true courage of this
sort of men, it is necessary to take away all that part of the danger which passion or prejudice conceals from them; and this
part is very considerable. Propose the plunder of a city to
the same soldier who would mount with fear to the assault,
avarice will fascinate his eyes; he will wait impatiently for
the hour of attack; the danger will disappear; and his intrepidity will be in proportion to his avarice. A thousand other
causes produce the effect of avarice : the old soldier is brave,
because the custom of being in a danger, from which he has
always escaped, renders it almost nothing in his view; the victorious soldier marches to the enemy with intrepidity, because
he does not expect much resistance, and believes that he shall
triumph without danger. This is bold, because he thinks himself fortunate; that, from an opinion of his own valour; and a
third, because he thinks himself very expert. Courage is seldom founded on a true contempt of death. Thus, the man,
who is intrepid with a sword in his hand, will be often a coward
at fighting with pistols. Remove the soldier who braves
death in battle into a ship, and he will look with horror on a
tempest, because he really sees nothing but destruction.

Courage is often then only the effect of a man's not having a clear view of the danger he confronts, or of his being entirely ignorant of it. How many are there, who are seized with terror at the noise of thunder, and would be afraid to pass a night in a wood at a distance from the high road, while there are none found who do not pass in the night without fear from Paris to Versailles? However, the blunder of a postillion, or the meeting an assassin on the high road, are accidents more common, and consequently more to be feared, than a clap of thunder, or meeting an assassin in a distant wood. Why then is fear more common in the first case than in the last? It is because flashes of lightning, and the noise of thunder, as well as the darkness of woods, present every instant to the mind images that give us the idea of danger, which do not arise in our minds in the road from Paris to Versailles. There are few men who can support the presence of danger: its appearance has such an effect upon them, that we have seen men, ashamed of their cowardice, kill themselves, though they had not the power to revenge an affront. The face of their enemy silenced in their breast the cries of honour; which to obey, they must by alone working up this sensation in their minds, and then seizing the moment of their rage, to give themselves death, if I may so express myself, without perceiving what they are about.

Thus, to prevent the effect produced by the sight of danger in almost all mankind, people at war are not content to range their soldiers in an order that renders their flight very difficult; in Asia, they heat them with opium, in Europe with brandy, and encourage them with the sound of the drum, or by their united shouts*. By these means, on concealing a part of the danger to which they are exposed, they place their love of honour in an equilibrium with their fear. What I have said of the common soldiers, I also say of the officers; among the

---

† Marshal Saxe, in his Reveries, speaking of the Prussians, says, that a custom they use, of loading their muskets as they march, is a very good one. Diverted by this employment, he adds, the soldier becomes less capable of attending to his danger.

Y Y

most brave, there are few who, in bed* or on the scaffold, consider death with a tranquil eye.   What weakness did Marshal
Biron, so brave in the field, betray at the execution of his
sentence !

In order to support the appearance of death, it is necessary
to have a disgust for life, or to be carried away by such strong
passions as determined Calanus, Cato, and Portia, to kill themselves.   Those, animated by these strong passions, love life only
on certain conditions; their passions do not conceal from them
the danger to which they expose themselves : they see it as
it is, and brave it.   Brutus resolves to free Rome from tyranny;
he assassinates Cæsar, raises an army, and fights Octavius; he
is conquered, and kills himself: life is insupportable without
the liberty of Rome.

Whoever is susceptible of such strong passions, is also capable of performing the greatest actions; he not only braves
death, but also pain.   This is not the case with men who give
themselves death from a disgust of life ; they merit almost as
much the name of wise as of courageous; most of them would
be without courage amidst the agonies of torture, for they have
not life and strength enough to support pain.   The contempt of
life is not the effect of a strong passion, but of the absence of the
passions; it is the result of a calculation, by which they prove
to themselves, that it is better not to be than to be unhappy.
Now this disposition of mind renders them incapable of great
things.   Whoever is disgusted with life, employs himself but
little about the affairs of this world.   Thus, among so many
Romans, who voluntarily embraced a violent death, there are
few, who, by the killing of tyrants, would have dared to

Speaking of a people called the Æries, who painted their bodies in a
frightful manner, he adds, why does Tacitus say, that in battle
the eyes are first conquered?   It is because a new object recalls more
distinctly to the soldier's memory the image of death, of which he had
before but a confused view.

* If the young in general shew more courage on a death-bed, and
greater weakness on the scaffold, than the old, it is because in the
first case, young men preserve more hope; and in the second, suffer
a greater loss.

have rendered themselves useful to their country. In vain do they say, that the guards which on all sides surrounded the palaces of tyranny forbad their access: their hands were disarmed by the fear of punishment. Such men drowned themselves, or opened their veins; but they did not expose themselves to cruel torments; no motive could determine them to it.

It is the fear of pain that explains to us whatever is fantastical in this species of courage. If the man has such resolution, as to blow out his brains with a pistol, and would shrink at stabbing himself with a dagger, and has an aversion to certain kinds of death, this only proceeds from a fear, either true or false, of suffering greater pain.

The principles above established, I think, afford a resolution to all questions of this kind, and prove, that courage is not, as some pretend, an effect of the different temperature of climates, but of the passions and wants common to all men. The bounds of my subject do not permit me to treat here of various names given to courage; such as those of bravery, valour, intrepidity, &c. These are only the different ways in which courage is shewn.

This question being discussed, I pass to the second. Whether, as it is pretended, we ought to attribute the conquests of the northern nations to the peculiar strength and vigour with which nature has endowed them.

Experience will be of little service in ascertaining the truth of this opinion; for, hitherto, no sufficient proof has presented itself to a scrupulous inquirer, that nature has given greater strength to her productions in the north than to those in the south. If the north has its white bears and its orax, Africa has its lions, its rhinoceroses, and its elephants. They have not caused a certain number of negroes of the gold coast of Senegal to wrestle with an equal number of Russians or Finlanders: they have not weighed the inequality of their strength, by the different weights they are capable of lifting. So far are they from having any thing settled in this respect, that, if I were to attack prejudice with prejudice, I might oppose, to whatever has been said on the strength of the northern nations, the praise given to that of the Turks. People can then no otherwise support the opinion they have of the strength and courage of the people of the north, but by the history of their conquests; and even here all nations may, from the same pretensions, justify them by the same reasons, and believe that each is equally favoured by nature.

If we have recourse to history, we there see the Huns quit the Palus Meotis to enslave the nations situated to the north of their country: we there see the Saracens descend in crowds from the burning sands of Arabia, to scourge the earth, subdue the nations, triumph over Spain, and spread desolation even into the heart of France; we there see the same Saracens break, with their victorious hands, the standards carried in the crusades, and the nations of Europe, by repeated attempts in Palestine, multiply their shame and defeats.

If I direct my view to other regions, I still see the truth of my opinion confirmed, as well by the triumphs of Tamerlane, who, from the banks of the Indus, pursues his victories even to the frozen climates of Siberia; by the conquest of the Incas, and by the valour of the Egyptians, who, in the time of Cyrus, were esteemed as the most courageous of all people, and proved themselves at the battle of Tembreia worthy of their reputation; and, in short, by those Romans, who carried their victorious arms even into Sarmatia and the island of Britain.

Since then victory has flown alternately from the south to the north, and from the north to the south; since all nations have been by turns conquering and conquered; since, as history informs us*, the people of the north are not much less sensible of the burning heat of the south than the people of the south are of the piercing cold of the north, and both make war with equal disadvantage in climates so different from their own; it is evident, that the conquests of the northern nations are absolutely independent of the particular temperature of their climates; and that people search in vain into physical causes for

---

* Tacitus says, that, if the northern nations bore cold and hunger better than the southern, these last supported heat and thirst better than they.

The same Tacitus says, in his Manners of the Germans, that they could not support the fatigues of war.

a fact where the moral one is so simply and naturally explained.

If the north has produced the last conquerors of Europe, it is because fierce and savage nations, such as those of the north, are *, as the Chevalier Toland remarks, infinitely more courageous and warlike than people indulged in luxury, softness, and subject to arbitrary power, as were then the Romans†. Under the last Emperors, the Romans were no longer that people, who, being the conquerors of the Gauls and Germans, held the south also subject to their laws; for then those masters of the world had sunk under the same virtues that had made them triumph over the universe.

But, in order to subdue Asia, little more, it is said, was necessary than to carry chains there. The rapidity with which they conquered it, I reply, does not prove the cowardice of the people of the south: what cities ever defended themselves with more obstinacy than Marseilles, Numantia, Saguntum, and Rhodes? Did not the Romans, in the time of Crassus, find the Parthians enemies worthy of their courage? It is then to the slavery and softness of the Asiatics that the Romans owed the rapidity of their success.

---

* Olaus Vormius, in his Danish Antiquities, confesses, that he drew most of his knowledge from the rocks of Denmark, that is, from the inscriptions engraved upon them in Runic or Gothic characters. These rocks formed a series of history and chronology, that composed almost the whole library of the north.

In order to preserve the memory of some events, they made use of unhewn stones of a prodigious size; some of these were thrown confusedly together, and to others they gave some symmetry. We see many of these stones on Salisbury Plain in England, which served as a sepulchre to the princes and heroes of the Britons, as is proved from the great quantity of bones and armour that has been found there.

† "If the Gauls," says Cæsar, "were formerly more warlike than the Germans, and now yield to them the glory of arms, it is because the former, being instructed by the Romans in commerce, are become rich and civilized."

"What has happened to the Gauls," says Tacitus, "has happened to the Britons; these two nations have lost their courage with their liberty."

When Tacitus says, that the monarchy of the Parthians was less formidable to the Romans than the liberty of the Germans, it is to the form of government in the last that he attributes the superiority of their courage. It is then to moral causes, and not to the particular temperature of the countries of the north, that we ought to attribute the conquests of the northern nations.

CHAP. XXIX.

OF THE SLAVERY AND ALLEGORICAL GENIUS OF THE EASTERN NATIONS.

EQUALLY shocked by the heavy yoke of despotic power, and the long and shameful patience of the people who groan under it, the western nations, proud of their liberty, have recourse to physical causes to explain this political phænomenon. They have maintained that the luxury of Asia produced only men without strength and courage, and that, delivered up to brutal desires, they are only born for slavery. They have added, that the countries in the south are therefore only capable of adopting a sensual religion.

Their conjectures are contradicted by history and experience : we know that Asia has produced very warlike nations; that love does not weaken courage *; that the nations most sensible of its pleasures have often been, as Plutarch and Plato observe, the most brave and courageous ; that the ardent desire of women can never be considered as a proof of the

---

* " The Gauls," says Tacitus, " loved women, and treated them with the greatest respect ; they even considered them as something divine, and therefore admitted them into their councils, and deliberated with them on state affairs. The Germans treated theirs in the same manner ; their decisions seemed to be received by them as so many oracles. Under Vespasian, one Velleda, and, before her, one Aurinia, and several others, were treated with the same veneration. In fine," says Tacitus, " the Germans owed to their associating with women both their courage in battle and their wisdom in councils."

weakness of the constitutions of the Asiatics*; and that, in short, long before Mahomet, Odin had established, among the most northern nations, a religion perfectly like that of the prophet of the south†.

Being forced to abandon this opinion, and to restore, if I may use the expression, souls and bodies to the Asiatics, people have thought to discover in the natural situation of the eastern nations the cause of their slavery : in consequence of which, they have considered the south as a vast plain, whose extent furnishes tyranny with the means of keeping their people in subjection. But unhappily this opposition is not confirmed by geography : we know the south of the globe abounds in mountains; that the north, on the contrary, might be considered as a vast plain desert, and covered with woods, as were probably the plains of Asia.

After having in vain exhausted physical causes for the foundation of the eastern despotism, it is proper to have recourse to moral causes, and consequently to history. This informs us that the nations, by becoming civilized, insensibly lost their courage, their virtue, and even their love of liberty; that every society, immediately after its institution, according to the different circumstances in which it was placed, marched with a slower or more rapid pace towards slavery. Now the southern nations, being the first assembled in society, must consequently have been the first subject to despotic power; because to this every species of government tends, and it is a form which every state preserves till its entire destruction.

But, say those who believe the world more ancient than we do, how does it happen that there are still republics upon earth ? To this it may be replied, that if all societies, by being civilized, tend to despotism, all despotic power tends to depopulation. The climates subject to this power, after a certain number of ages becoming uncultivated and depopulated, are changed into deserts; the plains in which were

---

* According to the Chevalier Beau-jeu, the northern nations have always been addicted to the pleasures of love. Ogerius, in Itinere Danico, says the same thing.

† See in chap. xxv. the exact conformity between these two religions.

cities of immense extent, or where sumptuous edifices were raised, became by little and little covered with forests, in which some families took refuge, who insensibly formed new nations of savages; and this succession must constantly preserve republics upon earth.

I shall only add to what I have just said, that, if the people of the south have been longer slaves, and if the nations of Europe, except the Muscovites, may be considered as free, it is because these nations have been more lately polished : because, in the time of Tacitus, the Germans and Gauls were still no more than a kind of savages, and that, unless a nation be at once driven to slavery by force of arms, this will not be accomplished till after a long succession of ages, and by insensible but continued attempts made by tyrants to extinguish in the hearts of their subjects that virtuous love which all mankind naturally have for liberty, and thus to debase the mind, so far as to make it bow to oppression and slavery. When once a people have become thus unhappy, they are no longer capable of any noble and generous actions *. If the nations of Asia are the contempt of Europe, it is because time has subdued them to a despotism incompatible with a certain elevation of mind. It is the same despotism, so destructive to every species of genius and abilities, that has made people regard the stupidity of certain nations of the East as produced by a defect in their organization. It would, however, be easy to perceive, that the exterior difference observable, for instance, in the countenances of the Chinese and the Swedes, can have no influence on their minds; and that, if all our ideas, as Mr. Locke has shewn, proceed from the senses, the northern nations, having no greater number of senses than the Orientals, have by their natural conformation equal mental capacities.

---

* In these countries magnanimity never triumphs over revenge. We do not see in Turkey what happened some years ago in England. The young pretender, being pursued by the king's troops, found an asylum in the house of a person of distinction, who, being accused of having afforded a retreat to the pretender, was summoned to appear before his judges: he did so ; and, on his appearance, said—" Suffer me, before I answer any questions, to ask, which of you, if the pretender had taken refuge in his house, would have proved so base and ab-

CHAP. XXX.

OF THE SUPERIORITY OF CERTAIN NATIONS IN DIFFERENT SCIENCES.

THE natural situation of Greece is always the same, why then are the Greeks at present different from what they were formerly? It is because the form of their government is changed; like water which assumes the shape of all the vessels into which it is poured, the character of nations is susceptible of all forms, and in every country the genius of the government constitutes the genius of the nation.* Now, under the republican government, what country ought to be more fruitful of great generals, politicians, and

---

* Nothing is generally more false and ridiculous than the portraits drawn to represent the characters of different nations. Some paint their own nation after the particular society they frequent, and consequently represent the people as gloomy or gay, dull or witty. Methinks I hear the order of friars, called the Minims, ask, what is the taste of the French with respect to cookery? and they reply, that every body in France eats oil. Others copy what a thousand writers have said before them; they have never examined the changes necessarily produced in the character of a people, by those which happen in the administration, and the alteration of manners. It has been said, that the French are gay; and this will be repeated to eternity. They do not perceive, that the misfortunes of the times having obliged the princes to lay considerable taxes on the country people, the French nation cannot be gay, because the peasants, who alone compose two thirds of the nation, are in want, and want can never be gay : that even, in regard to the cities, the necessity, it is said, the police of Paris is under of defraying a part of the expence of the masquerades performed on holidays at St. Anthony's gate, is not a proof of the gaiety of the artists and the citizen ; spies may contribute to the safety of Paris ; but being carried too far, they diffuse a general diffidence through the minds of the people, that is absolutely incompatible with joy, on account of the ill use that may be made of them : the youth, being forbid to enter a tavern, have lost a part of that gaiety, which has frequent need of being animated by

heroes, than Greece? Without speaking of statesmen, what philosophers must have been produced in a country where philosophy
was so much honoured? Where King Philip, the conqueror of Greece,
wrote to Aristotle:· "I return thanks to the Gods, not for their
having given me a son, but for having caused him to be born while
thou art living. I entrust thee with his education; and hope thou
wilt render him worthy of thee, and of me." What letter could
be more flattering than that of Alexander, the master of the
world, who, when ready to mount the throne of Cyrus, thus wrote
to him: "I am informed that thou art going to publish thy treatises on Acroatics. What superiority shall I now maintain over other
men? The sublime sciences thou hast taught me will become
common, and yet thou knowest that I had rather surpass men in
the knowledge of these noble subjects than in power. Adieu."

But philosophy was not honoured in Aristotle alone. We know
that Ptolemy, king of Egypt, treated Zeno as a sovereign, and
sent ambassadors to him; that the Athenians erected a mausoleum
to that philosopher, at the public expence; that before Zeno's
death, Antigonus, King of Macedonia, thus wrote to him:—
"Though fortune has raised me to the highest post, though I
surpass thee in grandeur, I acknowledge that thou surpassest me
in wisdom and in virtue. Come then to my court; thou shalt be
of use not only to a great king, but also to the whole Macedonian
nation. Thou knowest what an effect the power of example has
on the people; they are the servile imitators of our virtues, and

---

wine: that, in short, good company, by banishing gross joy from
their assemblies, have banished the true. Thus most foreigners find a
great difference between the real character of our nation, and that it has
obtained abroad. If gaiety ever dwells in any part of France, it is certainly on the ramparts in festival days; yet the people there are too wise
to be esteemed gay; for joy is always somewhat licentious. Besides,
gaiety supposes ease; and the true sign of the ease of a people is what
certain persons call their insolence; that is, their knowing the rights of
humanity, and what man owes to man: a knowledge never acquired
by those who are discouraged, and rendered timid by poverty. Ease
defends its rights, but indigence gives them up.

he who inspires princes with them, gives them to the people: Farewell." Zeno replied: " I applaud the noble ardour with which thou art animated: in the midst of the festivity, pomp, and pleasures with which kings are surrounded, it is beautiful to desire wisdom and virtue. My great age; and the bad state of my health, will not permit me to repair to thee; but I send thee two of my disciples: listen to their instructions. If thou hearest them, they will shew thee the path of wisdom and true happiness. Farewell,"

It was not philosophy alone, but to all the arts that the Greeks paid such homage. A poet was so extremely admired in Greece, that the Athenians, by an express law, forbad their leaving the country on pain of death.* The Spartans, whom certain authors have taken a pleasure in representing as virtuous men, but less polished, and not so ingenious as the other Greeks, were no less sensible than they to the beauties of the arts and sciences.† Passionately fond of poetry, they invited to them Archilochus, Xenodames, Xenocritus, Polymnestes, Sacadas, Periclitus, Phrynis, and Timotheus.‡ So great was their esteem for the poems of Terpander, Spendo, and Alcman, that their slaves were forbid to sing them; they would have looked upon this as a profanation of divine

---

* A poet in the Marian islands is considered as a very surprising man, and this character alone renders him respected by the nation.

† Indeed, they had an abhorrence for all poetry tending to enervate their minds and weaken their courage. They drove Archilocus from Sparta, for saying in verse, that it was more wise to fly, than to die in arms. His exile was not the effect of their indifference for poetry, but of their love of virtue. The care taken by Lycurgus to collect the works of Homer; the statue of Laughter raised in the midst of Sparta, and the laws he gave to the Spartans, prove that this great man had no design of rendering them a dull and stupid people.

‡ Among the Lacedæmonians Cynetho, Dionysodotus, Areus, and Chilo, one of the seven wise men, distinguished themselves by their poetic talents. The poetry of the Spartans, says Plutarch, was simple, masculine, and full of energy; it was animated with that fire proper to fill the soul with warmth and courage.

things. They were not less skilled in the art of reasoning than that of painting their thoughts in verse: " Whoever," says Plato, " converses with a Spartan, were he even the meanest among them, might find him at first coarse ; but if he entered into a subject, he will hear him speak with a dignity, a precision, and a delicacy, that renders his words like so many sharp arrows. Any other Greek besides would appear but like a stammering infant." Thus they learnt from their most early youth to speak with elegance and purity. To justness of thinking, they added the graces and delicacy of expression ; that their answers being always short and just, might be poignant and agreeable. Those who, through precipitation or slowness, made either a bad answer, or none at all, were instantly punished. Bad reasoning was chastised at-Sparta with as much severity as in other places was shewn to a bad conduct. Nothing, therefore, could impose on the under-standing of this people. A Spartan, exempt from the cradle from the capricious humours and peevishness of childhood, was in his youth freed from all fear, he walked with assurance in solitude and darkness ; and being less superstitious than the other Greeks, they cited their religion before the tribunal of reason.

It was impossible that the arts and sciences should not have shone with the greatest lustre in such a country as Greece, where so general and so constant an honour was paid to them. I say, so constant, in order to anticipate the objection of those who pretend, with the Abbé Dubos, that, in certain ages, such as those of Augustus and Lewis XIV. certain winds blow over great men as they bring flights of uncommon birds. In favour of this opinion they allege the pains some sovereigns have vainly taken to revive the arts and sciences in their dominions.* If the efforts of these

---

* Sovereigns are apt to think, that by a word, or by a law, they can suddenly change the spirit of a nation, and, for instance, render a cowardly and indolent people, courageous and active. They are ignorant that diseases in the state, which are long contracting, require much time in curing ; and that in the body politic, as well as in the human, the impatience of the prince and the sick persons often oppose the cure.   1

princes, I reply, were not successful, it was because they were not constant. After some ages of ignorance, the soil of the arts and sciences is sometimes so wild and uncultivated that it cannot produce truly great men, till it has been first grubbed up by several generations of the learned. Such was the age of Lewis XIV. in which great men owed their superiority to the learned who had preceded them in the study of the arts and sciences; a study in which these learned would not have succeeded, had they not met with the favour of our kings, as is proved by the letters-patents of the 10th of May 1543, in which Francis I. expressly forbids cursing, and using invectives against Aristotle *, and by the verses which Charles IX. addressed to Ronsard.†

I shall only add one word to what I have just said, which is, that as fireworks rapidly flying through the air, disseminate it with

---

* In the flourishing ages of the church, some have raised the books of Aristotle to the dignity of the divine text, and others have compared him with Jesus Christ ; some have advanced, in printed theses, that were it not for Aristotle, religion would want its principal explications. They have sacrificed to him many critics, and among others, Ramus : this philosopher having caused a work to be printed, under the title of Censure on Aristotle, all the old doctors who, ignorant from their station, and obstinate through ignorance, saw themselves, in a manner, driven from their patrimony, and, therefore, caballed against Ramus, and caused him to be sent into exile.

† These are the verses the monarch wrote to that poet :

> L'art de faire des vers, dût-on s'en indigner,
> Doit être à plus haut prix que celui de régner ;
> Ta lyre, qui ravit par de si doux accords,
> T'asservit les esprits dont je n'ai que les corps ;
> Elle s'en rend le maître, & te fait introduire
> Où le plus fier tyran ne peut avoir d'empire.

That is, the art of poetry, whoever it offends, is of greater value than that of swaying the scepter ; the ravishing harmony of thy lyre renders minds subject to thee, while I reign over bodies : it renders thee master, and thy pleasing sway is felt, where the power of tyranny cannot reach.

stars, and having for a moment enlightened the horizon, vanish, and leave nature in a more profound darkness; so the arts and sciences, in many countries, do no more than blaze, disappear, and abandon the people to the darkness of ignorance. The ages most fruitful in great men, are generally followed by an age in which the arts and sciences are less happily cultivated. In order to discover the cause, we must not have recourse to natural philosophy, but to morality. In fact, if admiration is always the effect of surprise, the more great men are multiplied in a nation, the less are they esteemed, the less is excited in them the spirit of emulation, the less are their efforts to attain to perfection, and the farther distant they are from it. After such an age it becomes necessary that a country should lie fallow during several ages of ignorance, to render it again fertile in great men.

It appears then, that we can only attribute the superiority of certain nations over others in the arts and sciences, to moral causes; and that there are no people privileged in point of virtue, genius, and courage. Nature, in this respect, has not made a partial distribution of her favours. Indeed, if the greater or less strength of mind depended on the different climate of countries, it would be impossible, considering the age of the world, but that what was in this respect most favoured, should by its progress have acquired a great superiority over all others. The esteem which different nations have by turns obtained, with respect to genius, and the contempt into which they have successively fallen, prove the little influence climates have on the mind. I shall even add, that if the place of our birth determined the extent of our intellects, moral causes could not here give us so simple and natural an explication of the phænomena that depended on physics. Upon which I shall observe, that, if there are no people to whom the climate of their particular country, and the small difference it must produce in their organization, have at present given any constant superiority over other nations, we may at least suspect, that the trifling differences to be found in the organization of the individuals of which a nation is composed, cannot have a more sensible influence on their minds.* Every thing concurs to prove the truth of this proposition. It seems that the most complicated problems of this kind present themselves only to the mind, in order to be resolved by the application of the principles I have established.

Why do men of moderate abilities almost always reproach illustrious men with being guilty of a very extraordinary conduct? It is because genius is not the gift of nature; and that a man, who embraces a kind of life that nearly resembles that of the rest of the society, does not require an higher degree of understanding than theirs; because a man of genius spends his time in study and application, and that a life so different from that of others will always appear ridiculous. Why is the present age more knowing than those which preceded it? And why is genius less common? Why, as Pythagoras says, do we see so many people take the thyrsis, and so few animated by the spirit of the god who carries it? It is because men of learning being too often forced from their closets by want, and obliged to enter into the world, there they diffuse knowledge, and form men of abilities; but they necessarily lose the time, which, by being spent in solitude and reflection, would have given a greater extent to their genius. The man of learning is like a body, that, having been forcibly struck against other bodies, loses the force it communicates to them.

These are the moral causes that give us an explanation of all the various phænomena of the mind; and inform us, that, like the fiery particles which lie inclosed in gunpowder, and remain

---

* If it cannot be strictly shewn, that a difference of organization has not any influence on the abilities of the men whom I commonly call well organized, we may at least assure ourselves, that this influence is inconsiderable, that they may be considered as those qualities which are of such small importance, that we neglect them in algebraical calculations; and that, in short, we may very well explain by moral causes, what has been hitherto attributed to natural ones, without any person's being able to explain them by those causes.

there without action, if no spark sets them in motion, the mind remains without action, till it is actuated by the passions; that the passions often render a man who is stupid a man of sense, and that we owe all to education.

If, as it is pretended, genius is a gift of nature, why among the men of certain employments, or those who were born, or have long lived in the country, are there none who excel in poetry, music, and painting? Why does not the gift of genius supply in men, entrusted with employments, the loss of time taken up by their posts? And in country gentlemen, why does it not counterbalance the conversation of the small number of men of abilities, who are only to be found in the capital? Why have the great no genius for any thing but what has long engaged their application? Is it not evident, that, if the man of genius does not preserve the same superiority on other subjects, it is because he has not made them the objects of his attention? For the man of genius has no advantage over other men but the habit of application, and a method of study. What is the reason, why among great men there are so few great ministers? It is because to the multitude of circumstances that must necessarily concur to form a great genius, there must be united a concurrence of circumstances proper to raise this man to the genius of a minister. Now the union of these circumstances, so extremely uncommon among all nations, is almost impossible in countries where merit alone does not entitle a person to the highest posts. Therefore, if we except Xenophon, Scipio, Confucius, Cæsar, Hanibal, Lycurgus, and perhaps about fifty statesmen in the whole world, whose minds might really stand the test of strict examination, all the others, and even some of the most celebrated in history, whose actions have made the greatest noise, notwithstanding all the encomiums lavished on their extensive talents, were but men of very common capacities. It is to the force of their character in life, more than to that of their minds, that they owe their fame.* The

---

* The force of characters, which are often unjust, render a person in political affairs more proper for performing great things, than persons

little progress made in legislation, the indifference of several works that are almost unknown, left by Augustus, Tiberius, Titus, Antoninus, Adrian, and Charles V. and which they have composed on subjects in which they ought to have excelled, too plainly prove the truth of this opinion.

The general conclusion of this discourse is, that genius is common, and the circumstances, proper to unfold it, very extraordinary. If we may compare what is profane to what is sacred, we may say in this respect, Many are called, but few are chosen.

The inequality observable among men, therefore, depends on the government under which they lie; on the greater or less happiness of the age in which they are born; ou the education; on their desire of improvement, and on the importance of the ideas that are the subject of their contemplations.

The man of genius is then only produced by the circumstances in which he is placed.* Thus all the art of education consists in

---

of great genius whose characters are unknown. It is necessary, says Cæsar, rather to execute than to deliberate upon bold enterprises. However these great characters are more frequent than great geniuses. A strong passion is sufficent to form a great character, but it is only one means of acquiring a great genius. Thus among three or four hundred ministers, or kings, we commonly find one great character; while we are not always sure of finding one great genius among two or three thousand, that is supposing, that such a genius as that of Minos, Confucius, and Lycurgus, &c. are only proper for forming legislators.

* The opinion I advance must appear very pleasing to the vanity of the greatest part of mankind, and therefore, ought to meet with a favourable reception. According to my principles, they ought not to attribute the inferiority of their abilities to the humbling cause of a less perfect organization, but to the education they have received, as well as to the circumstances in which they have been placed. Every man of moderate abilities, in conformity with my principles, has a right to think, that if he had been more favoured by fortune, if he had been born in a certain age or country, he had himself been like the great men whose genius he is forced to admire. Yet, however favourable this opinion may be to the mean abilities of the greatest

placing young men in such a concurrence of circumstances as are proper to unfold the buds of genius and virtue. A love of paradoxes has not led me to form this conclusion; but the desire of promoting the happiness of mankind. I am convinced that a good education would diffuse light, virtue, and consequently, happiness in society; and that the opinion, that genius and virtue are merely gifts of nature, is a great obstacle to the making any farther progress in the science of education, and in this respect is the great favourer of idleness and negligence. With this view, examining

part of mankind, it must generally displease; because, there is scarcely a man who thinks he has only moderate abilities, and that he has any degree of stupidity, since he every day with great pleasure thanks nature for the particular care she has taken of his organization. Consequently, there is scarcely a man who will not treat as a paradox, principles that openly shock his pretensions. Every truth, which shocks pride, must for a long time wrestle with that passion, before it can triumph over it. People are just only when they have an interest in being so. If the citizen exaggerates less the advantages of birth than the man of quality, if he makes a truer estimate of its real value, it is not because he is wiser; his inferiors have too often reason to complain of his being guilty of that ridiculous haughtiness for which he abuses the great: the justness of his judgment is then only the effect of his vanity; since in this case, it is his interest to be on the side of reason. I will farther add to what I have said, that the principles above established, supposing them to be true, will still meet with opposition from all who cannot admit them without abandoning ancient prejudices. When we are arrived at a certain age, laziness exasperates us against every new idea that imposes upon us the fatigue of examination. A new opinion finds partizans only among those men of genius, who being still too young to have wedded themselves to their ideas, or to have felt the sting of envy, greedily seize the truth where ever they find it. They alone, as I have already observed, render themselves witnesses in behalf of the truth, introduce it, present it, and establish it in the world; from them alone a philosopher may expect some praise: most of the other men are corrupted by laziness or envy.

1

the effects which nature and education may have upon us, I have perceived that education makes us what we are; in consequence of which I have thought that it was the duty of a citizen to make known a truth proper to awaken the attention, with respect to the means of carrying this education to perfection. And to cast the greater light on so important a subject, I shall endeavour, in the following discourse, to fix, in a precise manner, the ideas we ought to form on the different faculties of the human mind.

ESSAY IV.

OF THE DIFFERENT FACULTIES OF THE HUMAN MIND.*

———

CHAP. I.

OF GENIUS.

AMONG the many authors who have written on genius, most of them have considered it as a fire, an inspiration, and a divine enthusiasm; and these metaphors they have taken for definitions.

But however vague these kind of definitions may be, the same reason that makes us say that fire is hot, and induces us to place in the number of its properties the effect it has upon us, has made us give the name of fire to all the ideas proper to kindle and move our passions.

Few men have perceived, that these metaphors, which are applicable to certain kinds of genius, such as that of poetry or eloquence, are not so to the genius of reflection, such as that of Locke and Newton.

In order to obtain an exact definition of the word genius, and in general, of all the names given to the mental faculties, we must obtain more general ideas, and, for this purpose, listen with great attention to the judgments formed by the public.

The public equally places in the rank of men of genius, Descartes, Newton, Locke, Montesquieu, Corneille, Moliere, &c. The name of genius given to such different men, supposes, there re-

———

* The subject of this discourse as expressed by our author is, " The different names given to the Esprit," a word which cannot be literally translated, and signifies not only the mind, but its faculties.

fore, a common quality, which characterizes what is called genius.

In order to know what this quality is, let us consider the etymology of the word genius, since it is commonly by these etymologies, that the public most clearly shew the idea they fix to words.

That of genius is derived from GIGNERE, GIGNO; I bring forth, I produce; it always supposes invention, and this quality is the only one which belongs to all the different kinds of genius.

Inventions and discoveries are of two kinds. The one which we owe to chance, such as those of the mariner's compass, gunpowder, and in general almost all the discoveries we have made in the arts.

The other which we owe to genius: and here we ought to understand by the word discovery, a new combination, or a new relation perceived between certain objects, or ideas. A person obtains the title of a man of genius, if the ideas which result from this combination form one grand whole, are fruitful in truths, and are of importance with respect to mankind.* Now the subjects which employ our reflections generally proceed from chance. This has a greater share than we imagine in the success of great men, since it furnishes the more or less interesting subjects upon which they treat; and it is the same chance which has caused them to be born at a time, when these great men were capable of improving their abilities.

It must be observed, that every inventor of an art or science, which he draws in a manner from its cradle, is always surpassed by the man of genius, who follows him in the same study, and

---

* The novelty, and singularity of ideas are not sufficient to merit the title of genius; it is also necessary that these new ideas should be beautiful, general, or extremely interesting in these particulars, a work of genius principally differs from a mere original work, chiefly characterized by its singularity.

this second by a third, and so on, till the art has made a certain progress. When it has arrived at the last degree of perfection; or, at least, to the degree necessary to render it considered as perfect among the people, then he who has given it its last degree, obtains the title of genius; though he may not have advanced the art in greater proportion, than those who preceded him: The having a genius, therefore, is not sufficient to obtain a title to it.

From the tragedies on the passions to the poets Hardy and Rotrou, and till the Mariamne Tristan, the French theatre successively acquired many degrees of perfection. Corneille was born at a time, when the perfection he added to that art rendered it complete ; Corneille is therefore a genius. *

I by no means pretend by this observation, to diminish the glory of this great poet; but only to prove, that the law of continuity is always exactly observed, and that there are no breaks in nature. † We may apply to the sciences, the observation made on the drama.

Kepler discovered the laws by which bodies ought to gravitate towards each other ; Newton, by the happy application of this to

---

* Not but that tragedy was, in the time of Corneille, capable of new improvements : Racine has shewn, that they may be written with more elegance ; Crebillon, that they may have more fire ; and Voltaire has beyond all contradiction made it appear, that there might be introduced into them greater pomp and shew, if the stage, which is always crouded with spectators, did not oppose this kind of beauty, so well known to the Greeks.

† There are a thousand forces of illusion of this kind. A man is perfectly acquainted with a foreign language, we will suppose the Spanish. If the Spanish writers are then superior to us in the drama, the French author, who improves himself by reading their works, though he surpasses his model ever so little, must, to his ignorant fellow-countrymen, appear a very extraordinary man : and no doubt is made, but he has carried the art to that high degree of perfection, to which it would have been impossible for the human mind to have at first raised it.

the heavenly bodies, which a very ingenious calculation enabled him to make, confirmed the existence of these laws. Newton, therefore, lived in a proper period, and was placed in the rank of men of genius.

Aristotle, Gassendi, and Montaigne, had a confused view, that we owe all our ideas to our sensations: Locke cleared up, searched into this principle, and established its truth by an infinite number of applications, and hence Locke is a genius.

It is impossible that one great man should not have been preceded by another.* Works of genius are like some of those superb monuments of antiquity, which executed by several generations of kings, bear the name of him who finished them.

But if chance, that is, the chain of effects of whose causes we are ignorant, has such a share in the glory of men, who have rendered themselves illustrious in arts and sciences; if it determines the instant in which each ought to be born, in order to receive the name of a man of genius; has not this chance still greater influence on the reputation of statesmen?

Cæsar and Mahomet have filled the earth with their renown. The latter is by half the globe respected as the friend of God; and in the other he is honoured as a great genius: however this Mahomet, a mere dealer in cattle in Arabia, without learning, without education, and himself in part the dupe of the fanaticism he inspired, was forced, in order to compose the ridiculous work named the Koran, to have recourse to some Greek monks. Now, how is it possible, not to acknowledge, that such a man owed to

---

* I may even say accompanied by some great men. Whoever is pleased to consider the human mind, must see in every age, five or six men of abilities, who apply themselves to the discoveries made by a man of genius. If the honour remains in the possession of the last, it is because this discovery under his management is more fruitful, than in that of others; because he conveys his ideas with more strength and clearness; and because, in short, we always see, from the different manner in which men take an advantage of a principle or discovery, to whom that principle or discovery belongs.

chance his being placed in times and circumstances proper to produce the revolution in which this bold adventurer did little more than lend his name.

Who doubts but this same chance, so favourable to Mahomet, did not contribute to the glory of Cæsar? I do not pretend to lessen the praises due to that hero: but Sylla had, like him, humbled the Romans. The actions of war are no where so circumstantially mentioned, as to enable us to judge, whether Cæsar was really superior to Sertorius, or any other captain. If he was the only Roman who has been compared to the conqueror of Darius, it is because both subdued many nations. If the glory of Cæsar has tarnished that of the great captains of the republic, it is because his victories laid the foundations of the throne, which Augustus established;* because his dictature was the period when the slavery of the Romans began; and because he produced a revolution in the world, of so astonishing a nature, that it must necessarily add to the fame he had merited by his great talents.

What part soever I give to chance, whatever share it has in the reputation of great men, it however can do nothing for those who are not animated by a lively desire of glory.

This desire, as I have already observed, makes men support, without pain, the fatigue of study and reflection. It endues a man with that constancy of attention, necessary to render him illustrious, in any art or science whatsoever. To this desire per-

---

* Not but that Cæsar was one of the greatest generals, even according to the severe judgment of Machiavel, who erases from the list of celebrated captains all those who with small armies have not executed great and new things.

" If to excite their enthusiasm," adds that celebrated author, " we see great poets take Homer for a model, and when they write, ask themselves, had Homer this thought, how would he express himself? So great generals, the admirers of some great captain of antiquity, imitate Scipio, and Ziska, one of whom was proposed by Cyrus, and the other by Hannibal for a model."

sons owe that boldness of mind, which enables them to cite, before the tribunal of reason, the opinions, prejudices, and errors, consecrated by time.

It is this desire alone, which, in the arts and sciences raises us to the perception of new truths, or procures us new amusements. This desire, in short, is the soul of the man of genius : it is the source of what appears ridiculous in him,* and of his success ; a success

---

* Every man absorbed in deep reflection, and employed about great and general ideas, lives in the forgetfulness of those forms, and in the ignorance of those customs, which compose the knowledge of a great part of the world ; and thus almost constantly appears ridiculous. Few men perceive that the knowlege of little things generally supposes the ignorance of those that are great ; that every man who lives like the rest of the world, has no ideas but those that are common to all ; that such a man cannot raise himself above the abilities of the common people; and that, in short, genius always supposes a man to have a lively desire of glory, which, rendering him insensible to all other desires, opens his mind only to the love of knowledge.

Anaxagoras is an example of this. Being pressed by his friends to place his affairs in order, and for that purpose to employ some hours of his time, " O my friends, he replied, you ask what is impossible. How can I divide my time between my affairs, and my studies, when I prefer one ·drop of wisdom, to whole‑tuns of riches?"

Corneille was doubtless of the same opinion, when a young man, to whom he had promised his daughter, and whose affairs put him under the necessity of breaking off the marriage, went in the morning to Corneille, and without ceremony entered his closet : " I come, said he, Sir, to retract my promise, and to give you the motives of my conduct.———Why, Sir, replied Corneille, could not you, without interrupting me, talk of all that to my wife? Go up to her : I understand nothing at all of these affairs."

There is scarcely a man of genius, of whom some such circumstance might not be mentioned. A domestic enters in a fright the closet of the learned Budeus, and tells him, the house is on fire: " Well, says he, inform my wife of it. I do not interfere in household affairs."

commonly owing to the obstinacy with which he concenters himself in one kind of study. One science is sufficient to fill the whole capacity of one mind; it, therefore, neither has nor can have an universal genius.

The length of the reflections necessary to render a person superior in one kind of study, compared with the shortness of life, chews us the impossibility of excelling in many.

Besides, there is only one age, namely that of the passions, in which we can conquer the first difficulties that forbid access to to each science. This age being past, we may learn still to manage, with more dexterity, the instruments we have always made use of, the better to unfold our ideas and to present them to public view; but we are incapable of the necessary efforts for clearing a fresh soil.

Genius, of whatever kind, is always the effect of an infinite number of combinations, that can only be formed in early youth.

A taste for study suffers no distraction. It is to the retreat to which this taste confines illustrious men, that they owe that simplicity of manners, and those simple unexpected answers, which so often furnish men of moderate abilities with the pretence of ridiculing men of genius. I shall upon this subject mention two passages of the celebrated la Fontaine. One of his friends, who had doubtless his conversion much at heart, lent him one day the epistles of St. Paul. La Fontaine read them with avidity, but being naturally of a mild and humane disposition, he was shocked at the seeming severity of that apostle's writings, and shutting the book, returned it to his friend, saying, " I restore you your book : this St. Paul is not a man after my mind." It was with the same simplicity, that one day comparing St. Augustin to Rabelais, " How, cried la Fontaine, can men of taste prefer the reading of St. Augustin to that of Rabelais, so sprightly and so amusing ?"

Every man who is concentered in the study of interesting objects, finds himself alone in the midst of the world, he always acts like himself, and scarcely ever like anybody else; consequently, he must almost always appear ridiculous.

Moreover, by genius, I do not merely understand the discoveries made in the sciences or the invention, with respect to the matter and plan of the work, there is also a genius of expression. The principles of the art of writing are so obscure, so few and imperfect, that no one can obtain the title of being a celebrated writer, without being really an inventor.

La Fontaine and Boileau have employed but little invention, in relation to the subjects of which they have treated: yet both of them have been justly esteemed men of genius; the first, from the simplicity and agreeable manner in which he has formed his narrations; the last, from the correctness, strength, and poetic style, which runs through his works. Whatever reproaches are cast on Boileau, we are forced to confess, that by infinitely improving the art of versification, he has really merited the title of an inventor.

Among the different kinds of genius to which people apply themselves, some are more desirable than others. In poetry, for instance, the genius of expression is, if I may use the term, the genius of necessity. The epic poet, the most rich in the invention of a subject, is not read if he is void of the genius of expression; on the contrary, a poem, where the versification is good, and the piece abounds with poetic beauties, though otherwise without invention, will always meet with a favourable reception from the public.

This is not the case with philosophical works: in these, the first merit is that of the subject. In order to instruct mankind, it is necessary to present to them a new truth, or to shew them the connection that subsists between truths, that appear separate. In works of instruction, the beauty and eloquence of the diction, and an agreeable arrangement form only a secondary merit. Thus among the moderns we have seen philosophers without strength, grace, and even clearness of expression, obtain great reputation. The obscurity of their writings, may, for some time, condemn them to oblivion; but at length they rise from it: there, sooner or later, appears a penetrating mind, which seizing the truths contained in their works, frees them from the obscurity with which they are covered, and clearly explains them.   A genius like this, shares with the inventors the merit and glory of their discoveries.   He is a labourer, who digs up a treasure, and divides with the proprietor of the land, the riches he finds buried there.

After what I have said of the invention required in the subject, and of the genius of expression, it is easy to explain, how a celebrated writer may compose a bad work: it is sufficient, that the genius with which he writes, should be only a secondary one.   For this reason, a celebrated poet may be a bad philosopher, and a good philosopher, a bad poet; a writer of a romance may be a bad historian, and an excellent historian compose a bad romance.

The conclusion of this chapter is, that though genius always supposes invention, all invention, however, does not suppose genius.   In order to obtain the title of a man of genius, it is necessary, that his invention should be employed about objects that are general and important; and that he should be born at a time, when, by his talents and discoveries, he may make a figure in the learned world, by carrying to perfection the arts and sciences.

The man of genius, is then, in part, the work of chance; it is chance which, always in action, prepares the discoveries, insensibly bring truths together, that are always useless when too far separated, and which gives birth to the man of genius at the very instant, when the truths, already brought together, afford him general and clear principles: genius seizes these, presents them to the public, and some part of the empire of the arts and sciences is enlightened.

Chance then discharges, with respect to genius, the office of those winds, which, dispersed at the four corners of the earth, there charge themselves with the inflammable matter that compose the meteors: this matter dispersed loosely through the air, produces no effect, till the moment, when, by contrary winds, its particles impetuously clash against each other; then the lightning kindles its flashes fast through the air, and the horizon is in a blaze.   1

CHAP. II.

OF IMAGINATION AND SENTIMENT.

MOST of those, who have hitherto treated of the imagination, have too much confined and restrained the signification of the word. To obtain a clear idea of this term, let us consider its etymology; it is derived from the Latin IMAGO, image.

Many have confounded the memory and the imagination. They have not perceived, that there are no words exactly synonimous; that the memory consists in a distinct rememberance of the object presented to us, and the imagination in a conbination, a new assemblage of images, and proper relations perceived between these images, and the sensations they would excite. If this be terror, the imagination gives being to the sphinx and to the furies. If this be astonishment or admiration, it creates the garden of the Hesperides, the enchanted island of Armida, and the palace of Atalanta.

Imagination is then the invention with respect to images,* as genius with respect to ideas.

The memory, which is only the exact remembrance of the objects presented to us, differs no less from the imagination, than a portrait of Louis XIV. done by le Brun, differs from a picture of the conquest of Franche Comte.†

---

* We give the title of a man of a lively imagination, to him who expresses his ideas by strong images. It is true, in conversation we generally confound imagination with invention and passion. It is, however, easy to distinguish the man of warm passions, from the man of a strong and lively imagination, since it almost always proceeds from the want of imagination that a poet who excels in tragedy or comedy, so often makes but a very indifferent figure in an epic or lyric poem.

† It must be remembered that Louis XIV. is painted in this picture.

It follows from this definition of the imagination, that it is employed scarcely about any thing else, but in descriptions, pictures, and decorations. In all other cases, the imagination can only serve to cloke the ideas and sentiments we represent. It formerly played a much greater part in the world; it explained almost all the phænomena of nature. It was from the urn on which a naiad rested that the rivers flowed, which winded along the vallies; the forests and plains were loaded with verdure, by the care of the napeæ and the dryades; the rocks torn from the mountains, were rolled into the plains by the orcades; the powers of the air, under the name of genii, or demons, unchained the winds, and let loose the storms on the countries they would ravage.

Though in Europe, people no longer explain the phænomena of nature by the imagination; though they make no other use of it, than to give a greater clearness and beauty to the principles of the sciences, and though they expect to discover the secrets of nature only by experiments, we must not imagine that all nations are equally enlightened in this respect. Imagination is still the philosophy of India: it is she, who, in Tonquin, has fixed the instant of the formation of pearls;* it is she, who, by peopling the ele-

---

* Imagination, supported by some obscure and ridiculous traditions, teaches in relation to this subject, that a king of Tonquin, a great magician, had formed a bow of pure gold, and that all the arrows shot from it carried death. Armed with this bow he routed an army. A neighbouring king attacked him with more numerous forces : he experienced his power, and was defeated ; he concluded a treaty, and obtained for his son the daughter of the conqueror. Amidst the intoxication of the first night, the bridegroom conjured his spouse to substitute in the room of her father's magic bow, another perfectly like it. This the imprudence of love promised ; she executed her promise, and did not suspect her being guilty of a crime. But scarce was the son-in-law armed with the wonderful bow, when he marched against his father-in-law, defeated him, and forced him to fly with his daughter to the sea coast. There a demon appeared to the king of Tonquin, and let him know the author of his misfortune. The father enraged,

ments with demi-gods, creating at her pleasure demons, genii, fairies, and inchanters, in order to explain the phænomena of the natural world, has, with a bold wing, often raised herself to its origin. After having long run over the immeasurable deserts of space, and of eternity, she is at length forced to stop at a point; at this point time begins. The dark, thick, and spiritual air, which, according to the Taautus of the Phœnicians, covered the vast abyss, is filled with love for its own principles; love produces a mixture, and this mixture receives the name of desire; this desire conceives the aqueous corruption; this corruption contains the seed of the universe, and of all living creatures. Intelligent animals, under the name of Zophasemin, or the contemplators of the heavens, received their being: the sun was kindled, the earth and seas were warmed with its rays; they reflected them, and enflamed the air: the winds blew, the clouds arose, struck against each other, and from their shock proceeded thunder and lightning; the noise awakened the intelligent animals, who affrighted, began to move, and fled, some into the caverns of the earth, and others into the abyss of the ocean.

The same imagination, which, joined to the principles of a false philosophy, had in Phœnicia thus described the formation of the universe, in several other countries brought chaos into order, by a thousand different ways.*

---

seized his daughter, and drew his scimetar: she in vain protested her innocence, she found him inflexible. She then foretold, that all she drops of her blood should be changed into pearls, whose whiteness should render future ages a witness of her imprudence, and her innocence. She was silent, the father struck; the metamorphosis began; and the coast stained with this parricide, is still that where they fish for the finest pearls.

* They assert in the kingdom of Lao, that heaven and earth subsisted from all eternity. According to them, sixteen terrestrial worlds are subject to ours, and the most elevated are the most delightful. A flame sent forth, every thirty-six thousand years, from the abyss of the firmament, surrounds the earth, as the bark of a tree incompasses the

In Greece, it inspired Hesiod, who, when full of his enthusiasm, said, "In the beginning were Chaos, black Erebus, and Tartarus. Time did not yet exist, when eternal night, which, on heavy and extended wings, roved through the immense plains of space, suddenly stopped at Erebus: she there deposited an egg: Erebus received it into her bosom, hatched it, and Love sprang from thence. He arose on his golden wing, united himself to Chaos: and this union gave being to the heavens, to the earth, to the immortal gods, to men, and to animals. Already Venus, conceived in the sea, arose on the surface of the waters; all animated bodies stopped to contemplate her; the emotions which Love had

---

trunk and resolves it into water. Nature, for some moments reduced to this state, is revived by a genius of the first heaven. He descends on the wings of the winds, their breath makes the waters retire; the moist earth is dried; the forests and plains are covered with verdure, and the earth resumes its primeval form.

At the last conflagration, which, the inhabitants of Lao say, preceded the age of Xaca, a mandarin named Pontabobamy-suan, cast himself upon the surface of the waters: a flower swam on their immensity; the mandarin perceived it, and cut it with his scimetar. By a sudden metamorphosis, the flower cut from its stalk changed into a virgin: nature had never produced any thing so beautiful. The mandarin conceived the most violent passion for her, and made known his tenderness. The love of virginity rendered the maid insensible to the tears of her lover. The mandarin admired her virtue; but not being able to deprive himself of her sight, placed himself at some distance from her, where reciprocally darting ardent glances at each other, they had such an effect, that the maid conceived, and brought forth without losing her virginity. To provide nourishment for the new inhabitants of the earth, the mandarin caused the waters to retire; he excavated the vallies, raised the mountains, and lived among mankind, till at length leaving the earth, he flew towards heaven : but the gates were shut against him, and not opened till he had endured a long and severe penance on earth. Such is the poetic picture, given in the kingdom of Lao, of the generation of beings; a picture that is varied by different nations, so as to be more or less grand or fantastical, but it is always formed by the imagination.

impressed on all nature, were then directed towards beauty. Now order, regularity, and design, were first known in the universe."

Thus in the first ages of Greece imagination built the palace of the world. Now more wise in her conceptions, she suffers us to arrive at the knowledge of its foundation by the information of history. Instructed by an infinite number of errors, she no longer interferes in the explication of the phænomena of nature; but, in consequence of experiments, she applies herself only to descriptions and pictures.

It is there that she creates those beings, and those new scenes which poetry, by its turns, the magnificence of its expressions, and propriety of words, renders visible to the eyes of the reader.

Are bold paintings required? Imagination is sensible that the grandest pictures, should they be incorrect are even the most proper to make an impression; that people prefer to the mild and pure light of the lamps burning before the altars, the mingled explosions of fire, ashes, and smoke, darted from Mount Ætna.

Is a voluptuous picture required? Imagination conducts Adonis into the midst of a grove: he there sees Venus sleeping on a bed of roses; the goddess awakes; the blush of modesty covers her cheeks; a slight robe conceals a part of her beauties; the ardent Adonis is enraptured with the sight; he seizes the goddess; he triumphs over her resistance; the veil is snatched with an impatient hand, Venus is naked, the alabaster of her body is exposed to the eye of desire: and here the picture remains loosely terminated, leaving to caprice, and the varied fancies of love, the choice of attitudes and caresses.

Is it necessary to represent a simple fact under a shining image? to shew, for instance, the dissentions among the citizens? Imagination will represent Peace leaving the city in tears, with the olive hanging withered over her eyes. Thus in poetry, imagination shows how to represent every thing by short images, or allegories, which are properly only continued metaphors.

3 c

In philosophy, the use that may be made of the imagination is infinitely more limited: it there serves only, as I have said above, to throw a clearer and more agreeable light on principles. I say clearer; because men who understand very well what they mean, when they pronounce the words that represent sensible objects, as an *oak*, the *ocean*, the *sun*, do not understand the meaning of the terms *beauty*, *justice*, *virtue*, whose signification includes a great number of ideas. It is almost impossible for them to affix the same complex ideas to the same word, and hence arises the eternal and hot disputes, that have so often stained the earth with blood.

The imagination, which endeavours to clothe abstract ideas, and the principles of the sciences, with sensible images, gives therefore clearness and charms to philosophy.

It equally embellishes works of sentiment. When Ariosto conducts Rolando into the grotto, whither Angelica is to repair, with what art does he adorn it? On every side are inscriptions engraved by love, beds of turf prepared by pleasure; the murmur of rivulets, the freshness of the air, the purfume of flowers, are all united to excite the desires of Rolando. The poet knew that the more this grotto was embellished, the more pleasure it promised, and the sweeter delight it infused into the soul of the hero, the more violent would be his despair, when he should learn the falsehood of Angelica; and the more would this picture raise in the minds of his readers those tender emotions, to which their pleasures are attached.

I shall conclude this piece on the imagination with an oriental fable, which is perhaps in some respects incorrect, but very ingenious, and extremely fitted to prove how much the imagination may sometimes add charms to a sentiment. It is a fortunate lover, who, under the veil of an allegory, ingeniously attributes to his mistress the love he has offered her, and the perfections he admires.

"I was one day in the bath: an odoriferous earth, an animated hand passed into mine. I asked, art thou musk? art thou

1

amber? It replied, I am but common earth, but I have had some connexion with a rose; its beneficent virtue has penetrated me; without that I should still be only common earth."*

I have, I think, clearly determined what we ought to understand by imagination, and shewn several ways the use that may be made of it. I now pass to sentiment.

The moment when passion is awaked with the greatest strength, the strong feelings which it excites in us are called sentiments. Thus we understand by passion only a continuity of mental feeling, or sentiments. A man's passion for a woman, is only the duration of his desires, and sentiments, with respect to her.

This definition being given in order to distinguish the different ideas affixed to the word sentiment, it must be observed that it is frequently used in an indeterminate sense, and often confounded with sensation: we must recollect that there are appetites and passions; the first are immediately given by nature, these are hunger, thirst, &c.; the others not being immediately given by nature, suppose the establishment of society, as ambition, pride, the love of luxury, &c. hence I distinguish two kinds of sentiments. One of which has a relation to the natural wants, and are termed sensations; the other to the passions, and are particularly called sentiments. It is of the last species, that I speak in this chapter.

In order to form a clear idea of this subject, it must be observed that there are no men without desires, and consequently without sentiments; these sentiments are either weak or lively. When they are only weak, we shall consider them as not having any at all. We allow sentiments only to those who are strongly affected. If we are affrighted, if our fear does not precipitate us into greater dangers than those we would avoid, and allows us the full use of our reason, we can never be charged with being fearful men. What I say of the sentiment of fear, that I also say of love and ambition.

---

* See the Gulistan, or the Empire of Roses, by Saadi.

It is only to the passions, that man owes those ' '' ' emotions and transports, to which we give the name of sentiment.

We are animated by these passions, when a single desire governs the mind, and imperiously commands all the subordinate desires. Whoever yields successively to different desires, deceives himself, if he thinks he is possessed with strong passions : he mistakes inclinations for passions.

The despotic power, if I may be allowed the term, of a desire to which all the others are subordinate, is therefore in us what characterizes passion. There are, consequently, but few men of strong passions, and but few capable of lively sentiments.

Frequently the manners of a people, and the constitution of a state, oppose the expanding of the passions and sentiments.   How many countries are there, where certain passions cannot shew themselves, at least, by actions! In an arbitrary government, always subject to a thousand revolutions, the great are almost constantly scorched by the fire of ambition; but this is not the case in a monarchy, where the laws are put in force. In such a state the ambitious are chained, and we see none but the intriguing, to whom I do not give the title of ambitious. Not but in these countries there are an infinite number of people who have the seeds of ambition; but, except in some singular circumstances, they die away, without ever shooting forth. Ambition in these men, is like those subterraneous fires kindled in the bowels of the earth, when they burn without explosion, till the moment when the waters penetrate to them, where, being rarefied by the fire, they rise, burst open the mountains, and shake the foundations of the earth.

In countries where the seeds of certain passions and sentiments are choked, the public can only know and study them by pictures exhibited by celebrated writers, and principally the poets.

Sentiment is the soul of poetry, and above all of the drama. Having marked out the signs by which greater painters, and men of lively sentiments, may understand the passions, it is proper to observe, that neither these, nor the sentiments, can ever be well painted by those who have never felt them. If they place a hero in a situation proper for his shewing all the force of the passions, in order to draw a true picture, they themselves must be affected with the same sentiments whose effects they describe, and draw the model from their own hearts. If they are without passions, they can never seize the precise point which a sentiment attains, and never surmounts:* they always fall short, or go beyond nature.

Besdes, in order to succeed here, it is not sufficent to be in general susceptible of the passions, they must also be animated by that which they paint. One kind of sentiment does not make us divine another, and we always express that but poorly, which we feel but weakly. Corneille, whose soul was more elevated than tender, paints great politicians and heroes better than lovers.

It is principally to truth, that painters of the passions and sentiments owe their fame. I know, however, that happy situations, noble maxims, and elegant verse, have sometimes obtained great success on the stage; but whatever merit there is in this success, it is in the drama only a secondary merit.

The verses in which the character is expressed in tragedies, make the greatest impression upon us. Who is not struck with that scene, where Catiline answers the reproach of being an assassin, made him by Lentulus:

Crois que ces crimes
Sont de ma politique, & non pas de mon cœur :
. . . .
Forcé de se plier aux mœurs de ses complices.

Believe that these crimes
Proceed from policy, and not my heart:
Forced to yield to the manners of my accomplices.

---

* In theatrical works, nothing is more common than to express the sentiment with spirit. Would they paint virtue, they make the hero perform actions which surpass his motives. There are few dramatic poets free from this fault.

It is necessary, he adds, that the chief of a conspiracy should successively assume all characters. If I had only such as Lentulus in my party,

> *Et s'il n'étoit rempli que d'hommes vertueux,*
> *Je n'aurois pas de peine a l'etre encore plus que eux.*

And was it only filled with virtuous men,
I should find no pain in surpassing them.

What a character is included in these two last lines! What a chief of a conspiracy, is a man so much master of himself, as to be according to his choice either virtuous or vicious! What an ambition is that, which, in spite of the usual inflexibility of the passions, can make the proud Catiline stoop to assume all characters! Such an ambition proclaims the destroyer of Rome.

Such verses are always inspired by the passions. He who is not susceptible of them, ought to renounce all attempts to paint them. But it is asked, by what marks shall the public, who are often but little capable of judging of what falls short, or exceeds nature, know the great painters of the sentiments? By the manner, I reply, in which they express them. By means of reflection and memory, a man of genius may form a good judgment of what a lover ought to do or say in a particular situation; he may substitute the expression of the sentiment for the sentiment itself: but he is in the situation of a painter, who in the description of the beauty and form of a woman, might draw her portrait; and might perhaps make a fine picture; but not a true resemblance. Mere genius can never divine the language of the heart.

Nothing can be more insipid to an old man, than the conversation of two lovers. The man insensible, but witty, is the case of the old man; the simple language of the heart appears to him flat; he seeks, in spite of himself, to raise it by some ingenious strokes, which always discover, that he does not feel what he describes.

When Peleus braves the wrath of heaven, when the bursts of thunder proclaim the presence of the God, his rival, and Thetis, struck with fear, in order to calm the suspicions of her jealous lover, says:

> *Va, fuis ; te montrer que je crains,*
> *C'est te dire assez que je t'aime :**

> Go, fly; and let my tender fears impart
> The trembling apprehensions of my heart:

We perceive that the danger in which Peleus found himself was too sudden for Thetis to be in so tranquil a situation, as to give this ingenious turn to her answer. Terrified at the approach of a god, who, with a single word, could reduce the lover to nothing, and pressed with the eager desire of seeing him gone, she had properly only time to cry, Fly, I adore thee.

Every phrase ingeniously turned, is at the same time a proof of wit, and a want of sentiment. The man intirely agitated by a passion which he strongly feels, does not trouble himself about the manner in which he expresses it; the most simple is that which first occurs.

When Cupid, weeping at the knees of Venus, asks her to grant him Psyche, and the goddess laughs at his grief, Cupid says:

> *Je ne me plaindrois pas, si je pouvois mourir.*

> I should not complain, were it possible to die.

When Titus declares to Berenice, that the Destinies have ordained that they should be separated for ever,† Berenice answers:

---

* If in this verse of Ovid :

> *Pignora certa petis, do pignora certa timendo,*

the sun says nearly the same thing to Phaeton; it is because Phaeton is not yet mounted in his chariot, and consequently is not in the moment of danger.

† In the English tragedy of Cleopatra, Octavia rejoins Antony: and it is natural that Antony should find his love revive for her: this Cleopatra fearing, Antony comforts her :—"The difference," says he to her,

Pour jamais !——que ce mot est affreux quand on aime !

For ever !——A word how frightful when we love !

When Palmira says to Seide, that in vain she attempted by her prayers to move her ravisher, Seide replies:

Quel est donc ce mortel insensible a tes larmes ?

What is then this mortal insensible to thy tears?

These verses, and in general, all those expressive of the sentiments are simple, both in the turn and the expression. But wit, void of sentiment, would always lead us far from this simplicity, and even sometimes turn a sentiment into a maxim.

How may we prevent ourselves from being in this respect the dupe of wit? It is the business of wit to observe, to generalize observations, and to draw from them conclusions or maxims. Accustomed to this progress, it is almost impossible for the man of genius, who has never been in love, and would paint that passion, to avoid turning sentiments into maxims. Thus Fontenelle has made one of his shepherds say:

L'on ne doit point aimer, lorsqu'on a le cœur tendre.

When we have a tender heart, we ought not to love.

An idea common to him with Quinalt, who expresses himself very differently, when he makes Atys say:

---

between Octavia and Cleopatra !"—" Oh, my lord," replies she, " a much greater difference between my condition and her's : if Octavia be slighted at present, still Octavia is thy wife ; a never dying hope dwells in her soul, drys her tears, and comforts her in misfortune. To-morrow Hymen may place thee again in her arms. But what is my destiny ! A moment's suspension of love in thy heart, and all my hopes are fled. She can sigh, and fawn on the beloved object, hope to move him, flatter herself with a return of love——I cannot——one single instant of indifference, and there's an end of all to me ; immense space and eternity will for ever separate me from thy love."

Si j'amois un jour, par malheur,
Je connois lien mon cœur,
Il seroit trop sensible.

If ever Cupid wounds my heart,
So well I know its tender part,
My sure misfortune it must prove,
And I shall lose myself for love.

If Quinault has not turned the sentiment of Atys into a maxim, it was because he was sensible that a man warmly affected, does not amuse himself with generalizing his ideas.

It is not in this respect with ambition as with love. Sentiments in ambition may be united with wit and reflection: the cause of this difference is produced by the different objects proposed to these two passions.

A lover desires the favours of her whom he loves. Now these favours are not granted to the sublimity of his wit, but to the excess of his tenderness. The lover in tears and despairing at the feet of his mistress, is the eloquence most proper to move her. This is the intoxication of the lover, by which he prepares and seizes those moments of weakness, which puts the finishing stroke to his happiness. Wit has no share in the triumph: it is then a stranger to the sentiment of love. Besides, the excess of the lover's passion promises to afford a thousand pleasures to the object beloved. It is not so with the ambitious; for his ambition promises no pleasure to his accomplices. If a throne be the object of his desires, and in order to mount it, he must be supported by a powerful party; in vain would he lay before the eyes of his partizans all the excess of his ambition; they would hear him with indifference, did he not assign to each the share he was to have in the government, and prove how much it would be for their interest to raise him to his wishes.

The lover, in short, depends only on the object beloved; a single moment procures his felicity; reflection has no time to enter a heart, the more warmly agitated as it approaches nearer the attainment of its desires. But the ambitious, in order to execute

3 D

his projects, has continual need of the assistance of all sorts of men : and to make a proper use of them, he must know them : besides, his success depends on projects artfully managed, and long prepared.   What abilities are required to concert and pursue them ?   The sentiment of ambition is there necessarily connected with abilities and reflection.

The dramatic poet may then render faithfully the character of the ambitious, by sometimes putting into his mouth those sententious verses, which, that they may strongly strike the spectator, ought to be the result of a lively sentiment and profound reflection.   Such are those verses, where, to justify his audacity, Catiline says to Probus, who accuses him with imprudence :

> *L'imprudence n'est pas dans la temerité,*
> *Elle est dans un projet faux & mal concerté;*
> *Mais, s'il est bien suivi, c'est un trait de prudence*
> *Que d'aller quelquefois jusques a l'insolence.*
> *Et je sais, pour dompter les plus imperieux,*
> *Qu'il faut souvent moins d'art que de mépris pour eux.*

Imprudence consists not in rashness,
But in false and ill-concerted projects;
If 'tis properly tim'd, 'tis a stroke of prudence
Sometimes even to proceed to insolence.
I know to tame the most imperious,
Often requires less art than contempt.

What I have said of ambition shews in what different doses, if I may use the term, wit may be applied to the passions.

I shall conclude with this observation, that our manners, and the form of our government, not permitting us to give ourselves up to strong passions, such as ambition and revenge, our painters commonly employ themselves in representing the sentiments of sensible men, as love, filial and paternal tenderness; which, for this reason, has almost taken intire possession of the French theatre.

CHAP. III.

OF WIT.

WIT is nothing but an assemblage of new ideas and combinations.   Had we made in any one kind all the combinations possible, we could in that species carry no farther either our invention,
or our wit; we might be learned, but we could not be witty.   It
is then evident, that if there were no discoveries to be made, all
would be science, and wit would be impossible : for we should
have ascended up even to the first principles of things.   Being
once arrived at those general and simple principles, the knowledge
of the facts, that had raised us to them, would be no more than
a frivolous science, and all the libraries filled with these facts would
become useless.   We should then possess all the materials of politics and legislation, that is, have extracted from all histories the
small number of principles, which being proper to preserve among
mankind the greatest equality possible, would one day give birth
to the best form of government.   It would be the same with
natural philosophy, and in general with all the sciences.

Then the human understanding, scattered in an infinite number
of works, would be concentered by an able hand in a small volume
of principles, nearly as the spirit of the flowers diffused through
vast plains, are, by the art of chemistry, easily concentered in a
bottle of essence.

The human mind, indeed, is in every science very far from
having arrived at the term here supposed, and I freely confess
that we shall not soon be reduced to the sad necessity of being
only learned; and that, in short, thanks to human ignorance, we
shall long be permitted to have wit.

Wit then always supposes invention.   But what difference, it is
asked, is there between this kind of invention, and that which
obtains for us the title of a genius? In order to discover this, let
us consult the public.   In morality and in politics, they, for

instance, honour with the title of men of genius, both Machiavel, and the author of the Spirit of Laws; and give the title of men of great wit to Rochefaucault and la Bruyere. The only sensible difference between these two kinds of men is, that the first treat of the most important subjects, connect more truths together, and form a greater assemblage of them than the second. Now the union of a greater number of truths, supposes a greater quantity of combinations, and consequently a more uncommon person. Besides the public are fond of seeing all the consequences that can be drawn from a principle: they ought then to reward with a superior title, like that of genius, whoever procures them this advantage, by uniting an infinite number of truths under the same point of view. Such is in philosophy, the sensible difference between genius and wit.

In the arts, people express by the word talent, what in the sciences is meant by the word wit; or it seems that the difference is very small.

Whoever either models himself after the great men who have already preceded him in the same course, does not surpass them, or has not written a certain number of elegant pieces, has not made sufficient efforts of mind, nor given sufficient proofs of invention to merit the title of a genius. Consequently we place in the list of men of talents or abilities Reynard, Vergier, Campistron, and Flechier; while we quote as men of genius Moliere, la Fontaine, Corneille, and Bossuet. I shall even add on this subject that people sometimes refuse to the author, the title they grant to the work. A tale, or a tragedy has great success, and they say of these works that they are full of genius, without daring sometimes to grant the title to the author. In order to obtain it, it is necessary to have, like Fontaine, in an infinite number of small peices, the value of a great work; or, like Corneille and Racine, have composed a certain number of excellent tragedies.

The epic poem is, in poetry, the only work, the extent of which supposes a degree of attention and invention, sufficient to adorn a man with the title of a genius.   4

There remains two observations to be made before I conclude this chapter. The first is, that in the arts, people give the name of wit only to those, who being without a genius, or talent of one kind, transfuse into their works those of another : such are, for instance, the comedies of Fontenelle, which being destitute of the comic genius and talent, sparkled with philosophic beauties. The second is, that invention belongs so necessarily to wit, that we have not hitherto, by any epithets applicable to a great wit, pointed out those who have filled useful employments, that did not require invention. The same custom, which gives the epithet of good to a judge, a receiver of the revenues, * or an able arithmetician, permits us to apply the epithet of sublime to the poet, the legislator, the geometrician, and the orator. Wit then always supposes invention. This invention, more elevated in genius, supposes a more extensive view, and consequently more of that constancy and boldness of character, which strikes out new paths.

Such is the difference between genius and wit, and of the general idea we ought to affix to the latter.

This difference being established, I should observe, that we are forced, by a dearth of language, to take this word in a variety of acceptions, which are only distinguished by the epithets prefixed to the word wit. These epithets being always given by the reader, or the spectator, are constantly relative to the impression made upon him by a certain kind of ideas.

If people have so often, and perhaps without success, treated on this subject, it is from their not having considered wit under the same point of view; and from their having taken the epithets refined, masculine, sparkling, &c. joined to the word wit, for real and distinct qualities; and, in short, from their not having

---

* I do not say that good judges, or good receivers of the revenue, have not wit; but only that they have it not in the quality of judges, or receivers; unless we confound the quality of judge, with that of the legislator.

considered these epithets as expressing the different effects upon us, and the various species of ideas, and different manners of conveying them. To d s erse the darkness spread over this subject, I am going in the following chapters to endeavour to determine, in a clear manner, the different ideas that ought to be affixed to the epithets often united with the word wit.

CHAP. IV.

OF REFINED AND STRONG WIT.*

In natural philosophy, we give the epithet fine, or refined, to what we cannot perceive without some trouble. In morality, that is, in ideas and sentiments, we also give the name of fine and refined, to what cannot be perceived without some efforts of the mind, and great attention.

The Miser of Moliere suspects his valet of having robbed him, and not finding any thing in his pockets, says; "Give me what thou hast stolen, without searching." This speech of Harpagon's is fine, it is strongly characteristic of the miser; but it was difficult to discover it there.

In the opera of Isis, when the nymph Io, to soothe the complaints of Hierax, asks him: "Are your rivals better treated than you?" Hierax replies:

Le mal des mes rivaux n'egale pas ma peine.
La douce illusion d'une esperance vaine
Ne les fait point tomber du faîte du bonheur :
Aucun d'eux, comme moi, n'a perdu votre cœur :
   Comme eux, a votre humeur severe
   Je ne suis point accoutumé.
   Quel tourment de cesser de plaire,
   Lorsqu'on a fait l'essai du plaisir d'etre aimé !

---

* The title of this chapter is, *De l' esprit fin, de l' esprit fort.*

Oh! what to mine, my rivals' pain!
Like me, they have not hop'd in vain;
Like me, they have not lost your love;
They no such wretchedness can prove.
Your scorn they only yet have felt,
While I have hop'd your heart to melt.
Tormenting thought! no hopes of ease,
Tho' once belov'd, I cease to please!

This sentiment is nature; it is also fine; it is concealed in the bottom of the heart; and it required the eyes of a Quinault to perceive it there.

From sensations let us pass to refined ideas. We understand by a *refined idea*, a *refined* consequence drawn from a general idea.* I say a consequence: because an idea no sooner becomes fruitful in truths, than it loses the name of a refined idea, and is called a principle, or general idea. People say, the principles, and not the refined ideas, of Aristotle, Locke, Newton, and Descartes. Not but that in order to ascend like these philosophers, from observations to observations, till we have acquired general ideas, requires great delicacy of mind, that is, much attention. This attention, (let me be permitted to observe by the way), is a microscope which enlarges objects, without deforming them, makes us perceive an infinite number of resemblances and differences, invisible to the eye that is not attentive. Wit of every kind is properly no more than an effect of the attention.

But not to ramble from my subject, I shall observe, that every idea and every sentiment, the discovery of which supposes that an author has great delicacy of thought, and much attention, will not receive the name of refined, if this sentiment, or this idea, be examined upon the stage, or delivered in a simple and natural manner; for the public do not give the name of refined, to what they understand without any effort of the mind. They never

---

* Fontenelle's works furnish a thousand examples of this.

point out by the epithets they unite with the word wit, any thing farther than the impressions made upon them, by the ideas and sentiments presented to them.

This being considered, we understand by a refined idea, an idea which escapes the penetration of most readers: now it escapes them, when the author skips over the intermediate ideas, necessary to make them conceive that which he offers them.

Such is this sentence, which Fontenelle repeats so often:— " People would destroy almost all religions, if those who professed them were obliged to love one another.*" A man of wit easily supplies the intermediate ideas, which connect together the two propositions included in this sentence :† but there are few men of wit.

We also give the name of refined ideas to those that are dressed in obscure, enigmatical, and far-fetched terms. We, in general, affix the epithet fine, less to the species of ideas, than to the manner of expressing them.

In the eulogium on Cardinal Dubois, when speaking of the care

---

* That which may be true of a false religion, is not applicable to ours, which commands us to love our neighbour.

† It is the same with this other phrase, used by M. de Fontenelle : " In writing," says he, "I have always endeavoured to understand my-self." Few men really comprehend the force of this sentence. They do not, like him, perceive all the importance of a precept, the observation of which is so difficult. Without mentioning people of ordinary understandings, among such men as Malebranche, Leibnitz, and the greatest philosophers, how many are there who, for want of making use of this sentence, have not endeavoured to understand themselves, to de-compound their principles, in order to reduce them to simple and clear propositions, which they cannot perform without knowing whether they do, or do not understand themselves? They have support-ed themselves on these vague principles, the obscurity of which must be always suspected by every one who has Fontenelle's words habitually present to his mind. For want of having, if I may use the term, dug into the virgin earth, the immense edifice of their system has sunk in proportion as they have raised it.

he took of the education of the Duke of Orleans, M. de Fontenelle says, " That this prelate had laboured every day to render himself useless ;" it is to the obscurity of the expression, that this sentence owes its refinement.

In the opera of Thetis, when that goddess, to revenge herself on Peleus, whom she believes unfaithful, says :

> *Mon cœur s'est engagé sous l'apparance vaine*
> *Des feux que tu feignis pour moi ;*
> *Mais je veux l'en punir, en m'imposant la peine*
> *D'en aimer un autre que toi ;*

> My heart was obtained by the semblance vain,
>   Of the passion thou feignedst for me ;
> But to punish myself, I will suffer the pain
>   Of loving another like thee ;

it is still certain that this idea, and all the ideas of this kind, owe the name of refined, which is commonly given them, to the enigmatical turn in which they make their appearance, and consequently, to a small effort of mind required to comprehend them. Now an author writes only to be understood : every thing then in the style which renders him obscure, is a fault ; and all refined turns of expression are therefore blameable ; * we should then be

---

* I am very sensible that refined turns have their admirers. What every body easily understands, say they, every body believes they themselves could have said ; clearness of expression is therefore a want of address in the author, who ought always to spread some clouds over his thoughts. Flattered by piercing this cloud, which is impenetrable to common readers, and with perceiving truth through the obscurity of the expression, a thousand men praise with so much the more enthusiasm this manner of writing, as under the pretence of making an eulogium on the author, they make one on their own penetration ; this fact is certain. But I maintain, that we ought to depise such praises, and resist the desire of deserving them. Is a thought finely expressed ? there are at first few men who understand it ; but at length it is generally understood. Now as soon as the enigma of the expression is dis-

more attentive to give a simple and natural turn to an idea, in proportion† as that idea is more refined, and may more easily escape the notice of the reader.

Let us now affix our attention on the kind of wit expressed by the epithet strong.

A strong idea, is one that is interesting and proper to make a lively impression. This impression may either be produced by the idea itself, or the manner in which it is expressed. *

A very common idea, delivered in a striking expression, or image, may make a very strong impression upon us. The abbot Cartaut, comparing Virgil to Lucan says; " Virgil is only a priest raised in the midst of the grimaces of the temple; the sniveling, hypocritical, and devout character of his hero, dishonours the poet; his enthusiasm seems to be kindled by the flame of the lamps suspended before the altars; while the bold enthusiasm of Lucan is set on fire by the lightning." What strikes us forcibly, is what is understood by the epithet strong. Now the great and strong have this in common, that they make a lively impression upon us, and hence they are often confounded.

To fix clearly the different ideas that ought to be formed of grandeur and strength, I shall separately consider the meaning of these terms, first, in ideas; secondly, in images; and, thirdly, in sentiments.

A grand idea is one that is generally interesting: but the ideas of this kind are not always those that affect us in the most lively manner. The axioms of the Portico, or the Lyceum, though interesing to all mankind in general, and consequently to the Athe-

---

covered, this thought is by men of sense reduced to its intrinsic value, and placed much below it by men of moderate abilities : ashamed of their want of penetration, they always look upon it with an unjust contempt, to revenge the affront done to their sagacity, by the fineness of the turn.

* In Persia they represent the unequal powers of different poets, by the epithets painters and sculptors.; and therefore say, a poet-painter, a poet-sculptor.

nians; must not, however, have made so great an impression upon them as the speech of Demosthenes, when that orator reproached them for their cowardice. " You ask one another, said he, is Philip dead? Well, of what importance is it to you, Athenians, whether he be dead or living? When heaven shall have delivered you, you yourselves will soon be another Philip." If the Athenians were more struck at the speech of their orator, than at the discoveries of their philosophers, it was because Demosthenes presented them with ideas more suitable to their present situation, and consequently those, in which they were more immediately concerned.

Now the men, who are in general only sensible of the present moment, will be always affected in a more lively manner by this kind of ideas, than with those, which on account of their being grand and general, belong less immediately to the situation in which they are placed.

Thus those pieces of eloquence proper to fill the soul with emotion, and those orations so strong, because they discuss the actual interest of a state, are not, and cannot be, of such extensive and durable use, as the discoveries of a philosopher, which are equally suited to all times and places.

In relation to ideas, the only difference between the great and the strong is, that the one is more generally, and the other more warmly interesting.*

Does the enquiry relate to those beautiful images, those descriptions, or those pictures, intended to strike the imagination? The strong and the great have this in common, that they present to us grand objects.

• Tamerlane and Cartouche were two robbers, one of whom ravaged the world with four hundred thousand men, and the other

---

* People sometimes say of a method of reasoning, that it is strong; but this is when it relates to something in which they interest themselves. Thus we do not give this name to geometrical demonstrations, which of all reasonings are doubtless the strongest.

with four hundred; the first attracts our respect, and the last our contempt. *

What I say of morals, I apply to physics. Every thing which in its own nature is little, or becomes such on being compared with those that are great, makes scarcely any impression upon us.

Let Alexander be painted in the most heroic attitude at the moment when he rushes on the enemy, if the imagination places at the side of the hero one of those sons of war,† which growing every year a cubit in circumference, and three or four in height, might heap Ossa upon Pelion; Alexander is no more than a pretty puppet, and his fury becomes ridiculous.

But though the strong is always grand, the grand is not always strong. A decoration, either of the temple of the Destinies, or a heavenly festival, may be grand, and even sublime; but it will affect us less strongly than a description of Tartarus. The picture of the Glory of the Saints does not astonish the imagination so much as the Last Judgment of Michael Angelo.

The strong is then produced, by the grand united to the terrible. Now if all men are more sensible of pain than of pleasure; if violent pain silences every agreeable sensation, while a lively pleasure cannot stifle within us the sensation of violent pain, the strong must make a more warm impression, and we must be more struck with the picture of Hell, than this one of Olympus.

In regard to pleasure, imagination excited by the desire of the greatest happiness is always inventive, and some charms in Olympus are always wanting.

Does the subject require the terrible? Imagination has not the same interest in the invention of scenes of horror, this is less difficult; Hell is always sufficiently terrible.

------

* Every thing becomes ridiculous without strength, and every thing is ennobled with it. What a difference is there between the roguery of a smuggler, and that of Charles V.?

† In the eyes of this same giant, that Cæsar who said of himself, *Veni, vidi, vici,* and whose conquests were so rapid, would appear to crawl upon the earth, with the slowness of a star fish, or a snail.

Such, in decorations and poetical descriptions, is the difference between the great, and the strong. Let us now examine, whether in dramatic pictures, and the painting of the passions, we shall not find the same difference between these two kinds of wit.

In tragedy we give the name of strong to every passion, to every sentiment that affects us forcibly; that is, to all those of which the spectator may be the sport, or the victim.

No body is sheltered from the stroke of revenge and jealousy. The scene of Atreus, who presents his brother Thyestes with a cup filled with the blood of his son; the fury of Rhadamistus, who, to deliver the charms of Zenobia from the lascivious looks of the conqueror, drags her bleeding into the Araxes, affords two pictures, which, in the opinion of every one, are more terrible than that of an ambitious man seated on the throne of his master.

In this last picture, a private person sees no danger that can happen to himself. None of the spectators are monarchs: the misfortunes frequently occasioned by revolutions are not so imminent as to stike terror. The spectator must then consider such a sight with pleasure.* This spectacle charms some by letting them see, in the most elevated ranks, the instability of happiness which creates a certain equality among all conditions, and comforts the lower class for the inferiority of their state. It pleases the others by flattering their inconstancy: an inconstancy, which being founded on the desire of bettering their condition, makes the hope of a more happy state glitter in their eyes, by the overthrow of empires, and shews them a possibility, as a possibility at hand. It, in short, delights most men by the grandeur of the picture it represents, and by their being forced to interest themselves

---

* To this cause, we ought, in part, to refer the admiration conceived for those scourges of the earth ; for those warriors whose valour overturns empires, and changes the face of the world. We read their history with pleasure ; but we rejoice that we were not born in their time. It is with these conquerors as with those black clouds streaked with lightning, the thunder of which darting from them, roars and rends the trees and rocks. Seen near, the sight freezes us with terror ; seen at a distance it fills us with admiration.

in the fate of the hero virtuous and worthy of esteem, placed by the poet on the stage. The desire of happiness which always makes us consider esteem as the means of being more happy, creates in us a kind of identity with such a personage ; this identity is the more perfect, and we interest ourselves so much the more warmly in the happiness, or unhappiness, of a great man, in proportion as that great man appears to us more worthy of esteem ; that is, as his ideas and sentiments are more analogous to our own. Every one acknowledges in a hero, the sentiment with which he himself is affected. This pleasure is the greater, when the hero plays the greatest part ; when he, like Hannibal, Sylla, Sertorius, and Cæsar, triumphs over a people, on whose destiny that of the earth depends.

Objects always strike us in proportion to their grandeur. If we represent on the stage the conspiracy of the Genoese, and that of Rome ; if we trace with a hand equally bold, the characters of the count Fieschi and Catiline ; if we give them the same force, the same courage, the same spirit, and the same elevation : I say, that the bold Catiline will gain almost the whole of our admiration ; the grandeur of his enterprize will be reflected on his character, and render him great in our eyes, and our illusion will make us even desire his happiness.

In fact, we shall always believe ourselves the more happy, as we shall be more powerful, as we shall reign over a great number of people, as more men will have an interest in preventing and satisfying our desires, and as by being the only persons free upon earth, we shall be surrounded by a universe of slaves.

These are the principal causes of the pleasures we receive from the painting of ambition, of that passion which obtains the name of great only from the great changes it produces on the earth.

Though love has sometimes occasioned the like ; though it decided the battle of Actium in favour of Octavius ; though, in an age nearer to our own, it has opened the ports of Spain to the Moors ; and though it has successively overturned and raised an infinite number of thrones ; these great revolutions are not, however, so much the necessary effects of love as they are of ambition.

Thus the desire of grandeur, and the love of our country, which last may be considered as a more virtuous ambition, have always received the name of great, preferable to all the other passions: a name, which being conferred on the heroes inspired by these passions, has been at length given to Corneille, and the celebrated poets, who have painted them. Whence I observe that the passion of love is not less difficult to paint than that of ambition. To manage the character of Phædra with as much address as Racine has done, certainly requires as many ideas and combinations, and as much wit, as to trace in Rodogune the character of Cleopatra. The name of great, then, depends less on the ability of the painter, than on the choice of his subject.

It follows from what I have said, that if men are more sensible of pain than of pleasure, the objects of fear and terror must, with respect to ideas, pictures, and passions, affect them more strongly than objects formed for the general astonishment and admiration. The great is then, in every kind, that which universally strikes ; and the strong, that which makes a less general, but more lively impression.

The discovery of the compass, is, without dispute, of more general use to mankind, than the discovery of a conspiracy ; but this last is infinitely more important, with respect to the nation where the conspiracy is formed.

The idea of strength being once determined, I shall observe, that men being only able to communicate their ideas by words, if the strength of the expression is not answerable to that of the thought, however strong that thought may be, it will always appear weak, at least to those indued with a vigour of mind sufficient to supply the faintness of an expression.

Now to give strength to a thought, it is necessary, first, that it should be expressed in a clear and precise manner: every idea clothed in an ambiguous expression, is an object perceived through a fog; the impression is not distinct enough to be strong. Secondly, It is necessary that this thought should, if possible, be represented by an image, and that the image be exactly suited to the thought. 4

In fact, if all our ideas are presented by our sensations, we ought to convey our ideas to other men by the senses; and as I have said in the chapter on Imagination, to speak to the eyes, in order to be understood by the mind.

To strike us strongly, it is not even enough that an image be just and exactly adapted to an idea; it must be great without being gigantic: *such is the image employed by the immortal author of the Spirit of Laws, when he compares tyrants to the savages, who, with an ax in their hand cut down the tree, when they would gather the fruit.

It is also necessary, that this grand image, should be new, or at least presented under a new aspect. It is the surprise excited by its novelty, which fixing our whole attention on an idea, gives time to make a stronger impression upon us.

We, in short, attain the last degree of perfection in this kind when the image under which we present an idea is in motion. The moving picture is always to be preferred to a picture of an object at rest; it excites in us more sensations, and consequently makes a more lively impression. We are less struck with the the calm air, than with a tempest.

It is then to the imagination, than an author owes, in part, the strength of his expression; by its assistance, he transmits into the soul of his readers, all the fire of his thoughts. If the English in this respect, attribute to themselves a great superiority over us, they owe this advantage less to the peculiar strength of their language, than to the form of their government. People always use strength of expression in a free state; where men conceive the most noble thoughts, and may express them with as much boldness as they conceive them. This is not the case in monarchies: in these countries, the interest of certain bodies, that of some men in power, and more frequently still, false and little

* The excessive greatness of an image, sometimes renders it ridiculous. When the psalmist says, "that the mountains skipped like rams," this grand image makes but a small impression upon us, because there are few men whose imaginations are sufficiently strong, to form a clear and lively picture of mountains skipping about like sheep.

politics, oppose these flights of genius. Whoever in these governments conceives grand ideas, is often forced to conceal them, or at least to enervate their strength by ambiguous, enigmatical, and weak, expressions. Thus Lord Chesterfield, in a letter addressed to the Abbé de Gausco, says, speaking of the author of the Spirit of Laws, "It is a pity that the president Montesquieu, doubtless restrained by the fear of the ministry, has not had the courage to speak out. We perceive upon the whole, what he thinks on certain subjects; but he does not express himself with sufficient clearness and strength: we should have better known what he thought, if he had composed it at London, and had been born in England."

This want of strength in expression does not however proceed from a want of genius in the nation. Every thing that appears trifling to those in place, is with disdain abandoned to genius: I may cite a thousand proofs of this truth. What force of expression is there in some of Bossuet's orations, and in some of the scenes of Mahomet! a tragedy which, notwithstanding the criticisms made upon it, is perhaps one of the finest works of the celebrated M. de Voltaire.

I shall conclude with a passage from the abbé Cartout, full of that strength of expression, of which it has been thought that our language is not capable. He there discovers the causes of the superstition of the Egyptians.

"How could this people avoid being highly superstitious? Egypt, says he, was the country of enchantment; imagination was there perpetually struck by the grand machines of the marvelous, and nothing was to be seen but knights of terror and admiration. The prince was an object of astonishment and fear, like the thunder which gathers in the depths of the clouds, and seems there to roll with greater grandeur and majesty: it was from the most retired part of his labyrinths and his palace, that the monarch dictated his will. The kings never shewed themselves without the terrifying and formidable apparatus of a power sprung from a divine original. The death of the kings was an apotheosis: the earth sank under the weight of their mausoleums. By these powerful gods, Egypt was covered with superb obelisks, filled with wonderful inscriptions, and with enormous pyramids, whose summits were lost in the air: by these beneficent gods those lakes were formed which secured Egypt against the inundations of nature.

" More formidable than the throne and its monarchs, the temples and their pontiffs still farther imposed on the imagination of the Egyptians. In one of these temples was the colossus of Serapis. No mortal dared to approach it. To the duration of this colossus was connected that of the world : whoever had broken this talisman, would have replunged the earth into its first chaos. No bounds were set to credulity ; every thing in Egypt was enigma, wonder, and misery. All the temples gave oracles ; all the caverns belched forth horrible howlings ; every where were seen trembling tripods, the Pythia in a rage, victims, priests, and magicians, who, invested with the power of the gods, were entrusted with their vengeance.

" The philosophers, armed against superstition, rose up against it : but, soon engaged in the labyrinth of too abstracted metaphysics, disputes divided their opinions ; interest and fanaticism took advantage of it, and produced the chaos of their different systems ; from thence sprang the pompous mysteries of Isis, Osiris, and Horus. Then, covered with the mysterious and sublime darkness of theology and religion, the imposture was undiscovered. If some Egyptians perceived it, by the glimmering uncertain light of doubt, revenge, always suspended over the head of the indiscreet, shut their eyes to the light, and their mouths to the truth. Even the kings, who, in order to shelter themselves from all insult, had at first in concert with the priests, raised up about the throne terror, superstition, and the phantoms in their train ; the kings, I say, were themselves terrified at them, and soon entrusted the temples with the sacred depositum of the young princes : fatal epocha of the tyranny of the Egyptian priests! No obstacle could then oppose their power. Their sovereigns were encircled from their infancy with the bandage of opinion ; free and independent as they were, while they saw nothing in these priests but cheats and mercenary enthusiasts, they became their slaves and victims. The people, the imitators of their kings, followed their example, and all Egypt fell prostrate at the feet of the pontiff and the altar of superstition."

This magnificent picture, by the abbé Cartout, proves, I think, that the weakness of expression with which we are reproached, and which on certain occasions is visible in our writings; cannot be attributed to a want of natural genius.

CHAP. V.

OF A LUMINOUS, EXTENSIVE, AND PENETRATING, WIT; AND OF TASTE.

IF we believe certain people, genius is a kind of instinct, that may, without the knowledge of him who is possessed of it, render him capable of producing the greatest things. They place this instinct much below the light of wit, which they take for universal intelligence. This opinion, supported by some men remarkable for wit, is not however yet adopted by the public.

In order to arrive at some conclusions on this subject, it is necessary to attach clear ideas to the term, luminous wit.

In physics light is a body which renders objects visible. The light of wit is then that which renders our ideas visible to common readers. It consists in disposing all the ideas that concur to prove a truth in such a manner, that we may easily comprehend them. The title of luminous wit is then granted by the gratitude of the public to him who enlightens them.

Before M. de Fontenelle, most of the learned, after having scaled the sharp summit of the sciences, found themselves there alone, and deprived of all communication with other men. They had not smoothed the road of the sciences, nor marked out a path for ignorance to walk in. Fontenelle, whom I do not consider here in a light which places him in the rank of men of genius, was, if I may use the term, the first who established a bridge of communication between learning and ignorance. He perceived that the ignorant themselves might receive the seeds of all truths: but that, for this purpose, address ought to be used to prepare their minds for it; that a new idea, to use his own expression, is a wedge which we cannot drive in at the broad end, he therefore made use of all his endeavours to present his ideas with the greatest clearness; he succeeded in this: the turf of weak minds was suddenly kindled, and the gratitude of the public bestowed on him the title of a luminous wit.

What must be done to produce such a prodigy? Simply to observe the progress of ordinary minds: to know that every thing leads and contributes towards it; that, in relation to ideas, ignorance is always constrained to yield to the immense power of the insensible progress of light; which I compare to those slender roots, which, insinuating themselves into the crannies of the rocks, there grow, and cause them to split. It is also necessary to perceive, that nature is only a long chain, and that, by the assistance of the intermediate ideas, we may raise minds of moderate abilities, nearer and nearer, till they reach the highest ideas.*

The light of wit is therefore only the talent of bringing thoughts nearer to each other, of uniting the ideas, already known, with those that are less known, and of giving these ideas in clear and determinate expressions.

This talent is in philosophy what versification is in poetry. All the art of the versifier consists in giving the thoughts of

---

* There is nothing that men may not understand. However complicated a proposition may be, it is possible, by the assistance of analysis, to reduce it to a number of simple propositions, and these propositions will become so evident, that a man will be unable to deny them, without contradicting himself, and without saying, that a thing may and may not be at the same time. Every truth may be brought to this conclusion; and, when this is done, no eyes will be shut against the light. But what time and observation are necessary to carry the analysis to this point, and to reduce for certain the truths to such simple propositions! This is the labour of all ages, and of all men of learning, who are constantly employed in the investigation of truth, and uniting several ideas, while the public wait for the success of the discoveries, in order to seize the truths they propose.

the poets with force and harmony; all the art of a luminous wit is in expressing, with great clearness, the ideas of the philosophers.

These two talents neither suppose nor exclude genius nor invention. If Descartes, Locke, Hobbes, Bacon, have this light of wit united to genius and invention, all men are not so happy. The light of wit is sometimes only the interpreter of the philosophical genius, and the organ by which it communicates, to common minds, ideas too much above their understanding.

If people have sometimes confounded luminous wit with genius, it proceeds from their both enlightening mankind, and their not having fully perceived that genius was the centre and focus to which this kind of wit attracts the luminous ideas which are reflected on the multitude.

In the sciences, genius, like a bold navigator, searches for and discovers unknown regions. It is the business of the luminous wits, to draw slowly after their steps the heavy mass of common minds.

In the arts, genius, more free than the light of wit, may be compared to a proud courser, that, with a rapid foot, pushes into the thickest part of the forest, and bounds through the thickets and over the quagmires. Incessantly employed in observing him, and wanting the activity to follow him in his course, the luminous wit waits at some opening, there observes him, and marks some of the steps he has imprinted on the ground; but can only fix on a small number.

In fact, if in the arts, such as eloquence and poetry, a luminous wit might give all the fine rules, from the observation of which must result perfect poems or discourses, eloquence and poetry would no longer be arts of genius; we should become great poets, and great orators, as we become good arithmeticians. Genius alone can seize all those fine rules which secure its success. The inability of the light of wit, to discover every thing, is the cause of its little success in the very art in which it has often given excellent precepts. It happily accomplishes some of the conditions necessary for making a good work, but it omits the principal.

M. de Fontenelle, whom I quote, in order to illustrate this

idea by an example, has certainly given excellent precepts. That great man, however, not having, in his art of poetry, treated either of versification or of moving the passions, it is probable, that, by observing the fine rules that he has prescribed, he would have composed none but dull tragedies.

It follows from the difference established between genius and the light of wit, that the human race is not obliged to the latter for any discoveries, and that luminous wit does not extend to the bounds of our ideas.

This kind of wit is then only a talent, a method of conveying, in a clear manner, our ideas to others. Upon which, I shall observe, that all men, who would concentrate themselves in one art, and express with clearness only the principles of that art; as for instance, music or painting, would not be reckoned among the luminous wits.

In order to obtain this title, it was necessary, either to diffuse light upon something extremely interesting, or upon a number of different subjects. What is called light, always supposes extensive knowledge. This kind of wit ought, for this reason, to impose even on men of learning, and in conversation have the advantage over genius.

Let one of these luminous wits be placed in an assembly of men, celebrated for their skill in the different arts and sciences; if he speak of painting to a poet, of philosophy to a painter, or of sculpture to a philosopher, he will express his principles with more precision, and exhibit his ideas with greater clearness, than these illustrious men would express them to each other, and thence he would obtain their esteem. But let this man go, and talk of painting to a painter, of poetry to a poet, or of philosophy to a philosopher, and he would appear no more than a person of clear but limited understanding, and well versed in common place. There is only one case in which luminous and extensive wits may be reckoned among the men of genius: that is, when they are well skilled in some sciences, and, perceiving the relations that subsist between them, they reduce them to their common and more general principles.

What I have said establishes a sensible difference between

penetrating, luminous, and extensive, wits: these last cast a rapid view over an infinite number of objects; the others, on the contrary, attach themselves to few objects; but they dive to the bottom of them; they survey in depth the space which the extensive wits run over in surface. The idea I affix to the word penetrating agrees with its etymology. The property of this kind of wit is to pierce into a subject; but, if it has dived to a particular depth, it then loses the name of penetrating, and assumes that of profound.

" Profound wit, or the genius of the sciences, is," says Mr. Formey, " the art of reducing ideas, already distinct, to other ideas still more simple and clear, till we have the last solution possible. Whoever could know," adds Mr. Formey, " to what a point every man has carried this analysis, would have the gradual scale of the depth of all minds."

It follows from this idea, that the shortness of life will not permit a man to be profoundly skilled in many sciences; that wit is less extensive, in proportion as it is more penetrating and profound, and that there is no such thing as a universal wit.

In regard to penetrating wit, I observe, that the public grants this title only to the illustrious men, who employ themselves in the sciences in which they are more or less initiated; such are morality, politics, metaphysics, &c. With respect to painting or geometry, a person is considered as penetrating only by those who are proficients in that art or science. The public, too ignorant to set a value on these different kinds of penetration with respect to the mind of a particular person, judge of his works, and never apply to his abilities the epithet of penetrating; they wait before they praise him, till, by the solution of some difficult problems, or the drawing of some fine picture, a man has deserved the title of a great geometrician or a great painter.

I shall add but one word to what I have said, which is, that sagacity and penetration partake of the same nature. A person appears endued with great sagacity, when, having long meditated, and had habitually present to his mind, the subjects most commonly treated of in conversation, he searches into them with vivacity. The only difference between penetration and sagacity of mind is, that this last supposes more quickness of conception, and that the person has more lately studied the questions that afford proofs of his sagacity. A person has so much the more sagacity in relation to any subject, as he has more profoundly and more lately been employed about it.

Let us now pass to taste,—the last subject I propose to examine in this chapter.

Taste, taken in its most extensive signification, is, in relation to works, the knowledge of what merits the esteem of mankind. Among the arts and sciences there are some with regard to which the public adopt the opinion of men of skill, and never of themselves pronounce any judgment; such are geometry, mechanics, some parts of natural philosophy, and painting. In these arts and sciences, the only men of taste are the persons versed in them; and taste is in these various kinds only the knowledge of the truly beautiful.

This is not the case with respect to those works of which the public are, or believe themselves to be, judges, as poems, romances, tragedies, moral discourses, politics, &c. In these various kinds we ought not to understand by the word taste the exact knowledge of that beauty proper to strike people of all ages and countries; but the more particular knowledge of what pleases the public in a certain nation. There are two methods of arriving at this knowledge, and consequently two different kinds of taste. One which I shall call habitual taste: such is that of most players, who, by the daily study of the ideas and sentiments proper to please the public, are rendered very good judges of theatrical works, and especially of those which resemble the pieces already published. The other is a rational taste, founded on a profound knowledge of human nature, and the spirit of the age. The men endued with this last kind of taste are particularly qualified to judge of original works. He who has only an habitual taste must be void of taste whenever he is destitute of objects of comparison. But this rational taste, which is doubtless superior to that I call habitual, is only acquired, as I have already said, by long study both of the public taste, and of the art or science in which a person pretends to the title of a man of taste. I may then, by applying to taste, what I have said of wit, conclude that there is no such thing as universal taste.

The only observation that remains on the subject of taste is, that illustrious men are not always the best judges of it, in that very kind where they have had most success. What, it may be asked, is the cause of this literary phænomenon? To this I reply, it is with great writers as with great painters, each has his manner. M. de Crebillion, for instance, sometimes expresses his ideas with a force, a heat, an energy, peculiar to himself. M. de Fontenelle presents them with an order, a clearness, and a turn, remarkable of his own; M. de Voltaire expresses them with an imagination, grandeur, and continued elegance. Now each of these illustrious men, necessitated by his taste to consider his own manner as the best, must, consequently, set a greater value on the man of moderate abilities, who seizes it, than on the man of genius, who has a taste of his own. Hence arrives the different judgments often formed on the same work by the celebrated writers and the public, who, having no esteem for imitators, would have an author be himself, and not another.

Thus the man of wit, who has perfected his taste in one kind without having composed himself or adopted another's manner, has commonly a surer taste than the greatest writers. No interest puts him under an illusion, and hinders his placing himself in the same point of view in which the public considers and forms a judgment of a work.

CHAP. VI.

OF A GENIUS FOR WRITING WITH ELEGANCE.

WHAT pleases in all ages and in all countries is called beautiful. But to form a more exact and distinct idea, perhaps it may be necessary to examine what it is in each art, and even in each part of an art, that constitutes beauty. From this examination we may easily deduce the idea of a beauty common to all the arts and sciences, from whence we may at length form an abstract and general idea of beauty.

If the public unite the epithet of beauty to the productions of the mind, these are called works of elegance; an elegance which consists in beauty. We must not, however, affix to this epithet the idea of that true beauty of which we have not yet given a clear definition. It is to works of entertainment that we particularly give the name of elegant. This kind of genius is very different from the instructive. Instruction is less arbitrary: for important discoveries in chemistry, natural philosophy, and geometry, equally useful to all nations, are equally esteemed. This is not the case with what is produced by a fine genius; the esteem, conceived for a work of this kind, ought to be differently modified among different nations, according to the difference of their manners and form of government, and of the progress which the arts and sciences have made. Every nation then attaches different ideas to the word elegant. But, as there are none where they do not compose poems, romances, theatrical pieces, panegyrics, histories*, and those works, in short, which employ the reader without fatiguing him, so there is no nation where, at least under another name, they do not know what we here mean by the capacity for elegant writing.

Whoever, in these several kinds, do not attain to the title of a génius, is comprehended in the class of elegant writers, when he joins grace and elegance to a happy choice of ideas. Despreaux said, speaking of the elegant Racine, "That it was only from my taste for the elegance of this author, that I learnt with difficulty to make verses." I certainly do not adopt Despreaux's judgment on Racine; but I think I may conclude from it, that it is principally in the clearness, the colouring, the expression, and in the art of representing our ideas, that consists

---

* I do not speak of those histories written with a view of instruction, such as the Annals of Tacitus, which, being filled with profound ideas on morality and politics, and not being to be read without some efforts of attention, cannot, for this reason, be so generally relished and felt.

that elegance of writing to which is given the name of beauty, only because it pleases, will really please, and most generally ought to do so.

In fact, if, as M. de Vaugelas remarks, there are more judges of words than of ideas, and if men are in general less sensible of the justness of reasoning than of the beauty of an expression *, it is to the art of expressing ourselves well that we ought to affix the title of elegant writing.

After having stated this idea, it will, perhaps, be concluded that a capacity of writing with elegance is no more than the art of writing elegantly upon nothing, and without a meaning. My answer to this conclusion is, that a work, void of sense, would be only a continued flow of harmonious sounds, that would obtain no esteem †; and, therefore, the public adorns with the title of elegant writers only those whose works are full of grand, sublime, or interesting, ideas. There is no idea which may be excluded from polite writing, if we except those, which, supposing too much preliminary study, are not thought suitable to the polite.

I do not pretend, in this answer, to cast any blemish on the glory of philosophers. Philosophic studies, beyond all contradiction, suppose stricter researches, closer reflections, more profound ideas, and even a particular kind of life. In the world we learn to express our ideas well; but it is in retirement that we acquire them. We there make an infinite number of observations on things, and in the world we only make them on the manner of expressing them. Philosophers ought then,

---

* I shall relate on this subject a saying of Malherbe. He was on his death-bed, and his confessor, to inspire him with the greater fervour and resignation, described to him the joys of heaven, but made use of low and mean expressions. The description being ended,— " Well," said he to the sick man, " do not you feel a great desire to enjoy these celestial pleasures?" " O, sir," replied Malherbe, " talk to me no more about them, your bad style gives me a disgust to them."

† A person would not now be quoted as a man of wit for writing a madrigal or a sonnet.

on account of the depth of their ideas, to be preferred to polite writers; but from these last are required so many graces,
and such elegance, that the necessary conditions to merit the
title of philosopher, or an elegant writer, are, perhaps, equally
difficult to be fulfilled. It appears, at least, that, in these two
kinds, illustrious men are equally rare. Indeed, in order to be
able to instruct and to please at the same time, what knowledge
does it require in language, and in the spirit of the age! What
taste, always to present ideas under an agreeable aspect! What
study, to dispose them in such a manner as to make the most
lively impression on the mind of the readers! What observations, to distinguish the particulars that ought to be treated at
large, from those, which, in order to be felt, have only need
of being presented! And what art constantly to unite variety
to order and clearness; and, as M. de Fontenelle says, to excite the curiosity of the mind to manage its laziness, and to prevent its inconstancy!

It is here the difficulty of succeeding, that is, doubtless, in
part, the cause of the little value polite writers commonly set
on works of mere reasoning. As the man of a contracted mind
perceives in philosophy nothing but a heap of puerile and
mysterious enigmas, and hates in philosophers the trouble
it would give him to understand them, so the polite genius
treats them scarcely with greater favour: he also hates, in their
works, the dryness and stiffness of instruction. Too much employed about writing well, and less solicitous about sense* than
about the elegance of the phrase, he acknowledges only those
to be good thoughts, where the ideas are happily expressed.—
The least obscurity shocks him. He is ignorant that a profound
idea, however clearly it is expressed, will be always unintelligible to common readers, when they cannot reduce it to such

---

* Nothing can be more disagreeable to a person who does not express himself happily, than to be judged by the elegant writers, or
even the half-wits. They make no account of his ideas, and only
judge of his words. How superior soever he may really be to those
who treat him as weak, he will never reform their judgment, and, in
their opinion, he will always pass for a fool.

propositions as are extremely simple; and that it is with these profound ideas as with the pure and limpid waters, which by their depth always lose their transparency.

Besides, among the elegant writers, there are some who, being the secret enemies of philosophy, countenance the opinion of men of limited understandings. The dupes of a little ridi_culous vanity, they, in this respect, adopt popular errors; and without esteem for the justness, profoundness, and novelty of the thoughts, they seem to forget that the art of elegant expression necessarily supposes, that a person should have something to say; and that, in short, an elegant writer may be compared to a jeweller, whose dexterity becomes useless if he has no diamonds to set.

The learned and the philosophers, on the contrary, give themselves up entirely to researches into facts or ideas, and are often ignorant of the beauties and the difficulties of the art of writing. They, consequently, set little value on an elegant writer; and their unjust contempt is principally founded on a great insensibility with respect to the species of ideas that enter into the composition of elegant performances. They are almost all, in some respects, like that geometrician, before whom a great eulogium was made on the tragedy of Iphigenia; this eulogium excited his curiosity; he desired the person to lend him the tragedy; but, having read some scenes, he returned it, saying, "For my part, I cannot think what you find so beautiful in this work; it proves nothing."

The learned Abbé de Longuerue was nearly in the same case with this geometrician: poetry had no charms for him; he equally despised the grandeur of Corneille and the elegance of Racine: he had, he said, banished all the poets from his library *.

In order to be equally sensible of the merit both of ideas and

---

* "There are," says the same Abbé de Longuerue, "two works on Homer, worth more than Homer himself; the first is, Antiquitates Homericæ; the other, Homeri Gnomologia, per Duportum. Whoever has read these two books, has read all that is good in Homer, without suffering the fatigue of his sleepy tales."

expressions, we ought, like Plato, Montaigne, Bacon, Montesquieu, and some of our philosophers, whose modesty prevents my naming them, to unite the art of writing with the art of thinking well; an uncommon union, never to be found but in men of great genius.

After having pointed out the causes of the contempt which some of the learned and some of the polite writers respectively entertain for each other; I ought to shew the causes of the contempt into which polite writers fall, and must daily do so, rather than those of any other kind.

The taste of our age for philosophy has filled it with writers of dissertations, who, though dull, heavy, and tiresome, are, however, full of admiration for the profoundness of their judgments. Among these writers there are some who express themselves very ill: they suspect it; they know that every one is a judge of elegance and clearness of expression, and that, in this respect, it is impossible to impose upon the public; they are then forced, from a regard to their own vanity, to renounce the title of elegant writers, in order to assume that of good writers. They have heard that a good writer sometimes expresses himself in an obscure manner; they are sensible, therefore, that, by limiting their pretensions to the title of good writers, they may always hide the absurdity of their reasonings under the obscurity of their expressions, and that this alone is a certain way of preventing their being convicted of folly: thus they seize it with avidity, concealing as much as possible from themselves, that the want of elegance is the only thing that can give them a claim to being good writers, and that writing ill is no proof that they think well.

The judgment of such men, rich and powerful as they often are *, would yet make no impression on the public, if they

---

* In general, those who without success have cultivated the arts and sciences, if they are raised to the highest posts in the state, become the most cruel enemies of the men of letters. To decry them, they prompt the fools to do so; they would annihilate that kind of genius in which they have not succeeded. We may say, that in letters, as well as in religion, apostates are the greatest persecutors.

were not supported by the authority of certain philosophers, who being, like the polite writers, jealous of an exclusive esteem, do not perceive that every different kind of writing has its particular admirers ; that there are every where found more laurels than there are 'heads to be crowned with them : that every nation has, at its disposal, funds of esteem sufficient to satisfy all the pretensions of illustrious men ; and that, in short, by inspiring a disgust against polite writing, they arm against all the great writers the contempt of persons of mean capacities, who, having an interest in despising wit, comprehend equally under the name of a fine writer, which is scarcely more known to them, both the learned and the philosopher, and, in general, all the thinking part of mankind.

CHAP. VII.

OF THE SPIRIT OF THE AGE.

This kind of spirit does not at all contribute to the advancement of the arts and sciences, and would have no place in this work, if it did not fill a very great one in the heads of an infinite number of men.

Wherever the people are held in no consideration, what is called the spirit of the age is only the spirit of the persons who give the lead, that is, the men of distinction and the courtiers.

The men of distinction and the polite writers both express themselves with elegance and purity, and both are commonly more solicitous about expressing themselves well, than about thinking justly : however, they neither do, nor ought to discourse, on the same subjects *, because they have different objects in view. The elegant writer, greedy of the public esteem, ought either to exhibit grand pictures, or to present such ideas as are of importance to mankind in general, or at least to his

---

* A thousand agreeable strokes in conversation would be insipid to the reader. " The reader," says Boileau, " would make a profit of his amusement."

own nation. A person of distinction, satisfied, on the contrary, with the admiration of those that give the lead, employs
himself only in presenting agreeable ideas to what is called
good company.

I have said in the second discourse, that we can talk in company only of things or persons; that good company are commonly
superficial; that they employ themselves scarcely about any
thing but persons; that praise is burdensome to whoever is not
the subject of it, and that it makes the auditors yawn. Thus
those, who compose the polite circles, give a malignant inter-
pretation to the actions of men, seize their weak side, turn into
a jest things the most serious, laugh at every thing, and throw
a ridicule upon all ideas contrary to those agreeable to the company. The spirit of conversation is then reduced to the talent
of agreeable defamation, especially in this age, in which every
body pretends to wit, and believes he has a great deal; in
which no one can mention the superiority of another, without
wounding the vanity of every one else; in which they distinguish the men of merit, from the man of mean abilities, only
by the manner in which they defame him; in which they are
in a manner agreed to divide the nation into two classes, the
one that of brutes, who a: the most numerous, the other that
of fools, and comprehend in this last class all those whom
they cannot help acknowledging to be possessed of abilities.

Besides, defamation is now the only resource they have left
for praising themselves and the company. Every one is desirous of doing this: whether he blame or approve, whether
he speak or be silent, he is always making his own apology;
for every man is an orator, who, by his discourse or his actions, is perpetually making his own panegyric. There are
two ways of praising ourselves; one, by saying things to our
own advantage; the other, by speaking ill of our neighbours.
Cicero, Horace, and, in general, all the ancients, were more
frank in their pretensions, and openly gave themselves the
praises they thought they deserved. Our age is become more
delicate on this article. It is only by the ill we see of another,
that we are now permitted to make our own eulogium. It is

by making a jest of a fool, we indirectly boast our own wit. This manner of praising ourselves is doubtless the most directly opposite to good manners; however, it is the only one in use. Whoever says of himself the good he thinks, is puffed up with pride, and every one shuns him. Whoever, on the contrary, praises himself by the evil he says of others, is a charming man; he is surrounded with grateful auditors; they share with him the praises he indirectly gives himself, and incessantly applaud the fine speeches which deliver them from the vexation of being obliged to offer incense to their own vanity. It appears, that, in general, the malignity of the world proceeds less from the design of doing an injury, than from people's desire of raising an opinion of their own merit. Thus, this vice is easily indulged and put in practice, not only by the polite, but by men of narrow and contracted minds, whose intentions are still more odious. The man of merit knows, that the person of whom they say no ill, is, in general, one of whom they can say no good; that those who do not love to praise, have commonly been themselves but little praised: he is, therefore, not desirous of their commendations: he considers stupidity as a misfortune, on which stupidity always seeks to be revenged. " Let them prove a fact against me," said a man of great wit; " let them talk as ill of me as they please, I shall not be sorry for it; it is proper that every one should amuse himself." But if philosophy pardons malice, it ought not, however, to applaud it. To these indiscreet applauses we owe such a number of mischievous persons, who, in other respects, are sometimes a very good sort of people. Flattered by the praises bestowed on malice, and by the reputation for wit which it procures, they do not know how to place a proper esteem on the goodness that is natural to them: they would render themselves formidable by the severity of their satire: they have unhappily so much wit as to succeed in it: they, at first, became wicked to give themselves an air, and afterwards remain so by habit.

O you who have not yet contracted this fatal custom, shut your ears to the praises given to those satirical strokes, that are as prejudicial to society as they are common. Consider the impure sources from whence detraction springs*. Recollect, that, indifferent with respect to the ridicule of a particular person, the great man only employs himself about great things; that old and wicked appear to him as ridiculous as old and charming; that, among persons of distinction, those who deserve to be great must soon be disgusted with that taste for slander, which is held in abhorrence by other nations †: aban-

---

* One is guilty of slander because he is ignorant and lazy; another, because, tired of himself, conceitedly fond of talking humourously, and shocked at the least fault, he is habitually unhappy: it is more to his humour than to his wit that he owes the severity and keenness of his expression; *Facit indignatio versum.* A third is naturally splenetic; he slanders his neighbours, because he thinks them his enemies. O what grief to live perpetually with the objects of his hatred! He places his pride in not suffering them to impose on him: he sees none but what are villains or disguised cheats: he says so, and he frequently says true; but he is sometimes deceived. Now, I ask, if we are not equally dupes, when we take vice for virtue, as when we take virtue for vice? The happy age is that in which a man is the dupe of his friends and his mistresses. Woe to him whose prudence is not the effect of experience? A premature distrust is the certain sign of a depraved heart, and an unhappy temper. Who knows, whether he is not the most senseless of all mankind, who, that he may not be the dupe of his friends, exposes himself to the punishment of perpetual distrust? People, in short, defame others to shew their wit: it is not said, that satirical wit is only the wit of those who have none at all; but, in fact, what is the wit that only subsists in the ridicule of others, and a talent in which we cannot excel without the eulogium bestowed on wit becoming a satire on the heart? How can we puff ourselves up with our success, where, if we have preserved any virtue, we ought every day to blush at those smart strokes which our vanity makes us applaud, and which it would force us to despise, were it attended with more knowledge.

† It is only in France, and in good company, that we represent, as a man of wit, a person whom they will not allow to have common sense. Thus a foreigner, always ready to deprive us of a great general, an illustrious writer, a celebrated artist, or an able manufacturer, will never take from us a polite companion *(un homme du bon ton.)* Now what sort of a wit is that, which no nation will have any thing to do with?

don it then to little minds, to whom defamation is a want. Born the enemies of those of a superior genius, and jealous of the esteem they cannot attain, they know that, like those base plants that can only bud and grow on the ruins of palaces, they can only rise by the fall of great reputations, and, for that reason, they take pains to destroy them.

These men of contracted minds are very numerous. Formerly the people were inspired with envy only by their equals; at present every one aspires to wit, and believes that the public are entirely filled with envy at his merit. People no longer read for instruction, but to criticize. Now, among all works, there are none that can hold out against this disposition of readers. Most of them, employed only in searching for faults, are like those unclean animals that are sometimes found in cities, and ramble there only to grovel in the kennels. Are they still ignorant that it requires no less wit to discover the beauties than the faults of a work, and that " in books," as an English author says, " we ought to search for ideas, and set a great value on the book, when we have found a considerable number of them?"

All the injustice of this kind is the necessary effect of folly. What difference, in this respect, is there between the conduct of a man of genius, and that of a narrow mind? The first takes an advantage of every thing. There sometimes escapes from a person of mean abilities truths which the wise seize upon: the man of genius, who knows this, hears him without disgust; he commonly regards, in this conversation only, the good he has said, and the man of mean abilities what he has said that is bad or ridiculous.

The man of genius, perpetually sensible of his ignorance, finds instruction in almost every book: on the contrary, the man of a narrow mind, too ignorant and too vain to feel the want of instruction, receives none from any of the works of his cotemporaries; and, to speak modestly, he knows, he says, that no books can teach him any thing* : he even goes

---

* " The wise," says the Persian proverb, " know and inquire; but the ignorant do not even know what to inquire about."

so far as to maintain that every thing has been thought of and
said ; that authors do nothing but repeat after one another;
and that they only differ in their manner of expression.   O ye
envious! might one say, is it to the ancients that we owe print-
ing, clocks, glass, fire-engines?   Who, besides Newton, in
the last age, fixed the laws of gravitation?   Does not elec-
tricity every day afford an infinite number of new phænomena?   There are, according to you, no discoveries left to
be made : but in morality itself, and even in politics, where
every thing ought perhaps to have been said, is the species
of luxury and commerce of most advantage to a nation yet
determined?   Are their bounds fixed?   Have they discovered the means of preserving in a nation at the same time
the spirit of commerce and that of war?   Have they pointed
out the form of government most proper to render men happy?
Have they only made the romance of a good legislation *,
such as might serve for a colony established on some desert
coast in America?

---

* We do not even understand the principles we repeat every day:
to PUNISH and REWARD is a maxim; every body knows the words, but
few are acquainted with the sense.   Whoever could perceive its full
extent, might resolve, by the application of this principle, the problem of a perfect legislation.   How many things of the like kind do
we imagine we know and repeat every day, without understanding
them?   What a different signification have the same words in different mouths!

It is related of a young woman, in reputation for her sanctity, that
she passed whole days in prayer.   The bishop heard of it, and went
to see her.   "What are then the long prayers," said he, " to which
you consecrate your days?"—" I repeat my Pater-noster," said the
girl.   " The Pater-noster," replied the bishop, " is certainly an excellent prayer; but, in short, it is soon said."—" O my lord!" returned the girl, " what ideas of the grandeur, power, and goodness,
of God, are included in these two words, Pater-noster!—they are
enough for a week's meditation!"

I may say the same of certain proverbs; I compare them to tan-
gled chains; if we get hold of an end, we may wind off all the morals and politics; but this work requires a very dexterous hand.

Time, in every age, has presented some truths to man; but many of his gifts are still to be bestowed. We may then acquire an infinite number of new ideas. The maxim, that every thing has been thought of and said, is then false; it was invented first by ignorance, and has been repeated since by envy. There is no means which the envious, under the appearance of justice, do not employ to degrade merit. We know, for instance, that there is no truth that stands alone; that every new idea has a dependance on some ideas already known, to which it has necessarily some resemblance: yet from these resemblances, envy daily accuses the illustrious men our cotemporaries with plagiary *: when they declaim against plagiaries, they say, it is to punish the literary robbers, and to revenge the public. But, it might be replied, if you consulted only the public interest, your declarations would not be so warm; you would perceive that these plagiaries, though less worthy of esteem than the men of genius, are however of great use to the public; that a good work, in order to be generally known, ought to be divided into an infinite number of works, of less value.

---

* Under the name of love, Hesiod, for instance, gives us pretty nearly the idea of attraction; but in that poet it is only a vague idea: on the contrary, in Newton, it is the result of combinations and new calculations; Newton was then the inventor. What I say of Newton, I say equally of Locke: when Aristotle said—" NIHIL EST IN INTELLECTU QUOD NON PRIOS FUERIT IN SENSU," certainly he did not attach to this maxim the same ideas as Mr. Locke. This was neither more nor less in the Greek philosopher than a glimpse of a discovery to be made, and the honour of it was entirely to belong to an English philosopher. It is envy alone that makes us find in the ancients all the discoveries of the moderns. A phrase void of sense, or at least unintelligible before these discoveries, is sufficient to raise the cry of plagiary. They do not say, that, to perceive in a work a principle that nobody had found there before is properly making a discovery; that this discovery supposes, at least, in him who made it, a great number of observations which led to this principle; and that, in short, he who assembles many ideas in the same point of view, is a man of genius and an inventor.

In fact, if the individuals, of which the society is composed, ought to be ranged under several classes, that all, in
order that they may understand and hear, have different ears
and eyes, it is evident that the same writer, whatever be his
genius, cannot be equally suitable to them, and that there
should be authors of all classes *, such as Neuville, to preach
in the city, and Bridaine in the country. In morality, as in
politics, certain ideas are not universally felt, and their evidence not fully settled, that they have from the most sublime
philosophy descended to poetry, and from poetry into the
streets: they then become common enough to be useful.

Moreover this envy, which so often assumes the name of
justice, and from which nobody is entirely exempt, is a vice
peculiar to no nation: but it is commonly most active and
dangerous in the vain men of little minds. The man of superior abilities has but few objects of jealousy, and people of
distinguished rank are too fluctuating to obey the same sensation for a long time together: besides, they do not hate merit,
and particularly literary merit, which they often even protect;
their only pretence for making use of slander arises from their
desire of being agreeable, and of shining in conversation. In
this pretension properly consists the spirit of the age: thus,
there is nothing that they will not invent, to escape the reproach of being insipid.

A woman who has but little wit appears entirely taken up
with her dog; she speaks only of him; the pride of her visi-
tors offend her; they tax her with impertinence, but they are
to blame. She knows that a person makes some appearance in

---

* I shall mention on this subject a fact pleasant enough. A man
one day caused himself to be introduced to a magistrate, a person of
great wit. " What is your employment?" says the magistrate. " I
compose books," he answered. " But none of those books have yet
fallen into my hands," returned the magistrate. " I believe so,"
replied the author; " I do nothing for Paris. As soon as one of my
works is printed, I send the edition to America: I compose only for
the colonies."

society, when she has pronounced a number of words*, when she has performed a number of gestures, and made so much noise: her employment with her dog is therefore less an amusement to her than a means of concealing the meanness of her abilities: she is, in this respect, well advised by her self-love, which, on certain occasions, makes her put the best face on her folly.

I shall only add one word to what I have already said of the spirit of the age; and that is, that it is easy to represent it under a sensible image. Let an able painter be directed, for instance, to make allegorical pictures of the spirit of one of the ages of Greece, and of the actual spirit of our own nation. In the first picture, would he not be forced to represent the genius and spirit of Greece, under the figure of a man, who, with his eyes fixed, and his soul absorbed in profound meditation, remains in one of the attitudes given to the muses? In the second picture, would he not be under a necessity of painting the spirit of the French, under the appearance of the god of raillery; that is, in the figure of a man who considers every thing with a malicious laugh, and an eye of ridicule? Now these two pictures, so different in themselves, give us pretty exactly the difference between the spirit of the Greeks and ours. Upon which I shall observe, that in each age an ingenious painter would give to the spirit of a nation different features, and that the allegorical meaning of such pictures would be very agreeable and very curious with respect to posterity, who, with a glance of the eye, might judge of the esteem or contempt which in every age ought to be granted to the spirit of each nation.

---

* On this subject the Persians say—"I hear the noise of a mill, but I don't see the corn."

CHAP. VIII.

OF A TRUE UNDERSTANDING*.

In order to form constantly a just judgment on the different ideas and opinions of mankind, we ought to be exempt from all the passions which mislead the mind; we should have habitually present to our memories the ideas, the knowledge of which leads to that of all human truths: for this purpose, we should know every thing. Nobody does know every thing: we have therefore, only in certain respects, a true or solid understanding.

In dramatic writing, for instance, one is a good judge of the harmony and propriety of the verse, of the strength of the expression, and, in short, of all the beauties of style; but he is no judge of the justness of the plan. Another, on the contrary, is a connoisseur in the last particular; but he is neither struck with that justness, that propriety, nor that force of sentiment, on which depends the truth of the dramatic characters, and is the first merit of these pieces: I say the first merit, because the real utility, and consequently the principal beauty of this kind, consists in faithfully painting the effects produced by the strong passions.

We have then properly a solid understanding only in such things as have employed our thoughts.

We cannot then confound genius and an extensive and profound knowledge with a true understanding, without acknowledging that this last is liable to mistake, when it relates to those complicated propositions where the discovery of truth is the result of many combinations; where, to see distinctly, it is necessary to see a great deal, and where justness of thought depends on its extent: thus we commonly understand by a true understanding, only that kind of knowledge proper to

---

* In the extensive sense of true understanding is universal; but of this kind of understanding I do not treat in this chapter; I here take the word in its common acceptation.

draw just and sometimes new consequences, from those opinions that are presented to the mind, whether they be true or false.

In consequence of this definition, a solid understanding contributes little to the advancement of human knowledge; however, it merits some esteem. He who, departing from principles or opinions admitted, draws from thence consequences that are always just, and sometimes new, is an extraordinary man among the common people: he is even, in general, more esteemed by men of moderate abilities than persons of superior genius, who, too often calling men to the examination of received principles, and transporting them into unknown regions, must at one and the same time offend their laziness, and wound their pride.

Besides, however just the consequences may be that are drawn from a sentiment or a principle, I say, that, far from obtaining the name of a solid understanding, the person will always be mentioned as a fool, if that sentiment, or that principle, appear either ridiculous or foolish. A vapourish Indian imagined, that if he discharged his urine, he should overflow all Bisnagar. In consequence of this opinion, this virtuous citizen, preferring the safety of his country to his own health, continued to refrain from this necessary discharge; and was ready to perish, when a physician, a man of wit, entered, seemingly in a great fright, into his chamber: " Narsinga *," said he, " is in flames; it will soon be reduced to ashes: make haste, and let the stream flow." At these words, the good Indian reasoned justly, pissed, and passed for a fool †.

---

* The capital of Bisnagar.

† Persons of a solid understanding may consider the custom formerly practised, in order to decide the justice or injustice of a cause, by force of arms, as properly established. It may appear to them the just consequence of these two propositions: " Nothing happens but by the order of the Almighty, and God cannot permit injustice."— " If a dispute arose in relation to the property of some land on a per-

If such men are generally considered as fools, it is not solely from the drawing their reasonings from false principles, but from principles that are reputed such. In fact, the Chinese theologian, who proves the nine incarnations of Wisthnou, and the Mussulman, who, after the Koran, maintains, that the earth is carried on the horns of a bull, certainly found their opinions on principles as ridiculous as those of my Indian; yet each of them, in his own country, is esteemed a person of sense. What can be the reason of this? It is because they maintain opinions generally received. In relation to religious truths, reason loses all her force against two grand missionaries, Example and Fear. Besides, in all countries the prejudices of the great are the laws of the little. This Chinese and this Mussulman pass then for wise, only because they are fools of the common folly. What I have said

---

son's estate, if the case were not very clear on both sides, they chose champions to make it more so. The Emperor Otho, about the year 968, consulted his lawyers, to know if a line represented in a landscape ought to be complied with: as they were of different opinions, they nominated two bravos to decide this point of law, and the advantage falling to him who fought in behalf of the representation, the emperor ordered that should take place for the future."—Memoirs of the Academy of Inscriptions and Belles Lettres, tom. xv.

I might cite here, after the Memoirs of the Academy of Inscriptions, many other examples of different trials, appointed in those times of ignorance as judgments of God. I confine myself to the trial of cold water :—" After some prayers pronounced over the patient, they tied his right hand to his left foot, and his left hand to his right foot, and in this condition threw him into the water: if he swam, he was treated as a criminal, and if he sunk he was declared innocent. Upon this footing, they must find few guilty; because, the person being unable to make any motion, and his weight being superior to that of the water contained in the same space, he must necessarily sink. They were doubtless not ignorant of so simple a principle of statics, of which they made so common an experiment; but the simplicity of those times made them always expect a miracle, which they did not think that Heaven could refuse them, when it was proper to let them know the truth."—Ibid.

of folly, I apply to stupidity : he alone is mentioned as stupid who has not the stupidity in fashion.

Certain countrymen, it is said, erected a bridge, and upon it carved this inscription : "THE PRESENT BRIDGE IS BUILT HERE." Others resolved to draw a man out of a pit, into which he had fallen, and, letting down a cord with a slip-knot, pulled. him out strangled. If stupidity of this kind must always excite laughter, how can we seriously hear the doctrines of the Bonzes, the Brachmans, and Tallapoins ? Doctrines as absurd as the inscription on the bridge. How can we, without laughter, see the kings, the people, the ministers, and. even the great men, prostrate themselves sometimes at the foot of idols, and shew the most profound veneration for ridiculous fables ? How, in surveying voyages, can we avoid being astonished at seeing the existence of sorcerers and magicians as generally believed as the existence of God, and pass among most nations for a truth equally certain ? From what reason, in short, do not different absurdities, that are equally ridiculous, make the same impression upon us ? It is because people freely ridicule the stupidity from which they think themselves exempt, because nobody repeats after the countrymen—" The present bridge is built here:" and that the case is very different, when it relates to pious absurdity. Nobody believing themselves entirely free from the ignorance which produced it, they are afraid of laughing at themselves under another's name.

It is not, therefore, in general to absurdity of reasoning, but to the absurdities of a certain kind of reasoning, that we give the name of stupidity. We cannot then understand by this word any thing more, than an appearance that is but little common. Thus, people sometimes give the name of stupid to those whom they even allow to have a great genius. The knowledge of common things is the knowledge of common men, and sometimes the man of genius is, in this respect, grossly ignorant: eager to proceed to the first principles of the art or science he makes his study, and contented with seizing some of those new, primary, and general, truths, whence flow an infinite number of secondary ones, he neglects all other kinds of knowledge. Does he leave the bright path traced out by his genius? he falls into a thousand errors, and Newton writes a comment on the Apocalypse.

Genius enlightens some acres of that immense night which surrounds little minds; but it does not enlighten all. I compare the man of genius to the pillar which marched before the Hebrews, and was sometimes dark and sometimes luminous. The great man, always superior in one kind of study, necessarily wants abilities for many others; at least, if we understand here by abilities, an aptitude for instruction, which perhaps may be considered as knowledge begun. The great man by the habit of application, the method of study, and the distinction he is led to make between a half-knowledge and one that is entire, has certainly, in this respect, a considerable advantage over the common rank of men. These last, not having contracted the habit of reflection, and having known nothing deeply, believe themselves always sufficiently instructed, when they have obtained a superficial knowledge. Ignorance and folly easily persuade them, that they know every thing: both these are always attended with pride. The great man alone can be modest.

If I straighten the empire of genius, and shew the bounds in which nature forces it to be inclosed, it is to make it more evidently appear, that the man of understanding, who is much inferior to one of genius, cannot, as is imagined, always decide with strict truth on the various subjects of reasoning. Such an understanding is impossible. The property of a true understanding is to draw exact consequences from received opinions: now these opinions are, for the most part, false, and the understanding never proceeds so far as to an examination of them: a true understanding is then, most frequently, only the art of reasoning falsely according to method: perhaps this kind of understanding is sufficient to make a good judge; but it can never make a great man. Whoever is endued with it, commonly excels in no kind of study, and cannot be commended for any one talent. He often obtains, it is said, the esteem of persons of ordinary abilities. I confess it: but their esteem making him conceive too high an idea of himself, it becomes the source of errors; of errors, from which it is impossible for him to free himself. For, in fine, if the mirror of all counsellors, the most polished and discreet, cannot make a man sensible of his own deformity, who can disabuse a man, and make him quit the too high opinion he has conceived of himself, especially when that opinion is supported by the esteem of most of those who surround him? It is still modest enough for him, not to esteem himself, till after he has obtained the eulogium of others. Hence arises that confidence which a man of understanding places in his own knowledge, and that contempt for the great men whom he often regards as visionaries, as men of systematic minds and wrong heads *.

O ye men of solid understanding! might one say, when you treat as wrong-headed persons those great men, who at least are so superior to you in that kind of study which the public most admire; what opinion, think you, must the public have of you, whose abilities extend no farther than to the drawing of some petty consequences, from principles that may be either true or false, the discovery of which is but of small importance? Always in an extasy at beholding your little merit, you are, you say, not subject to the errors of celebrated men. True, because it is necessary either to run, or at least to walk, before one can fall. When you boast of the justness of your understanding, methinks I hear cripples glory in making no false steps. Your conduct, you add, is often wiser than that of the men of genius. Yes; because you have not within you that principle of life and of the passions, which equally produces great vices, great virtues, and great talents. But are you more worthy of commendation for this? Of what importance is it to the public, whether the conduct of a particular person be good or bad? A man of genius, had he vices, is still more worthy of esteem than you: in fact, he serves his country either by the innocence of his manners, and the virtuous example he sets, or by the knowledge he diffuses abroad. Of these two ways of serving his country, the last, without doubt, most directly belongs to ge-

---

* Saying that a man has a wrong head, is frequently saying, without knowing it, he has more wit than we have.

nius, and is at the same time that which procures the greatest advantages to the public. The virtuous example given by a particular person is scarcely of use to any besides the small number of those with whom he converses : on the contrary, the new light the same person spreads over the arts and sciences is a benefit to the whole world. It is then certain, that the man of genius, even though his probity should be very imperfect, would have a greater right than you to the gratitude of the public.

The declamations of the men of solid understanding, against those who are distinguished by their genius, must doubtless at times impose on the multitude : nothing is more easy than to deceive them. If the Spaniard, at the sight of the spectacles which some of his teachers constantly wear on their noses, persuades himself, that these doctors have almost pored themselves blind with reading, and that they are very wise ; if we every day take vivacity of gesture for that of wit, and taciturnity for knowledge ; we may also take the usual gravity of the men of understanding for an effect of their wisdom. But the delusion vanishes of itself, and we soon call to mind that gravity, as Mademoiselle de Scudery says, is only a secret of the body, to conceal the defects of the mind *. There are then properly none but these men of understanding, who are long dupes to the gravity they effect. Moreover, if they believe themselves wise, because they are serious ; if, inspired by pride and envy, when they decry genius, they believe that it proceeds from justice ; no body in this respect can escape from error. These mistaken sentiments are every where so general, that I believe I shall gratify the desire of the reader, by consecrating to this examination some pages of this work.

---

* " The ass," says Montaigne, on this subject, " is the most serious of all animals."

CHAP. IX.

OF MISTAKEN OPINIONS.

LIKE a ray of light which is composed of a collection of rays, every sentiment is composed of an infinite number of sentiments, which concur to produce a particular volition of soul, and a particular action of the body. Few men have the prism proper to separate this assemblage of sentiments: consequently people often believe themselves animated either by one sentiment alone, or by different sentiments from those by which they are moved. This is the cause of so many mistaken opinions, and the reason why we are almost always ignorant of the true motives of our actions.

In order the better to shew the difficulty of escaping these mistaken opinions, I shall represent some of the errors in which we are involved by a profound ignorance of ourselves.

CHAP. X.

HOW FAR WE ARE LIABLE TO MISTAKE THE MOTIVES BY WHICH WE ARE DETERMINED.

A MOTHER idolizes her son; " I love him," says she, " for his own sake." However, one might reply, you take no care of his education, though you are in no doubt that a good one would contribute infinitely to his happiness: why, therefore, do not you consult some men of sense about him, and read some of the works wrote on this subject? " Why, because," says she, " I think I know as much of this matter as those authors and their works." But how did you get this confidence in your own understanding? Is it not the effect of your indifference? An ardent desire always inspires us with a salutary distrust of ourselves. If we have a suit at law of considerable consequence, we visit counsellors and attorneys, we consult a great number, and examine their advice. Are we attacked by any of those

lingering diseases, which incessantly place around us the shades
and horrors of death? We see physicians, compare their opinions, read physical books, we ourselves become little physicians. Such is the conduct prompted by a warm interest.
With respect to the education of children, if you are not influenced in the same manner, it is because you do not love your
son as well as yourself. "But," adds the mother, "what
then should be the motive of my tenderness?" Among fathers and mothers, I reply, some are influenced by the desire of perpetuating their name in their children; they properly love only their names: others are fond of command, and
see in their children their slaves. The animal leaves its young
when their weakness no longer keeps them in dependence;
and paternal love becomes extinguished in almost all hearts,
when children have, by their age or station, attained to independence. "Then," said the poet Saadi, "the father sees
nothing in them but greedy heirs," and this is the cause, adds
some poet, of the extraordinary love of the grandfather for his
grand-children; he considers them as the enemies of his
enemies.

There are, in short, fathers and mothers, who make their
children their playthings and their pastime. The loss of this
plaything would be insupportable to them; but would their
affliction prove that they loved the child for itself? Every body
knows this passage in the life of M. de Lauzun: he was in the
Bastile; there, without books, without employment, a prey to
lassitude and the horrors of a prison, he took it in his head to
tame a spider. This was the only consolation he had left in his
misfortune. The governor of the Bastile, from an inhumanity
common to men accustomed to see the unhappy *, crushed the
spider. The prisoner felt the most cutting grief, and no mo-

---

* The habit of seeing the unhappy renders men cruel and merci-
less. In vain do they say, that they are cruel with regret, and that
their duty imposes upon them the necessity of being severe. Every
man who, from a regard to justice, can, like an executioner, kill one
of his own species in cold blood, would certainly assassinate for his
own personal interest, were he not afraid of the hangman.

ther could be affected by the death of a son with a more violent sorrow. Now whence is derived this conformity of sentiments for such different objects? It is because, in the loss of a child, or in the loss of the spider, people frequently weep for nothing but for the lassitude and want of employment into which they fall. If mothers appear in general more afflicted at the death of a child than fathers employed in business, or given up to the pursuit of ambition, it is not because the mother loves her child more tenderly, but because she suffers a loss more difficult to be supplied. The errors, in my opinion, are, in this respect, very frequent; people rarely cherish a child for its own sake. That paternal love* of which so many men make a parade, and by which they believe themselves so warmly affected, is most frequently nothing more than an effect, either of a desire of perpetuating their names, of the pride of command, or the fear of lassitude and inaction.

Such a mistaken opinion persuades the devout fanatics, that to their zeal for religion they owe their hatred to philosophers, and the persecutions they kindle against them. But it may be said, either the opinion which shocks you in philosophical works is false or it is true. In the first case, you ought to be

---

* What I say of paternal love may be applied to metaphysical love, so much boasted of in our old romances. We are, in this respect, subject to many mistaken opinions. When a person imagines, for instance, that he loves only the soul of a woman, it is certainly her person that he desires, and here, to satisfy his wants, and especially his curiosity, he is rendered capable of every thing. This truth may be proved from the little sensibility most spectators shew at the theatre for the affection of a man and his wife, when the same spectators are so warmly moved by the love of a young man for a young woman. What can produce these different sensations, if it is not the different sensations themselves have experienced in these two relations? Most of them have felt, that, as they will do every thing for the favours desired, they will do little for the favours obtained; that, in the case of love, curiosity being once gratified, they easily comfort themselves for the loss of one who proves unfaithful, and that then the misfortune of a lover is very supportable. Whence I conclude, that love can never be any thing else but a disguised desire of enjoyment.

animated with that mild virtue which religion supposes, and to prove philosophically its falsehood; this you also owe to Christianity. "We require not of you," says St. Paul, "a blind obedience; we teach, we prove, we persuade." In the second case, that is, if this philosopher's opinion be true, it is not contrary to religion: to believe that it is would be blasphemy. Two truths cannot be contradictory; and truth, says the Abbé de Fleury, can never injure truth. But this opinion, the fanatical devotee will say, cannot be reconciled with the principles of religion. You think then, it may be replied, that every thing which resists the efforts of your mind, and which you cannot reconcile with the doctrines of your religion, is really inconsistent with those doctrines? Do you not know that Galileo* was unworthily dragged to the prison of the inquisition,

---

* The persecutors of Galileo, doubtless, believed that they were animated with a zeal for religion, and were the dupes of that belief. I, however, confess, that if they had been scrupulously examined and asked, Why the church reserved to herself the right of punishing the errors of a man by the dreadful torment of fire, while she grants an inviolable asylum to crimes near the altars, and declares herself, in a manner, the protectress of assassins? If they had been farther asked, why the same church, by her toleration, seems to favour the crimes of those fathers, who, without pity, mutilate their children, whom in temples, concerts, and on the stage, they devote to the pleasure of some delicate ears? and that, in fine, had they perceived, that ecclesiastics themselves encourage unnatural fathers to perpetuate their crime, by permitting these unfortunate victims to be received into the churches, and hired to serve in them at a high price? they would then necessarily have agreed, that a religious zeal was not the only passion by which they were actuated. They would have been sensible that churches were made a refuge for criminals only to preserve, by this means, a greater credit with an infinite number of men, who would look with respect upon the monks, as the only protectors that could save them from the rigour of the laws; that they punished Galileo for the discovery of a new system, only to be revenged for the involuntary injury done them by a great man, who, perhaps, by enlightening the human race, and appearing more learned than the clergy, might lessen their credit with the people. It is true, that, even in Italy, people recollect with horror the treatment of the philosopher by the inqui-

for having maintained that the sun is placed in the centre, and does not move round the earth; that his system first offended the weak, and appeared directly contrary to that text of Scripture, " Sun, stand thou still ?" However, able divines have since made Galileo's principles agree with those of religion. Who has told you, that a divine more happy or more enlightened than you, will not remove the contradiction, which you think you perceive between your religion and the opinion you resolve to condemn? Who forces you by a precipitate censure to expose, if not religion, at least its ministers, to the hatred excited by persecution? Why, always borrowing the assistance of force and terror, would you impose silence on men of genius, and deprive mankind of the useful knowledge they are capable of dispensing?

You obey, you say, the dictates of religion. But it commands you to distrust yourselves, and to love your neighbour. If you do not act in conformity to these principles, you are then not actuated by the spirit of God*. But you say, by whom then are we inspired? By laziness and pride. It is laziness, the enemy of thought, which makes you averse to those opinions, which you cannot, without study and some fatigue of attention, unite with the principles received in the schools; but which

---

sition. As a proof of this truth, I quote part of the poem of the priest Benedetto Menzini, printed and publicly sold at Florence. The poet addresses himself to the inquisitors who condemned Galileo : " What," says he, " was your blindness, when you unworthily dragged this great man to your dungeon ! Is this the pacific spirit recommended to you by that holy apostle, who died in exile at Patmos ! No : you were always deaf to his precepts. Let us persecute the wise; this is your maxim. Proud mortals, under an exterior that inspires only humility, you, who speak with so soft a voice, and yet dip your hands in blood, what mischievous demon introduced you among us !"

* If the same devout fanatic, mild in China, and cruel at Lisbon, preaches in different countries toleration or persecution, according as he is there more or less powerful; how can he reconcile such a contradictory conduct with the spirit of the gospel; and not perceive, that under the name of religion, he is inspired by the pride of command?

being proved to be philosophically true, cannot be theologically false.

It is pride, which is ordinarily carried to a greater height in the bigot than in any other person, which makes him detest in the man of genius the benefactor of the human race, and which exasperates him against the truths discovered by humility.

It is then this laziness and this pride, which, disguising themselves* under the appearance of zeal†, render them the persecutors of men of learning; and which in Italy, Spain, and Portugal, have forged chains, built gibbets, and held the torch to the piles of the inquisition.

Thus the same pride, which is so formidable in the devout fanatic, and which in all religions makes him persecute, in the name of the Most High, the men of genius, sometimes arms against them the men in power.

After the example of those Pharisees, who treated as criminals the persons who did not adopt all their decisions, how many viziers treat, as enemies to the nation, those who do not blindly approve their conduct! Drawn into this error, by a mistaken opinion common to almost all mankind, there is no

---

* If we except luxury, of all the sins most prejudicial to mankind; but which consists in an act which it is impossible to conceal from ourselves, though we are under an illusion with respect to all the rest. Every other vice we transform into so many virtues. We take the desire of grandeur, for elevation of soul; avarice, for œconomy; defamation, for the love of truth; and an ill-humour, for a laudable zeal. Thus most of these passions are pretty commonly allied to bigotry.

† Those divines who believe that the popes have a right to dispose of thrones, also imagine themselves animated with a pure zeal for religion. They do not perceive that a secret motive of ambition is blended with the sanctity of their intentions; that the only means of commanding kings is to consecrate the opinion that gives the pope a right to depose them, in case of heresy. Now ecclesiastics being the sole judges of heresy, the court of Rome, says the Abbé de Longuerue, have made use of it at their pleasure, against all the princes who displease them.

vizier who does not take his interest for that of the nation; who does not maintain, without knowing it, that to humble his pride, is to insult the public; and that to blame his conduct, with whatever precaution it be done, is to excite disturbances in the state. But you deceive yourselves, it may be replied; for, in forming this judgment, you consult only your vanity, and not the general interest. Are you ignorant that a virtuous citizen can never see with indifference the evils occasioned by a bad administration? As legislation is the most useful of all the sciences, ought it not, like every other science, to be improved by the same means? Is it not by removing the errors of Aristotle, Averroes, Avicenna, and all the inventors in the sciences and arts, that people have improved these arts and these sciences? To resolve to cover the faults of the administration with the veil of silence is then to oppose the progress of the legislation, and consequently the happiness of mankind. It is the same pride, masked under the name of the public welfare, which makes you advance this maxim, that a fault being once committed, the divan ought always to maintain it, and that authority ought not to submit. But, if the public welfare be the principal object proposed by every prince and every government, ought they to make use of authority in the support of folly? The maxim you establish can only signify, I have given my advice, and would not, by suffering the prince to be informed of the necessity of changing his conduct, clearly prove to him that I have given him bad counsel.

There are few men who escape illusions of this kind. How many persons, who have good intentions, are dishonest for want of examining themselves! If there are some to whom the bodies of others, if I may use the term, are diaphanous, and who equally penetrate into their hearts, and into their own, the number of these is but small. In order to obtain a true knowledge of ourselves, we should observe, and for a long time study, our own hearts. The persons of strict morals are the only persons who concern themselves about this examination; most other men are ignorant of this study.

Among those who declaim with such heat against the singularities of men of wit, how many are there who believe themselves solely animated by the love of justice and truth! However, let me ask, why do you attack with such fury a ridicule which is frequently attended with no injury to any one? A man affects singularity. Laugh at him, and welcome : you would thus behave to a person without merit, and why should you not treat a man of genius in the same manner? It is because his singularity attracts the attention of the public : now their attention being once fixed upon a person of merit, it is employed about him; they forget you, and your pride is wounded. This is the secret principle both of the respect you affect to shew for the customs of the world, and of your hatred of singularity.

You will tell me, perhaps, that what is extraordinary makes an impression, and that this adds to the fame of the man of wit; that simple and modest merit is less esteemed, which is an injustice you are willing to revenge by decrying singularity. But does envy, I reply, prevent your perceiving where affectation is, and where it is not? In general, men of superior abilities are but little subject to it; a lazy and thoughtful disposition may be attended with singularity, but will never produce much appearance of it. The affectation of singularity is then very uncommon.

What activity does it require to support a singular character? What knowledge of the world must such a person have, nicely to choose such a ridicule as will render him neither despicable nor odious to other men; to adapt that ridicule to his character and proportion it to his merit? For, in short, it is only a particular degree of genius that is allowed to be particularly ridiculous. Have we this? we may make use of it; the ridicule, far from injuring us, is of service. When Æneas descended into hell, in order to pacify the monster that watched at its gates, that hero, by the advice of the Sybil, provided himself with a cake, which he tossed into the mouth of Cerberus. Who knows whether merit, in order to appease the hatred of its cotemporaries, ought not thus to cast into the mouth of envy the cake of ridicule? Prudence requires this, and even human nature renders it necessary. If there appeared a perfect man, it would be necessary for him, by some great foilies, to soften the hatred of his fellow-citizens. It is true, that in this respect we may trust to nature, since she has provided every man with a sufficient number of faults to render him supportable.

A certain proof, namely envy, under the name of justice, is let loose against the follies of men of genius, so that all their singularity does not offend us. A gross singularity, that flatters the vanity of a man of moderate abilities, by making him perceive that the man of merit has faults from which he is exempt, by persuading him that all men of genius are fools, and that he alone is wise, is a singularity always very proper to conciliate his good-will. Let a man of genius, or instance, dress himself in a particular manner, most men who do not distinguish wisdom from folly, and know it only by the length of a peruke, will take him for a fool; they will laugh at him, but like him the better for it. In exchange for the pleasure they find in ridiculing him, they will freely allow him the praise that is his due. People cannot frequently laugh at a man without talking much of him. Now this, which would ruin a fool, increases the reputation of a man of merit. They do not laugh at him without acknowledging, and perhaps even exaggerating, his superiority, with respect to his distinguishing excellence; and by outrageous declamations, the envious, unknown to themselves, even contribute to his glory. What gratitude do I owe you?" will the man of genius freely say; " your hatred makes me friends! The public will not long be deceived by the motives of your anger: you are offended, not by my singularity, but at my reputation. If you dared, you would, like me, be singular: but, you know, that an affected singularity is extremely flat in a man without wit; your instinct informs you, either that you have not, or at least that the public does not grant you, the merit necessary to appear particular. This is the true cause of your abhorrence of singularity*. You resemble those artful women who, incessantly exclaiming against the indecency of all modern dresses proper to shew the shape, do not perceive that they owe their respect for ancient fashions only to their personal deformity."

Whatever we have that is ridiculous, we always conceal from ourselves; we only perceive it in others. I shall mention on this subject a fact pleasant enough, which is said to have happened in our days. The Duke of Lorraine gave a grand entertainment to his whole court. The supper was served up in a vestibule, which opened on a parterre. In the midst of the supper, a lady thought she saw a spider: she was seized with fear, screamed out, left the table, fled into the garden, and fell down on the grass. At the moment of her fall, she heard somebody near her; this was the duke's prime minister. " O Sir!" said she, " you revive my courage : how much am I obliged to you! I was afraid I had been guilty of an impertinence."—" O Madam! who could stay there?" replied the minister: " but tell me, was it a very large one?"— " Dear Sir! it was quite frightful."—" Did it fly near me?" added he. " What do you mean? the spider fly!"—" How," returned he, " is it only for a spider that you make all this to

---

* To the same cause we ought to attribute the love which almost all fools affect to have for probity, when they say, we fly the men of wit, they are bad company, and dangerous men. But it may be said, the church, the court, the magistracy, and the treasury, furnish men as worthy of censure as the academies. Most men of learning have not even an inclination to become knaves. Besides, the desire of esteem, which always supposes the love of study, serves them, in this respect, as a preservative. Among the men of learning, there are few whose probity is not confirmed by some virtuous actions. But even supposing them as great cheats as the blockheads, the qualities of the mind may at least compensate for the vices of the heart; but the fool has nothing to atone for them. Why then do they fly from the men of genius? It is because they are humbled by their presence, and take that for a love of virtue which is only an aversion to persons of superior abilities.

do? Go, Madam, you are very weak: I thought it had been a batt." This fact is the history of all mankind: we cannot support our own ridicule in another; we reciprocally offer abuse, and in this world it is always absurdity that laughs at folly. Thus, after Solomon, one is always tempted to cry out—" All is vanity." On this vanity depends most of our mistaken opinions. But as it is more particularly in affairs of advice, that these mistakes are more easily perceived, after having exposed some of the errors into which we are thrown by a profound ignorance of ourselves, it must still be of use to shew the errors into which we are sometimes precipitated by the ignorance of others.

CHAP. XI.

OF ADVICE.

EVERY man whom we consult always believes that his counsel is dictated by friendship. He says so; most men believe him upon his word, and their blind confidence but too often leads them into error. It would, however, be very easy to undeceive ourselves in this particular; for we love but few people, and would advise all the world. From whence does this madness of giving advice derive its source? From our vanity. Most men have the folly to believe themselves wise, and much more so than their neighbours, and therefore they are pleased with every thing that confirms this opinion. Whoever consults us, is agreeable to us, for this is a confession of inferiority which flatters our vanity. Besides, what opportunities does our being consulted give us to display our maxims, our ideas, and our sentiments, to talk much of ourselves, and to our own advantage! Thus there is nobody who does not take advantage of it. More employed about the interest of our vanity, than about the interest of the person who comes to consult us, he commonly leaves us without being instructed, or enlightened; and our counsels have been our own panegyric. Thus our advice is almost constantly dictated by vanity, and hence we would correct all the world.

Upon this subject, a philosopher replied, to one of these persons eager to give his advice—" How should I correct my faults, when thou thyself hast not corrected the desire of giving correction?" If it was in fact friendship alone that gave counsel, this, like all other lively passions, would make known when and how we ought to give advice. In the case of ignorance, for example, there is no doubt but advice may be very useful: a physician, a counsellor, a philosopher, and a politician, may each, in their separate professions, give excellent advice. In every other case it is useless, and often even ridiculous, because people, in general, always propose themselves for a model.

Let an ambitious man consult a person of moderate desires, and propose to him his views and projects: " Abandon them," the latter will say; " do not expose yourself to dangers and vexations without number; but deliver yourself to sweet and peaceful employments." To this the ambitious man will reply—" If I had still my choice to make, I might follow your advice; but my passions are fixed, my character formed, and my habits settled. I would make the best of them, so as to promote my own happiness; and upon this point I would consult you." In vain would he add, that the character being once formed, it is impossible to change it; that the pleasures of a man of moderate desires are insipid to one filled with ambition; and the minister disgraced, would die with lassitude and inaction. Whatever reason he alledged, the man of moderate abilities would constantly repeat—" You ought not to be ambitious." Methinks I hear a physician say to his patient, " Sir, do not have a fever."

The old men constantly use the same language. When a young man consults them, in regard to the conduct he ought to observe—" Fly," say they, " plays, operas, balls, the assemblies of the women, and every frivolous amusement: imitate us, and employ yourself entirely about making your fortune." But the young man will reply—" I am still fond of pleasure; I love women to distraction; how then shall I renounce them? You must be sensible that at my age this pleasure is an appetite." Whatever he can say, an old man will never comprehend that the enjoyment of a woman is so necessary to the happiness of a young man. Every sensation, which we do not experience we cannot allow to exist The old man no longer seeks pleasure, and pleasure no longer seeks him. The objects with which he was incessantly employed in his youth, insensibly retire from his sight. Man then may be compared to a vessel that sails with a fair wind in a high sea; it gradually loses sight of the persons that stand on the shore, and soon disappears from their eyes. Whoever considers the ardour with which men propose themselves for models, may imagine that he sees a number of persons swimming upon a great lake, and being carried by different currents, lift up their heads above the water, crying to each other—" It is me you must follow, and there you must land." Held fast by chains of brass, fixed to a rock, the wise man contemplates their folly, crying—" Do you not see that, drawn by different currents, you cannot land at the same place?" To advise a man to say this, or to do that, is commonly nothing more than—" I would act in that manner, or I would speak thus." Thus the words in Moliere—" You are a goldsmith, master Josse;" applied to the pride of setting ourselves up for an example, is more general than is imagined. There is not a blockhead but would take upon himself to direct the conduct of the man of the greatest genius*. Methinks, I see the chief of the Natches†, who every morning, at the rising of Aurora, walks out of his cabin, and marks out for the sun, his brother, the course he is to take.

But, say you, the man who is consulted may, doubtless, be

---

* He who is not an equerry gives no advice about breaking horses. But we are not so diffident in cases of morality: without having studied it; we believe ourselves very learned, and able to give advice to the whole world.

† A savage nation.

under an illusion, and attribute to friendship, what is only the
effect of vanity; but how can this illusion pass upon him who
consults him? Why is not he in this respect enlightened by
his own interest? It is because he readily believes that others
take an interest in his concerns which they really do not;
because most men are weak, and, not being able to conduct
themselves, they have occasion for others to mark out their
conduct, and it is very easy, as observation proves, to communicate to such a person the high opinion the adviser has of
himself. This is not the case with one who has a firm mind.
If he consults, it is because he is ignorant: he knows that in
every other case, and particularly what relates to his own
happiness, he ought to consult none but his own judgment.
In fact, if the goodness of advice depends upon an exact
knowledge of the circumstances, in which those whom we
advise are placed, to whom can a man better apply than to
himself? As a warm interest enlightens us with respect to all
the subjects of our inquiries, who can be more enlightened
than we, in regard to our own happiness? Who knows whether, on the characters being formed, and the habits fixed,
each person is not able to conduct himself as well as possible,
even though he should appear a fool? Every body knows the
answer of a famous oculist: a countryman went to consult
him, and found him sitting at table, eating and drinking
heartily: " What must I do for my eyes?" said the peasant.
" You must abstain from wine," replied the oculist. " But it
seems to me," returned the peasant, walking up nearer to him,
" that your eyes are not much better than mine, and yet you
drink."—" Truly," replied the oculist, " that is, because
I am fonder of drinking than of being cured." How many
men are there, like this oculist, whose happiness depends
on passions that must plunge them in the greatest misery;
and yet, however, if I may venture to say so, would be
fools, did they endeavour to be more wise. There are
men, and experience has shewn that they are pretty
numerous, who are so miserable, that they can no otherwise be happy than by performing actions that lead to the

grave*. But it may be answered, there are also men who, for want of wise advice, daily commit the grossest faults ; and good advice, doubtless, might make them escape these misfortunes. But, I say, that they would commit more considerable ones still, if they gave themselves up inconsiderately to the counsels of others. Whoever blindly follows them, must observe a conduct full of inconsistencies, commonly more fatal than the excess even of the passions.

A person, by abandoning himself to his disposition, spares, at least, the useless efforts he might make to resist it. However violent the tempest may be, when we sail before the wind we support without fatigue the impetuosity of the sea: but if we resolve to struggle against the waves, and turn the side of the vessel to the storm, we shall always find the sea more rough and dangerous.

Inconsiderate advice precipitates us too often into the abyss of misfortune. Hence we ought often to call to mind this saying of Socrates: " May I," says that philosopher, " always be on my guard against my masters, and my friends, constantly preserve my soul in a tranquil situation, and obey none but reason, the best of counsellors !" Whoever hears reason, is not only deaf to bad counsel, but also weighs, in the balance of doubt, the counsels even of those men who are respectable by their age, their dignity, and their merit, yet consider themselves as of too much importance, and, like the hero of Cervantes, have a corner of folly, to which they would bring every thing.

If advice is ever useful, it is when it puts us in a condition to judge better for ourselves: if it is prudent to desire it, it is only so when it is asked of those wise men †, who, knowing

---

* If, as Pascal says, habit is a second, and perhaps a first nature, it must be acknowledged, that a guilty habit, once confirmed, will last as long as life.

† Every age, perhaps, produces not above five or six men of this kind ; and yet in morals, as well as in physic, we consult the first good woman. We do not say that morality, like each of the other sciences, requires much study and reflection. Every one believes that he understands it, because there is no public school in which it is to be learned.

the scarcity and value of good counsel, are very frugal in giving it. In fact, in order to give such as will be of use, it requires the greatest care to dive into the character of the man : what knowledge is necessary for the adviser to have of his taste, his inclinations, the sensations by which he is animated, and the degree to these inward feelings by which he is affected ? What skill to foresee the faults he would commit and the circumstances in which he may be placed by fortune, and to judge, in consequence of this, whether the fault he would correct, would not be changed into a virtue, in the station in which he will probably be placed ? This is the picture of those difficulties which render the wise so reserved on the article of giving advice. Thus it is only of those, who scarce even give any, that we ought to demand it. All other counsels may be justly suspected.

But is there any mark by which we may know the counsels of a wise man? Yes, doubtless there are. All the passions have a different language. We may then, from the advice itself, form a judgment of the motive from which it was given. In most men, as I have said above, it is dictated by pride ; and the counsels of pride, which are always humbling, are scarcely ever followed. Pride gives them ; pride resists them. It is the anvil which makes the hammer fly back. The art of making them relished, which of all the arts among mankind is, perhaps, the least improved, is absolutely unknown to pride. It does not examine : its counsels, and its decisions, are proofs of its ignorance. " Mortals," cries the proud man, " listen to me : superior in understanding to others, I speak ; let them attend, and rely on my knowledge : to reply, is to offend me." Thus always full of a profound respect for himself, whoever resists his advice is a conceited fellow, who wanted flatterers and not friends. "Vain man," might they reply, "on whom ought this reproach to fall but on thyself, who behaves with such violence to those, who do not, by a blind difference to thy decisions, flatter thy presumption? Learn that it is thy ill temper that saves thee from the vice of flattery. Besides, what would'st thou mean by that love of flattery, with which all men reciprocally reproach each other, and of which, particularly the great, and principally kings, are accused?" Every body, doubtless, hates praise when he believes it to be false: people then love flatterers only in the quality of sincere admirers. Under this it is impossible not to love them, because every one believes that his actions are laudable and worthy of praise. Whoever disdains eulogiums, suffers at least people to praise him on this account. When they detest the flatterer, it is because they know him to be such. In flattery it is not then the praise, but the falsehood, which shocks us. If the man of abilities appears less sensible of eulogiums, it is because he more frequently perceives their falsehood: but let an artful flatterer praise him, persist in praising him, and sometimes seem to mingle blame with the eulogiums he bestows, the man of genius will, sooner or later, be his dupe. From the artist to the prince, every one loves praise, and consequently delicate flattery.

But it may be asked, have not kings been seen to bear, with gratitude, the severe representations of a virtuous counsellor? Yes, without doubt; but these princes were jealous of their glory; they were warmly desirous of promoting the public welfare; and this disposition forced them to invite to their courts, men animated by the same passion, that is, men who would give them no counsels but what were favourable to the people. Now, if such counsellors flatter a virtuous prince, at least in the object of his passion, if they do always flatter him in the means he makes use of to satisfy it, such a liberty cannot offend him. I say more, such a truth may sometimes flatter him: it is the pleasing blow of a mistress.

Let a man go to a miser and tell him, you are to blame, you place your money out very badly; if you was to employ it in such a manner, you would find your account in it: far from being shocked at such frankness, the miser would be pleased with the author of it. In disapproving his conduct, he flatters him in what is most dear to him, that is, in the object of his passion. Now, what I say of the miser may be applied to the virtuous king.

In regard to a prince who is not in love with glory, or the public welfare, this prince can draw to his court none but such men as may instruct him in relation to the objects of his desires, as his taste, his prejudices, his views, his projects, and his pleasures: he will then be surrounded by none but vicious men, to whom the public dislike gives the name of flatterers*. All virtuous men fly far from him. To require that they should assemble about his throne, would be to demand an impossibility, and to resolve to produce an effect without a cause. Tyrants and great princes ought to determine themselves by the same motives, in the choice of their friends; they differ only in the passion by which they are animated.

Every man would then be praised and flattered; but all would not have it done in the same manner; and it is only in this particular that the difference between them consists. The proud are not free from this desire: what stronger proof can there be of this, than the haughtiness with which they decide, and the blind submission they require? It is not thus with the wise man: his self-love is not shewn in a insolent manner; and if he gives advice, he does not require that it should be followed. Sound reason always suspects that it has not considered an object in all its views. Thus in these counsels are always found some expressions of doubt proper to shew the situation of the mind. Such are these phrases: I believe that you ought to conduct yourself in such a manner: such is my advice: such the motives on which I form my opinion: but adopt nothing without examination, &c. From this manner of giving advice, we may discover the wise man: he alone can succeed with men of abilities; and if he has not always the same success with men of meaner intellects, it is because these last, being often uncertain, require a person to put an end to their irresolution, and determine for them; they confide more in folly, delivered with a firm voice, than in the wisdom that speaks with hesitation.

The friendship which advises, assumes nearly the same voice with that of wisdom, it only unites the expression of that passion

---

* "Most princes," says the poet Saadi, "are so indifferent with respect to good counsel, and have so seldom need of virtuous friends, that it is always a sign of a public calamity, when these virtuous men appear at court. They are never called but in an extremity, and commonly at the instant when the state is without resource."

with that of doubt. Is the advice resisted, or does the friend proceed so far as to despise it? it then makes itself better known, and, after having made its representations, it cries with Pylades, " Let us go, my lord; let us carry off Hermione."

Every passion has then its turns, its expression, and its particular manner: therefore, the man who, by an exact analysis of the phrases and expressions used by the different passions, should give the signs by which we might know them, would doubtless highly deserve the gratitude of the public. Then we might, from the multitude of sensations produced by each act of the will, distinguish, at least, that which rules over us. Till that time men will be ignorant of themselves, and will fall into the grossest errors.

CHAP. XII.
OF GOOD SENSE.

THE difference between wit and good sense proceeds from the different causes by which they are produced. The one is the effect of strong passions, and the other of the absence of those very passions. The man of good sense does not commonly fall into any of those errors into which we are drawn by the pasions, neither does he receive any of those beams of light that are owing to warm passions. In the current of life, and in such things where a perfect view may be obtained by an indifferent eye, the man of good sense does not deceive himself in relation to those questions that are a little complicated, where, in order to perceive and discover the truth, some efforts must be made, and some fatigue of attention endured; the man of good sense is blind: deprived of the passions, he finds himself at the same time deprived of that courage, of that activity of soul, and of that continued attention which alone can enlighten him. Sense supposes then no invention, nor consequently any wit: and here, if I may venture to use the term, sense ends where wit begins*.

* It will be found, that I here distinguish wit from good sense, which are sometimes confounded in the ordinary use of these words.

We ought not, however, to conclude from hence, that good sense is so very common. The men without passions are rare. Solid judgment, which of all the faculties of the mind is, beyond contradiction, the nearest to good sense, is not free from the passions. Besides, the blockheads are not less susceptible of them than the men of wit. If all pretend to good sense, and even assume the character, we shall not believe them upon their word. M. Diafoirus says, " I judge by the heaviness of my son's imagination, that he will in time have a good judgment." People always want good sense, when they have no other pretensions to it than their want of wit.

Is the body politic sound? The men of good sense may be called to great places, and fill them worthily: but if the state be attacked by a disease, the men of good sense are extremely dangerous. Mediocrity preserves things in the state in which it found them. Every thing is left to go on as it will: the silence of these people conceals the progress of the evil, and opposes the effectual remedies that might be brought against it: they commonly do not make known the disease till it is become incurable. In regard to those secondary places, where they are not intrusted with the management, but the punctual execution, they are commonly very proper for them. The only faults they commit are those of ignorance, which, in inferior places, are almost constantly of little importance. As to their particular conduct, it is not masterly, but it is always reasonable. The absence of the passions, preventing all the light derived from these passions, makes them at the same time avoid all the errors to which the passions would precipitate them. Sensible men are in general more happy than those influenced by strong passions: in the mean time, the indifference of the first renders them less happy than the man of an amiable disposition, who, being born sensible, has by age and reflection weakened that sensibility; but his heart is still open to the weakness of others: his sensibility revives for them, and he enjoys the pleasure of being sensible without being less happy. Thus he is more amiable in the eyes of all his fellow-citizens, who are pleased with his weakness.

However rare good sense may be, the advantages it procures

are only personal; they cannot be extended to the human race. The man of good sense cannot pretend to the public gratitude, nor consequently to glory. But prudence, it is said, which is one of the attendants of good sense, is a virtue which it is for the advantage of all nations to honour. This prudence, so boasted of, and sometimes so useful to individuals, is not, with respect to a whole nation, a virtue so desirable as is imagined. Of all the gifts heaven could bestow upon a people, the most fatal, without dispute, would be that of prudence, if it were rendered common to all the citizens. What, in fact, is the prudent man? He who keeps evils at a distance; an image strong enough for what balances in his mind the presence of a pleasure that would be fatal to him. Now let us suppose, that prudence were to descend on all the heads that compose a nation: where would be found the men who, for five-pence a-day, would in battle confront death, fatigue, and diseases?— What woman would present herself at the altar of Hymen to expose herself to the trouble of child-bearing, to the pain and danger of delivery, to the humours and contradiction of a husband, and to the vexations occasioned by the death or ill-conduct of children? What man, in consequence of the principles of his religion, would not despise the fleeting pleasures of this world, and, entirely devoting himself to the care of his salvation, seek only in an austere life the means of increasing the felicity that is to be the reward of sanctity? What man would not choose, in consequence of this, the most perfect state, and that in which his salvation would be least exposed? would he not prefer the palm of celibacy to the myrtles of love, and bury himself in a monastery *? It is then to imprudence that posterity owes its existence. It is the presence of pleasure, its all-powerful view, that braves distant misfortune, and destroys foresight: it is, therefore, to imprudence and folly that heaven

---

* When it was inquired in China, whether the missionaries should be allowed to preach freely the Christian religion, it is said, the men of letters, assembled on this subject, saw no danger in it. They did not foresee, said they, that a religion, in which celibacy is the most perfect state, could be very extensive.

attaches the preservation of empires, and the duration of the world. It appears, that, according to the actual constitution of most governments, prudence is only desirable in a very small number of citizens; that reason, a synonimous word to good sense, and so much boasted of by mankind, deserves but little esteem; that the wisdom, which is supposed to belong to it, tends to inaction; and that its apparent infallibility is often no more than an apathy. I, however, confess, that the title of a person of good sense, usurped by an infinite number of people, certainly does not belong to them.

If we say of almost all the stupid, that they are men of good sense, it is, in this respect, with them as with the ordinary women, who are always mentioned as mighty good. We freely boast of the merit of those who have none: we represent them in the most favourable light, and persons of superior abilities in a light the most disadvantageous. How many men bestow the greatest praises on good sense, which they place above wit! In reality, every one would place a higher esteem on himself than on others, and the men of moderate abilities, perceiving that they are nearer to good sense than to wit, set little value upon the latter, and consider it as a trifling endowment: and hence the proverb is so often repeated by men of moderate abilities: " An ounce of good sense is worth a pound of wit ;" a phrase by which every one of them would insinuate, that at the bottom they have more wit than any of our celebrated men.

CHAP. XIII.

OF THE SPIRIT OF CONDUCT.

THE common object of men's desires is happiness: and it is the business of conduct, or the art of conducting themselves, that renders them happy. This art appears less an endowment of the mind than an effect of wisdom, of the regulation of our temper, and the moderation of our desires. The greatest part of mankind, tormented by their passions, or languishing under the calm of lassitude, may be compared, the first to a vessel, buffeted by the tempests of the north; and the second, to a ship stopped by a calm in the midst of the seas of the torrid zone. To her assistance, one calls upon the calm, and the other upon the winds. In order to sail happily, it is necessary for them to be driven by a wind that is always equal. But all I might say, in this respect, on happiness, would have no relation to the subject on which I treat.

People have hitherto understood, by the spirit of conduct, only the art of guiding themselves to the various objects they have in pursuit.

In a republic, such as that of the Romans, and in every government where the people are the distributors of favours, and where honours are the reward of merit, the spirit of conduct is nothing less than genius and great abilities. This is not the case in governments where favours are in the hands of men, whose greatness is independent of the public happiness: in these countries, the spirit which directs the conduct is only the art of becoming useful or agreeable to the dispensers of favours; and it is less to this spirit, than to his turn of mind, that a man commonly owes this advantage. The most favourable and most necessary disposition for succeeding with the great, is a temper pliable to all characters and circumstances. Were a man void of abilities, such a disposition, assisted by favourable circumstances, would be sufficient to make his fortune. But it may be said, that nothing is more common than such characters; therefore, there is nobody who may not make his fortune, and obtain the good will of the great man, by becoming the minister of his pleasures, or his spy. Chance must then have a great share in the fortunes of men. It is chance which makes us fathers, husbands, and the friend of the beauty that is offered, and who pleases the patron; it is chance which places us near a great man at the moment when he wants a spy. " Whoever is without honour and without humour," said the Duke of Orleans, the late regent, " is a perfect courtier." According to this definition, it must be allowed, that the perfect man, in this kind, is only rare in regard to humour.

But, if great fortunes are, in general, the work of chance, and if man no otherwise contributes to obtain them than by stooping to the mean and base actions necessary to procure them, it must, however, be confessed, that wit has sometimes a share in our elevation. The first, for example, who by importunity has made a patron; he who, improving the haughty temper of the placeman, has drawn upon himself those rough speeches, which dishonours him who pronounces them, and forces him to become the protector of the person he has offended; he, I say, has introduced invention and wit into his conduct. It is the same with the first, who has perceived that, in order to rise in the house of the man in power, he must condescend to be the but of ridicule, and sell, at as high a price as he can, his being despised and made a buffoon.

He who thus makes use of the vanity of another, to obtain his ends, is endowed with the spirit of conduct; The man of address, in this kind, proceeds constantly towards his interest; but always under the shelter of another's interest. He is an able man, if, in order to arrive at the end he proposes, he takes a road which seems to lead from it. This is the means of lulling to sleep the jealousy of his rivals, who do not awake till they can be no obstacle to his projects. How many men of wit have played the fool, rendered themselves ridiculous, and have affected the greatest stupidity before their superiors, who are too easily deceived by the base persons who can stoop to this meanness? How many men have, consequently, arrived at the highest fortune, and must have done so? In fact, all those who are not animated with an extreme love for glory, cannot, in point of merit, even love any but their inferiors.—This taste derives its source from a vanity common to all men. Every one would be praised; now of all praises, the most flattering is, without dispute, that which most evidently proves our own excellence. What gratitude do we owe to those who discover to us defects, that, without being prejudicial to us, assure us of our superiority? Of all flattery this is the most artful. At the court of Alexander it was dangerous to appear too great. " My son, make thyself little before Alexander," said Parmenio to Philotas: " give him sometimes the pleasure of reproving thee: and remember, that to thy apparent inferiority thou wilt owe his friendship." How many Alexanders are there in the world, who have a secret hatred to superior talents * ! The man of mean abilities is beloved. " Sir," said a father to his son, " you would succeed in the world, and yet believe that you have great merit. To humble your pride, know to what qualities you must owe your success: you are born without vices, without virtues, without character; your knowledge is little, your mind is limited; what a right, O my son, have you to the good will of mankind!"

But whatever advantage mean abilities procure, and whatever access it opens to fortune, wit, as I have said above, has sometimes a share in our elevation: why then have the public no esteem for this kind of wit? It is, I reply, because they are always ignorant of the arts made use of by the person of intrigue, and scarcely even know whether he owes his elevation to his wit or to mere chance. Besides, the number of ideas, necessary for a person to make his fortune, is not immense. But what knowledge, say they, is necessary to improve upon mankind? The man of intrigue, I reply, knows perfectly the person he wants to make use of, though he is not acquainted with the rest of the world. Between the man of intrigue and the philosopher, we, in this respect, find the same difference as between the courier and the geographer. The first knows, perhaps, better than M. Danville the shortest way to Versailles; but he does not know the surface of the globe like that geographer. Let an artful man of intrigue be obliged to speak in public, and in an assembly of the people; he will be there as silly, as misplaced, and as silent, as a superior genius, when before a great man; he is ambitious of know-

---

* A courtier belonging to Emanuel, King of Portugal, being ordered to write a dispatch, the prince composed one upon the same subject, and, having compared them, found that of the courtier the best: this he told him. The courtier only replied by a profound bow, and went to take leave of his best friends: "There is nothing more for me to do at court," said he; " the king knows I have more wit than he."

ing mankind in all ages and all countries, and despises the art
of knowing a particular man. The man of intrigue has not
then a knowledge of mankind, which would be of no use to
him. His view is not to please the public, but some men in
power, who have often mean intellects, and too much wit would
be prejudicial to his design. To please the people of ordinary
understandings, we ought, in general, to give into common
errors, to conform to established customs, and to resemble the
rest of the world. A person of an elevated genius cannot
stoop so low. He chooses rather to be the bank which opposes
a torrent, though he should be overwhelmed by it, than a light
bough floating about on the surface of the water. Besides,
the man of great abilities, with whatever address he masks
himself, can never so exactly resemble one that is ignorant, as
an ignorant man resembles himself. They are more sure of a
person when he takes, than when he pretends to take, errors
for truth.

The number of ideas, supposed by the art of conducting
ourselves, is not then very extensive: but should it require
more, the public would have no esteem for this kind of genius.
The man of intrigue makes himself the centre of nature; to
his own interest alone he refers every thing; he does nothing
to promote the public welfare: if he obtain high employments,
he then enjoys the respect always annexed to power, and especially to the fear he inspires; but he cannot attain the reputation that ought to be considered as flowing from the gratitude
of the people. I even add, that the abilities, by which he arrived at his high post, seem suddenly to abandon him. He is
raised to great employments only to dishonour them: because
the spirit of intrigue, necessary to obtain them, has no relation
to that strength and depth of genius necessary to discharge
them worthily. Besides, the spirit of intrigue is united to a
certain meanness that must still render him despicable in the
eyes of the public.

Not but that people may unite in great intrigues with an
extraordinary elevation of mind. If, after the example of
Cromwell, a man is desirous of mounting a throne, the power
and lustre of a crown, and the pleasures annexed to govern-

vernment, may doubtless, in his eyes, ennoble the baseness of his plots, since they efface the horror of his crime in the opinion of posterity, who places such a one in the rank of the greatest men: but if, by an infinite number of intrigues, a man endeavour to raise himself to those little posts which he can never deserve; if he be mentioned in history by the name of villain, or cheat, he is rendered despicable, not only in the eyes of honest men, but also in those of persons of understanding. He ought to be a little man who desires little things.— Whoever finds himself above want, without being by his rank entitled to the first posts, can have no other motive than that of glory, and has no other part to choose, if he be a man of abilities, than to shew himself steadily virtuous.

The man of intrigue ought then to renounce the public esteem. But it may be said, that he is fully recompensed for the loss of it, by the happiness annexed to a great fortune. People deceive themselves, I reply, if they think him happy; for happiness is not an appendage of great places; it depends only on the agreement between our dispositions and the circumstances in which fortune has placed us. It is with men as with nations, the most happy are not always those that make the greatest figure in the world. What nation more fortunate than the Swiss! Among these wise people the happy do not throw every thing into disorder by their intrigues; contented at home, they employ themselves but little about others; they are not found in the road of ambition; a part of their time is taken up in study; they are but little known, and the obscurity of their happiness renders it secure.

It is not thus with the man of intrigue; the ministers sell him dear the titles with which they adorn him. What does the patron require from him? The perpetual sacrifice of the will is the only homage that can please him. Like Saturn, Moloch, and Tuisco, if he dared, he would be honoured by none but human sacrifices. The pain endured by those he protects is an agreeable sight to the protector; this informs him of his power, and makes him conceive a higher opinion of himself. Thus it is only to the most painful attitudes that most nations have attached the sign of respect.

Whoever would, by his intrigues, rise to the possession of great employments, must devote himself to humiliations. Ever restless, he can at first only perceive happiness in the perspective of an uncertain futurity; and it is from hope, that reviving dream of men awake and unhappy, that he must expect his felicity. When he has obtained it by suffering a thousand mortifications, he commonly revenges what he has felt, by his severity and cruelty towards the unhappy, refuses them his assistance, renders their misery a crime, reproaches them for it, and believes that, by this reproach, he makes his inhumanity considered as an act of justice, and his fortune as derived from merit: he does not, however, enjoy the pleasure of convincing any one that this is the truth.

How can we be assured that the fortune of a man is the effect of this conduct, especially in those countries that are entirely despotic, where of the vilest slave they make a vizier; where riches depend on the will of the prince, and on a momentary caprice, the cause of which is not always perceived? The motives, which in this case determine the sultans, are almost constantly concealed; historians relate only the apparent motives, they are ignorant of the true ones; and, in this respect, we may, after M. de Fontenelle, assert, that history is only a fable, which people consider as true.

In a comparison between Cæsar and Pompey, if, as Balzac says, speaking of their fortune,

One is the workman, and the other the work!

it must be acknowledged, there are but few Cæsars, and that, in arbitrary governments, chance is almost the only god of fortune. Every thing there depends on a moment, and on the circumstances in which a person is placed; and this, perhaps, as in the East, has given the greatest credit to the doctrine of fatality. According to the Mussulmans, destiny keeps every thing under her empire, places kings on the throne, drives them from thence, fills their reign with happy or unhappy events, constitutes the felicity or unhappiness of all mortals. According to them, wisdom and folly, or the virtues and vices of a man, make no change in the decrees engraven on the tables of light *. To prove this doctrine, and, consequently, to shew that the most criminal is not always the most unhappy, and that one proceeds to punishment by the same road which leads another to fortune, the Indian Mahometans relate a remarkable fable.

Want, say they, formerly assembled a number of men in the deserts of Tartary. Deprived of all, said one, we have a right to all. The law, which strips us of necessaries to augment the superfluities of some rajahs, is unjust. Let us struggle with injustice. A treaty can no longer subsist where the advantages cease to be mutual. We must force from our oppressors the wealth they have forced from us. At these words the orator was silent; a murmur of approbation ran through the whole assembly; they applauded the speech; the project was noble, and they resolved to execute it. They divided about the means. The bravest rose first: force, said they, has deprived us of all; it is by force we must recover all. If our rajahs have by their tyrannic injustice snatched from us even what is necessary, so far as to require us to lavish upon them our substance, our labour, and our lives, why should we refuse to our wants what the tyrants permit to their injustice? At the confines of these regions, the bashaws, by the presents they require, divide the profits of the caravans; they plunder the men enslaved by their power and by fear. Less unjust and more brave than they, let us attack men in arms; let valour decide the victory, and let our riches be, at least, the price of our courage. We have a right to them! Heaven, by the gift of bravery, points out those who should shake off the fetters of tyranny. Let the husbandman, without strength or courage, plow, sow, and reap: it is for us that he has gathered in the harvest.

Let us ravage,—let us pillage the nations! We consent to all, cried those who, having more wit and less courage, feared

---

* The Mussulmans believe that every thing, which is to happen to the end of the world, is written on a table of light called Louh, with a pen of fire called CALAM-AZER, and the writing above is named CAZA, or ÇADAR, that is, THE INEVITABLE PREDESTINATION.

to expose themselves to danger; yet let us owe nothing to force, but all to imposture. We shall receive without danger from the hands of credulity, what we shall in vain, perhaps, attempt to snatch by force. Let us clothe ourselves with the name and the habit of the bonzes, or the bramins, and encompass the earth; we shall see every one eager to supply our wants, and even our secret pleasures.

This party appeared base and cowardly to those who were fierce and courageous. Being divided in opinion, the assembly separated; one party spread itself into India, Tibet, and the confines of China. Their countenances were austere, and their bodies macerated. They imposed on the people, they taught, they persuaded, they divided families, caused the children to be disinherited, and applied their substance to themselves. The people gave them lands, built them temples, and settled upon them great revenues. They borrowed the arm of power, in order to make the man of understanding bow to the yoke of superstition. In short, they subdued all minds by keeping the sceptre carefully concealed under the rags of misery and the ashes of penance.

During this time, their old brave companions retired into the deserts, surprised the caravans, attacked them sword in hand, and divided among themselves the booty.

One day, when, doubtless, the battle had not turned to their advantage, the people seized one of these robbers; they conducted him to the next city; they prepared the scaffold; they led him to execution. He walked with a firm step, till he found in his way and knew again, under the habit of a bramin, one of those who had separated from him in the desert. The people respectfully surrounded the bramin, and conducted him to his pagod. The robber stopped at seeing him: "Just Gods!" cried he, "though equal in crimes, what a difference is there in our destiny! What do I say? Equal in crimes! In one day he has, without fear, without danger, without courage, made more widows and orphans sigh, and deprived the empire of more riches, than I have pillaged in the whole course of my life. He had always two vices more than I, cowardice and falsehood; yet I am treated as a villain—he honoured as a saint; they drag me to the scaffold, him they lead to his pagod; me they impale, him they adore!"

Thus do the Indians prove, that there is neither happiness nor unhappiness in this world.

CHAP. XIV.

OF THE EXCLUSIVE QUALITIES OF THE MIND AND SOUL,

My view in the preceding chapters was to affix clear ideas to the several qualities of the mind; I propose in this to examine, if there are talents that must necessarily exclude each other. This question, it is said, is determined by facts; no person is, at the same time, superior to all others in many different kinds of knowledge. Newton is not reckoned among the poets, nor Milton among the geometricians: the verses of Leibnitz are bad. There is not a man who, in a single art, as poetry, or painting, has succeeded in all the branches of it. Corneille and Racine have done nothing in comedy comparable to Moliere: Michael Angelo has not drawn the pictures of Albani, nor Albani painted those of Julius Romano. The genius of the greatest men appears then to be confined within very narrow limits. This is, doubtless, true: but I ask, what is the cause? Is it time, or is it wit, which men want to render themselves illustrious in the different arts and sciences?

The progress of the human mind, it is said, ought to be the same in all the arts and sciences: the operations of the mind are reduced to the knowledge of the resemblances and differences that subsist between various objects. It is then by observation that we obtain, in all the different kinds of study, the new and general ideas on which our superiority depends. Every great physician, every great chemist, may then become a great geometrician, a great astronomer, a great politician, and the first, in short, in all the sciences. This fact being stated, it will, doubtless, be concluded, that it is the short duration of human life that forces superior minds to limit themselves to one kind of study.

It must, however, be confessed, that there are talents and qualities possessed only by the exclusion of some others. Among mankind some are filled with the love of glory, and are not susceptible of any other of the passions: some may excel in natural philosophy, civil law, geometry, and, in short, in all the sciences that consist in the comparison of ideas. A fondness for any other study can only distract or precipitate them into errors. There are other men susceptible not only of the love of glory, but an infinite number of other passions: these may become celebrated in several different kinds of study, where the success depends on being moved.

Such is, for instance, the dramatic kind of writing: but, in order to paint the passions, we must, as I have already said, feel them very warmly: we are ignorant both of the language of the passions and of the sensations they excite in us, when we have not experienced them. Thus ignorance of this kind always produces mediocrity. If Fontenelle had been obliged to paint the characters of Rhadamistus, Brutus, or Cataline, that great man would certainly have fallen much below mediocrity.

These principles being established, I conclude that the love of glory is common to all who distinguish themselves in any kind of study whatsoever; since that alone, as I have proved, is sufficient to make us support the fatigue of thought. But this passion, according to the circumstances in which fortune has placed us, may be united to other passions. The men in whom this union subsists, can never have any great success, if they give themselves up entirely to the study of one science, as, for instance, morality, where, in order to see well, we must see with an attentive but indifferent eye: in this science it is indifference which holds the balance of justice. In disputes, it is not the parties, but an indifferent person who is taken for judge. What man, for instance, that is capable of loving violently, would, like M. de Fontenelle, approve the crime of infidelity? "In an age," says that philosopher, "when I was most amorous, my mistress left me for another lover. I heard of it, and was enraged; I went to her, and loaded her with reproaches: she heard me, and laughing, said, "Fontenelle, when I took you, it was doubtless pleasure that I sought: I found more with another. Is it to the least degree of pleasure tha' I ought to give the preference? Be just, and answer me." " On my faith," said Fontenelle, " you are in the right; and though I am no longer your lover, I will still be your friend." Such an answer supposes but little love in Fontenelle: the passions do not reason so justly.

We may then distinguish two different kinds of the arts and sciences, the first of which supposes a mind free from every other passion but that of glory; and the second, on the contrary, supposes a mind susceptible of a variety of passions. There are then exclusive talents; and the ignorance of this truth is the source of much injustice. We desire that men shall have contradictory qualities; we demand impossibilities from them; and would have the stone that is thrown remain suspended in the air, without obeying the laws of gravitation.

Let a man, for instance, like M. de Fontenelle, contemplate, without severity, the wickedness of mankind ; let him consider it, let him rise up against crimes without hating the criminals, and people will applaud his moderation; and yet, at the same instant, they will accuse him of being too lukewarm in friendship. They do not perceive, that the same absence of the passions, to which he owes the moderation they commend, must necessarily render him less sensible of the charms of friendship.

Nothing is more common than to require contradictory qualities from men. This is occasioned by our blind love of happiness: we would be constantly happy, and thence would have the same objects assume every instant the form we think most agreeable. We have seen various perfections scattered among different objects ; hence, we would find them united in one, and taste a thousand pleasures at once. For this purpose, we would have the same fruit have the lustre of the diamond, the odour of the rose, the taste of the peach, and the coolness of the pomegranate. It is then the blind love of happiness, the source of an infinite number of ridiculous wishes, that makes men desire qualities that are absolutely impossible to be blended together. To destroy this fruitful seed of unjust expectation, it is necessary to treat this subject in a pretty extensive manner. It is only by pointing out, in conformity to the end I propose, both the qualities absolutely exclusive, and those that are too seldom found united in the same person for us to have a right to desire them, that a man can be at once rendered more enlight- ened, and more indulgent.

A father would have his son unite to great talents a most wise conduct. But do you know, I ask, that you desire to have in your son qualities that are almost incompatible? Know, that if some singular concourse of circumstances have sometimes united them in the same man, yet they are very seldom blended toge- ther; that great abilities always suppose strong passions; that strong passions produce a thousand irregularities; and that, on the contrary, what is called good conduct, is almost always the effect of the absence of the passions, and consequently the ap- pendage of moderate abilities. It requires strong passions to form the great, of what kind soever. Why do we see so many countries barren of great men? Why so many little Catos, so wonderful in early youth, who have commonly in advanced age only common abilities? From what reason, in short, is the world so full of ingenious children and stupid men? It is be- cause in most governments the citizens are not inflamed by strong passions. Well, I consent, the father will say, that my son shall be animated by them; it will be sufficient for me to direct them towards certain objects of study. But do you per- ceive, I reply, the hazard of the desire? It is expecting that a man with good eyes should perceive only the objects you point out to him. Before you form any plan of education, you ought to be fully determined within yourself, and know what you desire most for your son, whether great abilities or a wise conduct. Is it to a good conduct that you give the preference? Believe that strong passions would be a fatal gift to your son, and especially among a people, where, by the constitution of the government, the passions are not always directed towards virtue; stifle therefore within him, if possible, all the seeds of passions. But I shall then, the father will reply, give up the hope of rendering him a man of merit. Doubtless you will. If you cannot resolve upon this, restore him the passions, and endeavour to direct them to laudable pursuits: but expect to see him perform great things, and sometimes commit the greatest faults.   There is no medium in a man of strong passions; and it is chance which generally determines his first steps.   If the men of strong passions become illustrious in the arts, if the sciences preserve some empire over them, and if they sometimes observe a wise conduct; it is not so with the men of strong passions, whose birth, character, dignities, and riches, call them to the first posts in the world.   The good or bad conduct of these is almost entirely subject to the empire of chance; according to the circumstances in which they are placed, and the moment of their birth, their qualities change into vices and virtues. Chance makes at its pleasure an Appius or a Decius.   In M. de Voltaire's tragedy, Cæsar says, " If I was not the master of the Romans, I should be their avenger.

" Had I not been Cæsar, I should have been Brutus."

Give to the son of a cooper, wit, courage, prudence, and activity : among republicans where military merit opens a door to grandeur, you will make a Themistocles or a Marius*: at Paris you will only form a Cartouche.

Let a man bold, enterprizing, and capable of executing the most desperate resolutions, appear when the state, ravaged by powerful enemies, seems without resource; if success favours his enterprizes, he is a demi-god: at any other time, he is no more than a madman or a fool.

To these different ends are we frequently conducted by the same passions.   This is the danger to which the father exposes himself, whose children are susceptible of these strong passions, which so often change the face of the world.   It is, in this case, the conformity of their minds and dispositions, with the

---

* Lu-cong-pang, founder of the dynasty of Han, was the first of a gang of robbers; he made himself master of a town; attached himself to the service of T-cou: became the general of armies, defeated T-sin, rendered himself master of several cities; took the title of king; and fought and disarmed the princes, who revolted against the empire: by his clemency more than by his valour he restored the peace of China, was acknowledged emperor, and is mentioned in the Chinese history as one of their most illustrious princes.

station in which they are placed, that make them what they are. Every thing depends on this conformity. Among those ordinary men, who, by important services, cannot render themselves of use to the world, crown themselves with glory, nor pretend to the general esteem, there are none who would not be of advantage to their fellow-citizens, and acquire a right to their gratitude, were they but placed in the posts most suitable to them: it is on this subject that Fontaine says,

> Un roi prudent & sage
> De ses moindres sujets sait tirer quelque usage.

That is,

A wise and prudent king
Will turn to his own advantage the abilities of his meanest subjects.

Let us suppose, for instance, that a place of consequence is vacant. A person must be nominated to fill it; and it requires one that can be depended upon. He who is proposed has but little wit; besides, he is indolent. This, I say, signifies nothing to him who nominates him: give him the place. A good conscience is often indolent; activity, when it is not the effect of the love of glory, is suspicious; the knave, always agitated by remorse and fear, is incessantly in action. " Vigilance," says Rousseau, " is the virtue of vice."

A place is ready to be disposed of: it requires assiduity. He who is proposed is a sloven, disagreeable, and burthensome to good company: so much the better; assiduity will render his being a sloven a virtue.

I shall not expatiate any farther on 'this subject'; but conclude with what I have said above, that a father, by requiring the greatest talents from his son, joined to the wisest conduct, desires that he should have the principle of irregularity, and yet that he should never swerve from a regular conduct.

Not less unjust with respect to despotic princes than the father with respect to his son, throughout all the East there are people who require from their sultans many virtues, and more particularly great knowledge: yet what can be more unjust? Are you ignorant, might one say to these people, that knowledge is the reward of much study and reflection ?—Study and reflection are painful : the people then must make use of all their endeavours to preserve the prince from them ; he must then give way to his laziness, if he is not animated by a motive so powerful as to make him triumph over it. What can this motive be ? Nothing but the desire of glory. But this desire, as I have proved in the third discourse, is itself founded on the desire of the pleasure procured by glory, and the general esteem. Now, if the sultan, in quality of a despotic prince, enjoys all the pleasures which glory can promise to other men, the sultan is then without desires, and nothing can kindle in him the love of glory : he has not a motive sufficient to enable him to undergo the tiresome task of business, and to expose himself to that fatigue of attention, necessary to his obtaining instruction. To require knowledge from him, is to desire that the rivers should run back to their source, and to expect an effect without a cause.

All history justifies this truth. Let us open that of China : we there see revolutions rapidly succeed each other. The great man, who raises himself to the empire, has for his successors princes born in purple, who, not having the same powerful motives as their father to render themselves illustrious, sleep on the throne ; and most of them lose it by the third generation, frequently without having any other crime to reproach themselves with but that of indolence.

I shall mention only one example of this*. Li-t-ching, a man of an obscure birth, took up arms against the emperor T-coug-ching, placed himself at the head of the malecontents, raised an army, marched to Pekin, and surprised that city. The empress and the queens strangled themselves; the emperor stabbed his daughter, and retired into a distant part of his palace, where, before he put an end to his life, he wrote these words on the lappet of his robe : " I have reigned seventeen years : I am dethroned, and in this misfortune see nothing but the punishment of heaven, justly offended at my indolence.

* See the History of the Huns, by M. de Guignes, tom. I. p. 74.

I am not, however, the only one guilty : the great men of my court are still more so than I; it is they, who, by concealing from me the knowledge of the affairs of the empire, have dug the pit into which I am fallen. With what face shall I appear before my ancestors? How support their reproaches? O ye, who have reduced me to this dreadful situation! take my body, cut it in pieces, I consent to it; but spare my poor people: they are innocent, and already unhappy enough, in having had me so long for their master."

A thousand of the like instances, found in history, prove that luxury and softness influence almost all those, who, by their ·birth, are armed with arbitrary power. The atmosphere spread over these thrones, and the despotic sovereigns who sit upon them, seem to be filled with a lethargic vapour, which seizes all the faculties of their souls. Thence they are seldom reckoned among great kings, except when they have cleared the way to the throne, or been long instructed in the school of misfortune. They always owe their knowledge to the interest they have in acquiring it.

Why are little princes generally more able men than the most powerful despotic sovereigns? It is because they have, in a manner, their fortunes to make ; because they are obliged, with an inferior force, to resist that which is superior ; because they live in the perpetual fear of having their dominions taken from them; and because their interest, being more strictly united with that of their subjects, must enlighten them with respect to the various parts of the legislation. Thus they are in general much more busily employed in training up soldiers, contracting alliances, and in peopling and enriching their provinces. Thus we might, in consequence of what I have said, prepare geographi-political maps of the merit of the princes in the several empires of the east, Their understanding, measured by the scale of their power, would decrease in proportion to the extent and the strength of their empires, to the difficulty of penetrating into them, and, in short, to the more or less absolute authority they have over their subjects ; that is, to the more or less pressing interest they have in being enlightened. This scale being once calculated and compared

with observation, it would certainly afford very just conclusions: the Sophies and Moguls would, for example, be placed
in the rank of the most stupid princes; because, excepting
some singular circumstances where they have accidentally had
a good education, the most powerful must commonly be the
most ignorant.

To require an eastern despotic prince to consult the happiness of his people, and with a strong arm and steady hand to
hold the helm of government, would be to desire that the arm
of Ganymede should wield the club of Hercules. Let us suppose that an Indian was, in this respect, to make some remonstrances to the Mogul. " Of what dost thou complain ?" might
he reply. " Can'st thou without injustice require, that I should
be more enlightened than thyself with respect to thy own interest? When thou didst invest me with supreme power,
couldst thou believe that, forgetting pleasure for the painful
honour of rendering thee happy, I and my successors would
not enjoy the advantages attached to arbitrary power? Every
man loves himself preferably to all others; thou knowest this.
To require then, that, deaf to the voice of care and the cry of
my passions, I should sacrifice them to thy interest, is to endeavour to subvert the order of nature. How can'st thou imagine,
that, being able to do every thing, I would never do any thing
unjust? The man fond of the public esteem, thou sayest, makes
a different use of his power. I confess it; but of what importance is glory, and the esteem of the public to me? Is there
one pleasure granted to virtue, that is refused to power? Besides, the men passionately fond of glory are scarce, and this
is not a passion that descends to their successors. This ought
to have been foreseen, and thou shouldst have been sensible,
that, by arming me with an arbitrary authority, thou has cut
the knot of mutual dependence, which binds the sovereign to
the subject, and that thou has separated my interest from thine.
Imprudent, in placing in my hand the sceptre of despotism;
cowardly, in not daring to snatch it from me; be at once
punished for thine imprudence and thy cowardice: know, that
if thou breathest, it is because I permit thee: learn that every

instant of thy life is a favour. Vile slave, thou wert born, thou livest, for my pleasures. Bend under the weight of thy chain, cringe at my feet, languish in misery, die! I forbid thee to complain: such is my will."

What I have said of sultans, may in part be applied to their ministers: their knowledge is, in general, in proportion to the interest they have in acquiring it. In the countries where the cries of the public may depose them, great abilities are necessary, and they are obliged to acquire them. On the contrary, among the public, where the people have neither credit nor the least influence, they deliver themselves up to idleness, and are contented with that kind of merit necessary to make their fortunes at court; a merit absolutely incompatible with great abilities, from the opposition found between the interest of the courtiers and the general interest. It is in this respect with ministers as with men of learning. It is a ridiculous pretence to aim at the same time at glory and passions: before they compose their works, they ought always to choose, whether they would have the esteem of the public, or that of the courtiers. It must be known, that in most courts, and especially in those of the east, the men are from their infancy swathed and confined in their swaddling clothes of prejudice and arbitrary constraint; that most minds are bound up so, that they cannot rise to be great; that no man, who is born and lives near despotic thrones, can escape the general contagion, and he is under a necessity of never having any but mean ideas.

Thus, true merit resides far from the palaces of kings. It never approaches but in times of misfortune, when the princes are forced to invite it. At any other time, want alone may draw men of merit to the court; but in this situation there are few who preserve the same strength and elevation of mind. Want is too nearly allied to guilt.

It follows from what I have been saying, that it is demanding an impossibility to require great talents of those, who, by their state and situation, cannot be animated by strong passions. But how many of these demands are made every day? People complain of the corruption of manners; we ought, say they, to form virtuous men, and they would have the citizens warmed with the love of their country, and yet see in silence the misfortunes occasioned by a bad legislation. They do not perceive, that this is requiring a miser not to exclaim against a robber, when he his carrying off his strong box. They do not observe, that those, who, in certain countries are called wise men, are always indifferent with respect to the public welfare, and are consequently without virtue. It is with equal injustice, as I am going to prove in the following chapter, that people demand of men, not only talents, but qualities and habits, contrary to each other, and which cannot subsist together.

CHAP. XV.

OF THE INJUSTICE OF THE PUBLIC IN THIS RESPECT.

PEOPLE require that an equerry, accustomed to point his toes to his horse's ears, should have them as well turned as a dancer at the opera-house; they would have a philosopher, solely employed in strong and general ideas, write like a woman of distinction, or even be superior, for instance, in the epistolary style, where, in order to write well, it is necessary to write agreeably without a subject. They do not perceive that this is demanding the union of talents that are almost incompatible; and that there is no woman of wit who is not, in this respect, superior to the most celebrated philosopher.

It is, with the same injustice that people expect the man who has never read or studied, and has spent thirty years of his life in dissipation of thought, should suddenly become capable of study and meditation: they ought, however, to know, that it is the habit of meditation to which we owe the capacity for meditating, and that this capacity is lost when we cease to make use of it. In fact, when a man, though habituated to labour and application, finds himself suddenly trusted with too great a part of the administration, a thousand different objects will pass rapidly before him: he can only cast a superficial glance on each affair, and for this very reason, after a certain time, he will become incapable of a long and close attention. We have not, therefore, a right to require an equal attention from a minister. It is not for him to pierce to the first principles of morality and politics; to discover, for instance, how far luxury is useful in a state, what changes it may introduce in the manners of a people, and in the constitution ; what kind of commerce ought to be encouraged ; by what laws we may in the same nation reconcile the spirit of commerce with that of war, and render it at the same time rich at home, and formidable abroad. The solution of such problems requires leisure, and a habit of reflection : now, how can a person think much when he has much to execute ? . We ought not then to require from a man in a high post, that invention that supposes close application. What we have a right to demand from him is a just, lively, and penetrating, wit, and which, in matters of debate in relation to politics and philosophy, is capable of striking out the truth, and seizing it with strength ; and of being so fertile in expedients as to carry into execution the projects he adopts : for this last reason he ought to add to this wit a firmness and constancy not to be shaken.

The people are not always sufficiently grateful for the advantages they receive from ministers: being ungrateful through ignorance, they do not know what courage is necessary to do good, and to triumph over the obstacles which personal interest places against the general happiness*. Thus,

---

* At the moment when a person is nominated to be a minister, one of the first commissioners of Versailles, who is commonly a man of much wit, addresses him to this purpose : You love what is good, and you are now enabled to do it. A thousand projects, of use to the public, will be presented to you, and you will desire that they may succeed : take care however of undertaking any thing before you have examined it, whether the execution of these projects will require only small sums, little care, and but little probity. If the money required for the success of one of these projects be considerable, the affairs under your management will not permit you to apply to it the necessary funds and to lose your disbursements. If the success depend on the vigilance and probity of those you employ, fear lest

courage enlightened by probity, is the principal merit of men in high posts. In vain do the people flatter themselves with the hopes of finding in them a fund of knowledge; they cannot be deeply versed in any affairs that have not been the subject of their contemplations before they obtained great employments: now these affairs are necessarily but few in number. To be convinced of this, let us follow the life of those who are designed for high posts. At sixteen or seventeen years of age they leave the college, learn to ride the great horse, and to perform their exercises; then spend two or three years in the academies, and the schools of law; the study of the law being ended, they purchase a place. In order to discharge the duty of it, it is not necessary to instruct themselves in the law of nature and nations, and the public law, but to consecrate all their time to the examination of some particular causes. They pass from thence to the government of a province, where, over-burthened by daily details, and fatigued by giving audiences, they have no time for reflection. They at length rise to superior places, and find that, after thirty years exercise, they have only the same kind of ideas as they had at twenty or twenty-two years of age. Upon which I shall observe, that voyages made to the neighbouring nations, in which they might compare the differences to be found in the form of government, and in the legislation, genius, commerce, and manners, of the people, would be, perhaps, more proper to form statesmen than the education actually given them. I shall expatiate no farther on this subject, but shall conclude this chapter with considering the men of genius; because it is chiefly in them that people desire exclusive qualities and abilities.

Two causes, equally powerful, lead to this injustice; the one, as I have said above, is the blind love of our own happiness, and the other is envy.

---

they force you to be under a difficulty in the choice of proper persons; fear also that you are going to be surrounded by knaves; it requires a very penetrating eye to discover them; and the first, but at the same time the most difficult, knowledge of a minister, is that of knowing how to make a proper choice.

Who has not condemned Cardinal de Richlieu for that excessive love of glory that rendered him greedy of every species of success? Who has not ridiculed the ardour with which, if we may believe Dumaurier*, he desired canonization; and the order given in consequence of it to his confessors, to publish every where that he had never committed a mortal sin? In short, who has not laughed at being informed that, at the same instant inflamed with a desire of being thought to excel in poetry as well as in politics, that cardinal caused Corneille to be asked to give up to him the honour of writing the CID? It was however to this love of glory, so often condemned, that he owed his great abilities for the administration. If we have not since seen a minister make pretensions to so many kinds of glory, it is because we have yet had only one Cardinal de Richlieu.

The resolution to centre in one single desire the action of the strong passions, and to imagine, that a man inflamed with a love of glory should be contented with one single species of success, when he believed he had it in his power to obtain it in several, is to desire that a piece of excellent land should produce only one kind of fruit. Whoever has a strong love of glory, is secretly conscious that the success of political projects sometimes depends on chance, and often on the folly of those with whom he treats: he would have it more personal. Now, without a ridiculous and stupid pride, he cannot disdain the glory acquired by learning, to which so many great princes and heroes have aspired. Most of them, not satisfied with immortalizing themselves by their actions, have resolved to do it by their writings, and at least to leave to posterity precepts on the art of war and in politics, in which they have excelled. How should they avoid being ambitious of this honour? These great men loved glory, and no one is ambitious of obtaining it without desiring to communicate to mankind the ideas that ought to render us in their eyes still more worthy of esteem.

* See Memoires pour servir à l'Histoire de la Hollande, article Grotius.

How many proofs of this truth are to be found in history! Xenophon, Alexander, Hannibal, Hanno, the Scipios, Cæsar, Cicero, Augustus, Trajan, the Antoninuses, Comnenes, Elizabeth, Charles V., Richlieu, Montecuculi, du Guay-Trouin, and the Count de Saxe, by their writings resolved to enlighten the world, and shade their heads with different kinds of laurels.

If now it cannot be conceived how men, entrusted with the administration of the world, found time to think and write; it is, I reply, because business is soon concluded, when they do not deviate into particulars, and affairs are taken by their true principles. If all great men have not composed, all have at least protected men of learning, and were under a necessity of doing it, because, being in love with glory, they knew that the great authors bestowed it. Thus, Charles V. founded an academy before Richlieu: thus, the fierce Attila himself assembled about him the learned of all kinds; the Caliph Aaron Al-Raschid had them at his court, and Tamerlane established the academy of Samarcand. What a reception did Trajan give to merit! Under his reign people were allowed to think, to speak, and to write, every thing; because the writers, struck with the lustre of his virtues and abilities, could not avoid being his panegyrists: very different in this respect were Nero, Caligula, and Domitian, who, from a contrary reason, imposed silence on the men of learning, lest in their writings they should transmit to posterity the vices and disgrace of those tyrants.

I have shewn in the examples above-mentioned, that the same desire of glory to which great men owe their superiority, may, with respect to genius, make them aspire to universal monarchy. It is, doubtless, possible to unite greater modesty to abilities: for these qualities are not in their own nature exclusive, though they are so in some men. There are those who cannot be deprived of this vain opinion of themselves, without having the seeds of their genius lost. This is a defect, and envy takes the advantage of it, in order to discredit merit; she is pleased with pulling men in pieces, sure of always finding, by this means, some disfavourable side, under which she may present them to the public. We cannot too often recollect, that it is with men as with works; that we ought to judge of them together; that there is nothing perfect on earth; and that, if we were to describe the virtues and defects of each man's mind and character by ribbons of two opposite colours, there is not a man who would not be speckled with those two colours. Great men are like those rich mines where gold is always found more or less mixed with lead. It is necessary then, that the envious should sometimes say to himself: If it be possible to degrade this gold in the opinion of the public, what value ought they to set on me, who am a mine of mere lead! But the envious will be always deaf to such advice. Dexterous at seizing the least faults committed by the men of genius, how often have they accused them with not being so agreeable in their manners as the rest of the world? They will not recollect, as I have said above, that, like those animals that remain in the deserts, most of the men of genius live in retirement, and that it is in the silence of solitude that truth unveils herself to their sight.

Now all men who by their kind of life are thrown into a particular chain of circumstances, and who contemplate objects under a new face, cannot have in their minds either the good qualities, or defects, common to ordinary men. Why does a Frenchman resemble another Frenchman more than a German, and a German much more than a Chinese? Because these two nations by their education, and the resemblance of the objects presented to them, have an infinitely greater connection with each other than with the Chinese. We are what we are made by the objects with which we are surrounded. To expect that a man who sees other objects, and leads a life different from mine, should have the same ideas as I have, would be to require contradictions, and to desire that a staff should not have two ends.

What injustice of this kind is done to men of genius! How often are they accused of folly, at a time when they give a proof of the highest wisdom! Not but men of genius have often, as Aristotle says, a corner of folly. They are, for instance, subject to represent the art they cultivate as of greater importance than it really deserves*. Besides, the strong passions which genius supposes, may sometimes render their conduct irregular : but, though this is the seed of their errors, it is also the seed of their knowledge. Men of a cold disposition, void of passions and abilities, do not fall into the irregularities of the man of strong passions. But it ought not to be imagined, as their vanity would persuade them to believe, that, before they take a resolution, they calculate the advantages and inconveniences of it : were this the case, these men would only be determined in their conduct by reflection; but experience informs us that they are always moved by sensations, and that in this respect the men of cold dispositions are the same as the rest. To be convinced of this, let us suppose that one of them is bit by a mad dog: they send him to the sea; he is put into a bark; they are going to plunge him. He runs no risk : he is sure of it, and knows that in this case his fear is altogether unreasonable; he says so himself. They dip him in the water. Reflection no longer acts upon him; the sensation of fear takes possession of his mind, and to this ridiculous fear he owes his cure. Reflection is then in men of a cold disposition, as well as in other men, subject to sensation. If men of a cold constitution are not liable to such frequent deviations as the men of strong passions, it is because they have fewer principles of motion; and, in

---

* They have frequently an exclusive esteem for them. Among even those who distinguish themselves only in the most trifling arts, there are some who think that there is nothing done well in their own country but what is done by them. I cannot help mentioning, on this subject, a saying attributed to Marcel. A very celebrated English dancer, arrived at Paris, and went to pay a visit to Marcel. " I came," said he, " to pay you the respect which all the men of our art owe to you: allow me to dance before you, and to improve by your advice."—" Freely," said Marcel. Immediately the Englishman performed a thousand difficult steps and cross capers. Marcel looked at him, and suddenly cried out—" Sir, people jump in other countries; they only dance at Paris; but, alas! poor kingdom! we can do nothing well but that!"

this respect, it is only to the weakness of their passions that they owe their wisdom. However, what a high esteem do they conceive of themselves! With what respect do they think they inspire the public, who suffers them to enjoy the title of men of sense, and never call them fools, because they are never mentioned. How can they, without shame, thus spend their lives in watching for what is ridiculous? If they discover any thing in a man of genius, and he commit the slightest fault, though it should be, for instance, paying too high a price for the favours of a woman, what a triumph is it for them! They assume a right from thence to despise him. Yet, if in the woods, if in solitude and danger, fear has often in their eyes exaggerated the greatness of danger, why may not love exaggerate pleasure, as fear exaggerates perils? Are they ignorant that there is properly none but himself that can be the just appraiser of his own pleasure; that men being animated by different passions, the same objects cannot appear of the same value to different eyes; that sentiment alone can judge of sentiment; and that the desire of always citing to the tribunal of cold reason, is assembling the diet of the empire, in order to determine upon cases of conscience? They ought to be sensible that before they pass sentence on the actions of a man of genius, they should at least know what are the motives that determine him; that is, the force by which he is drawn: but, for this purpose, they should know both the power of passing, and the degree of courage necessary to resist, them. Now, every man that stops to make this examination may soon perceive that the passions alone may fight against the passions; and that these rational people that pretend to conquer them give to very weak inclinations the name of passions, in order to obtain the honours of a triumph. In fact, they do not resist the passions, but escape from them. Wisdom is not in them the effect of knowledge, but of an indifference equally barren of pleasure and of pain. The absence of unhappiness is the only felicity they enjoy, and a kind of reason, which serves them for a guide on the sea of human life, makes them avoid the rocks only by steering at a distance from the fortunate isle of pleasure. Heaven arms men of a cold disposition with only a buckler for defence, and not with a sword to conquer.

Let reason direct us in the important affairs of life; but let us abandon the little affairs of it to our tastes and our passions. He, who would ever consult reason, will be incessantly employed in consulting what he ought to do, and never do any thing; he will always have before his eyes the possibility of all the misfortunes with which he is surrounded. The pain and daily irksomeness of such a consultation would, perhaps, be more to be feared than the evils from which it might deliver him.

Whatever reproaches are made to men of wit, however attentive envy is to depress them, and to discover their personal and trifling faults, in order to shade the lustre of their glory, the men of genius ought to be insensible to such attacks, and to perceive that they are often snares which envy lays to divert them from their studies. Of what importance is it to be incessantly representing their inattention as a crime? People ought to know that most of those little attentions, so much recommended, have been invented by the indolent, to serve as the employment of their idle hours; that there is no man endued with a sufficient attention to become illustrious in the arts and sciences, if that attention is to be employed about an infinite number of trifles; besides, as what is called attention procures no advantage to a nation, so it is for the public interest that a learned man should make a discovery at no more than fifty attempts at least.

I cannot help mentioning on this subject a fact said to have happened at Paris. A man of learning had for his neighbour one of those indolent people so troublesome to society; this last, tired of himself, went one day to pay a visit to the man of letters, who received him in a very agreeable manner, and, with great politeness, continued tired of him, till, being weary of staying any longer in the same place, the idler took his leave, in order to plague somebody else. He was no sooner gone than the man of learning returned to his studies, and forgot his vexation. Some days after he was accused of not having returned the visit he had received, and taxed with the want of politeness; upon which he, in his turn, went to see the idler. " Sir," said he, " I am informed that you complain of me : however, you know that it was being weary of yourself that brought you to me. I, who tire nobody, received you as well as I could; it is then you who are obliged, and I who am taxed with unpoliteness. Be yourself the judge of my proceedings, and see whether you ought not to put an end to complaints that prove nothing, but that I have not, like you, occasion for visits, and have neither the inhumanity to plague my neighbour, nor the injustice to defame him after I have tired out his patience." How many are there to whom we might apply the same answer! How many idlers require from men of merit that respect, and those abilities, that are incompatible with their employments, and take upon them to demand contradictions!

A man has spent his life in negociations, and the affairs in which he has been employed have rendered him circumspect : let this man go into the world, they would have him wear that air of freedom which the constraint of his situation has made him lose. Another man is of an open disposition, and has pleased us by his frankness: he is required suddenly to change his character, and to become circumspect, at the precise moment when it is desired. People are always for having impossibilities performed. There is, doubtless, a neutral state in which a man is found to have all the qualities that are not absolutely contradictory; and I am sensible that a singular concourse of circumstances may bend us to opposite habits; but this is a miracle, and we ought not to reckon upon miracles. In general, we may assure ourselves that every thing depends on the dispositions of men; that their good qualities are blended with their faults, and that there are certain vices of the mind annexed to certain stations.

Let a man possess an important post; let him every day have a hundred affairs to decide ; if no appeal be made against his judgment, and his decisions be never disputed, it is certain that in time pride will take possession of his soul, and he will have the greatest confidence in his own understanding. This will not be the case where a man has his opinions frequently debated and contradicted in council by his equals; or with a learned man, who, being sometimes mistaken in relation to subjects which he has thoroughly examined, will necessarily contract the habit of suspending his judgment*; this supposition, which, being founded on a salutary distrust of our own understandings, makes us penetrate to those hidden truths that are seldom perceived by a proud and superficial glance. It seems as if the knowledge of truth was only to be purchased by this wise distrust of ourselves. The man who refuses to doubt is subject to a thousand errors: he has himself set bounds to his mind. One of the most learned men in Persia being asked, how he had acquired so much knowledge, replied, " By freely asking what I did not know."—" Examining one day a philosopher," says the poet Saadi, " I pressed him to tell me from whom he had acquired his knowledge." " From the blind," he replied, " who do not lift up their feet without having first felt with their staff the earth that was to support them."

What I have said on exclusive qualities, both with respect to nature and contrary habits, is sufficient for the object I had in view. I am now to shew the use that may be made of this knowledge. The principal is, to learn to make the best advantage of the mind, and of this I am going to treat in the following chapter.

---

* It might, perhaps, be wished that, before men were raised to high posts, they would better perceive the difficulty of doing well; they would learn to distrust their own understandings; for, by applying this distrust to business, they would manage it with more attention.

CHAP. XVI.

THE METHOD OF DISCOVERING THAT KIND OF STUDY FOR WHICH WE ARE BEST QUALIFIED.

In order to know our abilities, we must examine with what kind of objects chance and education have principally charged the memory, and what degree of love we have for glory. Upon this combination we may determine the kind of study to which we ought to apply ourselves.

There is no man entirely destitute of knowledge. According as we have in the memory more physical or historical facts, more images or sentiments, we shall have a greater or less aptitude to natural philosophy, politics, or poetry. Is it to this last art that a man would apply himself? He may become so much the greater painter in this kind of writing, in proportion as the magazine of his memory is better furnished with the objects that enter into the composition of a certain species of pictures. A poet, born in those rugged climates of the north, with a rapid wing incessantly traverses the black storms : his eye never wanders through smiling valleys ; he only knows eternal Winter, who, with his hair whitened by the hoar frost, reigns over barren deserts : the echoes only repeat to him the howling of bears : he sees nothing but the snow and the ice thrown up in heaps ; fir-trees, as old as the earth, cover with their dead branches the lakes which wash their roots. Another poet, born, on the contrary, in the fortunate climate of Italy, where the earth is strewed with flowers, the zephyrs with their breath gently move the fragrant groves ; he sees the rivulets winding their silver streams through the verdant meadows ; art and nature unite to adorn the cities and fields, and every thing seems formed to please the eye and ravish the senses. Can we doubt that the last of these two poets would draw more agreeable pictures ? and the first pictures more bold and terrible ? However, neither of these poets would compose these pictures, were they not animated by an ardent love of glory.

The objects which chance and education place in our memory are indeed the primary matter of the mind; but it remains there dead and inactive, till it is put into a ferment by the passions. It then produces a new assemblage of ideas, images, or sentiments, to which we give the name of genius, wit, or talents.

After having discovered what is the number, and what the species of objects deposited in the magazine of the memory, before we can determine on any kind of study, we must calculate to what a degree we are sensible of glory. We are liable to mistake in this particular, and to give the name of passion to mere inclination; nothing, however, as I have already said, is more easily distinguished. We have a strong passion when we are animated with a single desire, and all our thoughts and actions are subordinate to it. We have only inclinations when the mind is divided by an infinite number of nearly equal desires. The more numerous these desires are, the more moderate are our inclinations; on the contrary, the less our desires are multiplied, the more nearly do they approach to unity, and the more do these inclinations become lively, and the readier to be changed into passions. It is then the unity, or at least the pre-eminence of one desire over all the others, that constitutes passion.

The passions being once determined, we must know their strength, and, for this purpose, examine the degree of enthusiasm we feel for great men. This is in early youth a pretty exact standard of our love of glory. I say in early youth, because, being then more susceptible of the passions, we deliver ourselves the more freely up to our enthusiasm. Besides, we have then no motives to degrade merit and abilities, and we may still hope to see esteemed in ourselves what we esteem in others: this is not the case with those who are grown up to manhood. Whoever has attained to a certain age without having any merit, always indulges the contempt of abilities, to comfort himself for the want of them. In order to be a judge of merit, we should be entirely disinterested, and, consequently, not have yet experienced the sensation of envy. We are but little susceptible of it in early youth : therefore, young people commonly look upon great men with the same impartial eye as posterity. It is generally necessary for us to renounce the esteem of the men of our own age, and expect it only from those who are young. It is from their praises that we must state the value of our merit, and by the praises they give great men, we may form a judgment of the value of theirs. As we esteem in others only such ideas as are analogous to our own, our respect for wit is always proportioned to the wit we have ourselves; we celebrate great men only when we are made to be great. Why did Cæsar weep on his stopping before the bust of Alexander? It was because he was Cæsar. Why do not we weep at the sight of the same bust? It is because we are not Cæsar.

We may then, from the degree of esteem conceived for great men, measure the degree of our love of glory, and, consequently, come to a resolution in the choice of our studies. The choice is always good, wherever the strength of the passions is proportioned to the difficulty of the success. Now it is more difficult to succeed in any one art or science in proportion to the number of men employed in it, and to their having carried it nearer to perfection. Nothing can be more bold than to enter into the same course in which Corneille, Racine, Voltaire, and Crebillon, have rendered themselves illustrious. To be distinguished in it, a person must be capable of the greatest efforts of mind, and, consequently, be animated by the strongest love of glory. He who is not susceptible of this extraordinary degree of passion, ought not to enter the lists with such rivals, but to apply himself to a kind of study in which it is more easy to succeed. There are in natural philosophy, for instance, uncultivated lands, and subjects on which the men of great genius, at first employed about more interesting objects, have only in a manner cast a superficial glance. In this, and all other of the like kinds of study, the discoveries and the success are within the reach of almost all minds; and these are the only ones in which the weak passions are capable of obtaining success. He, who is not intoxicated with the love of glory, ought to seek for it in winding paths, and particularly to avoid the roads beaten by the men of the greatest understandings. His merit, if compared with that of these great men, will be eclipsed by their lustre, and the public, prejudiced against him, will refuse him even the esteem he deserves.

The reputation of the man of weak passions depends, therefore, on the address with which he avoids being compared with those who, burning with a stronger passion for glory, have made greater efforts of genius. By this address, the man of weak passions, who has, however, in his youth contracted a habit of labour and reflection, may sometimes, with a very small degree of genius, obtain a very great reputation. It appears then, that, to reap the greatest advantage possible from his genius, the principal attention ought to be comparing the degree of the passion with which a man is animated, with the degree of the passion supposed by the kind of study to which he applies himself. Whoever is, in this respect, an exact observer of his own mind, must escape from the numerous errors into which men of merit sometimes fall. We shall not, for instance, see him engage in a new kind of study at a time when age has abated the ardour of the passions. He will perceive that, by passing successively through different arts and sciences, he can never become any thing more than universally superficial; that this, universality is a rock to which vanity leads, and upon which men of genius are often wrecked ; and that, in short, it is only in youth that we are endowed with that indefatigable attention which dives even to the first principles of an art or science: an important truth, the ignorance of which often stops genius in its course, and opposes the progress of the sciences.

In order to reap advantage from this idea, we ought to recollect, that the love of glory, as I have proved in my third discourse, is kindled in our breasts by the love of natural pleasures; that this love is never more warmly felt than in early youth ; and that it is, consequently, in the spring of life, that we are susceptible of a more violent love of glory. We then feel in ourselves the glowing sparks of virtues and abilities: health and strength, which circulate in our veins, bring with them the sentiment of immortality; the years appear then to pass with the slowness of ages; we know, but we do not feel, that we must die, and thence we are more ardent to procure the esteem of posterity. It is not so when age cools our passions: we then have a perspective view of the gulph of the grave, and the shades of death, mingling with the rays of glory, tarnish their lustre. The universe then in our eye changes its form: we cease to have an interest in it, and do nothing of importance. · If we still follow the course in which the love of glory made us first enter, it is from our giving way to habit; for habit has become stronger while the passions were growing weaker. Besides, we are afraid of the lassitude of indolence; and, to preserve ourselves from it, continue to cultivate the sciences, the ideas of which, being familiar, are combined in our minds without difficulty. But we are incapable of the strong attention required in a new kind of study. Are we arrived to thirty-five years of age, we cannot, from being a great geometrician, become a great poet; from a great poet, a great chemist; from a great chemist, a great politician. Yet, at that age a man is raised to a high post; but if the ideas, with which he has already charged his memory, have no relation to the ideas required in the place he possesses, either the place does not require much wit or abilities, or that man will not fill it worthily.

Among the magistrates, who are sometimes too much involved in the discussion of private disputes, is there one who can with superiority fill the first places, if he do not in his retired hours profoundly study the subjects relative to his employment? The man, who neglects to pass through these studies, mounts to high places only to dishonour them. Is this man of an arbitrary and despotic temper? the enterprizes he will form will be severe, foolish, and always prejudicial to the public. Is he of a mild character, and the friend of mankind? he will not dare to undertake any thing. How can he run the hazard of making any changes in the administration? We do not walk with a firm step in ways unknown, and interrupted by a thousand precipices. The firmness and courage of the mind depend always on its extent. The man, fruitful in the means of executing his projects, is bold in his conceptions: on the contrary, the man, barren of resources, necessarily contracts a habit of timidity, which folly takes for wisdom. It is very dangerous to touch too often the machine of government, and there are also times in which the machine, if it is not furnished with new springs, will stop of itself: the ignorant workman dares to undertake nothing, and, therefore, the machine destroys itself. This is not the case with the able artist; he knows how to preserve it by repairing it with a bold hand. But a wise boldness supposes a profound study in the science of government; a study that is fatiguing, and of which we are only capable in early youth, and, perhaps, in countries where the public esteem promises many advantages. Wherever this esteem is barren of pleasures, it produces no great talents. The small number of illustrious men, who, from the chance of an excellent education, or a remarkable chain of circumstances, are rendered in love with this esteem, then desert their country, and this voluntary exile presages its ruin: they are like those eagles whose flight proclaims the approaching fall of the antique oak from which they retire.

I have said enough on this subject; and shall conclude, from the principles established in this chapter, that all the mental abilities are produced by the objects placed in our memory, and by those objects being put into a fermentation by the love of glory. It is then, as I have already said, only by combining the species of objects with which chance and education have charged our memories, with our love of glory, that we can really know the strength and kind of our genius. Whoever scrupulously observes himself in this respect, finds that he is nearly in the same situation with those able chemists, who, on being shewn the substances with which the retorts are filled, and the degree of heat that has been given them, can foretell the result of the process. Upon which I shall observe, that, if there be an art of exciting in us strong passions, if there be easy means of filling the memory of a young man with a certain species of ideas and objects, there are, consequently, certain methods of forming men of genius.

This knowledge of the nature of the mind may then be very useful to those who are animated with the desire of becoming illustrious: it may furnish them with the means of doing it; teach them, for instance, not to diffuse their attention upon too great a variety of objects, but to fix it entirely on the ideas and objects relative to the science in which they would excel. Not that they ought, in this respect, to carry their scruples too far: for men are not profoundly skilled in any science, if they have not made excursions into every thing analogous to that they cultivate. We ought even to fix for some time our attention on the first principles of several sciences. It is of use to follow the uniform progress of the human mind in all the different arts and sciences, and also to consider the universal chain which binds together all the ideas of man. This study gives greater strength and extent to the mind; but we ought only to consecrate a small part of our time to it, and to fix our principal attention on the particulars of the art or science we cultivate. He who in his studies listens to an indiscreet curiosity, seldom obtains a great reputation. Let a sculptor, for instance, be from his taste equally drawn towards the study of sculpture and politics, and, consequently, charge his memory with ideas that have no relation to each other, I maintain that the sculptor will be certainly less skilful, and less celebrated, than he would have been, had he always filled his memory with objects analogous to the art he professes, and had not united in himself, if I may venture thus to express myself, two men, who can neither communicate their ideas nor converse together.

Moreover, this knowledge of the mind may not only be of use to individuals, but also to the public: it may enlighten ministers with respect to the knowledge of making a proper choice, and enable them to distinguish men of superior abilities. They will know, in the first place, the species of objects about which a man is employed; and, in the second, the passion he has for glory, the strength of which, as I have already said, is always proportioned to his abilities, and almost constantly to the merit of those with whom he converses.

He who neither loves nor esteems those who, by their actions or works, have obtained the general esteem, is certainly a man without merit. The little analogy between the ideas of a dunce and a man of genius prevents all society between them. In relation to merit it is a curse to be too much pleased with the conversation of men of mean abilities.

After having considered the mind in so many various relations, I ought, perhaps, to trace out the plan of a good education, and perhaps a complete treatise on this subject should have been placed at the conclusion of this work. If I avoid this labour, it is because, supposing that I could really point out the means of rendering men better, it is evident, that, from the actual manners of the people, it would be almost impossible to make use of them. I shall therefore content myself with casting a rapid glance over what is called education.

CHAP. XVII.

OF EDUCATION.

The art of forming men is in all countries so strictly connected with the form of the government, that, perhaps, it is impossible to make any considerable change in public education, without making the same in the constitution of states.

The art of education is no other than the knowledge of the means proper to form strong and robust bodies, and wise and virtuous minds. As to the first object of education, we should take example from the Greeks, who honoured bodily exercises, and with whom these were considered as medicinal. As to the means of rendering the mind more enlightened, more strong and virtuous, I believe that, having shewn the importance of making a proper choice of the objects placed in the memory, and the facility with which we may kindle the strong passions, and direct them to the general welfare, I have sufficiently pointed out to the intelligent reader the plan that should be followed to perfect the public education.

We are, in this respect, too far distant from any thoughts of a reformation, for me to enter into particulars, which are always tedious when they are useless. I shall content myself with observing, that we do not, in this respect, attend to the reformation of the most gross abuses, and those that are the most easily corrected. Who doubts, for instance, that, in order to reap the greatest advantage in our power, we ought to make the best distribution of our time possible? Who doubts, that the success depends, in part, on the œconomy with which it is managed? And what man, convinced of this truth, does not perceive, at the first glance, the reformation that might be made in this respect in the public education?

We ought, for example, to consecrate some part of our time to the rational study of the national language. What can be more absurd than to lose eight or ten years in the study of a dead language, which we immediately forget after leaving the colleges; because it is almost of no use in the course of life? In vain is it said, that, if young men are kept so long in the colleges, it is not so much to teach them Latin, as to make them contract the habit of labour and application. But, to bend them to this habit, might not there be proposed a study less irksome and disagreeable? Is there not reason to fear the extinguishing or blunting that natural curiosity, which in early youth warms us with the desire of learning? How much would this desire be strengthened, if, in the age when we are not yet distracted by strong passions, they were to substitute in the room of the insipid study of words, that of natural philosophy, history, mathematics, morality, poetry, &c.

The study of the dead languages, it is replied, in part answers this purpose. It subjects us to the necessity of translating and explaining authors; it consequently furnishes the heads of young men with all the ideas contained in the best works of antiquity. But, I reply, is there any thing more ridiculous than to consecrate many years to placing in the memory some facts or ideas, that we, by the assistance of translations, might engrave upon it in two or three months? The only advantage that can be derived from eight or ten years study is then the very uncertain knowledge of those delicacies of expression in the Latin tongue, that are lost in a translation. I say very uncertain; for, in short, how long soever we study the Latin tongue, we shall never know it so perfectly as we know our own. Now if, among our learned men, there are very few sensible of the beauty, strength, and elegance, of a French expression, can we imagine that they are more happy in relation to a Latin one? May, we not suspect that their learning, in this respect, is only founded on our ignorance, our credulity, and their boldness; and that were the manes of Horace, Virgil, and Cicero, to appear, the most elegant discourses of our orators would seem to them to be written in an almost unintelligible jargon?

I shall not, however, lay any stress on this suspicion, and will agree, if they will have it so, that a young man, on his leaving the college, is well instructed in the delicacies of the Latin tongue: but even upon this supposition I will ask, whether they ought to pay for this knowledge the price of eight or ten years labour; and if, in early youth, in the age when curiosity is not obliged to struggle with any passion, when we are consequently more capable of application, these eight or ten years consumed in the study of words, would not be better employed in the study of things, and especially in things that have a relation to the situation in which a person will probably be placed? Not that I adopt the too austere maxims of those, who believe that a young man ought to be solely confined to the studies suitable to his station. The education of a young man ought to have a reference to the different paths he may take, for the genius should be left free. There are even branches of knowledge of which every citizen ought to be possessed; such are the principles of morality, and the laws of his country. All that I require is, that the memory of a young man be principally charged with the ideas and objects relative to the employment he will probably embrace. What can be more absurd, than to give exactly the same education to three different men, one of whom is to enjoy some little place in the revenue, and the two others the first places in the army, the magistracy, or the administration? Can we, without astonishment, see them employed in the same studies till they are sixteen or seventeen years of age, that is, till they enter into the world, and till diverted by pleasure they become incapable of application?

Whoever examines the ideas with which the memory of

young men are loaded, and compares their education with the station in which they are to be placed, will find it as foolish as it would have been in the Greeks, to have given only a master of the flute to teach those who were to be sent to the Olympic games, to dispute the prize of running or wrestling.

But it may be asked, that if we might make a much better use of the time spent in education, why do we not attempt it? To what cause can we attribute our indifference in this respect? Why do we put from infancy the pencil in the hand of the designer? Why place at that age the fingers of the musician on the strings of the violin? Why do both these artists receive an education so suitable to the arts they are to profess, while we neglect so much the education of princes, of great men, and, in general, of all those who by their birth are entitled to important posts? Are we ignorant that the virtues, and particularly the learning, of the great, has an influence on the happiness or unhappiness of nations? Why then do we abandon to chance so essential a part of the administration? It is not, I reply, from there not being in the colleges a great number of learned men, who are equally sensible of the faults in education, and the remedies that should be applied to them: but what can they do without the assistance of the government? Now governments ought to trouble themselves but little about the cares of public education. We ought not in this respect to compare great empires with little republics. Great empires seldom feel the pressing want of a distinguished genius: great states support themselves by their own bulk. This is not the case with a republic, for instance, like that of Sparta, which, with a handful of citizens, was obliged to support the enormous weight of the armies of Asia. Sparta, therefore, owed her preservation only to the great men who successively arose in her defence; and being from thence constantly employed in forming new defenders, the principal attention of the government was fixed on the public education.

Great states are seldom exposed to such dangers, and the same precautions are not taken for their security. The greater or less want of any thing is in every instance the exact standard of the efforts of the mind made to procure it. But it may be said, that there is no state, even among those who are most powerful, where a want of great men is not sometimes felt. This is doubtless true; but this want not being habitual, no care is taken to prevent it. Foresight is not the virtue of great states: persons in important posts have too much business upon their hands to attend to the public education; whence it necessarily becomes neglected. Besides, how many obstacles does personal interest, in great empires, raise up against the production of men of genius? Yet men might even there become well instructed; for nothing prevents taking advantage of early youth, in order to plant in the memory of young men the ideas relative to the posts they may happen to possess: but never will they form men of genius; because these ideas are barren, if not fertilized by the love of glory. In order to kindle this love in our minds, it is necessary that glory, like money, should procure an infinite number of pleasures, and that honours should be the reward of merit. Now the interest of the powerful does not permit them to make so just a distribution: they would not accustom the citizens to consider favours as a debt due to abilities, and consequently they seldom grant them to merit: they perceive that they shall obtain so much the more gratitude from those they oblige, as they are less worthy of their favours. Injustice then must often preside in the distribution of favours, and the love of glory become extinguished in all hearts.

Such are in great empires the principal causes of the scarcity of great men; of the indifference with which they are considered, and of the little care taken of the public education. Great, however, as the obstacles are which, in these countries, oppose the reformation of the public education, yet in monarchies, such as most of those in Europe, these obstacles are not insurmountable: but they become so in governments absolutely despotic, such as those of the East. What means are there in those countries of improving education? There can be no education without having an object in view, and the only one that can be proposed is, as I have already said, to render citizens stronger, more enlightened, more virtuous, and, in short, more proper to contribute to the happiness of the society in which they live. Now, in arbitrary governments, the opposition despotic princes think they perceive between their interest and the general interest, does not permit them to adopt a system so conformable to the public utility. In these countries, there is then no object of education, and consequently no education. In vain would they reduce it to the sole means of pleasing the sovereign; for what an education must that be, where the plan is to be traced after the ever imperfect knowledge of the manners of a prince, who may either die, or change his disposition, before the education is completed. In those countries, it would be in vain to labour after the reformation of the public education, till that of the sovereign's was perfected.

But a treatise on this subject ought doubtless to be preceded by a work, still more difficult to be wrote, in which it should be examined, whether it be possible to remove the powerful obstacles which personal interest always raises up against the good education of kings. This is a moral problem, which, in arbitrary governments, such as those of the East, is, I believe, not to be solved. The viziers, too jealous of reigning under the name of their masters, always keep the sultans in a shameful and almost invincible ignorance; and they keep from them every man capable of instructing them. Now, where the education of princes is thus abandoned to chance, what care can be taken of that of private persons? A father desires to raise his sons: he knows that neither knowledge, nor abilities, nor virtues, will ever open them a way to fortune; and that princes never believe they have occasion for men of genius and learning: he will then desire for his sons neither knowledge nor abilities; he will even have a confused idea, in such governments, that a person cannot be virtuous with impunity. All the precepts of his morality will then be reduced to some vague maxims, which having but little connexion with each other, cannot give his children clear ideas of virtue; for he will be in this respect afraid of giving them precepts too severe and too determinate. He will have a glimpse that a rigid virtue would be injurious to their fortunes; and that if two things, as Pythagoras says, render a man like the gods, the one promoting the public welfare, and the other speaking truth, he who modelled himself by the gods would certainly be ill treated by men.

This is the source of the contradiction to be found between the moral precepts, which even in countries subject to despotic power, people are forced by custom to give to their children, and the conduct they prescribe to them. A father says in general, and as a maxim, " Be virtuous:" but he says to them, without knowing it, " Do not mind this maxim, be a fearful and cautious villain; and have no more honesty (as Moliere says) than is just sufficient to save you from being hanged." Now, in such a government, how can they perfect even that part of education, which consists in rendering men more firmly virtuous? There is no father, who, without contradicting himself, can answer the pressing arguments that a virtuous son might offer on the subject.

To illustrate this truth by an example, suppose that, under the title of bashaw, a father designs his son for the government of a province, and that, ready to take possession of that post, his son says to him—" O my father! the principles of virtue I have acquired in my infancy have budded in my soul. I depart to govern men: it is their happiness which I shall make my only aim. I shall not lend a more favourable ear to the rich than to the poor. Deaf to the menaces of the powerful oppressor, I shall always hear the complaints of the weak under oppression, and justice shall preside in all my judgments."

" O my son!" how amiable does the enthusiasm of virtue render youth! but age and prudence will teach thee to moderate it. We ought, doubtless, to be just: yet to what requests art thou going to be exposed! To how many little acts of injustice must thou be blind! If thou art forced to refuse the great, what graces, my son, ought to accompany thy refusal! Elevated as thou art, a word from the sultan can reduce thee to nothing, and confound thee in the throng of the vilest slaves. The hatred of an eunuch, or an icoglan, may destroy thee; think, therefore, of treating them with respect."

" Shall I respect injustice? No, father! The Sublime Porte frequently requires a too burdensome tribute from the people: I shall not listen to its views. I know that a man is under obligations to the state only in proportion to the interest it takes in his preservation; that the unfortunate owe nothing to it; and that affluence itself, which supports the taxes, requires a wise economy, and not prodigality. Upon this point I shall enlighten the divan."

" Abandon this project, my son; thy representations would be vain; it must always be obeyed."

" Obeyed! No, rather let .me resign to the sultan the place with which he honours me."

" O my son! a foolish enthusiasm for virtue leads thee astray. Thou wilt ruin thyself, and the miseries of the people will not be removed: the divan will nominate in thy place a man of less humanity, who will discharge thine office in a more severe manner."

" Yes, injustice will doubtless be committed; but I shall not be the instrument. The virtuous man entrusted with the administration, either does well, or retires: the man more virtuous still, and more sensible of the miseries of his fellow-citizens, snatches himself from the converse of cities, into deserts, forests, and even among the savages; he flies from the odious aspect of tyranny, and the too-afflicting sight of the misfortunes of his equals. Such is the conduct of virtue. I should have, thou sayest, no imitators: I am not sure of that: thy secret ambition makes thee think so, and my virtue makes me doubt it. But I would not have my example followed. Did the zealous Mussulman, who first proclaimed the law of the divine Prophet, and braved the fury of tyrants, take care, in marching to punishment, that he was followed by other martyrs? Truth spoke from his heart, he owed it an authentic testimony, and he paid it. Do we owe less to humanity than to religion? And are its doctrines more sacred than the virtues? But suffer me to examine thee in my turn:

if I associate myself with the Arabs, who plunder our caravans, may I not say to myself, whether I live with these robbers, or separate myself from them, the caravans will be nevertheless attacked? yet, living with the Arab, I shall soften his manners; I shall oppose, at least, the useless cruelties he commits on the travellers; I shall do my duty without adding to the public misery. This reasoning is thine; and if neither my nation nor thyself can approve it, why then shouldst thou permit, under the name of Bashaw, what thou forbiddest under that of Arabs? O my father! my eyes are at length opened; I see that virtue does not inhabit despotic states, and that in thy breast ambition stifles the cry of equity. I cannot proceed to grandeur by trampling justice under my feet. My virtue defeats thy hopes: my virtue becomes odious to thee, and thine hopes being deceived, thou givest it the name of folly. It is still to thee that I must refer it; fathom the abyss of thy soul, and answer me. If I sacrifice justice to pleasure and wanton caprice, by what power wilt thou recal to my mind those austere maxims of virtue I learned in my youth? Why is thine ardent zeal grown cool, when I am required to sacrifice this same virtue to the orders of a sultan, or a vizier? I dare to answer this question: it is because the lustre of my grandeur, the unworthy price of a base obedience, would be reflected on thyself: thou wouldst then overlook the crime; but if thou didst discover it, thou wouldst think it only my duty."

It is evident that, pressed by such reasonings, it would be very difficult for a father not to perceive a manifest contradiction between the principles of sound morality and the conduct prescribed to his son. He would be forced to confess that, by desiring the grandeur of his son, he has, in an implicit and confused manner, exhorted him to devote himself entirely to his advancement, and to sacrifice to it even justice and humanity. Now, in the Asiatic governments, where, out of the mire of servitude they draw the slave who is to command the other slaves, this desire must be common to all fathers. What man would then endeavour, in those empires, to mark out the plan of a virtuous education, which no parent

3 s

would give to his children? What madness but to pretend to form minds filled with magnanimity in countries, where men are not vicious from a general propensity to vice, but because vice is rewarded and virtue punished? What can be hoped for, in this respect, from a people among whom we can only cite as honest men, those who are ready to become so as soon as ever the form of the government will admit of it? Where, besides, nobody being animated with a spirit of patriotism, there cannot be any man truly virtuous? In despotic governments they ought then to renounce the hope of forming men celebrated for their virtues or abilities. This is not the case in monarchies, where, as I have already said, this may be doubtless attempted with some hope of success; but it ought at the same time to be acknowledged, that the execution would be the more difficult, in proportion as the constitution of the monarchy approached nearer to the despotic form of government, or the manners of the people were more corrupt.

I shall not expatiate any farther on this subject, but shall content myself with recalling to the mind of the zealous citizen, who would form more virtuous and more learned men, that the whole problem of an excellent education is reduced, first, to the fixing, in each of the different states where fortune has placed us, the kind of objects and ideas that ought to be placed in the memories of young men; and, secondly, to the determining the most certain means of inflaming them with a love of glory and the public esteem.

This problem being solved, it is certain that the great men that are now produced by a fortuitous concourse of circumstances, will become the work of the legislature, and that, by leaving it less in the power of chance, an excellent education may infinitely multiply the abilities and virtues of the citizens in great empires.

FINIS.